THE CANADIAN LEGAL SYSTEM

Second Edition

by

GERALD L. GALL

B.A., LL.B.

Member of the Ontario Bar
Faculty of Law
The University of Alberta

With Chapter 8
The Quebec Legal System
by Mr. Justice Paul Reeves
of the Quebec Superior Court

1983
CARSWELL LEGAL PUBLICATIONS
Toronto Calgary Vancouver

Gall, Gerald L.
The Canadian legal system
(Carswell student edition)
Bibliography: p.
Includes index.
ISBN 0-459-35800-6 (bound). — ISBN
0-459-35810-3 (pbk.)

1. Law - Canada.   I. Title   II. Series.

KE444.G34 1983   349.71   C83-091290-8

TO
**My wife Karen
and my children
Melanie and Wendy**

FOREWORD

There is a story in the life of Martin Buber, the eminent philosopher, which appears to me to have relevance in the present context.

In the middle 1930's, when Hitlerism was bringing an ethical black-out to Germany and other countries, Martin Buber left Germany and came to live in Palestine, as it was then called. The Hebrew University of Jerusalem, sensing its good fortune in having this distinguished scholar within its midst, quickly arranged to add him to its faculty. One difficulty presented itself. The language of instruction of the Hebrew University was Hebrew. It was a language which Professor Buber, for all his awesome talents, did not speak. But exceptional situations give rise to exceptional remedies. The University authorities permitted Buber to give his lectures in German, with a translator present who rendered the subject matter into Hebrew. This was to be only a temporary arrangement, while Professor Buber immediately began the study of Hebrew to equip himself for the day when he would be able to teach in the University's official language.

That day did indeed come. One day a friend asked the great Professor how he was getting along with his lectures in Hebrew. Professor Buber replied, "I can lecture well enough in Hebrew to be understood. But I can't lecture well enough in Hebrew *not* to be understood."

That answer may have been given tongue in cheek. But it does draw attention to a frailty sometimes found in academic persons, namely, the deliberate desire to express themselves in language not readily comprehensible at a first reading. Such persons have elevated obscurity to the level of a principle.

When I read the work of an academic, I address myself to the question of whether the author belongs to the "obscurity" school or not. I addressed myself to that question in reading the present work. The verdict was one easy to reach and pleasant to announce. Professor Gerald Gall belongs to the "lucidity" school, not the "obscurity" school. Every page is written in clear, simple, translucent prose.

My joy with regard to the style of this book is exceeded only by my pleasure with its content. If, when I had put down the final page of The Canadian Legal System, I had been asked to state in one word what I liked best about this book, my answer would have been its *comprehensiveness*. For it deals with virtually every aspect of our legal system. With an economy of words the author has highlighted the essential features of the legal system of our country. Everything is there — the common law and statute law, the origin and development of equity, Canada's relationship to English law, our courts and the media, the adversarial system and its search for truth, the role of lawyers and judges in making the legal system work, the allegiance of bench and bar to codes of ethics, the doctrine of stare decisis and the role of decided cases as precedents, the problems involved in the interpretation of statutes, the function of administrative tribunals and their obligation to adhere to natural justice and rules of fairness, law in the computer age and the emergence of "jurimetrics", the function of legal aid in making possible greater access to the courts, and the recurring obligation of judges and lawyers to participate in programs of continuing legal education. These are only some of the topics in the book.

Do you ask about the civil law of Quebec? It's there, and Professor Gall acknowledges his gratitude to Mr. Justice Paul Reeves of the Quebec Superior Court for contributing that chapter. And the new Canadian Constitution, and its Charter of Rights and Freedoms, proclaimed by the Queen in Ottawa on April 17, 1982? It's there too. Indeed the author's chapter on this subject is one of the high points of the book. Any reader seeking enlightenment on the Constitution or the Charter could well make this chapter the starting point of his endeavours.

This brings me to a point that should be stated. Not all the topics in the book are explored in depth. The author probably had to make a choice. Should he deal more fully with the subjects before him, and thus end up with a book two or three times its present size? Or should he excise a number of those subjects, perhaps half, and give himself room to treat the remaining half in greater detail? Both of such courses have their obvious disadvantages. Instead, Professor Gall elected in favour of comprehensiveness, covering many topics, all of them adequately even if not completely. I think readers will agree that he made the wisest choice.

In his concluding chapter, dealing with new directions that law must take to meet the challenge of this technological age, Professor Gall says:

> "In short, to borrow the words of s. 1 of our new Charter of Rights and Freedoms, we must preserve and protect the 'free and democratic society' that Canadians cherish. By the pursuit of innovative new directions, we can ensure that the Canadian legal system will continue to endure as a cornerstone of liberty and democracy in Canada."

Professor Gall's book is itself a significant step towards the attainment of that high objective.

The Honourable Samuel Freedman
Former Chief Justice of Manitoba

June 1983

PREFACE TO THE SECOND EDITION

During the intervening six years since the publication of the first edition of this book, many significant changes in the Canadian legal system have taken place. The most important of these is the patriation of the Canadian Constitution, with, among other things, its entrenched Canadian Charter of Rights and Freedoms and a new domestic amending formula. But there have been other significant changes as well. These include a proliferation in the number of lawyers, with its attendant ramifications related to the delivery of legal services, and the institutional changes in our legal system arising out of the merger of certain courts and recent concern relating to the independence of the judiciary. Also, there have been many substantive changes in the law, as a result, naturally, of new legislation, but also as a result of the developing jurisprudence. There is no better example of the latter than the development of the doctrine of procedural fairness in administrative law.

Also during the intervening years, the writer has experienced personal changes. I would like to acknowledge the continued support and encouragement of my wife, Karen, to whom, together with my two daughters, both products of the intervening years, this book is dedicated. During this period, I served for 1½ years as the Associate Director and for 3½ years as the Executive Director of the Canadian Institute for the Administration of Justice, an organization with which many fine and dedicated persons have been associated. And that service provided me with an opportunity to gain a better understanding of our legal system and how it operates. In this connection, I wish to thank all those with whom I was associated during this period for assisting me in achieving that better understanding.

I would also like to express my appreciation to the various research assistants who, from time to time, aided me, and including the most recent assistant, Brenda Machny, who worked with me in the summer of 1982.

I wish to thank the administrative staff of the Faculty of Law at the University of Alberta, especially Robert Graham, Maureen Sexsmith and Anne Megan. I also wish to acknowledge the support of my colleagues, including the Dean of the Faculty of Law, Frank D. Jones, Q.C. Not to be forgotten are the University of Alberta law librarians who are always so helpful in assisting faculty members and students, and especially Patricia Rempel for her help with this new edition.

Probably the greatest thanks are due to the staff at Carswell for their patience, tolerance and understanding. More particularly, I want to thank, in Toronto, Alan Turnbull, Tom Clouston and James Lang, and in Calgary, Karen Flint, Karen McBean, Leslie McGuffin and Peter Enman. I am also grateful to Leslie McGuffin and Peter Enman for their fine editorial work on the second edition.

May I express my special thanks to the Honourable Mr. Justice Paul Reeves, of the Quebec Superior Court, who prepared the excellent chapter on the Quebec legal system, and to the Honourable Samuel Freedman, the retired Chief Justice of Manitoba and a legendary figure in the Canadian judiciary, who wrote the Foreword.

Finally, I wish to thank the many readers of my first edition, especially those who conveyed to me that the book enhanced their understanding of our legal system. The positive reaction to the first edition not only was personally and professionally satisfying, but also served to encourage me to write this second edition.

May, 1983   Gerald L. Gall
Edmonton, Alberta

PREFACE AND ACKNOWLEDGMENTS
TO THE FIRST EDITION

In taking on the task of writing a treatise on the entirety of the Canadian legal system, one is faced with formidable problems. First, although there are many English texts of this nature, there exists no substantial Canadian treatise on the Canadian legal system as such. One might look for direction to the various English texts, but one most certainly does not want to simply take an English model and apply it to the Canadian context. In short, the author is faced with a desire for some originality and freshness of approach. Secondly, and this probably represents the most difficult problem with which the author is faced, a decision must be made as to what to include in a book on a virtually open-ended topic. Indeed, some chapters in this book could be (and, in fact, at one time or another have been) a subject of a text or texts of their own.

As a result, whenever I received assistance in the undertaking of this project, such assistance, no doubt, was greatly appreciated. Accordingly, I would like to formally express my appreciation and to acknowledge the assistance of those who helped me undertake and complete this project.

First, I would like to express my appreciation to the Canadian Institute for the Administration of Justice for appointing me a Summer Research Fellow in the summer of 1976. That Institute sponsored and financed a research project which subsequently led to much of the contents of Chapters 7, 8 and 9 [now Chapters 9, 10 and 11] of this book. Those chapters, and the report of the research contained in those chapters, represent the work done as a Summer Research Fellow for that Institute. I would like to thank the Canadian Institute for the Administration of Justice for its sponsorship and support and to wish that organization, of which I am proudly a member, every success in its future endeavours. In this connection, may I sincerely thank all those members of the judiciary of the province of Alberta who participated in the above research project. Their thoughtful and interesting contributions were much appreciated and very helpful.

I would also like to thank three students who at various times in the course of this project served as summer research assistants. Specifically, those students are Alvin Esau, a former editor of the Alberta Law Review, Maureen Markley, a third-year law student, and Gail Black, a second-year law student. These students, whose bright, energetic and enthusiastic approach always cheered me, contributed to this text by way of a uniformly high quality of research. I am confident that all of these students will do well in their chosen career.

I would also like to thank the Administrative Professional Officer of the Faculty of Law at the University of Alberta, Robert Graham, for providing extra secretarial assistance during the final days and weeks in the typing of the manuscript. And, of course, many thanks to the various persons who provided that secretarial assistance for their fine work and cheerful attitude.

May I also express my appreciation to the library staff in the Faculty of Law for their work on various matters, from time to time, and to Professor Peter Freeman, the Law Librarian, for his review and comments in connection with part of the manuscript. I am also grateful to the Honourable Mr. Justice D. C. McDonald of the Supreme Court of Alberta who provided me with valuable materials from time to time.

I wish to acknowledge the editorial assistance of various members of the staff of my publishers, particularly Anne Milner. I also wish to acknowledge the kind patience of my editor in waiting for the manuscript through difficult periods of unintentional delay.

No acknowledgment of assistance would be complete, however, without reference to individuals who assisted me in a personal capacity. First, I would like to sincerely thank my father, Robert Gall, for his proof-reading and lay assessment of each chapter as I went along. Secondly, I would like to also sincerely thank my wife, Karen, to whom this book is dedicated, for her many hours of typing assistance and her very helpful suggestions, as well as her confidence at all stages in this project and, most importantly, her undying patience.

Finally, I would like to acknowledge the many persons from the bar, bench and law teaching profession who have contributed to my appreciation of the essential nature of the legal process in Canada. It is a personal judgment that law represents the only opportunity to achieve international peace and progress, domestic tranquillity, and major advancements in the quality of life. Law should, in my opinion, be regarded as this unique opportunity, and it is this view that I strongly espouse and which, in part, prompted me to write this book. I fervently hope that my readers and my students adopt this appreciation of our legal system and work to achieve this end.

To those embarking upon a study of law, either in a formalized law school setting, or in pursuit of a casual but concerned interest, may I wish you every success in your endeavours. I hope this volume, in at least some measure, makes your journey more pleasant and, at the very least, more understandable.

April, 1977   Gerald L. Gall
Edmonton

TABLE OF CONTENTS

xiv

12 FAIRNESS AND NATURAL JUSTICE IN THE ADMINISTRATIVE PROCESS

TABLE OF CASES

INTRODUCTION

Law essentially serves two functions in modern, western, industrial society. First, it serves to order and regulate the affairs of all "persons", be they individuals, corporations or governments. Secondly, law acts as a standard of conduct and morality, variously directed at individuals and groups, businesses and governments. In short, through both of these functions, the law seeks to promote and achieve a broad range of social objectives.

But law is not merely an abstract phenomenon. It can and does take many forms. Most important, our lives are ordered through a vast number of legislative enactments as well as an even far greater number of regulations passed thereunder. But, apart from this, much of the law may be found in the vast body of judicial pronouncements enunciated, most often by judges at appeal levels, in the decisions of our courts. This case law arises out of disputes in interpreting the complex and sometimes ambiguous language contained in statutory enactments or perhaps disputes as to the meaning or applicability of a particular rule of common law. The common law is that great body of law borne out of British legal tradition and built up and developed over centuries of judicial pronouncements.

Students of the law discover early that law is even more complex and flows from an even greater number of sources than depicted above. They also discover that, whatever the source, men must transmute this somewhat abstract notion of law into a breathing, living entity, with meaning and availability to all persons. This translating process has taken the form of creating intricately styled societal institutions. These institutions, in turn, must then function in the context of a complex and highly interwoven judicial system. The institutions must be manned by appropriately trained persons. And the entire machinery of interconnected institutions as part of a single, functioning system must operate in an orderly, efficient manner.

To do this, various customs, usages and conventions have been developed throughout the history of our British legal tradition. These include the notions of fairness and natural justice which are so vitally enshrined in the judicial administrative process. But our institutions have also been guided, not only by specific, technical procedural rules, but also by what might be described as prevailing judicial attitudes.

These attitudes, somewhat akin in nature to historically derived customs and usages, are the basis of our common law system and include such notions as precedent and stare decisis, as well as the rules and principles of statutory interpretation. Indeed, the very process of construing statutes and documents consumes much of the time and energy expended by judges and practitioners of the law.

Nonetheless, however perfect the foregoing model appears, perfection must ultimately depend upon the acceptance of the system by those it governs in order to achieve its desired objectives. A legal system must command the support of the members of society, for without general social acceptance it simply cannot function, at least not in the context of liberal, democratic society.

Finally, the law must be regarded, as Lon Fuller once wrote, "as a dimension of human life".[1] As such, it can compel society to take one of many possible directions, the two extremes of which are set out by Professor Fuller in his treatise *Anatomy of the Law:* .

> [Law] can appear as the highest achievement of civilization, liberating for creative use human resources otherwise dedicated to destruction. It can be seen as the foundation of human dignity and freedom, our best hope for a peaceful world. In man's capacity to perceive and legislate against his own defects we can discern his chief claim to stand clearly above the animal level. Philosophers of former ages have, indeed, not hesitated to see some kinship with the divine in man's ability to reorder his own faulty nature and in effect, to recreate himself by the rule of reason.
>
> A shift in mood and all this bright glitter surrounding the law can collapse into dust. Law then becomes man's badge of infamy, his confession of ineradicable perfidy.[2]

In Canada most people would agree that our legal system must strive to achieve the former direction of the two set out above. Indeed, presumably, that is the very motivation underlying any movement for law reform. Moreover, to regard law "as the foundation of human dignity and freedom" is philosophically and ideologically consistent with the basic, underlying values reflected in the new Canadian Charter of Rights and Freedoms. However, for Professor Fuller's former direction to be successfully achieved it is necessary that all persons working within the legal system possess a responsible awareness of the nature of the system, of the institutions within the system, of the roles expected of those persons manning these institutions, and of the judicial attitudes which bind all of the foregoing together into a single, complex, functioning entity. That entity is the legal process in Canada. And it is the essential task of students of the law to examine, understand and critically appraise this process.

---

[1] Fuller, *Anatomy of the Law* (Mentor, 1969), p. 9.
[2] *Ibid*.

1

THE NATURE OF LAW

Professor Philip S. James defines law as "a body of rules for the guidance of human conduct which are imposed upon and enforced among the members of a given state".[1] In offering that definition, the English legal scholar distinguished between the immutable laws of natural science and man-made law. He regards the latter as "a collection of rules of human conduct, prescribed by human beings for the obedience of human beings".[2] Professor James also discusses the somewhat vaguer distinction between man-made law and moral precepts. While it is indeed convenient for the student, upon embarking on a study of the Canadian legal system, to have a working definition of law such as that offered by Professor James, it is also a somewhat artificial starting point.

What is more important than a basic definition of law is the fundamental realization that law — be it in the nature of statutory law, judicial pronouncement, or otherwise — is merely one part of an overall functioning legal system. The positive law of a given state is but a single component of that overall system. As a result, the law must be studied in terms of its interrelationships with the various other components of the legal system. In short, it is far more important to begin a study of our legal system with a definition of the system as the sum of its constituent parts. In turn, it is of even more fundamental importance to provide a definitional framework to the very process by which that sum operates as a working and meaningful entity. An understanding of this process provides the clearest appreciation of the nature of the Canadian legal system and its constituent elements. Accordingly, an examination of the nature of law more appropriately becomes an examination as to the nature of the legal process itself.

The legal process may thus be considered as the vehicle by which our legal system operates in order to govern and enforce the conduct of the people of Canada and in order to promote the best interests of the people as a whole. As well, the legal process is the vehicle by which we resolve disputes in a just, orderly and peaceful fashion when they arise.

---

[1]*Introduction to English Law* (London: Butterworths, 1982), p. 5.
[2]*Ibid.*, p. 4.

It is also important to realize that the legal process is part of an overall complex of interacting processes that form the lifeblood of modern, western, industrial society. It is fundamental, but absolutely essential to appreciate this basic notion. Our society functions through the interaction of a complex matrix of highly interrelated processes. Our society can be looked at in terms of our economic system and the economic processes inherent within that system, or it can be examined in terms of our political system, including the political processes which define the nature of our political system. Even our individual interactions as well as our group and social interactions, according to the conventional wisdom espoused in the disciplines of psychology and sociology, are also part of this overall complex matrix that we call our society. In short, the legal process is but one of the many ongoing processes that make society function. In addition, it cannot be separated from the other processes in that all of the processes which define our society are highly interrelated and impinge on each other with assured regularity.

Professor R. I. Cheffins and lawyer R. N. Tucker define law having regard to the foregoing notion. As they stated in their recent treatise entitled *The Constitutional Process in Canada*:

> Law, in our view, is that part of the over-all process of political decision-making which has achieved somewhat more technical, more obvious and more clearly defined ground rules than other aspects of politics. It is still, however, an integral subdivision of the over-all political process. The student of politics, law and legal philosophy is concerned, among other things, with the question of allocation of all types of resources, and with questions of the relationships between individual citizens and the state, as well as the relationships between states. The study of the legal and political process in any nation is a study of how decisions are made, who makes them, what the decisions are, how they influence subsequent events, and how alternative decisions might have led to different results.

> One of the chief problems in any constitutional system is to decide when decisions should be made within formal legal channels, and when matters should be left to other more informal and usually more flexible arenas. This is one of the things a formal constitutional document attempts to determine. A constitution usually serves a variety of needs. First, it is a badge of nationhood, an indication that the nation has arrived on the national scene fully clothed with the appropriate legal garb. In addition, as already indicated, constitutions set up certain structures and assign them different authority. These structures are usually given such titles as Parliament, Congress, Courts, Executive Officers, Administration. Each of these various types of bodies irrespective of its title, is usually assigned some rather nebulous area of power.[3]

The authors make further reference to this fundamental but important notion as to the nature of the legal system when they define what they regard as the purpose of a constitution. As they stated:

> A constitution is more than a mechanical set of ground rules. It is a mirror reflecting the national soul. It reflects those values the country regards as important, and shows how

---

[3]*The Constitutional Process in Canada*, 2nd ed. (Toronto: McGraw-Hill Ryerson, 1976), p. 3.

these values will be protected. It is for the constitutional student to try to correlate and explain the extent to which the national idea is implemented within the day-to-day framework of political processes.[4]

It is obvious from the foregoing that when one, for example, reads a reported decision of a court of law, one is reading not only the judgment rendered by the court with respect to the facts presented by the opposing litigants, but also a judgment that must be regarded, realistically, as reflecting the judge's notion as to what constitutes public policy, the existing state of morality and the political and economic conditions of the day. The latter considerations, namely, prevailing political and economic conditions, often form a substructure or foundation upon which many decisions are based.

Consider, for example, the obscenity provisions in the Criminal Code of Canada and the cases decided pursuant to those provisions. The state of the law appears to be that a publication will be regarded as obscene if it involves an undue exploitation of sex, with such "undue exploitation" measured against national community standards. With the somewhat restrictive rules as to the admissibility of evidence, how can a judge from Edmonton, for example, who might never have been outside of his province throughout his lifetime, determine national community standards? In effect, that judge, under the guise of applying national community standards, is applying local standards with which he is familiar. Yet the judge must make this determination and it would be folly to believe that his own concept of the existing or prevailing state of morality did not enter his decision.[5]

A more important example relates to constitutional cases. To be sure, these vital national policy decisions have affected the very fabric of our constitutional order in Canada by defining the scope of the respective federal and provincial legislative jurisdictions. Indeed, questions as to federal and provincial relations on a given issue often end up in a court where prior settlement cannot be effected by negotiation and compromise. The decisions of the Supreme Court of Canada and the Judicial Committee of the Privy Council prior to 1949 certainly reflect or in some way relate to the prevailing political and economic conditions of the day. A conclusion of this sort is somewhat in accordance with a realist school of judicial philosophy. To adopt any other view, and to ignore other factors which enter into a judicial decision, would probably be somewhat misleading and would create a highly artificial impression.

Even if a novice, in embarking upon an examination of the legal process in Canada, subscribes to the basic notion that the law is system-

---

[4]*Ibid.*, p. 4.

[5]See, *e.g.*, *R. v. Sudbury News Service Ltd.* (1978), 18 O.R. (2d) 428, 39 C.C.C. (2d) 1 (C.A.), and *R. v. Pink Triangle Press* (1980), 51 C.C.C. (2d) 485, affirmed (*sub nom. Popert v. R.*) 19 C.R. (3d) 393, 58 C.C.C. (2d) 505, leave to appeal to S.C.C. refused 40 N.R. 6 (S.C.C.).

atic in nature, functioning as a continual process in the context of many interacting societal processes, this, in itself, does not render a totally accurate appreciation of the legal process in Canada. Aside from an understanding of the various roles of the persons in the legal system, of the institutions which form the basic structural components of that system, and of the various judicial attitudes which, through convention, essentially make the whole process operational, there is, however, one basic component, the absence of which will not allow a thorough understanding of the nature of the legal process. The roles of the persons who man the legal system, the various institutions within the system and the judicial attitudes which, through convention, make operational that system, will all be discussed in subsequent chapters, but before those discussions, it is essential for the new student of law to appreciate this additional entity within the process. It refers to the judicial philosophy or jurisprudence which, depending upon the particular school of thought adopted by an individual, undoubtedly affects the way in which a judge judges, a prosecutor prosecutes, a lawyer defends or advocates, and the way in which every citizen views the law and the legal system.

One perceives the issues and appreciates the consequences depending upon the particular philosophy that one espouses. An appreciation of the nature and function of the law is not an absolute. One must realize that nature and function are variables that depend upon which particular school of judicial philosophy or jurisprudence one holds. With that in mind, let us now consider some of the major schools of jurisprudence.

Probably the best illustration of the various schools of judicial thought is set out in the now classic fictitious case of the *Speluncian Explorers*.[6] The case was written by a noted legal scholar and proponent of the natural law school of thought, Professor Lon Fuller of Harvard University. Professor Fuller, using contrived facts,[7] modelled various judges' decisions arising out of those facts as a mirror of the various schools of jurisprudence. The case of the *Speluncian Explorers* is now a classical model of how particular facts in a particular dispute or matter are resolved in accordance with the way in which a judge perceives the nature and function of the law. As indicated, each judge resolves the questions before the court in terms of his own view of the appropriate judicial philosophy which ought to govern decision-making by a court. Aside from providing an excellent initial exposure to the science of jurisprudence, the case of the *Speluncian Explorers* drives home the fundamental notion that, given a constant set of facts, different judges may resolve the same problem in different ways, in accordance with different philosophies of law.

---

[6](1949), 62 Harvard L. Rev. 616.

[7]The fictitious case was, however, somewhat modelled after the real case of *R. v. Dudley and Stephens* (1884), 14 Q.B.D. 273.

In short, an examination of judicial philosophy is not merely an abstract, academic, and purely theoretical endeavour, but rather it is vital to an honest and full appreciation of the legal process as it operates in a real-life context.

The *Speluncian Explorers* case is not only illustrative of the various schools of jurisprudence reflected in the various judgments rendered by the members of the court, but it also serves to exemplify: (1) how judges participate in the legal process in accordance with their perception of the nature and purpose of law and the legal system; and (2) the ways in which judges resolve the great dilemmas they must face, in order to effect just results.

Part of a later chapter will be devoted to an examination of the role of judges in our legal system. But, for the present discussion, consider the above two matters in the context of the case of the *Speluncian Explorers*.

Briefly, the facts of that fictional case are as follows. Four men were trapped beneath the ground as the result of a cave-in. In order to survive until rescued it was necessary for them to choose, by lottery, and to eat one of their number. Although the original proponent of this technique of survival subsequently reversed his position, a scheme of chance was devised and the original proponent himself was the hapless victim. The surviving three men were later charged with murder and the "case" is a report of the decision of a final court of appeal considering an appeal against conviction (and the consequential sentence of execution).

One judge, adopting a positivist approach to law, simply interprets the written language of the governing statute literally and upholds the conviction. Another judge, obviously a proponent of natural law thinking, looks to a "state of nature" in which the men found themselves and rejects the notion that the men were bound by the regular, positive law of the land. Moreover, he argues against a literal interpretation of the governing statute. That judgment, incidentally, raises the broader (and currently relevant) question of the role, if any, of judges, in interpreting statutes, of "legislating". By that it is meant that some judges may interpret a statute in such a way as to subvert or twist the literal language of that statute to such an extent that they have, in fact, usurped the role of Parliament. (This approach is particularly noteworthy in view of the new role of Canadian judges under the Charter of Rights and Freedoms.) Further reference will be made to this concern in the subsequent chapter on statutory interpretation.

Another judge in the *Speluncian Explorers* case wishes to ignore the substantive issues, uphold the conviction, and exhort the Chief Executive to exercise his prerogative and grant executive clemency. Another judge, perplexed by the difficult issues he must face, simply withdraws from the case.

Finally, the remaining judge, in reflecting a variant of the philosophy of legal realism, based upon gossip that comes to his attention, urges his colleagues not to resort to an appeal to the Chief Executive for clemency, in that it has come to his attention that this would have the opposite effect on the Chief Executive.

The important point to appreciate in the present context is as follows. Five judges, viewing the same facts and considering the same body of law, have taken different approaches. Why? First, some judges have perceived the nature and purpose, and the role and function of law and the legal system in accordance with a particular school of legal philosophy to which they subscribe. Secondly, judges want to effect just results (although that notion will obviously differ from judge to judge), but the rigidities of the law often do not allow those results to ensue. This, historically, is the basis of the development of the law of equity. At any rate, in order to effect just results, when faced with onerous circumstances, judges might very well resort to exhorting the Chief Executive to offer the prerogative of clemency, as was done by Chief Justice Truepenny in the *Speluncian Explorers* case. But in real life, judges utilize all sorts of available techniques, such as distinguishing cases, ignoring precedent, and a variety of other devices. These techniques, too, will be discussed in the subsequent chapter on the rules and principles of statutory interpretation.

Many scholars and philosophers have laboured over thousands of years in order to categorize and define distinct schools of judicial thought. It is perhaps simplistic and preliminary to summarize, in this initial chapter, the major schools of jurisprudence. However, a student of the legal process in Canada should appreciate the major divisions of judicial thought and the difficulty faced by judicial philosophers over thousands of years in defining the theoretical parameters of the various schools of judicial philosophy. At the outset, it is important to recognize that:

> In jurisprudence we are not concerned to derive rules from authority and apply them to problems; we are concerned rather to reflect on the nature of legal rules, on the underlying meaning of legal concepts and on the essential features of legal systems.[8]

Basically, the three major schools of jurisprudence are the positive law school, the natural law school and the realist school of law. Again, it is important to realize that, first, there are many other schools of jurisprudence which provide an equally legitimate perception of legal systems and the legal process and, moreover, all of the foregoing schools have many variants (there is, for instance, no one absolute school of natural law). Furthermore, for example, one might classify the various schools of jurisprudence in terms of the following subdivisions: natural law, German transcendental idealism, analytical positivism, sociologi-

---

[8]*Salmond on Jurisprudence*, 12th ed. (1966), p. 1.

cal jurisprudence, American realism, Scandinavian realism, Marxian theory of law, and others. Accordingly, it is somewhat artificial to compartmentalize the many schools of jurisprudence into three major divisions; yet, at the same time, this compartmentalization does provide at least a fundamental understanding of the various divisions of legal thought.[9]

POSITIVISM

Basically, positivism, expressed in its simplest terms, regards valid law as the command of the sovereign law-giver, enforced through a system of sanctions imposed by the sovereign. But there is not, however, a single universally-accepted view of analytical positivism. Rather, there are many schools of positivist thought characterized by a common thread running through them. This common thread is a scientific attitude which, as Bodenheimer states, "rejects a priori speculations and seeks to confine itself to the data of experience".[10]

Generally, positivists such as Austin hold the view that there must be a strict separation between law and morality. Or, restated, the positivists emphasize what "is" the law, over considerations as to what "ought to be" the law. A positivist might ask whether a given law is a good law or a bad law, but it is purely a secondary consideration. In other words, legal validity depends only upon legal criteria and not upon moral criteria. A positivist will regard a bad law in the same way in which he will regard a good law.

As Bodenheimer put it, "it is characteristic of legal positivism that it contemplates the form and structure of the law rather than its moral and social content".[11]

The early positivists, particularly Bentham and Austin, should be contrasted with the more modern view of Hart. Hart, in *The Concept of Law*, is critical of the older Austinian view and presents an alternative perspective of positivist thinking. Kelsen, too, offers yet another view of positivism by constructing a theory under which the law is a system of norms which can be traced back to a fundamental source, Kelsen's *Grundnorm*.

Positivism probably represents the most widely held view of law, although obviously there is no one view of positivism that is satisfactory to all proponents who subscribe to this school of jurisprudence.

---

[9]Some, but certainly not all, of the major treatises on judicial philosophy are as follows: *Salmond on Jurisprudence, ibid.;* Friedmann, *Legal Theory* (1967); Dias, *Jurisprudence*, 4th ed. (1976); Lloyd, *Introduction to Jurisprudence*, 4th ed. (1979); Bodenheimer, *Jurisprudence* (1974); Hart, *The Concept of Law* (1961).

[10]*Jurisprudence* (1974), p. 92, footnote 6.

[11]*Ibid.*, p. 104. See also Hart, "Positivism and the Separation of Law and Morals" (1958), 71 Harvard L. Rev. 595.

NATURAL LAW

In his treatise *Introduction to Jurisprudence*, Lloyd categorizes natural law theorists as those "jurists who believe in some higher system to which mere positive law should conform".[12] Moreover, as he stated elsewhere, "We have a feeling of discontent with justice based on positive law alone, and strenuously desire to demonstrate that there are objective moral values which can be given a positive content."[13]

The problem, of course, with natural law is defining the particular nature of the natural law to which the positive law must conform. The danger is that anyone can invoke his version of the natural law in order to suit his purposes.

Historically, natural law thought can be traced to the ancient Greek and Roman philosophers, including Plato, Socrates and Aristotle. Many years later, St. Thomas Aquinas, inspired by Aristotle, developed a natural law theory based upon Christian theology. In short, Aquinas believed that there existed God-given objective moral values.

Essentially, the main characteristic of natural law is that a "natural law" is the law, and a "positive law" contrary to the law of nature is not the law. For example, St. Thomas Aquinas stated in *Summa Theologica* that "an unjust and unreasonable law and one which is repugnant to the law of nature, is not law but a perversion of law".[14] The opposite, of course, is believed by a positivist, namely, that the valid law is the positive law of the land, regardless of the invocation of a natural law.

To inquire as to the content of the natural law is essentially to investigate the written philosophy of the various theorists. And the writings often (but not always) reflect the historical period in which a particular philosopher wrote. For example, after the Reformation, philosophers such as Hobbes, Locke, Spinoza, Montesquieu, Grotius and Rousseau emphasized reason as the source of the natural law and placed less reliance on a theological content in the natural law.

The American Constitution (which was influenced by the philosophies of Locke and Montesquieu) is an example where the natural law is set out in statutory form and becomes the central component of the positive law of the land, to which all other positive laws must conform. Similar examples in Canada are the new Canadian Charter of Rights and Freedoms, as well as the Canadian Bill of Rights, although it should be remembered that both contain opting out provisions, while the latter can be repealed by a simple statutory enactment. A similar example, on the

---

[12]Lloyd, *Introduction to Jurisprudence*, 4th ed. (1979), p. 81.

[13]Lloyd, *The Idea of Law* (1973).

[14]Pt. II, 1st part, Q. 95, art. 2, at p. 25, footnote 6.

international level, of incorporating the natural law as a central component of the international positive law to which all other international laws must conform, is the Universal Declaration of Human Rights, enacted by the United Nations. The natural law might also be incorporated into a custom or usage, or prevailing attitude, such as the common law notion of natural justice. The particular conception of the natural law in all of the foregoing examples relates to a value-oriented perception of the natural law. In this model, law and morality should be mutually inclusive. The actual state of the law must conform to the ideal state of the law. The leading contemporary thinker in this school of jurisprudence is Professor Lon L. Fuller, the author of many works, including the fictional case of the *Speluncian Explorers*, discussed earlier.

Perhaps the best definition of natural law judicial philosophy is stated in *Salmond on Jurisprudence*[15] where the author states that the essence of natural law is as follows:

> The central notion is that there exist objective moral principles which depend on the essential nature of the universe and which can be discovered by natural reason, and that ordinary human law is only truly law in so far as it conforms to these principles.

REALISM

There are many schools of judicial realism, but essentially all these schools have the following theme in common. In analyzing the judicial process, it is not sufficient to merely conclude that a judge is deciding the cases of individual litigants having regard only to the particular facts adduced in evidence, as such facts are applied to cold, hard, legal rules, be they statutory in nature or in the nature of precedent cases at common law. There are, in short, other components to judicial decision-making. For example, the following elements have been suggested as constituting relevant input in judicial decision-making: the personality of the judge, the ability of the judge to distinguish, ignore and re-interpret precedent, the political or policy-making role of judges based upon a subjective perception of justice and equity by a particular judge, and the political, social and economic substructure that defines the context of a given case.

Some twentieth century proponents of judicial realism in the United States include Holmes, Pound, Cardozo and Frank. Legal realism, including the sociological school of law, subscribes to the view that the legal process is not an objective exercise in fact-finding, nor is it an objective exercise in applying the facts to the particular rules of law. While one might say that the realists are basically skeptics, one might also say that they appreciate the psychological or human element in judicial decision-making, and, to that extent, they appreciate the legal process as it in fact operates, not only as it should operate in theory.

---

[15]P. 15, footnote 5.

THE HOHFELDIAN SCHEME

The denotation of legal relationships in terms of the "rights" of one party vis-à-vis those of another is often misleading. That is so because the term "rights", in ordinary and commonplace usage, has given rise to a variety of meanings. Legally, however, the term has a more precise meaning. Indeed, in Canada, the term "civil rights" has a particular meaning constitutionally (see s. 92(13) of the Constitution Act, 1867). Nonetheless, confusion in terminology does exist. Jurisprudential theoreticians have directed themselves to this problem and have produced clever, novel and interesting results. For example, as Dias points out,[16] Bentham was the first to distinguish between a right and a liberty. Following this, Windscheid distinguished between a right and a power, while Bierling distinguished between a right, a liberty and a power. However, in 1902 Salmond analyzed right, liberty and power as well as duty, disability and liability, and, in essence, set the stage for the remarkable analysis of Wesley Newcomb Hohfeld.[17] In 1913, Hohfeld logically and brilliantly set out his scheme of jural relations (jural correlatives, jural opposites and jural contradictories).[18]

The Hohfeldian analysis has gained much respect for its brilliance and clarity although it has not been without criticism. Professor Arthur L. Corbin, writing in a foreword to Hohfeld's treatise on *Fundamental Legal Conceptions*, cited earlier, suggests why the Hohfeldian scheme has encountered some criticisms:

> Hohfeld's articles disturbed the mental complacency of professors of law as well as of students. This was due not only to the fact that mastery of his work is a severe disciplinary process, but also to the fact that they got the erroneous impression that his analysis of concepts and terms was offered as a method of determining social and legal policy — not only for the purpose of distinguishing between a right and a privilege, between a right and a power or an immunity, but also as a method of determining whether any of these jural relations existed or should exist.[19]

---

[16]*Jurisprudence* (London: Butterworths, 1970), p. 249. In a later edition of this work, the author, however, only states that it "is apparent from a work of Bentham, which was published only in 1945, that he too distinguished, clearly and convincingly, between claim and liberty". See Dias, *Jurisprudence*, 4th ed. (London: Butterworths, 1976), p. 34.

[17]See Llewellyn, *Jurisprudence (Realism in Theory and Practice)* (Chicago: University of Chicago Press, 1962), p. 491.

[18]This scheme was originally set out in Hohfeld, *Fundamental Legal Conceptions (As Applied in Judicial Reasoning)* (New Haven: Yale University Press, 1946), and was subsequently represented geometrically in a table prepared by Professor G. L. Williams. For an excellent discussion and explanation of the Hohfeldian scheme, see the following treatises:
(i)   Dias, *Jurisprudence*, 4th ed. (1976), p. 62;
(ii) Stone, *The Province and Function of Law* (Buffalo: William S. Hein and Co. Inc., 1968), p. 115;
(iii) Pound, *Jurisprudence*, Vol. IV (St. Paul: West Publishing Company, 1959), p. 77.
    Interestingly, Pound, in the above treatise, refers to Hohfeld's work as "an elaborate scheme . . . after the manner of Hegelian logic."

[19]Hohfeld, p. xi, footnote 8.

There is, moreover, a significant practical value in the mastery of the Hohfeldian analysis. Generally speaking, as Professor Corbin reminds us:

> One whose own mind is cloudy and confused is certain to convey only cloudy and confused thoughts to others, but the identification of a specific word that will convey an exact thought and no other is an almost necessary process in the clarification of one's own mind.[20]

Discussing the importance of an Hohfeldian analysis, Professor Corbin places it in its proper perspective:

> Hohfeld's analysis of concepts and his arrangement of terms does indeed give great aid to the analysis of legal problems and in breaking down our complex and variable terms. It solves no problem of social or juristic policy, but it does much to define and clarify the issue that is in dispute and this enables the mind to concentrate on the interests and policies that are involved, and increases the probability of an informed and sound conclusion.[21]

Despite some criticism, Hohfeld's work has gained a significant measure of acceptance and approval. The Hohfeldian vocabulary has been utilized regularly in the American Restatements, and, along similar lines, Dias suggests that although the courts may not be using the exact Hohfeldian language, they are thinking it. That is,

> what is important is not the words, but the ideas which they represent. One may think Hohfeld without talking Hohfeld. Every lawyer can utilize the analysis to keep his mind clear when grappling with problems, and may then state the result in any language he pleases.[22]

The following is a schematic representation of the Hohfeldian analysis incorporating, inter alia, the work of Sir John Salmond and Wesley Newcomb Hohfeld. The particular form of schematic representation, as set out on the following page, was originally devised in this geometric form by Professor G. L. Williams.

Consider, for example, the person who has fulfilled all the statutory requirements for the annual renewal of his driver's licence. Assume that upon the tendering of the appropriate fee, the government clerk has no discretion to refuse the granting of the renewal. Applying the Hohfeldian scheme, the presence of the right to have the licence renewed in the citizen implies the duty to renew in the clerk. In addition, the presence of the right to have the licence renewed in the citizen implies the absence of a privilege in the clerk not to renew. Finally, the presence of the duty in the clerk to renew implies an absence of a privilege in the clerk not to renew.

---

[20]*Ibid.*, p. viii.

[21]*Ibid.*, p. xi.

[22]Dias, 4th ed. (1976), p. 62.

THE HOHFELDIAN SCHEME

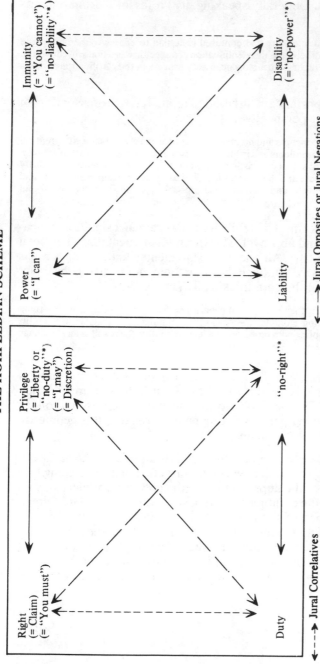

Right
(= Claim)
(= "You must")

Privilege
(= Liberty or
"no-duty")**
(= "I may")
(= Discretion)

Duty

"no-right"**

Power
(= "I can")

Immunity
(= "You cannot")
(= "no-liability")**

Liability

Disability
(= "no-power")**

→ Jural Correlatives
(i.e., the presence of a correlative in one person implies the presence of a corresponding correlative in another person. For example, the presence of a right in one person implies the presence of a duty in another person. The converse here is not necessarily true since duties may arise without correlative rights.)

→ Jural Opposites or Jural Negations
(For example, the presence of a duty in one person implies the absence of a privilege in that same person.)

→ Jural Contradictories
(For example, the presence of a right in one person implies absence of a privilege in another person.)

*This particular terminology was suggested in *Salmond on Jurisprudence.*

It can therefore be seen from the above that fundamental notions, such as "rights" and "duties", possess precise interrelationships in accordance with the Hohfeldian analysis. In examining the various legal sources of law, it is important to regard the legal rights and obligations and the related notions set out in those various sources of law with equal precision. Otherwise, we might fall prey to serious disorder. As Professor Ronald M. Dworkin of Yale University wrote, in an essay on positivism:

> Lawyers lean heavily on the connected concepts of legal right and legal obligation. We say that someone has a legal right or duty, and we take that statement as a sound basis for making claims and demands, and for criticizing the acts of public officials. But our understanding of these concepts is remarkably fragile, and we fall into trouble when we try to say what legal rights and obligations are.[23]

CONCLUSION

Clearly, then, there is no comprehensive philosophy of law acceptable to all persons, just as there is no comprehensive philosophy of life with universal acceptance. At the very least, the formulation of a philosophy of law is a function of a particular appreciation of the nature and purpose of law. And a given appreciation of the nature and purpose of law must, in turn, depend not only upon a keen intellectual insight, but also upon the philosopher's perception of the world in which he lives and his judgment of the values that ought to be promoted.

A detailed study of jurisprudence is beyond the scope of this book, but it is nonetheless important to realize that there is no one view as to the nature and purpose of law. Indeed, Derham, Maher, and Waller, in their treatise *An Introduction to Law*, state several definitions of law which have been offered throughout history:

(a) Law is the will of God Expressed in His commands revealed to man through His chosen instruments. Obedience to God's will is the supreme command.

(b) Law is in two great parts: Divine law, and human law. They may conflict. Differing theories were developed to explain man's duty if faced with a conflict between the dictates of the two.

(c) Law is the product of man's capacity to reason, and it consists of all those principles and rules which, by the use of reason, can be seen to be necessary for, or which can be seen to promote man's peaceful and happy life in a society of men.

(d) Law is in two great parts: Natural law and positive law. Natural law is the product of reason (as in (c) above) whereas positive law is made up of all the rules in force in actual legal systems. The two may sometimes conflict. Differing theories have been developed to explain man's duty when faced with a conflict between the two.

---

[23]"The Model of Rules" in *Law, Reason and Justice* (Essays in Legal Philosophy), Graham Hughes (ed.) (New York: New York University Press, 1969), p. 3.

(e) Law is the command of the sovereign. The sovereign is that person, or group of persons, in any independent human society who, owing no obedience to any outside body or person, enjoys the habitual obedience of all persons in his society.

(f) Law is the instrument man uses in his attempt to achieve justice in society.

(g) Law is an instrument of social engineering.

(h) Law is an instrument by which capitalist society ensures the suppression of the proletariat. With the establishment of communism, law will wither away.

(i) Law is what the courts declare to be the law.[24]

As suggested earlier, the perfect definition of law is elusive, but perhaps the most realistic approach is to avoid attempts at defining law at all. Rather, the law should be regarded as the core matter which those persons and those institutions in any legal system utilize in order to effect an ongoing process in regulating the affairs and conduct of persons in society. With this fundamental notion, it is probably unnecessary to search for an all-encompassing definition of law. Law is more than the setting for a great drama played by lawyers and judges. More accurately, it is the foundation for the infinite number of dramas played by all persons in society, every day of their lives.

The nature of law is not unlike the nature of the evolution of life. It had a beginning, it has many times changed throughout its long history, and it responds to changing needs and circumstances.

Even its destiny is analogous, for man has the power to adapt the law to the needs of a modern, mass, technocratic society, just as man has the technology to avoid environmental hazards which place his future in jeopardy. But law is more than this, for it is possible that man, through law, can control his destiny and improve the quality of life. More than anything else, an organized system of law represents this opportunity for man. From this somewhat lofty perspective, one, however, can easily retreat to an equally appropriate notion of law. For example, law may simply be regarded as the means of ensuring that criminals go to jail or that dogs, while outdoors, are kept on leashes. However one views the law, ultimately there is but one certain notion. Since virtually all aspects of life are affected by the omnipresent influence of the law, the law simply defies a single all-encompassing definition. And that, in itself, is a significant comment on the expansive and pervasive nature of law.

---

[24]"What Then is Law?", in *An Introduction to Law*, 3rd ed. (1977), p. 184.

SELECTED BIBLIOGRAPHY OF TREATISES
ON AN INTRODUCTION TO LAW

Allen, C. K., *Law in the Making*, 7th ed., Oxford: Clarendon Press, 1964.

Baker, J., *An Introduction to English Legal History*, London: Butterworths, 1971.

Brandon, S.; Duncanson, I.; Samuel, G., *English Legal History*, Sweet & Maxwell, 1979.

Claydon, J.; Galloway, D., *Law and Legality*, Toronto: Butterworths, 1980.

Derham, D. P.; F. K. H. Maher and P. L. Walker, *An Introduction to Law*, 3rd ed., Melbourne: Law Book Co., 1977.

Derrett, J. D. M., *An Introduction to Legal Systems*, New York: F. A. Praeger, 1968.

Deschenes, J., *The Sword and The Scales*, Toronto: Butterworths, 1979.

Eddey, K. J., *An Introduction to Public Law*, London: Butterworths, 1967.

Finch, J. D., *Introduction to Legal Theory*, 3rd ed., Sweet & Maxwell, 1979.

Fitzgerald, P.; McShane, K., *Looking at Law: Canada's Legal System*, Ottawa: Bybooks, 1979.

James, P. S., *Introduction to English Law*, 10th ed., London: Butterworths, 1979.

Kiralfy, A. K. R., *The English Legal System*, 6th ed., London: Sweet & Maxwell, 1978.

Lloyd, D., *The Idea of Law*, Middlesex: Penguin, 1979.

Newton, C. R., *General Principles of Law*, 2nd ed., Sweet & Maxwell, 1977.

Phillips, O. H., *A First Book of English Law*, 7th ed., London: Sweet & Maxwell, 1977.

Radcliffe and Cross, *The English Legal System*, 6th ed., London: Butterworths, 1977.

Raz, J., *The Authority of Law*, Oxford: Clarendon Press, 1979.

Sim and Scott, *"A" Level English Law*, 3rd ed., London: Butterworths, 1970.

Troller, A., *The Law and Order — An Introduction to Thinking About the Nature of Law*, Leyden, A. J. Sithoff, 1969.

Waddams, S. J., *Introduction to the Study of Law*, 2nd ed., Toronto: Carswell, 1983.

Walker, R. J., and M. G. Walker, *The English Legal System*, 4th ed., London: Butterworths, 1976.

Wilson, G., *Cases and Materials on the English Legal System*, London: Sweet & Maxwell, 1973.

2

THE DIVISIONS OF LAW

THE MAIN DIVISIONS OF LAW

The various sources of law will be discussed in the next chapter, but emerging from the various legal sources of law is not a single, homogeneous entity to which we can refer as "the law". Rather, what emerges is a complex paradigm, containing many divisions and subdivisions, each characterized in terms of its interrelationship with all other components of a complicated and integrated system. This conception of our legal system cannot, however, be defined in terms of a single, representative model. Rather it must be examined by reference to various degrees of abstraction.

From the most fundamental and general abstraction, "the law" may be broken down as follows:

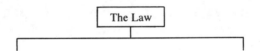

Positive law, as set out in the various legal sources of law.

All the other conceptions and notions of binding law (be they in the nature of natural law, morality, orthodox religious beliefs, or whatever form they might take).

Given that the student of the law is primarily concerned with the positive law, it is necessary to become more specific and define "the law" in terms of a more meaningful and less general abstraction. As such, the positive law may be subdivided as follows:

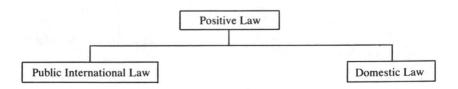

Public international law is concerned with the affairs of nations as members of the international community and the affairs of men within nations from the perspective of internationally recognized customs and conventions, rules and principles, and treaties and other obligations.

Domestic law, in this sense, refers to the positive law which governs the affairs of all persons within a sovereign, independent nation.

Owing to interjurisdictional variations in the substantive law, a body of rules has been developed in order to resolve those variations. These rules are sometimes referred to as "private international law" or, alternatively, "conflicts of law".

The positive, domestic law of Canada can now be subdivided in terms of two basic components. The first is concerned with the substantive legal principles set out in the various legal sources of law. The second is concerned with the mechanism by which the substantive law is brought into operation. That is:

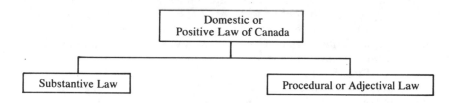

— That is, the law of civil procedure (including the rules of court), the law of criminal procedure, and the law of evidence.

The positive, domestic, substantive law of Canada is subdivided further in terms of yet a more specific abstraction:

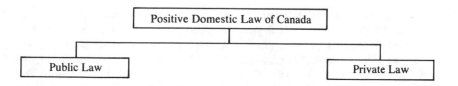

The public law is defined, essentially, as those areas of the law in which the public interest is primarily involved. There are, basically, four areas of public law:

1.   Constitutional law — Intrinsically, the public interest is involved in that, essentially, the fundamental questions of Canadian constitu-

tional law relate to the relationship between the various components of a federal state. Constitutional law now also includes considerations relating to the Canadian Charter of Rights and Freedoms and the protection of the fundamental freedoms guaranteed therein.

2.   Administrative law — Here, the public interest is involved in that although a private interest may be the subject of an administrative decision, that decision is based upon certain guidelines which promote and advance the public interest. For example, if a private interest, such as a radio station, applies to the administrative tribunal regulating that industry for a renewal of the station's licence, the tribunal will render its decision in accordance with the guidelines or terms of reference as set out in the tribunal's enabling legislation. Presumably, those terms of reference will provide the basis under which the private application for licence renewal will be decided. Of more importance, however, those terms of reference and the tribunal's exercise of authority under them will reflect what constitutes a benefit to the public interest at large.

3.   Criminal law — Here, the public interest is involved in the sense that crime is regarded as an offence against the state, against the people and against the public interest. That is why the police, as agents of the executive branch of government, conduct an investigation of an alleged crime. That is why a Crown attorney, as the agent of the provincial (or, on occasion, the federal) Attorney General, will prosecute a crime. That is why, in the event of a conviction, federal and provincial authorities will seek to rehabilitate, segregate, deter and punish the convicted person (and deter others, by way of example). And that is why various provincial criminal injuries compensation boards will render awards to innocent victims of crimes of violence, in part for reason of the state's failure to protect its subjects from the injuries arising out of criminal conduct.

4.   Taxation law — Here, the public interest is served by the collection of moneys needed to finance the operations of government and the conduct of public programmes.

The private law is defined, essentially, as those areas of the law in which the private interest is primarily involved. Of course, the public interest does enter into a court's consideration of essentially private matters. This occurs, for example, whenever a court entertains notions of "public policy". However, the above notwithstanding, private law encompasses those areas of the law where our legal system must resolve essentially private disputes.

Most of the workload faced by our courts occurs in the area of private law. Indeed, if one examines a typical Canadian law school curriculum, one will readily observe that the curriculum, and probably necessarily so, is heavily weighted towards a private law emphasis.

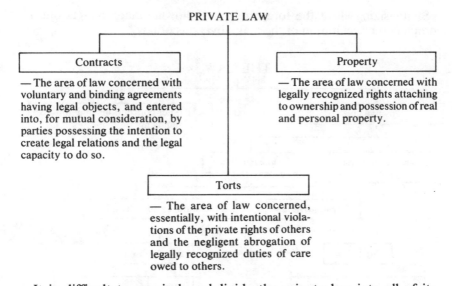

PRIVATE LAW

Contracts

— The area of law concerned with voluntary and binding agreements having legal objects, and entered into, for mutual consideration, by parties possessing the intention to create legal relations and the legal capacity to do so.

Property

— The area of law concerned with legally recognized rights attaching to ownership and possession of real and personal property.

Torts

— The area of law concerned, essentially, with intentional violations of the private rights of others and the negligent abrogation of legally recognized duties of care owed to others.

It is difficult to precisely subdivide the private law into all of its various components; however, in order to complete the picture, the above represents a more specific and detailed abstraction of the main divisions of law emerging out of and encompassing the various legal sources of law.

More specifically, the private law is also concerned with the following subdivisions.

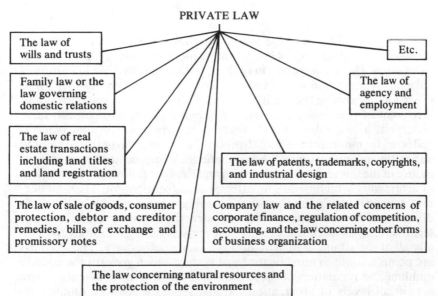

PRIVATE LAW

The law of wills and trusts

Family law or the law governing domestic relations

The law of real estate transactions including land titles and land registration

The law of sale of goods, consumer protection, debtor and creditor remedies, bills of exchange and promissory notes

The law concerning natural resources and the protection of the environment

The law of patents, trademarks, copyrights, and industrial design

Company law and the related concerns of corporate finance, regulation of competition, accounting, and the law concerning other forms of business organization

The law of agency and employment

Etc.

Synthesizing all of the foregoing, the following diagram sets out a complete representation of the main divisions of law.

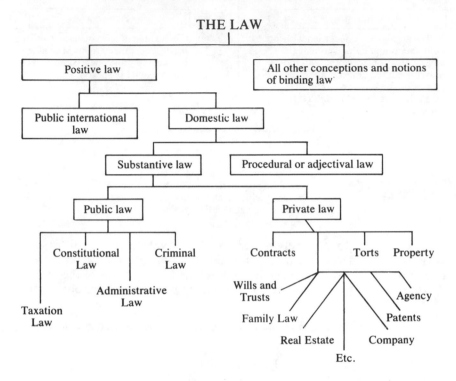

THE LAW

Having regard to all of the foregoing, the reader can appreciate that the various legal sources of law manifest themselves in terms of various categories. These categories may then, in turn, be classified in terms of various divisions and subdivisions. However, in attempting to achieve precision in defining the main divisions of the law, it is important not to lose sight of the reality that law is, as many perceptive persons have observed, a "seamless web" where a reverberation in one place is reflected by motion elsewhere. In short, however precise the attempt to define the main divisions of the law, one must appreciate the integrated nature of the law and the legal system and thus not fall prey to an element of artificiality which befalls an attempt at categorization. That intellectual danger notwithstanding, the foregoing representation of the main divisions of law, at various levels of abstraction, is representative of our legal system, as a complex entity, encompassing regulation over virtually all of the affairs of man in modern, industrial society. Those affairs are complex, and so must be the legal system which governs the orderly conduct and regulation of those affairs. That is why, in essence, there are, at all levels of abstraction, so many (and a growing number of) divisions of law. In short, out of the two fundamental legal sources of law, statutes and cases, emerges a complicated system, characterized by many divisions and subdivisions and directed at resolving the great problems and complexities that define modern society.

OTHER DISTINCTIONS

1. THE COMMON LAW

The reader should appreciate that the same words in different contexts possess different meanings. For example, the body of the case law is referred to as the common law. As such, the reliance upon the "common law" in a search for precedents in order to resolve new cases is a principal feature of the "common law system" of law. The reader should also be aware that there are two major sources of law: cases and statutes (and many cases, of course, also arise out of the interpretation of statutes). In defining the nature of the common law system, it would be misleading to ignore the importance of the statutes. Consider, for example, the following distinction between common law and statute law in the common law system.

> The common law has its foundation in those general and immutable principles of justice which should regulate the intercourse of men with men, wherever they may reside. The statute law emanates from the wisdom of the legislature of the day, varies with varying circumstances, and consists of enactment which may be beneficial at one time and injurious at another.[1]

2. THE DIFFERENCES BETWEEN THE COMMON LAW AND CIVIL LAW SYSTEMS

Nine provinces in Canada are said to be common law provinces; that is, the private law of those provinces is administered in accordance with principles associated with "common law" systems of law. On the other hand, Quebec's private law is administered in accordance with principles associated with "civil law" systems of law.

The common law and civil law systems have developed similarities, but their fundamental approaches to the law are substantially different. The civil law system begins with an accepted set of principles. These principles are set out in the civil code. Individual cases are then decided in accordance with these basic tenets. In contrast, the common law approach is to scrutinize the judgments of previous cases and extract general principles to be applied to particular problems at hand. This difference in approach helps to explain the different manner in which the two systems regard the doctrine of stare decisis. Owing to the doctrine of stare decisis, judges, in a common law system, are bound to follow precedent cases, decided by judges of higher courts, given a similar fact

---

[1]*Uniacke v. Dickson* (1848), 2 N.S.R. 287 at 289-90, per Justice Halliburton Peace.

situation in the precedent case and the case at hand. In contrast, however, in the civil law system, the codified principles, and not the cases, are supreme. As a result, theoretically at least, judges are not bound by previous decisions and may differ in their interpretation of the civil code. In deciding cases, a civil law judge is essentially applying the various codified principles to the cases at hand. In doing so, he must, of course, interpret those principles. But he need not rely on prior interpretation in a "precedent" case. Instead, he can choose to conduct his interpretation in accordance with the dictates of justice. He may even consider that an instant case is an exception to a particular codified principle.

Practically speaking, however, civil law judges do not ignore previous cases. There are several reasons for this. First, once a given principle, as set out in the civil code, has been given the same interpretation a number of times, a civil law judge would be risking reversal on appeal if he entertained a new analysis in interpreting the same principle. Secondly, judges do, in fact, follow previously decided cases because of the necessity of providing an element of predictability in the law. As will be seen at a later point in the book, the interests of certainty and predictability play an important role as rationales for the doctrines of precedent and stare decisis in the common law provinces.

It has been said that another major distinction between the two systems is that the civil law system is codified while the common law system is not. However, with the tremendous increase in the amount of legislation (both primary and subordinate legislation) in common law jurisdictions, that observation is no longer valid. The true difference between the common law and civil law systems may be found in the approach described above. Notwithstanding this, legislation in common law jurisdictions is not intended to be self-contained. In contrast, codified civil law is expected to replace all that has gone before and is intended to be a conclusive statement of the law. This attitude was demonstrated in the very beginnings of the civil law.

Fundamentally, the difference between the civil law system and the common law system relates not only to the importance of precedent in the common law system and the relative lack of importance of precedent in the civil law system, but also to the general approach taken by the courts in the two systems. In a common law system, the courts extract existing principles of law from decisions of previous cases, while in the civil law system, the courts look to the civil code to determine a given principle and they then apply the facts of an instant case to that principle. If the code is silent in respect of a given matter, a judge will then attempt to apply general principles contained in the code to the specific fact situation before him.

3. TERMINOLOGY

It is also important for the reader to realize, in initially confronting the Canadian legal system, that in the formal legal terminology, the same words have different meanings in different contexts. For example, we have referred extensively to the term "common law". The term "common law" means different things in different contexts. The common law system is often contrasted with the civil law system. On the other hand, we have referred to the common law in contrast with statute law as the two major legal sources of law in Canada. Moreover, civil law is often referred to not as a system, but as, essentially, private law. In this sense, civil law is often contrasted with criminal law. In the latter context, the civil law refers to, for example, rights and remedies in connection with the law of contracts, torts and real property. In other words, here, the civil law is concerned with rights and duties in connection with one's fellow citizens in a private capacity. This is contrasted with criminal law, which is concerned with the rights and duties enjoyed by the subject in connection with the state. As well, there are other connotations of the term common law. For example, its original meaning was the law common to all of England as opposed to merely local law. Also, the common law is often contrasted with the law of equity. Equity is, essentially, the branch of law which grew and developed in the old Courts of Chancery. The reader should appreciate the main connotations set out above, as well as possess an awareness that these fundamental words and phrases have different meanings in different contexts, although the same words and phrases are used.

4. CONCLUSION

From the above, it becomes obvious that our system of law is truly multi-faceted. A typical Canadian law school curriculum has some thirty or more available subjects taught. The vast number of areas of the law, including new, emerging areas, such as environmental and consumer law, makes it almost impossible for a lawyer to become an expert in all areas of the law. Indeed, the growing number of areas of the law is one reason why officially accredited specialization is a development predictably over the horizon. At the same time, all areas of the law remain interrelated. It has, for good reason, been said that the law is a "seamless web" — when it makes an impact in one of its areas, it causes reverberations elsewhere. Accordingly, although there are truly many divisions of law, they are in fact moulded together in the context of a single, multi-dimensional legal system.

3

THE SOURCES OF LAW

INTRODUCTION

The natural laws of physics require, in defining the concept of sound, that there be a source, a medium and a recipient. The positive laws which govern the affairs of man in society, like sound, also require a source, a medium and a recipient, in order to be real in more than a philosophical way.

The law, be it biblical or contemporary, requires a law-giver. Because law is not a single, homogeneous entity, but rather an amalgam of all kinds of entities of various natures, then it follows that each type of commandment or law that governs our behaviour may be traced to its own unique source or law-giver. In other words, just as there are many categorizations of law, there are many sources of law, each possessing its own unique nature.

As indicated above, the law, as a medium, requires a law-giver. Throughout history, there have been many renowned law-givers. Consider, for example, the following list of the great law-givers whose contributions to the development of law span many centuries and contribute to the growth of law in many nations.[1]

1. Hammurabi, 1950 B.C., Babylon
2. Moses, 13th century B.C., Egypt
3. Confucius, 551-479 B.C., China
4. Justinian, 483-565, Roman Empire
5. Mohammed, 570-632, Arabia
6. Grotius, 1583-1645, Holland
7. Napoleon, 1769-1821, France
8. Menes, 3100 B.C., Egypt
9. Solomon, 973-933 B.C., Israel
10. Lycurgus, 9th century B.C, Greece
11. Draco, 7th century B.C., Greece
12. Solon, 600 B.C., Greece
13. Augustus, 63 B.C.-14 A.D., Roman Empire
14. Charlemagne, 742-814, Roman Empire
15. St. Louis, 1214-1270, France
16. Blackstone, 1723-1780, England
17. John Marshall, 1755-1835, U.S.A.

---

[1]World Peace Through Law Center, "Renowned Law Givers and Great Law Documents of Humankind" (Washington, 1975).

The foregoing list of law-givers most certainly contains some of the greatest contributors in the development of law throughout history. In addition, however, there have also been, throughout history, great bench marks of legal documentation. Some of these documents are as follows:[2]

1. Ten Commandments, 13th century B.C.
2. Koran, 652, Arabia
3. Magna Carta, 1215, England
4. Declaration of Independence, 1776, U.S.A.
5. U.S. Constitution, 1787, U.S.A.
6. Bill of Rights, 1791, U.S.A.
7. Declaration of the Rights of Man and of the Citizen, 1791, France
8. Universal Declaration of Human Rights, 1948

To define the sources of law in Canada, one must assume, first, that what constitutes the law is merely the positive law of the land, without regard to any form or system of natural law, and, secondly, that the sources of that positive law represent the traditional law-givers in an Anglo-Canadian constitutional system. Specifically, those traditional sources will be discussed in detail in Chapter 4 in connection with the discussion on the Canadian constitutional system.

For the time being, however, it is important to consider, on a more general level, the various sources of law. The problem is, however, one of proper characterization and categorization. Since the sources of law are often set out in different ways, the result is that those sources are often difficult to define with precision. For example, consider the diagrammatical representations of the sources of law, as set out on the following pages by the leading authors of introductory texts in English law.

From these diagrams it is obvious that there exist not one, but many models of the various sources of law. Also, it is important to define what is meant by "source of law". One could be referring, of course, to the historical sources of law. In doing so, we would be looking to "the factors that have influenced the development of the law and to which the content of the law may be traced . . . for example, mercantile custom, religious beliefs, ideas of reasonableness, natural justice, conscience, public policy, borrowing from Roman civil law and Canon law, professional practice and juristic opinion."[3]

By inquiring into the sources of law, we could also be entertaining an examination as to what constitutes the "formal" sources of law. "A Formal Source of Law is that from which a system of law derives its validity, whether that be, for example, the general will or the will of a dictator".[4] This question of validity, as we saw in the first chapter, may

---

[2]*Ibid.*
[3]Phillips, *A First Book of English Law*, 7th ed. (London: Sweet & Maxwell, 1977), p. 117.
[4]Walker and Walker, *The English Legal System*, 4th ed. (London: Butterworths, 1976), p. 78.

SOURCES

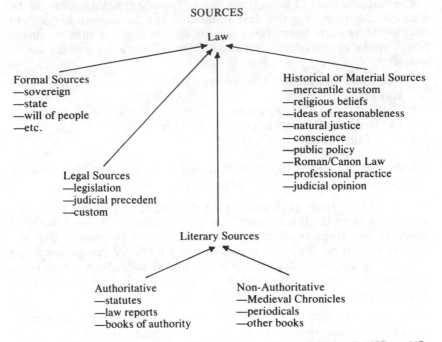

Phillips, *A First Book of English Law*, 7th ed. (London: Sweet & Maxwell, 1977), p. 117.

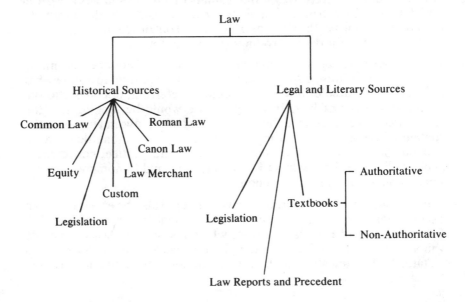

Walker and Walker, *The English Legal System*, 4th ed. (London: Butterworths, 1976).

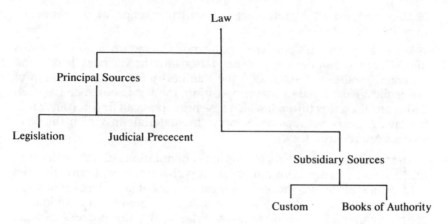

James, *Introduction to English Law*, 10th ed. (London: Butterworths, 1979), pp. 8-24.

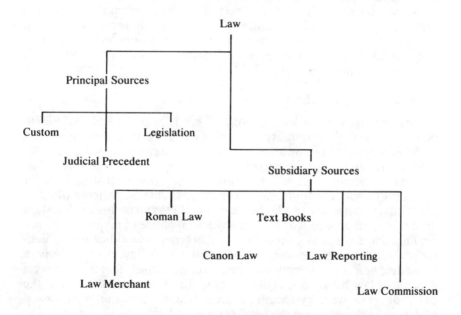

Sim and Scott, *"A" Level English Law*, 3rd ed. (London: Butterworths, 1970), p. 33.

be answered, in part, by reference to a particular school of jurisprudence to which one subscribes.

More likely, and this concerns us the most, by inquiring into "sources of law", one is conducting an examination into the various "legal" and "literary" sources. Essentially, the "authority for any proposition of law is the *legal* source of that proposition; the legal sources have been defined as the gates through which new principles can find entrance into the law. *Literary* sources are simply the materials in which the *legal* sources are recorded".[5]

The foregoing represents the various connotations of an inquiry into the "sources of law". Our inquiry, in this chapter, is primarily directed at an examination into the various legal sources of law. An examination of literary sources of law is, in effect, closely related to an examination of the techniques of legal research. Essentially, the process of legal research is the process by which, through an examination of the various literary sources of law, the legal sources of laws are discovered. And through an examination of the legal sources of law, we are able to discover the various rights, duties, powers and privileges which define the nature of control that the law exerts over human affairs. However, in order to appreciate that "nature of control", it is important first to appreciate what constitutes, in a somewhat philosophical but nonetheless useful way, the concepts of "rights", "duties", "powers", "privileges", and other related notions.

THE LEGAL SOURCES OF LAW

What are the various legal sources of law? To the extent that public policy and prevailing morality are part of our judicial system, one could perhaps conclude that the legal sources of law have no specific bounds. Indeed, prevailing morality might be a source of law. For example, in the obscenity sections under the Criminal Code, a judge must look at the prevailing Canadian community standards in order to determine whether a particular matter under adjudication constitutes an undue exploitation of sex. Moreover, a judge often takes judicial notice of many factors not contained in any specific formal source, in order to adjudicate a particular problem. And moreover, notions of public policy often underlie a given decision. Accordingly, one might, at the outset, feel that the legal sources of law have no specific bounds. But, in reality, that is not the case, for there are very specific sources which one should turn to and rely upon in determining the legal sources of law.

Basically, the two main sources of law are statutory enactments and cases adjudicated by courts. However, there are other legal sources of law as well. For example, at a later point in this chapter, brief mention will be made of the royal prerogative, custom and convention, and

---

[5]*Ibid.*

morality, as legal sources of law. For the time being, however, the two main sources of law are statutory enactments and cases adjudicated by judges in courts of law.

1. STATUTES

Statutes are the most important legal source of law. Under the major written component of the Canadian constitution, namely, the Constitution Act of 1982 (incorporating, among other things, the former British North America Act of 1867), there are eleven sovereign legislative bodies in Canada. One is the Parliament of Canada, and the others are the ten provincial legislatures. By the provisions of the Constitution Act, each is granted legislative authority to enact statutes, but the legislative competence of each is, however, specifically limited to certain classes of matters. It is important to realize that a sovereign legislative body can enact statutes pursuant only to its legislative competence. Such legislation is referred to as primary legislation, in that it is passed by the sovereign legislative body itself. However, there is another category of legislation in Canada, and this is referred to as subordinate legislation.

Subordinate legislation is legislation enacted by a person, body or tribunal, subordinate to a sovereign legislative body. Subordinate legislation takes many forms: by-laws, ordinances, statutory instruments, orders in council, rules and regulations. The body enacting subordinate legislation must do so only in accordance with the authority granted it under the enabling or governing legislation passed by the sovereign legislative body.[6] In short, a sovereign legislative body enacts governing legislation, and pursuant to that governing legislation, authority is granted to a delegate or a subordinate body to pass regulations, orders in council, by-laws, ordinances, rules, statutory instruments, and otherwise. A good example of a delegated authority is a municipal council. Pursuant to enabling provincial legislation, municipalities are created and municipal councils are granted authority to enact by-laws in accordance with the limitations set out in the enabling provincial legislation.

2. CASE LAW

The second major legal source of law is the decisions of courts in adjudicating particular matters. In deciding cases, judges, especially at the appellate levels, often set out in writing the material facts of the particular case, the issues of law involved and the reasons for decision, among other things. The reasons for decision, or ratio decidendi, may serve as a precedent for future courts to follow in the event that a similar fact situation is adjudicated again. The courts are bound to follow

---

[6]There are some restrictions on subordinate or delegated legislation and these restrictions are set out in Chapter 11 in connection with the discussion of statutes, and in Chapter 12 in dealing with an introduction to administrative law.

precedent cases in accordance with the doctrine of stare decisis. Accordingly, as a result of the operation of the doctrines of precedent and stare decisis, a body of case law has developed which acts as a guide for judges in deciding future cases. This body of case law is referred to as the common law. Because the common law is such a major legal source of law in the Canadian legal system, with the exception of the province of Quebec, the Canadian legal system is characterized as a common law system of law.[7] Essentially, the common law contains a set of principles enunciated through the decisions of courts over the past six hundred years. In other words, as new fact situations arise and as judges decide new cases, the existing principles are broadened, exceptions are developed, and the body of case law is expanded. In short, all of the case law and all of the principles and exceptions enunciated as part of that case law for the past six hundred years, initially in Great Britain, and subsequently in Canada, form the basis of the common law, the second major legal source of law in Canada.

Consider the following commentaries on the historical evolution of the common law:

This term, common law, which we have been using, needs some explanation. I think that it comes into use in or shortly after the reign of Edward the First. The word "common" of course is not opposed to "uncommon": rather it means "general", and the contrast to common law is special law. Common law is in the first place unenacted law; thus it is distinguished from statutes and ordinances. In the second place, it is common to the whole land; thus it is distinguished from local customs. In the third place, it is the law of the temporal courts; thus it is distinguished from ecclesiastical law, the law of the Courts Christian, courts which throughout the Middle Ages take cognisance of many matters which we should consider temporal matters — in particular marriages and testaments. Common law is in theory traditional law — that which has always been law and still is law, in so far as it has not been over-ridden by statute or ordinance. In older ages, while the local courts were still powerful, law was really preserved by oral tradition among the free men who sat as judges in these courts. In the twelfth and thirteenth century as the king's court throws open its doors wider and wider for more and more business, the knowledge of the law becomes more and more the possession of a learned class of professional lawyers, in particular of the king's justices. Already in John's reign they claim to be juris periti. More and more common law is gradually evolved as ever new cases arise; but the judges are not conceived as making new law — they have no right or power to do that — rather they are but declaring what has always been law.

The starting point, therefore, is an assumption, or a theory, or a fiction if you will, that the common law of England is a comprehensive body of rules by reference to which every conceivable problem can be determined. Only a small portion of that body of rules has at any particular time been "found" and set forth in judicial decisions for our guidance. The rest remains to be found and applied from time to time as circumstances require. It follows that, in theory at least, the common law never changes. When a rule of the common law is found and enunciated for the first time, that is not a new law. It has always been the law but is now found for the first time. When the ultimate court of appeal overrules a line of cases in the lower courts and enunciates a rule that was never enunciated before, that is not a change in the law. The law was always as it is now

---

[7]The doctrines of precedent and stare decisis are discussed in detail in Chapter 10.

revealed to us and we were in error, prior to the new decision, in thinking that it was something else.[8]

. . . .

As a practical fact, whenever the ultimate court of appeal enunciates a rule which was never enunciated before, something new has been created; in fact, a new rule of law has been added to the body of rules that previously existed or one of the old rules that existed in fact has been altered or abrogated. However it is the theory of our system of law that the ultimate court of appeal is finding and expounding the true rule of the common law as it has always been.[9]

On the other hand, as indicated in the previous chapter, in the province of Quebec, the legal system is based not on the British tradition of common law but rather on the French and Roman tradition of codification of law. The Quebec Civil Code is essentially a domestic adaptation of the Napoleonic or French Civil Code and, to some extent, also reflects the earlier Roman Code. This is not to say that the common law does not share those influences. Indeed, many statutes are a codification derived from some of the same historical sources. However, in the province of Quebec, codification represents the essential embodiment of the law, in that a judge need not abide by a precedent. He might, instead, rely on his own interpretation of a provision in the Quebec Civil Code.

The role of precedent and stare decisis in developing and evolving the common law and, in particular, in providing a mechanism by which the common law can respond to changing social conditions, is discussed in some detail in Chapter 10. In addition, reference should be made to a further discussion of the civil law system set out in the next chapter. But, for the time being, the reader ought to appreciate the importance of case law or the common law as a major legal source of law in Canada.

3. PARLIAMENTARY SOVEREIGNTY AND THE RELATION OF CASES TO STATUTES

Under the British doctrine of parliamentary sovereignty, Parliament can make or unmake any laws provided, in the Canadian context, that Parliament or a provincial legislature does so in accordance with the constitutional limitations set out in the Constitution Act of 1867. The doctrine of parliamentary sovereignty and some restrictions on the Canadian application of that doctrine are discussed in detail in Chapter 5. However, for the purposes of the present discussion, it is important to appreciate the sovereign power of Parliament or a provincial legislature to enact law. We have thus far defined the two major sources of law — statutory enactment and case law. The question then becomes: What is

---

[8]Maitland, *Constitutional History of England* (Cambridge: Cambridge University Press, 1908), pp. 22-23.

[9]Jackett, "Foundations of Canadian Law in History and Theory", in Lang (ed.), *Contemporary Problems of Public Law in Canada* (1968).

the relationship between the two? By virtue of the operation of the doctrine of parliamentary sovereignty, Parliament has the authority to repeal or modify any principles set out in the case law. Accordingly, in the event that a particular common law rule is antiquated or somehow in need of reform, the sovereign legislative body can enact legislation in effect to repeal, modify or alter (or perhaps codify) that common law rule. The various interpretation statutes do, however, contain provisions to the effect that a statute is remedial (rather than confirmatory) of an existing common law rule.

There is a second aspect to the relationship between statutes and cases. Much of the common law is developed, not solely through an adjudication of new fact situations with reference to past and settled principles of common law, but also out of an interpretation of existing statutory provisions. Statutory interpretation represents a major portion of the role and function of the judge. As such, there have been many rules and principles developed in order to assist the court in interpreting ambiguous statutory provisions. These rules and principles are discussed in detail in Chapter 11.

4. MISCELLANEOUS LEGAL SOURCES OF LAW

As indicated earlier, there are other legal sources of law, although they do not assume the importance that the foregoing sources of law possess. The first of these is the royal prerogative. Although, generally, the royal prerogative is not exercised without the advice and consent of the executive branch of government, it does, nonetheless, legally and constitutionally, represent another legal source of law. Actually, many powers are constitutionally vested in the Crown. In the Canadian context, these powers are vested in the Crown in right of the Dominion and in the Crown in right of the provinces. The powers of the Crown in right of the Dominion are vested in the Governor General of Canada, and the powers of the Crown in right of a province are vested in the Lieutenant Governor of a province. The powers vested in the Governor General of Canada have, historically, been set out in letters patent and letters of instruction issued by Westminster to the Governor General. The last letters patent issued to the Governor General were issued in 1947. In addition, there is case authority in Canada to the effect that the Crown in right of a province possesses the same power as the Crown in right of the Dominion. At any rate, there are certain prerogatives of the Crown which are historically derived and which presently exist. Most Crown prerogatives, however, have been abolished by virtue of statutory enactment. Moreover, once a statute repeals a Crown prerogative, it can never again be revived as a Crown prerogative. It may subsequently be revived in statutory form, but as a Crown prerogative it is lost forever.

Consider the following examples of Crown prerogatives. Before the abolition of the death penalty in Canada, there existed a Crown prerogative to commute the execution of a sentence of death to life imprisonment. Also, the Crown presently has the prerogative to pardon persons convicted of crimes. Thirdly, certain provinces possess a tortious immunity for the Crown; that is, by virtue of the Crown prerogative, the Crown may not be sued in tort. However, most provinces have either repealed or modified this Crown prerogative by statute, so that the Crown may be sued in tort, provided that certain notice requirements are satisfied and, in some provinces, provided that permission is obtained from the Crown to be sued in tort.

The Crown prerogative is probably best described as an historical vestige of colonial times. Notwithstanding this, however, the Crown prerogative does provide that certain powers reside in the Crown. But, as indicated earlier, most of these powers would not be exercised without the advice and consent of the executive. There might, however, exist some exceptions to this, and, as such, the Crown prerogative represents another legal source of law of which the reader should be aware.

Another miscellaneous legal source of law is that of custom and convention. Essentially, custom and convention is a legally recognized and legally enshrined practice or usage. It is, of course, difficult to determine at what point in time a practice or usage hardens or crystallizes into a custom or convention and, as such, becomes a legal source of law. Also, the occasions when this occurs are few. That notwithstanding, the English rule is that for a custom to be regarded as a legal source of law in a particular case, "the court must be satisfied of the validity of the custom on seven grounds".[10] The various grounds upon which a practice or usage will be considered to have crystallized into a custom or convention are as follows: continuous operation; open exercise; exercise conducted peaceably and as of right; reasonable, certain and obligatory in nature; consistency with other customs and compatibility with statutes.[11]

Note that continuous operation has come to mean that the custom must be traced back to at least 1189. As a result, it is fair to conclude that custom is rarely a legal source of law of significant import today. The major exception to this, however, is Canadian constitutional law, where custom or convention plays a very significant role.

Another legal source of law, to whatever extent courts will rely upon it, is juristic writings of notable scholars. However, to possess that

---

[10]Sim and Powell-Smith, *Questions and Answers on General Principles of English Law* (London: Butterworths, 1969), p. 10.

[11]The nature of convention in our legal system was considered at some length in *A.G. Man. v. A.G. Can. etc.*, [1981] 6 W.W.R. 1, 125 D.L.R. (3d) 1 (*sub nom. Reference re Amendment of Constitution of Can.*), 34 Nfld. & P.E.I.R. 1, 95 A.P.R. 1, 39 N.R. 1, 11 Man. R. (2d) 1 (S.C.C.). This matter is also discussed in Chapter 5 on the constitutional basis of legislative and judicial authority in Canada.

status (and not be regarded as merely another literary source of law) the writing must be authoritative and the author distinguished. Even then, as a legal source of law, juristic writings might fall prey to the concern that they do no more than offer opinion as to the state of the law.

The final legal source of law is that of morality. Assume that a judge, in the conduct of an adjudication, is not able to find a particular piece of legislation upon which to rely. And assume further that he is not able to find a case or judicial precedent which relates to the fact situation before him, nor is he able to find a custom or convention which is applicable. Then, the question arises as to the principles upon which a judge must rely in deciding that case. "It is the judge's duty to decide every case brought before him and he cannot refuse to do so on the pretext that there is no relevant statutory text [or other legal source of law] applicable to the fact."[12] In that situation, the judge "must find out for himself, he must determine what the law ought to be, he must have recourse to the principles of morality."[13] It should be obvious, however, that only rarely will a circumstance arise in which a judge will not have recourse to a more specific legal source of law.

5. CONSTITUTIONAL SOURCES OF LAW

In defining the various sources of the Canadian constitution, one identifies the various legal sources of law in a somewhat different manner than that outlined above. In doing so, one points to the major legal sources of law and isolates them in terms of more specific, but generically described, categories. For example, statutes, as a legal source of law, may be subdivided, constitutionally, in terms of the following categories: British statutes, especially the Canada Act of 1982 with its constituent components, including the Constitution Acts of 1982 (containing the Canadian Charter of Rights and Freedoms), and 1867 (the old B.N.A. Act); pre-Confederation colonial statutes; post-Confederation Canadian statutes; and quasi-constitutional Canadian statutes. Also, there are additional legal sources of law which have unique constitutional significance, such as letters of instruction to Governors General and letters patent. These constitutional/legal sources of law are discussed in Chapter 5; however, those readers who are interested in pursuing these matters further may consult the following source: Dawson, *The Government of Canada*, 5th ed., rev. by Ward (Toronto: University of Toronto Press, 1970), c. 4.

THE LEGISLATIVE PROCESS

This chapter has dealt essentially with statutes as the most important legal source of law. The enactment of legislation is the main task of our elected representatives at all levels. Accordingly, those persons who

---

[12]Kiralfy, *The English Legal System*, 6th ed. (1978), p. 71.
[13]Gray, *The Nature and Sources of Law* (1921), p. 302.

have not had occasion to engage in a study of political science should appreciate at least the very basic elements of the legislative process. Essentially, a bill is passed into law in accordance with the following procedures. The government introduces a proposed bill into the particular legislative body, at which time the bill is given a routine first reading, that is, it is introduced and then passed without debate. Then, at a future time, the bill is re-introduced by the minister responsible for the subject matter contained in the bill for a second reading. At this stage in the legislative process, the bill is made the subject of a full debate. In introducing the bill at second reading, the responsible minister usually sets out the rationale behind the proposed enactment. If the bill passes second reading, the effect of the successful vote is that the legislative body has approved the bill in principle. Then the bill is usually forwarded to the appropriate standing committee of the legislative body for any hearings and/or further considerations that the standing committee may wish to entertain. (In some cases, however, it is referred instead to a committee of the whole.) The bill is then re-introduced into the legislative body, at the so-called report stage of the legislative process, containing any amendments arising out of the recommendations of the standing committee.

At the third reading, any amendments arising out of committee are debated and the bill is then usually passed, with the principle enunciated at second reading intact, subject only to any detailed amendments made as a result of considerations by the standing committee. Provincially, at this point, the bill has now been enacted into law, subject to formal approval by the Lieutenant Governor. Federally, the whole process repeats itself in the Senate, after which the bill then goes to the Governor General for formal approval. In respect of the latter, it is possible that the bill emerging from Parliament might differ, to some extent, from the bill subsequently emerging from the Senate. If that is the case, any amendments passed in the Senate must be referred back to the House of Commons for approval. Also it is possible that a bill might originally be initiated in the Senate and then proceed through the House of Commons in accordance with the above procedure.

In addition to the foregoing, legislation may be introduced by private members of the House of Commons and/or Senate (by private members I am referring to members of the opposition and to backbenchers of the governing party). These bills, however, virtually always meet with failure and do not represent a significant component of the legislative process.

THE GROWTH OF PRIMARY AND SUBORDINATE LEGISLATION

In recent years there has been a major proliferation of legislative enactments at all levels of government. Because Parliament and the various provincial legislatures cannot possibly deal with every matter, and indeed lack the requisite expertise to do so, a common legislative practice is for the sovereign legislative body, be it Parliament or a provincial legislature, to enact governing or enabling legislation. Under that enabling legislation, the power to make statutory instruments — orders in council, regulations, by-laws, etc. — is delegated to an inferior body. That inferior body may be the cabinet, a minister of the cabinet, an administrative tribunal, a municipal council, or one of many other forms of inferior legislative authority. The inferior body may then enact subordinate legislation, in accordance with its terms of reference as set out in the enabling statute. In doing so, it may not, of course, exceed its jurisdiction as provided in the enabling statute.

There are certain additional constraints placed upon the delegated authority, including the rule of construction that the delegate may not re-delegate (as expressed in the Latin maxim delegatus non potest delegare). Even this rule of construction is subject to two exceptions, the first relating to an express provision in the enabling statute permitting a re-delegation, and the second to an implied delegation, the absence of which would prevent the operation of the intended legislative scheme.

The vast increase in both primary and delegated legislation represents a significant phenomenon in recent years. Probably it can best be understood in light of two possible explanations. First, as modern technology increases and as social problems become more complex, it follows that there must be, not only a legislative response, but often a complex legislative response. Often, such a response must be couched in technical language and must cover a wide range of activities in order to effect the desired regulation. Perhaps no better example can be found than the recent enactment of regulations under the Anti-Inflation Act. Secondly, it has been said that no aspect of human life and human affairs is not covered by law. Indeed, when a new problem arises, the modern tendency, on the part of the public at large and of our legislators, is to immediately demand legislation in order to resolve the problem. For example, one can cite many recent legislative enactments which regulate the affairs of business, in previously little or unregulated areas. One might point to the Foreign Investment Review Act, 1973-74 (Can.), c. 46, the 1975 amendments to the Combines Investigation Act, R.S.C. 1970, c. C-23, the Anti-Inflation Act, 1974-75-76 (Can.), c. 75, major revisions to the Income Tax Act, 1970-71-72 (Can.), c. 63, consumer protection legislation at all levels of government, and many others. On the other hand, one might argue that government intervention has decreased in terms of the regulation of private life and morality. For example, one can point to such recent examples as the liberalization of laws respecting abortion, homosexuality, divorce, attempted suicide, and others. The one exception to this latter notion, however, relates to the prevention of and protection against discrimination. This is an area where the state has interceded to an increasing extent in regulating private conduct.

In any event, there can be no doubt that the proliferation of statutory enactments has given rise to several problems. In the province of Alberta, at the beginning of 1974, there existed some 7,000 regulations contained in 25,000 pages (see the Report of the Select Committee of the Legislative Assembly on Regulations in the Province of Alberta, November 1974). A similar situation exists in every province. Generally speaking, the problem arising out of the vast number of regulations resolves itself into four specific concerns: the need for advance consultation by all regulation-making authorities; the important requirement that the regulations be made accessible both to government personnel and members of the general public; the need for a continuing consolidation and revision of all regulations presently in force; and finally, the need to scrutinize all regulations in order to ensure that they have been enacted in accordance with the terms of reference contained in the enabling statute and that they have not violated any rule of law or any provision contained under a bill of rights.

These concerns were articulated in the Report of the House of Commons Special Committee on Statutory Instruments under the chairmanship of Mark MacGuigan, M.P. As a result of that report, the Statutory Instruments Act was enacted by Parliament in 1971. Under s. 26 of that Act, provision was made that statutory instruments were to be referred to any committee of one or both Houses of Parliament established for the purpose of reviewing delegated legislation. Subsequently, a standing Joint Committee of the House of Commons and Senate on Regulations and other Statutory Instruments was established. It tabled its first major report in the House of Commons and Senate on 4th February 1977. In that report, the Committee "accused the government . . . of using its sweeping decision-making power to trample citizens' basic civil rights". It pointed to the 14,000 federal regulations in force.[14] When these 14,000 federal regulations are added, for example, to the 7,000 provincial regulations in Alberta, the amount of regulatory control, not to mention primary legislation, is clearly staggering. On the provincial level, these same concerns were articulated in the Report of the Select Committee of the Legislative Assembly on Regulations in the Province of Alberta. In addition, this whole question has been made the subject of research conducted by the Law Reform Commission of Canada.[15]

In connection with the question of advance consultation and scrutiny of regulatory enactments, all of the reports recommend that a standing committee of the various legislative bodies be established to conduct that function. Indeed, such a committee has been established federally as a result of the recommendations contained in the MacGuigan report.

---

[14]See the Edmonton Journal, 4th February 1977 (including editorial comment on 7th February 1977) and editorial comment in the Toronto Star, 5th February 1977.

[15]See Access to the Law (Toronto: Carswell/Methuen, 1975), by Dean Martin Friedland of the University of Toronto.

Accessibility is probably the most important concern arising out of regulatory proliferation. There is, of course, the problem that arises in connection with the existence of secret regulations. However, that problem aside, even in respect of public regulations, lawyers as well as members of the general public face difficulties due to the lack of consolidation of the thousands of regulations in force. In order to research a given point of law contained in a regulation, a lawyer often has to engage in a substantial time-consuming research project. One solution is of course, to provide for a continual or at the very least periodic consolidation of existing regulations in force. However, a better solution, which appears likely to be implemented at some time in the future, relates to the development of computer technology. Computerized information retrieval systems would revolutionize the process of legal research. Indeed, there has been considerable research in Canada in recent years exploring these possibilities.

We live in an age in which society has imposed certain demands. The 1970's might be regarded as the maturation of the consumer age, in which society has come to recognize the legitimate demands of consumers in ensuring protection at the market place and the preservation of the environment. Accordingly society has come to recognize that the law can no longer be regarded as falling within the monopolistic preserve of the legal profession. The law belongs to all people in contemporary society and every person has the right to know how the law affects him. This is not, of course, to say that lawyers do not now serve a useful function. Indeed, the opposite is true, for it is a function of the lawyer, in serving his clients, to translate the language of the law to an understandable form. But persons in modern society, as consumers in our legal system, want more than a mere translation. They want, first, the ability to understand the law themselves and this, essentially, is in the nature of an invocation to more precise draftsmanship. Secondly, the consumer in the legal system wants the law to be accessible to him. And clearly, to refer again to the Alberta example, with 7,000 regulations contained in 25,000 pages, not to mention the problem arising out of a lack of consolidation, the average citizen has little, if any, access to the law.

Perhaps the answer lies in computer technology. Perhaps it lies in fewer and simpler statutes. Perhaps we are simply "over-judicialized". Indeed there are over 10,000 crimes contained in federal statutes and regulations. Probably, the best answer lies in a more responsive legal professional disseminating legal information to all segments of the public and in servicing previously underserviced areas of the public. The answer also lies in ensuring that members of the legal profession, as educators, reformers and practitioners, maintain a continuous scrutiny of new and existing legislation. In order to serve the consumers of the legal system, the law must possess, at the very least, the fundamental characteristics of clarity and accessibility.

4

THE BRITISH LEGAL TRADITION

INTRODUCTION

The influence of the British legal tradition is felt by many of the institutions within our system; it is the British tradition that underlies many of the processes and attitudes which make our system operational. No stronger comment on the influence of the British legal tradition in the Canadian legal system can be made than that by the Honourable Chief Justice of Canada, Bora Laskin,[1] referring to a letter written over one hundred and twenty-five years ago:

> What a Toronto correspondent wrote in 1856 in a letter to the Law Times (28 L.T. 85) about England and Upper Canada has a familiar ring even today in respect of England and common law Canada; he said:
>
>> The laws of the two countries are almost identical. The practice or administration of the law is the same in each country . . . I do not invite an emigration of English lawyers, for in Upper Canada the profession is well supplied from native sources. But it will be a consolation to such members of the English Bar as may resolve to enter into competition in the colonies to know that they will labour under no disadvantage.[2]

There can be no doubt that the British influence on the Canadian legal system is very significant. However, it is also important to realize that the Canadian legal system, as a whole, consists of two major components. As indicated in an earlier chapter, the private law in nine of the provinces of Canada is governed by the common law system, while, in the province of Quebec, private law is governed by a civil law system. While the system of law in Quebec is not derived from the British legal system, it does possess an element of British influence. Unfortunately, most lawyers in the common law provinces do not possess more than a fundamental understanding of the civil law tradition in Quebec. Canada is a unique nation in that her citizens can experience the two major systems of law prevailing throughout the world. It is rarely mentioned in

---

[1] When he delivered the 21st series of Hamlyn Lectures on "The British Tradition in Canadian Law", in December 1969.

[2] *Ibid.*, p. xiii.

the recent and now renewed debate and controversy concerning the possible secession of Quebec from Confederation that within Confederation, as it presently exists, Canada is indeed fortunate in having both of the major systems of law in the world operate within her boundries. Accordingly, a later chapter will be directed at a major discussion of the Quebec legal system.

THE RECEPTION OF ENGLISH LAW IN CANADA

1. THE ORIGIN OF THE COMMON LAW

The common law system of law originated in feudal England at about the time of the Norman conquest. It became a practice at that time that the King, in the course of travelling throughout England, would listen to complaints of his subjects and resolve disputes in accordance with the particular customs of that local area of the country. Customs which were not local, but rather were known throughout the land, were called "common customs".

Eventually, responsibility for this adjudication fell to the King's body of advisors, who established three types of courts. First, there was the Court of Common Pleas, for the adjudication of private disputes, one individual against another. Secondly, there was the Court of King's Bench, for criminal matters. Finally, there was the Exchequer Court, in which monetary matters were resolved. The decisions of these courts subsequently became known and were regarded as the "common customs" or "common law" of the land. Eventually, they began to take on a formal aspect and the judges of the various courts held themselves bound by past decisions, and therein lay the origin of the common law as a body of jurisprudence or past decisions upon which judges rely in deciding the cases before them.

The common law of England subsequently spread to the colonies of the British Empire, including the British colonies in North America. Of the two major systems of law in the world, the common law system is not as extensively followed as the civil law system. However, the common law system governs the law in most of the English speaking world (except Scotland) and in many parts of the non-English speaking world, encompassing those nations that are presently or were formerly part of the British Commonwealth. The common tradition linking the common law world is this reliance on a body of case law that developed over centuries of judicial decision-making in solving current problems before the courts.

The mechanism by which the British colonies in North America adopted the common law system in general and the English law, as it existed at the time, specifically, is somewhat complicated. Generally speaking, the method by which English law was received in a British colony depended upon how that colony was acquired by Great Britain.

If it had been acquired by settlement, one set of rules would apply. If it had been acquired by conquest, another set of rules would apply. And if it had been acquired by treaty or cession, yet another set of rules would apply. In Canada, the reception of English law in the territories and in each of the provinces differed. No attempt will be made in this text to consider the complicated history of the reception of English law in detail. However, set out below is a brief and summary review of that history. In addition, interested readers may consult various writings which consider the history of the reception of English law in Canada in considerable detail.[3]

2. CONFEDERATION

Under the provisions of the British North America Act of 1867 (since renamed the Constitution Act of 1867), the Dominion of Canada was created. The original B.N.A. Act provided for a union of the then existing provinces of Canada, Nova Scotia and New Brunswick. Upon union, the province of Canada was divided into the province of Ontario (formerly called the province of Upper Canada) and the province of Quebec (formerly the province of Lower Canada), and these two provinces were united with Nova Scotia and New Brunswick. In addition, the original B.N.A. Act provided for the possibility of future admission of the provinces of Newfoundland, Prince Edward Island and British Columbia, as well as Rupert's Land and the North-Western Territory.

3. WESTERN PROVINCES

English law was first brought to the Canadian west by the Hudson's Bay Company under its Charter of 3rd May 1670. When British subjects settled a colony, they brought with them the existing English common law and statutory law.

Under the combined operation of the Rupert's Land Act, 1868 (U.K.), c. 105, the Manitoba Act, 1870 (Can.), c. 3, and the Order in Council of 23rd June 1870, the Hudson's Bay Company surrendered its land to the new Dominion. Rupert's Land and the North-Western Territory were admitted into the Dominion, and the province of Manitoba was created. The admission into the Dominion of Rupert's Land and the North-Western Territory and the creation of the province of Manitoba all became effective on 15th July 1870. That date is significant, moreover, for reason that it is the date when the province of Manitoba and the North-Western Territory received English law, as it existed at that time.

By virtue of an 1871 amendment to the Constitution Act of 1867, the Parliament of Canada had legislative authority to create new provinces

---

[3]In particular, see Laskin, *supra*, note 1, at p. 3; and Cote, "Reception of English Law" (1977), 15 Alta. L. Rev. 29, among others.

out of the existing territories. Pursuant to that authority the Alberta Act, 1905 (Can.), c. 3, created the province of Alberta and the Saskatchewan Act, 1905 (Can.), c. 42, established the province of Saskatchewan. Under those statutes, there was provision for the continuance of the law as it existed in the territories, and the reader will recall that in the territories, English law was received as it existed on 15th July 1870. As a result the effective date of the reception of English law in the provinces of Alberta and Saskatchewan was also 15th July 1870.

Generally speaking, the date of reception of English law for those colonies acquired by settlement is the date at which the colonial legislature, once established, enacted its first statute. The province of British Columbia acquired English law by settlement. The Law and Equity Act, R.S.B.C. 1979, c. 224, expressly provides for a reception of English law as it existed on 19th November 1858.

4. MARITIME PROVINCES

The Maritime provinces were also acquired by settlement and, therefore, the date for reception of English law is the date at which each of the colonial legislatures was instituted. For the provinces of New Brunswick[4] and Nova Scotia, this occurred in 1758; for the province of Newfoundland, in 1832. In Prince Edward Island, the colonial legislature was instituted in 1773; however, English law was actually received in 1763 pursuant to a royal proclamation.

5. CENTRAL CANADA

Although the province of Quebec is presently a civil law jurisdiction, for a short time it was ruled by English law. After Quebec fell to the British, English civil law and criminal law were introduced by the Royal Proclamation of 1763. Subsequently, although English criminal law remained, French civil law was reinstated by virtue of the Quebec Act, 1774 (Can.), c. 83.

Under the Constitutional Act, 1791 (Can.), c. 31, the provinces of Upper Canada and Lower Canada were created. In Ontario (Upper Canada), following the above enactment, a legislature was created and it enacted its first statute in 1792, under which the English civil law was made applicable to the new province. That Act was assented to on 15th October 1792, and that date is generally regarded as the date for the reception of English law in the province of Ontario.

---

[4]Arguably, in New Brunswick, the reception date is 1660. Lawyer Eric Teed, in correspondence dated May 1980, wrote:

New Brunswick has English law by virtue of the discovery of John Cabot in 1497 who claimed down to Virginia. There have been several cases which ruled 1660 was the date of reception of English law. The Maritimes have English law by virtue of English discovery of settlement prior to the French settlement, not by virtue of conquest.

6. OTHER SIGNIFICANT DATES

After the reception of English law in the "colonies" English legislation affected the "colonies" only if it was applicable to and intended to apply to the colony. Conversely, no colonial statute could be repugnant to any British statute or common law, and it would be inoperative to the extent of any repugnancy. However, upon the enactment of the Colonial Laws Validity Act, 1865, c. 63, the above doctrine of repugnancy applied only to colonial statutes which were repugnant to British statutes specifically directed at the colonies.

Significantly, following the enactment of the Statute of Westminster, 1931, c. 4, the British Parliament had no further capacity to legislate for Canada, unless Canada so requested. The English common law, however, still had a significant impact so long as Canadian courts considered themselves bound by decisions of the higher English courts under the doctrine of stare decisis. This was particularly so until the Supreme Court of Canada became the final court of appeal in respect of all criminal and civil matters in 1949.[5]

THE LAW OF EQUITY

With the reception of English law, Canada inherited not only the English common law but also the law of equity. Historically, the various courts established by the King's advisors, referred to earlier in this chapter, became very formal and rigid in applying the law and in providing the appropriate remedies in the course of adjudicating particular disputes. As a result many subjects would petition the King for extraordinary remedies, as the King was regarded as the fountainhead of justice. The King, in response to these petitions, would provide these extraordinary remedies in the appropriate circumstances. However, as this responsibility became increasingly burdensome, he transferred this jurisdiction for providing extraordinary remedies to his Chancellor. The Chancellor would then receive the various petitions and would dispense these remedies in the appropriate circumstances. By reference to "appropriate circumstances", one means, first, that owing to the rigidity of the rules under which the regular courts operated, they could not provide a remedy in a particular circumstance. Secondly, the petitioners had to fulfill certain preconditions. Eventually, the Chancellor, too, found this responsibility burdensome, and accordingly he transferred jurisdiction to special courts established for the sole purpose of granting those extraordinary remedies. These courts became known as the courts of

---

[5]For a more detailed examination of significant developments throughout the history of Canadian law, see Jackett, "Foundations of Canadian Law in History and Theory" in Lang (ed.), *Contemporary Problems of Public Law in Canada* (University of Toronto Press, 1968).

chancery. After a period of time, these courts, like the King's courts, became somewhat formalized and operated under a regime of rigid rules to which subjects had to adhere before the granting of these extraordinary remedies would be permitted.

In essence, what developed then were two systems of courts in England: the King's regular courts or courts of common law, and the courts of chancery or, alternatively expressed, the courts of equity. The reader will recall the various connotations given to the term "common law". This is yet another connotation, for here the term "common law" means a system of courts of common law providing common law remedies, as opposed to a system of courts of equity providing what are known as equitable remedies.

Parallel with the development of the two systems of courts was the development of two systems of law. The common law courts concerned themselves with the common law, while the courts of chancery concerned themselves with what became known as the law of equity. The extraordinary remedies dispensed by the latter system of courts became known as equitable remedies and the preconditions that had to be fulfilled before the courts of chancery would entertain a petition for an equitable remedy became known as the rules of equity. Probably the most important rule of equity is that a petitioner will not receive an equitable remedy unless he comes to the court "with clean hands". This means, essentially, that he must not taint his case by any wrongdoing whatsoever on his part. Examples of the more important of the equitable remedies are those of rescission and specific performance in the law of contract, but there are several others as well.

In the latter part of the last century, by virtue of the enactment of the Judicature Acts by the Parliament of Great Britain and by the legislative assemblies of the provinces of Canada, the courts of common law and the courts of equity merged, with the result that we now have only one system of courts dispensing both common law and equitable remedies. However, since a court will not now entertain an application for an equitable remedy unless the applicant has satisfied the various rules of equity referred to above, the distinction between law and equity is still important.

THE CANADIAN CONSTITUTIONAL SYSTEM

The Canadian constitutional system is the subject of a major discussion in Chapter 5; however, for our present purposes, we will examine that system in the context of the British legal tradition.

The major written portions of the Canadian constitution are the Constitution Acts of 1867 (the old B.N.A. Act) and 1982 (including the new Canadian Charter of Rights and Freedoms). The significance and content of the major constitutional changes of 1982 are discussed in the next chapter; however, in the preamble to the original B.N.A. Act, the drafters of our constitution included a provision to the effect that the various provinces, upon union, desired that Canada possess a constitution "similar in principle to that of the United Kingdom". Those operative words "similar in principle to that of the United Kingdom", have been known as the "Implied Bill of Rights" in the Canadian constitution.

The effect of the "Implied Bill of Rights" has been to import into our constitutional order various doctrines of British constitutional law.[6] Generally speaking, those words, contained in the preamble, incorporate into the Canadian constitutional system notions of fair play and fundamental freedoms (i.e., freedom of association and assembly, freedom of the press and freedom of speech). More specifically, however, those words import into our constitutional system three fundamental doctrines of British constitutional law. In particular, those fundamental doctrines are the doctrine of responsible government, the doctrine of rule of law and the doctrine of parliamentary sovereignty. The importance and effect of the latter two doctrines are discussed in detail in Chapter 5.

---

[6]See A.G. Can. v. Dupond, [1978] 2 S.C.R. 770, 5 M.P.L.R. 4, 84 D.L.R. (3d) 420, 19 N.R. 478 (*sub nom. Dupond v. Montreal*) (S.C.C.).

Per Beetz J. (For the majority — Martland, Judson, Ritchie, Pigeon and de Grandpre JJ. concurring):

In reply to the submission made by appellants that s. 5 and the Ordinance are in relation to and in conflict with the fundamental freedoms of speech, of assembly and association, of the press and of religion which were inherited from the United Kingdom and made part of the Constitution by the preamble of the B.N.A. Act or protected by the Canadian Bill of Rights, it should be remembered that:

(1) none of the freedoms referred to is placed above the reach of all legislation by the Constitution;

(2) none of these freedoms is a single matter coming within exclusive federal or provincial jurisdiction;

(3) these freedoms are distinct and independent of the faculty of holding assemblies, parades, gatherings, demonstrations or processions on the public domain of a city;

(4) the right to hold public meetings on a highway or in a park is unknown to English law; consequently it cannot have become part of the preamble of the B.N.A. Act;

(5) the holding of assemblies, parades or gatherings on the public domain is a matter which, depending on the aspect, comes under federal or provincial competence;

(6) the Canadian Bill of Rights does not apply to provincial and municipal legislation.

Laskin C.J.C. and Dickson and Spence JJ. dissented on other grounds.

See also D.A. Schmeiser, "The Entrenchment of a Bill of Rights" (1981), 19 Alta. L. Rev. 375 at 379:

[v]arious judges have also suggested the existence of an implied bill of rights in our constitution, at least until the recent rejection of that doctrine by the Supreme Court of Canada in Attorney General for Canada and Dupond.

In addition to the above, under the Canadian constitution, executive power vests in the Crown in Great Britain. However, the Queen now acts only through her representatives in Canada. As a result, in particular, executive authority at the federal level vests in the Governor General of Canada. Provincially, executive power vests in the various Lieutenant Governors of the respective provinces. In addition, there is case authority to the effect that the Crown in right of a province has the same executive authority as the Crown in right of the Dominion. Many of the executive powers vested in the Governor General and the Lieutenant Governors are set out specifically in the Constitution Act of 1867. In addition, traditionally the Queen's representatives in Canada have had their authority defined and communicated to them by way of letters of instruction and letters patent issued in 1947, with the result, essentially, that the Queen's representatives in Canada now have plenary executive authority, as the Queen does herself in the United Kingdom.

Notwithstanding the fundamental nature of the link between the exercise of executive authority in Canada and the Crown in Great Britain, the above is not a truly representative description of the constitutional and de facto exercise of executive power in Canada. This is so for reason of the conventional rules of Canadian constitutional law. In particular, although there are in the Constitution Act of 1867 various specific powers which are vested in the Governor General (such as, for example, the power to summon Parliament), in reality, under the conventional rules of Canadian constitutional law, the Governor General acts only upon the advice and consent of the Prime Minister and his cabinet. Also, for example, under the Constitution Act of 1867, the Crown has a legislative role, namely, to assent to legislation (or, alternatively, to refuse to assent to or to reserve assent of legislation). However, under the conventional rules of constitutional law, the power to refuse to assent or to reserve assent will, most likely, no longer be exercised. In short, executive power in Canada, with some limited exceptions, lies in the hands of the Prime Minister and his cabinet and, provincially, with the various premiers and their cabinets.

In addition to the foregoing, in Canada the Crown serves another function of considerable importance. Specifically, the Crown symbolically represents, to use the words of Chief Justice Laskin, the "personification of the State".[7]

OTHER COMPONENTS OF THE BRITISH LEGAL TRADITION IN CANADA

The Chief Justice, in the published version of the 1969 Hamlyn Trust Lectures referred to earlier, discusses other components of the Cana-

---

[7]Laskin, *supra*, note 1, at p. 119.

dian legal system which share a British legal tradition: the historical evolution of Canadian courts along British lines, including, inter alia, the independence of the judiciary and the use of the jury trial in Canada; the British influence on the development of the legal profession in Canada, including legal education, the admission to practice, and legal scholarship and research. In connection with the legal profession, it is important to appreciate that the practice of law in the United Kingdom differs somewhat from that in Canada. In the United Kingdom, persons are trained and admitted to the bar to practise as either a barrister or a solicitor, but not both. In contrast, however, in Canada a person is admitted to the bar of his or her respective province to practise as both a barrister and a solicitor.

In addition to all of the foregoing, there is one other matter of great significance in defining the British influence on Canadian law. Specifically, Canada has inherited through the operation of the doctrine of stare decisis a rich body of jurisprudence containing centuries of often brilliant reasoning in the decisions of English courts.[8]

Under the doctrine of stare decisis, Canadian courts, at least prior to 1949 when the Supreme Court of Canada became the final court of appeal in all criminal and civil matters, were bound to follow decisions of high English courts. In particular, the Supreme Court of Canada (and, by implication, all inferior courts) felt themselves bound to follow all decisions of the House of Lords and the Judicial Committee of the Privy Council. In 1949, however, the Supreme Court of Canada became the final court of appeal and thereafter there existed no resort to appeal to any English court. As a result, decisions of the House of Lords and the Judicial Committee of the Privy Council are no longer binding on Canadian courts. However, even to the present day, decisions of these courts, under the doctrine of stare decisis, remain highly persuasive. A fuller discussion of this is set out in detail in Chapter 10.

CONCLUSION

In summary, there can be no doubt that historically, and, to a lesser extent, presently, the British legal tradition plays a vital role in defining the nature of the Canadian legal system. Given that patriation of the Canadian constitution has occurred, as the Supreme Court of Canada continues to evolve and develop as the highest court in the nation and the final court of appeal,[9] and as Parliament and the provincial legislatures provide fresh and innovative solutions to present and future problems, it is reasonable to expect that the reliance on the British legal tradition

---

[8]For a discussion of the modern English barrister, see the Guardian, 30th July 1979.

[9]This process of development will, no doubt, be aided by the 1975 amendment to the Supreme Court Act, under which the court may pick and choose those cases of national or legal importance it wishes to decide.

will diminish in time. That prediction notwithstanding, the British tradition in the Canadian legal system is considerably more than a mere historical vestige. When one examines the Canadian legal system as a whole, as an organic, viable and operational structure, one will never be able to divorce that structure from its British origins.

Indeed, as Chief Justice Laskin stated[10]

> More than two hundred years have passed since English law and English legal institutions were rooted in a yet unborn Canada. Sustained at first by remote control from Westminster and by domestic control of colonial governors, the English tradition has survived Canadian legislative and judicial independence, and remains a vital and omnipresent force in Canadian law.

This chapter has reviewed the extent to which the British legal tradition pervades the Canadian legal system. As we expand our examination of that system, the truth of the foregoing will become evident. Indeed, as we shall see in the next chapter, the constitutional basis for the legislative and judicial authority in Canada is, to a significant extent, set out in a statute of the United Kingdom. Before 1982, that constitutional basis was set out in the old B.N.A. Act. In 1982, the enactment of the Canada Act by the U.K. Parliament provided Canadians with the so-called "new" constitution. The new constitution contains, among other things, the Canadian Charter of Rights and Freedoms and a domestic amending formula. These major developments are discussed in the next chapter. The Canada Act, which incorporates both the old B.N.A. Act of 1867 and the new instrument (including the Charter and the amending formula), states:[11]

> No Act of the Parliament of the United Kingdom passed after the Constitution Act, 1982, comes into force shall extend to Canada as part of its law.

Notwithstanding the above provision, the Canadian constitution, at least until it is dramatically amended in Canada, is embodied in a British statute. That in itself is a commentary on the importance of the British legal tradition in Canadian law and in the Canadian legal system.

---

[10]Hamlyn Lectures, *supra*, note 1, at p. 1.
[11]1982 (Eng.), c. 11, s. 2.

5

THE CONSTITUTIONAL
BASIS OF LEGISLATIVE
AND JUDICIAL AUTHORITY

INTRODUCTION

Professor R. I. Cheffins and lawyer R. N. Tucker discuss the purpose of a constitution in their treatise *The Constitutional Process in Canada* as follows:

> One of the chief problems in any constitutional system is to decide when decisions should be made within formal legal channels and when matters should be left to other more informal and usually more flexible arenas. This is one of the things a formal constitutional document attempts to do. A constitution usually serves a variety of needs. First, it is a badge of nationhood, an indication that the nation has arrived on the national scene fully clothed with the appropriate legal garb. In addition, as already indicated, constitutions set up certain structures and assign them different authority. These structures are usually given such titles as Parliament, Congress, Courts, Executive Officers, Administration. Each of these various types of bodies, irrespective of its title, is usually assigned some rather nebulous area of power . . .
>
> A constitution is more than a mechanical set of ground rules. It is a mirror reflecting the national soul. It reflects those values the country regards as important, and also shows how these values will be protected. It is for the constitutional student to try to correlate and explain the extent to which the national idea is implemented within the day-to-day framework of political processes. Every nation's approach to these legal and political problems has much in common with that of every other nation, and much that is peculiarly the nation's own. Every nation draws, to a considerable extent, on the experience of other nations. Similarly, no state can function legally and politically without some internal recognition that it is, in at least some ways, part of a world community. Thus there have developed between states narrow legal, and wider customary, methods of communication and organization, which affect the domestic political order.[1]

Essentially, Professor Cheffins and Mr. Tucker are maintaining that a constitution should be regarded as an integral part of the polity of a given nation. As such, a study of constitutional law ought to be conducted in the context of the Canadian political system. But also, that study ought

---

[1] 2nd ed. (1976), pp. 3-4.

to be conducted in the context of the social and economic underpinnings upon which Canadian society is founded.

THE CONSTITUTIONAL BASIS

Generally, the Canadian constitution is very complex and is derived from numerous sources. Prior to April 17, 1982, in terms of the most fundamental consideration, the Canadian constitution could be reduced to two major components — a written component and an unwritten component. The written component consisted primarily of three British statutes enacted by the Parliament of Great Britain. In order of enactment, those statutes were the Colonial Laws Validity Act of 1865, the British North America Act of 1867, and the Statute of Westminster of 1931. When taken together these three statutes provided the basic framework of the Canadian constitution and enshrined in our constitutional system the doctrine of ultra vires. Under the doctrine of ultra vires, the B.N.A. Act possessed a supremacy over all statutes enacted by the Parliament of Canada and by the legislatures of the ten provinces. The result of this was that any Act passed by Parliament or a legislature had to conform to the jurisdictional constraints set out in ss. 91 and 92 of the B.N.A. Act.

However, even then (i.e., prior to April 17, 1982) it was simplistic and incorrect to regard the B.N.A. Act as the total embodiment of the Canadian constitution. It was far more accurate to regard it instead as the main element of the written component of the constitution. In addition to the above, there were (and are) other elements of the written component of the Canadian constitution. For example, existing laws at Confederation are also elements of the written component in that they continue in force by virtue of s. 129 of the B.N.A. Act. Furthermore, legislation creating the provinces of Alberta, Saskatchewan and Manitoba must necessarily be regarded as an important element in the constitution. In addition, one usually regards letters patent and letters of instruction from Westminster to the colonial Governor before Confederation and to the Governor General since Confederation as part of the written constitution. Indeed, the creation of the office of the Governor General in Canada and the delegation of all Crown prerogative power to that office was effected by the issuance of the last letters patent in 1947. In addition, every statute and every regulation of Parliament and of the provincial legislatures is also regarded as a part of the written constitution.

Some persons argue that some regular statutes possess, by their very nature, a special status. These so-called quasi-constitutional statutes include the Canadian Bill of Rights, R.S.C. 1970, App. III, the Supreme Court Act,[2] R.S.C. 1970, c. S-19, provincial bills of rights and like statutes. Although these statutes are not entrenched in the constitution and could strictly be repealed at any time, they intrinsically occupy a special status for reason that their subject matters fall within the constitutional realm. Some statutes, like the Canadian Bill of Rights, contain primacy provisions which, in effect, require that all other statutes of the same legislative jurisdiction must conform to the substantive provisions contained in the statute possessing primacy, unless those other statutes specifically state that they shall operate notwithstanding the statute containing the primacy provision.

However, notwithstanding all of the foregoing, the B.N.A. Act was the most important component of the written constitution.

Reference was made above to April 17, 1982. That is the date Canada received a so-called "new" constitution. This major event in Canadian history followed a somewhat tumultuous series of events that have transpired over the past few years. Those events have been described in some detail in some recent publications, including McWhinney, *Canada and the Constitution 1979-1982: Patriation and the Charter of Rights* (Toronto: University of Toronto Press, 1982); Sheppard and Valpy, *The National Deal: The Fight for a Canadian Constitution* (Toronto: Fleet Books, 1982); Stevenson, *Unfulfilled Union: Canadian Federalism and National Unity*, Revised Edition (Toronto: Gage Publishing Limited, 1982); and Milne, *The New Canadian Constitution* (Toronto: James Lorimer & Company, 1982).

Essentially these events followed a decade of constitutional negotiations between the provinces and the federal government to restructure and modernize the Canadian constitution. However, after the failure, in September 1980, of the federal government and the ten provinces to reach an accord on a revised constitution, the federal government unilaterally proceeded with the placing before the Parliament of Canada of a new constitutional package. That package, of course, included a Canadian Charter of Rights and Freedoms. That Charter, among other things, attracted considerable debate. Hundreds of submissions were made to the Special Joint Committee of the Senate and House of Commons, a committee created to consider changes to the resolution then before Parliament containing the constitutional package. At the same time, there was much debate as to the wisdom of entrenching a bill of rights in the constitution and as to the quality of the proposed Charter of Rights and Freedoms. The debate embraced both sides of the Atlantic, as the British Government and Members of Parliament were strongly lobbied by Canadian politicians hoping to influence the manner in which Britain would deal with the Canadian request to enact the Charter. Much of the discussion centred on the unilateral nature of the federal action, and questioned whether the enactment by the Canadian Parliament of a resolution authorizing the Parliament of the United Kingdom to include a Charter of Rights and Freedoms in the new Canadian constitution

---

[2]The Supreme Court of Canada is, however, somewhat indirectly, given constitutional status in the Constitution Act of 1982. See later discussion.

infringed on provincial legislative powers under the B.N.A. Act. If so, the discussion then centred on whether a convention existed that the consent of the affected provinces was needed before the Parliament of Canada could make such a request. This issue was to some extent jurisprudential in nature, as the question whether such a convention existed directly led to the question of the status of convention in our legal system.

In any event, these issues were canvassed in three separate constitutional references made to the Courts of Appeal in the provinces of Manitoba, Newfoundland, and Quebec with an appeal therefrom to the Supreme Court of Canada.[2a] During this process, Parliament dealt with the resolution before it, making some significant changes in the Charter of Rights and Freedoms, largely as a result of submissions made to and recommendations made by the Special Joint Committee referred to earlier. Subsequently, the Supreme Court of Canada upheld the legality, though not the constitutionality (in the conventional sense) of the unilateral federal move to patriate the constitution with its entrenched Canadian Charter of Rights and Freedoms. Subsequent to this decision, the federal and provincial governments convened in a final effort to reach an agreement. This led to a breakthrough in which the federal government and all provinces except Quebec agreed to patriation of a somewhat revised package, the revisions including a new amending formula and some changes in the Charter of Rights and Freedoms. Further changes to the Charter, arising from a lobbying effort by native and women's groups, were later agreed to. The entire package was finally approved by the Parliament of Canada in December 1981 and then enacted by the Parliament of the United Kingdom, following which the patriation was effected by the signature of Her Majesty the Queen on the instrument of Proclamation on April 17, 1982. More specifically, a Joint Resolution of the House of Commons and the Senate was enacted in December 1981, after the consent of nine provinces was obtained. That Joint Resolution requested Her Majesty the Queen to place before the Parliament of the United Kingdom an Act called the Canada Act of 1982 (technically cited as 31 Elizabeth II). The Canada Act was passed by the United Kingdom Parliament and proclaimed in Ottawa on April 17, 1982 by Her Majesty the Queen.

The Act contains just four sections. The first section makes reference to Schedule B to the Canada Act. The second section provides that no Act of the Parliament of the United Kingdom shall extend to Canada from this point forward. The third section states that the English and French texts of the Canada Act are equally authoritative, and the fourth section merely provides that the name of the Act is the Canada Act. As a

---

[2a]See *The Supreme Court Decisions on the Canadian Constitution* (Toronto: James Lorimer & Co., 1981).

result, when looking at the substance of the so-called "new constitution", one must focus on Schedule B to the Canada Act, which is itself styled and cited as the Constitution Act of 1982. The Constitution Act of 1982 contains numerous parts. Part 1 is the Canadian Charter of Rights and Freedoms. Part 2 is concerned with the rights of the aboriginal peoples of Canada. Part 3 deals with equalization and regional disparities. Part 4 is more or less a transitional provision dealing with a constitutional conference. Part 5 contains the new domestic procedure for amending the Constitution of Canada. Part 6 provides for a specific amendment to the B.N.A. Act of 1867, now cited as the Constitution Act of 1867. Part 7 contains some important general provisions. Finally, the Constitution Act contains a Schedule, which is by virtue of s. 52(2) an integral part of the Act.

More specifically, s. 52(1) provides that the Constitution of Canada is the supreme law of Canada. Section 52(2) goes on to specify what constitutes the Constitution of Canada. It points out that the Constitution includes the Canada Act and its Schedule (namely, the Constitution Act of 1982 in its English and French texts and its Schedule) and any amendments to any of those instruments. The Schedule to the Constitution Act is therefore an integral part of the Constitution. It contains all of the British North America Acts passed since 1867. They have, however, been renamed as the various "Constitution Acts". The B.N.A. Act of 1867 is therefore brought forward as part of the Constitution as Item 1 in the Schedule to the Constitution Act of 1982. Accordingly, all the jurisprudence to date dealing with the division of legislative powers in ss. 91 and 92, as well as the other sections of the B.N.A. Act, is brought forward and remains as relevant now as it always has been.

This raises the question as to what is, in fact and in law, "new" about the so-called new Constitution. Since all the old provisions are brought forward as well as all the attendant jurisprudence, what is new is, essentially, the Charter of Rights and Freedoms. It is now an entrenched instrument forming an integral part of the Constitution and occupying a constitutional status amendable only by formal constitutional amendment. The second major "new" aspect of the Constitution is the domestic amending formula. There are some other "new" matters but they are not quite as important.

It should be emphasized that the B.N.A. Act and all the law dealing with the division of powers are brought forward and continue in force. However, there have been some minor changes. Sections 20, 50, 91(1) and 92(1) have been repealed and re-enacted as part of the Canadian Charter of Rights and Freedoms.

Essentially, the structure of the Charter follows a categorization scheme of civil liberties that has been widely accepted. Professors Trudeau and Laskin (as they then were) and later Professor Tarnopolsky (as he then was) and even later Professor MacGuigan (as he then was) have all had a part in the development of this categorization scheme, which is essentially a rationalization of the various cases concerning civil liberties. Those cases usually were decided on the basis of the division of powers, the courts using what has been described as the "power allocation" technique of protecting civil liberties. It is a rationalization in the sense that once a particular type of civil liberty is identified, it can then be categorized as to whether that type of civil liberty can be legislated federally or provincially. This rationalization arose out of an analysis of the jurisprudence in respect of the traditional categories of civil liberties. The four basic categories are the egalitarian civil liberties (which deal with equality under the law), the legal civil liberties (which deal with protections contained in the Criminal Code and other statutes), the political civil liberties (which deal with the fundamental freedoms, namely freedom of the press, freedom of speech, freedom of assembly and association and freedom of religion), and finally the economic civil liberties (which deal with the right to freely enter into contracts, the right to own property and the right to sue for damages in the event of a breach of a duty owed to a plaintiff, etc). These traditional categories have been followed in the drafting of the Charter, although the economic civil liberties were eventually taken out (an omission which created quite a political controversy at the time). In addition, new categories of civil liberties, including mobility rights, linguistic rights, multicultural rights, and aboriginal rights have been included in the Charter. Nonetheless, the Charter essentially reflects the various traditional categories which are now preserved within it.

1.   THE PROVISIONS OF THE CHARTER

1. The Canadian Charter of Rights and Freedoms guarantees the rights and freedoms set out in it subject only to such reasonable limits prescribed by law as can be demonstrably justified in a free and democratic society.

Structurally, the Charter begins in section 1, with the so-called "limitations clause" to which most other sections are referable. The theory behind having a limitations clause is that no right is absolute, and therefore the clause provides a court with a basis for placing limits on the exercise of particular rights. It is interesting to note that in the international spectrum, the one right which is recognized as immune from any forms of limitation is the protection against cruel treatment or punishment. In Canada, however, that provision in the Charter is still referable to section 1 and the limitation imposed by it.

2.   Everyone has the following fundamental freedoms:
   (a) freedom of conscience and religion;
   (b) freedom of thought, belief, opinion and expression, including freedom of the press and other media of communication;
   (c) freedom of peaceful assembly; and
   (d) freedom of association.

Section 2 of the Charter, which is broken down into four subsections, is concerned with the fundamental freedoms. It is expected that this section will have a considerable impact with respect to attacks on municipal by-laws. It is interesting to note that while freedom of conscience is included in s. 2 to protect persons who hold agnostic or atheistic views, its inclusion may be inconsistent with the Preamble, which is part of the Charter, and which recognizes "the supremacy of God".

3. Every citizen of Canada has the right to vote in an election of members of the House of Commons or of a legislative assembly and to be qualified for membership therein.

4. (1) No House of Commons and no legislative assembly shall continue for longer than five years from the date fixed for the return of the writs at a general election of its members.

(2) In time of real or apprehended war, invasion or insurrection, a House of Commons may be continued by Parliament and a legislative assembly may be continued by the legislature beyond five years if such continuation is not opposed by the votes of more than one-third of the members of the House of Commons or the legislative assembly, as the case may be.

5. There shall be a sitting of Parliament and of each legislature at least once every twelve months.

Sections 3 to 5 deal with the so-called democratic rights and those rights are concerned with the matters previously contained in ss. 91(1) and 92(1) of the former B.N.A. Act of 1867.

6. (1) Every citizen of Canada has the right to enter, remain in and leave Canada.
(2) Every citizen of Canada and every person who has the status of a permanent resident of Canada has the right
    (a) to move to and take up residence in any province; and
    (b) to pursue the gaining of a livelihood in any province.
(3) The rights specified in subsection (2) are subject to
    (a) any laws or practices of general application in force in a province other than those that discriminate among persons primarily on the basis of province of present or previous residence; and
    (b) any laws providing for reasonable residency requirements as a qualification for the receipt of publicly provided social services.
(4) Subsections (2) and (3) do not preclude any law, program or activity that has as its object the amelioration in a province of conditions of individuals in that province who are socially or economically disadvantaged if the rate of employment in that province is below the rate of employment in Canada.

Section 6 deals with a relatively new category of civil liberties, namely mobility rights.

7. Everyone has the right to life, liberty and security of the person and the right not to be deprived thereof except in accordance with the principles of fundamental justice.

8. Everyone has the right to be secure against unreasonable search or seizure.

9. Everyone has the right not to be arbitrarily detained or imprisoned.

10. Everyone has the right on arrest or detention
    (a) to be informed promptly of the reasons therefor;
    (b) to retain and instruct counsel without delay and to be informed of that right; and

(c) to have the validity of the detention determined by way of *habeas corpus* and to be released if the detention is not lawful.

11. Any person charged with an offence has the right
(a) to be informed without reasonable delay of the specific offence;
(b) to be tried within a reasonable time;
(c) not to be compelled to be a witness in proceedings against that person in respect of the offence;
(d) to be presumed innocent until proven guilty according to law in a fair and public hearing by an independent and impartial tribunal;
(e) not to be denied reasonable bail without just cause;
(f) except in the case of an offence under military law tried before a military tribunal, to the benefit of trial by jury where the maximum punishment for the offence is imprisonment for five years or a more severe punishment;
(g) not to be found guilty on account of any act or omission unless, at the time of the act or omission, it constituted an offence under Canadian or international law or was criminal according to the general principles of law recognized by the community of nations;
(h) if finally acquitted of the offence, not to be tried for it again and, if finally found guilty and punished for the offence, not to be tried or punished for it again; and
(i) if found guilty of the offence and if the punishment for the offence has been varied between the time of commission and the time of sentencing, to the benefit of the lesser punishment.

12. Everyone has the right not to be subjected to any cruel and unusual treatment or punishment.

13. A witness who testifies in any proceedings has the right not to have any incriminating evidence so given used to incriminate that witness in any other proceedings, except in a prosecution for perjury or for the giving of contradictory evidence.

14. A party or witness in any proceedings who does not understand or speak the language in which the proceedings are conducted or who is deaf has the right to the assistance of an interpreter.

Sections 7 to 14 are concerned with the legal rights or the various criminal protections contained in our criminal procedure. These legal rights are probably the most important part of the Charter and are deserving of the most attention.

15. (1) Every individual is equal before and under the law and has the right to the equal protection and equal benefit of the law without discrimination and, in particular, without discrimination based on race, national or ethnic origin, colour, religion, sex, age or mental or physical disability.

(2) Subsection (1) does not preclude any law, program or activity that has as its object amelioration of conditions of disadvantaged individuals or groups including those that are disadvantaged because of race, national or ethnic origin, colour, religion, sex, age or mental or physical disability.

. . .

28. Notwithstanding anything in this Charter, the rights and freedoms referred to in it are guaranteed equally to male and female persons.

Section 15 deals with equality rights and probably should be read together with s. 28. Section 15(1) provides for equal protection and equality under the law, while s. 15(2) provides for the legality of affirmative action programmes. Section 28 provides that, notwithstanding anything in the Charter, the rights and freedoms referred to in it are guaranteed equally to male and female persons. Aside from any protections it offers it is significant that s. 28 is effective immediately whereas s. 15 will not be effective until April 17, 1985. At that time, both ss. 15 and 28 will be operative with the possibility that s. 28 may have the effect of impacting upon the scope of the affirmative action provision of s. 15(2).

16. (1) English and French are the official languages of Canada and have equality of status and equal rights and privileges as to their use in all institutions of the Parliament and government of Canada.

(2) English and French are the official languages of New Brunswick and have equality of status and equal rights and privileges as to their use in all institutions of the legislature and government of New Brunswick.

(3) Nothing in this Charter limits the authority of Parliament or a legislature to advance the equality of status or use of English and French.

17. (1) Everyone has the right to use English or French in any debates and other proceedings of Parliament.

(2) Everyone has the right to use English or French in any debates and other proceedings of the legislature of New Brunswick.

18. (1) The statutes, records and journals of Parliament shall be printed and published in English and French and both language versions are equally authoritative.

(2) The statutes, records and journals of the legislature of New Brunswick shall be printed and published in English and French and both language versions are equally authoritative.

19. (1) Either English or French may be used by any person in, or in any pleading in or process issuing from, any court established by Parliament.

(2) Either English or French may be used by any person in, or in any pleading in or process issuing from, any court of New Brunswick.

20. (1) Any member of the public in Canada has the right to communicate with, and to receive available services from, any head or central office of an institution of the Parliament or government of Canada in English or French, and has the same right with respect to any other office of any such institution where
(a) there is a significant demand for communications with and services from that office in such language; and
(b) due to the nature of the office, it is reasonable that communications with and services from that office be available in both English and French.

(2) Any member of the public in New Brunswick has the right to communicate with, and to receive available services from, any office of an institution of the legislature or government of New Brunswick in English or French.

21. Nothing in sections 16 to 20 abrogates or derogates from any right, privilege or obligation with respect to the English and French languages, or either of them, that exists or is contained by virtue of any other provision of the Constitution of Canada.

22. Nothing in sections 16 to 20 abrogates or derogates from any legal or customary right or privilege acquired or enjoyed either before or after the coming into force of this Charter with respect to any language that is not English or French.

23. (1) Citizens of Canada
(a) whose first language learned and still understood is that of the English or French linguistic minority population of the province in which they reside, or
(b) who have received their primary school instruction in Canada in English or French and reside in a province where the language in which they received that instruction is the language of the English or French linguistic minority population of the province,

have the right to have their children receive primary and secondary school instruction in the same language.

(2) Citizens of Canada of whom any child has received or is receiving primary or secondary school instruction in English or French in Canada, have the right to have all their children receive primary and secondary school instruction in the same language.

Linguistic rights are contained in two separate categories. The first category, dealing with the official languages of Canada and New Brunswick[2b] is contained in ss. 16 to 22, while the second category, dealing with the controversial issue of minority language education rights, is contained in s. 23. After s. 23, the substantive protections of the Charter are more or less completed and the balance of the Charter is concerned with applicability and procedural matters.

> **25.** The guarantee in this Charter of certain rights and freedoms shall not be construed so as to abrogate or derogate from any aboriginal, treaty or other rights or freedoms that pertain to the aboriginal peoples of Canada including
>
> > (*a*) any rights or freedoms that have been recognized by the Royal Proclamation of October 7, 1763; and
> >
> > (*b*) any rights or freedoms that may be acquired by the aboriginal peoples of Canada by way of land claims settlement.
>
> **27.** This Charter shall be interpreted in a manner consistent with the preservation and enhancement of the multicultural heritage of Canadians.

There are, however, other substantive sections which deal with such matters as aboriginal rights in s. 25 and multicultural rights in s. 27, but the main human rights package is contained in ss. 2 through 23 inclusive.

> **24.** (1) Anyone whose rights or freedoms, as guaranteed by this Charter, have been infringed or denied may apply to a court of competent jurisdiction to obtain such remedy as the court considers appropriate and just in the circumstances.
>
> (2) Where, in proceedings under subsection (1), a court concludes that evidence was obtained in a manner that infringed or denied any rights or freedoms guaranteed by this Charter, the evidence shall be excluded if it is established that, having regard to all the circumstances, the admission of it in the proceedings would bring the administration of justice into disrepute.

Section 24 deals with enforcement, inasmuch as s. 24(1) provides a mechanism for an application to a court for a remedy in the event of a breach of a substantive right, while s. 24(2) deals with the exclusion of evidence obtained through a breach of a substantive right. The other procedural section that is of considerable importance is s. 52(1), about which more will be said later.

2. THE SIGNIFICANCE OF ENTRENCHMENT

> **52.** (1) The Constitution of Canada is the supreme law of Canada, and any law that is inconsistent with the provisions of the Constitution is, to the extent of the inconsistency, of no force or effect.

[2b]The Government of Manitoba recently announced it wished to propose an amendment to the Constitution making English and French the official languages of that province.

(2) The Constitution of Canada includes
    (a) the *Canada Act*, including this Act;
    (b) the Acts and orders referred to in Schedule I; and
    (c) any amendment to any Act or order referred to in paragraph (a) or (b).

(3) Amendments to the Constitution of Canada shall be made only in accordance with the authority contained in the Constitution of Canada.

. . .

32. (1) This Charter applies
    (a) to the Parliament and government of Canada in respect of all matters within the authority of Parliament including all matters relating to the Yukon Territory and Northwest Territories; and
    (b) to the legislature and government of each province in respect of all matters within the authority of the legislature of each province.

(2) Notwithstanding subsection (1), section 15 shall not have effect until three years after this section comes into force.

33. (1) Parliament or the legislature of a province may expressly declare in an Act of Parliament or of the legislature, as the case may be, that the Act or a provision thereof shall operate notwithstanding a provision included in section 2 or sections 7 to 15 of this Charter.

(2) An Act or a provision of an Act in respect of which a declaration made under this section is in effect shall have such operation as it would have but for the provision of this Charter referred to in the declaration.

(3) A declaration made under subsection (1) shall cease to have effect five years after it comes into force or on such earlier date as may be specified in the declaration.

(4) Parliament or a legislature of a province may re-enact a declaration made under subsection (1).

(5) Subsection (3) applies in respect of a re-enactment made under subsection (4).

The entrenchment of various provisions in a constitution is significant because of the legal status those provisions occupy after entrenchment. Section 52(1) states that the Constitution of Canada is the supreme law of Canada and that any law that is inconsistent with the provisions of the constitution is, to the extent of the inconsistency, of no force or effect. The result of that is that a constitutional challenge can now be based not only on whether a legislative body has exceeded its power under ss. 91 and 92, but also on whether it has violated substantive rights. This changes our constitutional orientation in Canada to one somewhat akin to that of the United States. In Canada, to date, we have only been concerned, by and large, with jurisdictional questions, namely, who has jurisdiction to pass what laws. However, we are now also concerned with the issue of whether those laws, in terms of their content or substance, conform to the Charter of Rights, which now forms an integral part of the Constitution. Thus, our orientation has changed from one of jurisdiction to one of jurisdiction and content. At the same time, the doctrine of parliamentary sovereignty has been preserved by virtue of the non obstante provision contained in s. 33 of the Charter, which provides that Parliament or a legislature may expressly declare that an act of Parliament or the legislature shall operate notwithstanding the Charter of Rights and Freedoms. Two things ought to be said about this provision. First, the notwithstanding clause applies only to certain sections of the Charter, namely, s. 2 and ss. 7 to 15, and to no other sections. Secondly, the political experience in Canada today indicates that it is not politically expedient to exercise this override option. For example, the human rights legislation of Alberta and Saskatchewan has contained similar such opting out provisions which have never been used in either of those two provinces. Federally, a similar provision exists in the Canadian Bill of Rights, but it has been used only once (and this in respect of the federal statute passed in 1971 replacing the application of the War Measures Act by temporary measures legislation imposed at the time). It is true that an opting out provision has been used a number of times in Quebec with respect to Quebec's human rights legislation. But Quebec ranks as an exception to the general experience elsewhere which strongly suggests that it is politically inexpedient to use an opting out provision.

26. The guarantee in this Charter of certain rights and freedoms shall not be construed as denying the existence of any other rights or freedoms that exist in Canada.

Notwithstanding the entrenchment of a Charter of Rights in the Constitution, there are rights that continue to exist under various federal and provincial laws. Indeed, this is anticipated in s. 26 of the Charter, which provides that rights and freedoms guaranteed in the Charter shall not be construed as denying the existence of any other rights and freedoms that exist in Canada. Accordingly, federally, the Canadian Bill of Rights continues in force, at least to the extent that any of the provisions of the Canadian Bill of Rights do not conflict with the rights contained in the Charter. The same is true of the various provincial bills of rights. For example, in Alberta the Individual's Rights Protection Act and the Alberta Bill of Rights also continue in force. This is significant in that there are some rights contained in these various provincial and federal enactments which are not contained in the Charter, and there are some rights which are contained in the Charter which are not contained in the various other human rights enactments.

In addition, it is important to realize that the Charter is drafted so as to avoid what Professor Tarnopolsky (as he then was) refers to as the "frozen concepts" interpretation of the Canadian Bill of Rights, which limits its applicability to rights which existed at the time of its enactment. The Charter is applicable to all rights — existing and newly-acquired.

It is also important to realize that other significant statutes do remain in force subject to their conformity to the Charter, and one of these is the federal War Measures Act.

3.   THE PROCESS OF CHARTER ADJUDICATION/INTERPRETATION

Essentially, there are three types of applications that can be made under the Charter. The first is an application under s. 24(1) for a remedy by an aggrieved party whose rights have been infringed. While the charging words differ from section to section (for example, the fundamental freedoms apply to "everyone", the democratic rights apply to "every citizen", the mobility rights apply, in one section, to "every citizen", and, in another section, to "every citizen of Canada and every person who has the status of a permanent resident of Canada", some of the legal rights sections apply to "everyone", while others apply to "every person", and yet another applies to "everyone", the equality rights section applies to yet another formulation, that is, "every individual"), the enforcement section, namely s. 24(1), applies to "anyone whose rights or freedoms have been infringed or denied".

The second type of application that may be made under the Charter is an application to exclude evidence under s. 24(2). The test that is applied is whether the use of such evidence (which was obtained in a manner that infringed or denied any rights or freedoms guaranteed by the Charter) "would bring the administration of justice into disrepute". That wording has recently been interpreted by the Supreme Court of Canada in the *Rothman*[3] decision.

The third type of application is provided for in s. 52(1), which provides that the Constitution of Canada is the supreme law of Canada and that any law that is inconsistent with the provisions of the Constitution is, to the extent of the inconsistency, of no force or effect. This invites our courts, upon application, to overturn legislation on the basis of the position of primacy occupied by the Constitution of Canada in our legal system. A question arises as to who may make an application under s. 52(1). Clearly, only persons whose rights have been infringed can make applications under ss. 24(1) and 24(2), but what is the scope of the locus standi requirements in order to apply under s. 52(1)? As a result of the decisions in *Thorson*,[4] *McNeil*[5] and *Borowski*,[6] it appears that almost any person can make an application to strike down legislation under s. 52. It should be pointed out that, while s. 24 provides a statutory right of standing to aggrieved persons, s. 52, as a result of the *Borowski* decision, seems to suggest that standing to challenge impugned legislation is discretionary.

---

[3]*Rothman v. R.*, [1981] 1 S.C.R. 640, 20 C.R. (3d) 97, 59 C.C.C. (2d) 30, 121 D.L.R. (3d) 578, 35 N.R. 485.

[4]*Thorson v. A.G. Can.*, [1975] 1 S.C.R. 138, 43 D.L.R. (3d) 1, 1 N.R. 225.

[5]*McNeil v. N.S. Bd. of Censors*, [1976] 2 S.C.R. 265, 32 C.R.N.S. 376, 55 D.L.R. (3d) 632, 12 N.S.R. (2d) 85, 5 N.R. 43.

[6]*Borowski v. Min. of Justice*, [1982] 1 W.W.R. 97, 24 C.R. (3d) 352, 39 N.R. 331 (S.C.C.). See also Blake, "Minister of Justice v. Borowski: The Inapplicability of the Standing Rules in Constitutional Litigation" (1982), 28 McGill L.J. 126, and Kushner, "Case Comment on Minister of Justice et al. v. Borowski" (1983), 17 U.B.C. L. Rev. 143.

An interesting issue arises as to whether notice is required under the appropriate provincial statutes before an Act can be declared unconstitutional. The conventional view is that notice is not required with respect to a s. 24(1) application, nor with respect to a s. 24(2) application for the exclusion of evidence. However, it is likely that notice will be required under the various provincial statutes with respect to any application under s. 52. However, the view has also been expressed that since the Constitution is supreme and since there is no notice provision contained therein, even provincial notice requirements are invalid as they do not conform to the Constitution. The prudent barrister probably would be wiser to give the requisite notice with respect to a s. 52 application before challenging a particular law, unless of course there are very special circumstances.

One of the more important issues relates to the evidentiary considerations in constitutional decision-making. Dr. Barry Strayer's view of the process of constitutional adjudication, as he uses that phrase in his book *Judicial Review of Legislation in Canada*,[7] is that in addition to the application of normal rules of statutory interpretation, there are special rules in respect of the process of constitutional adjudication. He makes a distinction between evidence adduced to prove so-called "adjudicative facts" and evidence designed to prove so-called "legislative facts" and argues that with respect to the latter, there should be a wider regime of admissibility. This would lead to a greater use of judicial notice, Brandeis briefs, amicus curiae interventions and generally the lessening of some of the stricture in the rules of evidence. This, of course, to some extent already exists in constitutional cases as evidenced by the decision, for example, in the *Anti-Inflation Reference*.[8] But in addition, there are words in the Charter which invite the courts to admit wider kinds of evidence. For example, in s. 1, there is a specific reference to the term "demonstrably justified". Whether something is demonstrably justified or not must surely be determined on the basis of either judicial notice, or evidence, or both, and that seems to invite consideration of a broader range of evidence than can be received. Elsewhere in the Charter, for example, in the section on minority language education, there is mention of the notion of "where numbers warrant". Obviously, a court has to receive demographic evidence in order to determine whether, in fact, the "numbers warrant" the expenditure of public funds to provide minority language education.

One of the most important aspects of our new Charter raises the question of what types of precedent are relevant and should be receivable by our courts. A language comparison between the Charter and the

[7]University of Toronto Press, 1968.
[8]*Reference re Anti-Inflation Act*, [1976] 2 S.C.R. 373, 68 D.L.R. (3d) 452, 9 N.R. 541.

Canadian Bill of Rights indicates some language similarity. Therefore, the existing jurisprudence under the Canadian Bill of Rights would be relevant. In other sections, the Charter is comparable to the U.S. Bill of Rights; therefore, American jurisprudence would also be relevant. But also, European precedents will assist a court in interpreting a Charter provision, since, for example, the limitations clause in s. 1 is borrowed heavily from various international instruments. In this connection, one might particularly refer to Justice McDonald's book, *Legal Rights in the Canadian Charter of Rights and Freedoms*,[9] with respect to a discussion of the various relevant international instruments.

There is a presumption of constitutionality or constitutional validity in our law. Does this presumption apply equally in respect of the Charter, that is, must the courts presume that an act is constitutionally valid when measured against the Charter with the onus of proof falling on those who allege that a given statute is constitutionally invalid? A reading of s. 24 together with s. 1 suggests very strongly that the onus of proof in alleging a violation of the Charter falls upon the person whose rights have been infringed. One cannot be sure what standard of proof will be required but the onus clearly, under s. 24, falls upon those who allege their rights have been infringed. Notwithstanding views to the contrary regarding an onus shift, it is submitted that, once the infringement has been proven, the onus then shifts, under s. 1, to the government to prove that the impugned enactment is a reasonable limit demonstrably justified in a free and democratic society.

One should also, in this context, refer to Canada's international obligations under the various international instruments. One should then consider whether there exists a presumption that our domestic statutes conform to our international obligations.

Consider the following key issues in connection with the process of Charter adjudication/interpretation.

(a) Role of the Judiciary

Clearly a major change in our legal system relates to the role of the judiciary. Previously our judges were largely responsible for the interpretation of our laws. Although that responsibility has not changed in and of itself, what has occurred is a usurpation of the doctrine of parliamentary sovereignty by a regime under which the final say on legislative policy rests with the judiciary pursuant to the power given judges under s. 52 of the Constitution Act. This role should be contrasted with the "construe and apply" mandate given the judiciary under the Canadian Bill of Rights,[9a] or the mandate given the courts under other human rights legislation. Plainly and simply there has been a shift from a regime of

---

[9]Toronto: Carswell, 1982.

parliamentary sovereignty to a system whereby the ultimate power rests in the Constitution as interpreted by a judge with powers under s. 24 to fashion new remedies in appropriate circumstances.

(b) Interpretation

Obviously, neither the federal Interpretation Act nor a provincial Interpretation Act can be binding on the interpretation of a constitution. They might be persuasive but they cannot be viewed as binding. Although the Constitution Act is technically a U.K. statute, it would be ironic to rely upon the United Kingdom Interpretation Act in interpreting the Canadian constitution in view of the symbolic significance of the act of patriation. Accordingly, the correct view is that all interpretation acts are relevant and persuasive but that none is binding, which leads to the conclusion that the judiciary must perhaps proceed on its own instincts rather than be bound by one particular instrument in interpreting the constitution.

(c) Generally

First, in connection with s. 1, there are various issues which ought to be raised. In respect of the question of "demonstrably justified in a free and democratic society", the issue arises as to who bears the onus of proving this. The view has already been expressed that the onus is on the government to justify its own legislation, but, legally, the matter has not yet been determined. As to what constitutes a free and democratic society, one might reflect upon the views of U.S. Circuit Court of Appeal Judge Aldisert, who says simply that it means Canada and therefore invites a consideration of Canadian traditions and history in order to determine what constitutes a free and democratic society and a reasonable limit therein. Others have expressed the view that, given, for example, the Japanese-Canadian chapter in our history, Canada is perhaps not the best example of a free and democratic society in interpreting s. 1.

With respect to the question of the application of the Charter, ss. 32 and 33 clearly indicate that the Charter applies to Parliament and the federal government, as well as to the legislatures and the provincial governments, but this raises the issue as to what constitutes "government". To what extent are Crown agencies and Crown corporations covered by the Charter? Does P.W.A. or Canada Development Corporation or the C.B.C. fall within this terminology? Professor Dale Gibson of the University of Manitoba argues that because the word "only" is not included

---

[9a]See Hovius, "The Legacy of the Supreme Court of Canada's Aproach to the Canadian Bill of Rights: Prospects for the Charter" (1982), 28 McGill L.J. 1. See also the Edmonton Journal, 11th April 1983.

in the charging words of s. 32, the private sector as well as the public sector may be covered by the Charter. Again, the matter has not yet been determined.

(d) New Terminology

The courts will have to interpret the terminology of the Charter, including some phraseology which is relatively new. The key areas of interpretation are as follows:

1. "Reasonable limits" in s. 1.

2. "Demonstrably justified in a free and democratic society" in s. 1.

3. "Principles of fundamental justice" in s. 7.

4. "Unreasonable search and seizure" in s. 8.

5. "Arbitrarily detained or imprisoned" in s. 9.

6. "Unreasonable delay" and "reasonable time" in s. 11.

7. "A court of competent jurisdiction" and "such remedy as the court considers appropriate and just in the circumstances" in s. 24.

As indicated earlier, the main constitutional concern in Canada prior to April 17, 1982 was with the jurisdiction to pass laws of the various sovereign legislative bodies. As of April 17, 1982, the constitutional orientation in Canada has changed to concern with content and jurisdiction, which is to say that the constitutionality or validity of laws will be tested on the basis of whether they conform to the jurisdictional constraints imposed by the division of legislative powers and whether they conform to the boundaries of content imposed by the Canadian Charter of Rights and Freedoms. Having examined the latter, our attention will now turn to examining the former, namely, the jurisdictional concerns that have been with us since 1867 and that will, no doubt, continue into the future.

The B.N.A. Act of 1867 (now renamed the Constitution Act of 1867) was primarily concerned with jurisdiction, but it was also concerned with questions relating to the establishment of a body politic for the new nation created at Confederation. In examining the provisions of the B.N.A. Act, it is important to bear in mind that this Act continues in force as the Constitution Act of 1867 by virtue of its (and all amendments thereto) inclusion in the Schedule to the Constitution Act of 1982, which specifically states in s. 52(2) that the Constitution of Canada includes, among other things, all the matters contained in the Schedule to the Constitution Act of 1982.

The B.N.A. Act of 1867 (hereinafter referred to as the Constitution Act of 1867) was extraordinarily vague in defining many of the elements of our constitutional system. In other words, a reading of the Constitution Act of 1867 alone by a stranger to the Canadian political system would in and of itself leave that person with a serious misimpression as to the nature of our political order. For example, the Constitution Act of 1867 mentions a governor, advised by a council, having what appears to be autocratic and dictatorial authority, including the power to convene Parliament, prorogue Parliament, dissolve Parliament, call an election, appoint senators, command the armed forces, and conduct many other responsibilities under provisions contained in the Act. It makes no mention of a Prime Minister, of a cabinet, or political parties. With limited exceptions, it makes no mention of the procedure by which constitutional amendments are effected. It is only through the application of the unwritten component of the constitution, comprised principally of conventions, customs and usages derived from British constitutional history and developed through the political and constitutional experience of Canada since attaining her nationhood, that the ambiguity and misimpression that arises out of a literal interpretation of the Constitution Act of 1867 may be resolved and corrected. In other words, the simplistic and autocratic impression arising out of a literal reading of the Constitution Act of 1867 is greatly modified by the application of the customs and usages which define accurately the nature of our constitutional system.

The principle features of the Constitution Act of 1867 are as follows:

(1) The preamble, which states essentially that our constitution is similar in principle to that of the United Kingdom;

(2) The provisions relating to the union of the four provinces of Nova Scotia, New Brunswick, Ontario and Quebec in 1867;

(3) The establishment of a federal executive;

(4) The establishment of a federal legislative body; this includes the Senate and the House of Commons;

(5) The establishment of provincial executives;

(6) The establishment of provincial legislatures;

(7) The distribution of legislative powers;

(8) Miscellaneous provisions relating to such matters as education, language rights, courts, agricultural marketing, etc.

The essential values which are promoted by the Constitution Act of 1867 relate, primarily, to a desire on the part of the drafters of our constitution to achieve a strong central government. It is interesting to note that the opposite notion was promoted in the drafting of the United States Constitution, a document which emphasized strong states' rights. Ironically, one might argue that the original American desire for strong states' rights has, throughout the nation's history, been transformed, de facto, into a strong central government, while the original Canadian notion of a strong central government has been transformed into an increase in provincial power. However, it is clear that a strong central government was one of the initial concerns arising from such practical considerations as, for example, the achievement of efficiency in expanding trade and commercial enterprises and the creation of a strong defence against the United States.

In addition, one can imply certain values promoted by the Constitution Act of 1867 from a reading of the preamble to the Act, which contains what has been termed "the implied Bill of Rights". The preamble states, essentially, that the drafters of our constitution desired to establish a constitution similar in principle to that of the United Kingdom, which has been interpreted as importing into the Canadian constitutional system certain values contained in the British system. These values include the principles enunciated in the Magna Carta, the British Bill of Rights, and the Petition of Rights, and refer to such notions as freedom of speech, freedom of association and assembly, freedom of the press, and fair play. However, more importantly, and more specifically, this implied Bill of Rights has imported into our constitutional system the British doctrines of parliamentary sovereignty, the rule of law, and responsible government.

The doctrine of parliamentary sovereignty means that Parliament is supreme and can make or unmake any law. The British view of parliamentary sovereignty is best stated by Professor A.V. Dicey in his classic treatise *Introduction to the Study of the Law of the Constitution*, and has subsequently been restated by Professor Wade. In brief, the Diceyan-Wade model of parliamentary sovereignty contains the following two essential elements:

(a) that Parliament can make or unmake any law; and

(b) that no body or person has a right to override or set aside the legislation of Parliament.[10]

The key question is whether the Diceyan-Wade model of parliamentary sovereignty applies to the Canadian federation. If it does, Parliament would, of course, be supreme only in respect of those matters coming within the legislative competence of the Parliament of Canada under the provisions of the Constitution Act of 1867 and the provinces would be sovereign only in respect of those matters which fall within provincial jurisdiction under the provisions of the Constitution Act of 1867. This modification notwithstanding, is it reasonable to assume that the Diceyan-Wade model of the doctrine of parliamentary sovereignty applies in all other respects to the Canadian federation? Although the

---

[10]10th ed. by E.C.S. Wade (London: Macmillan Papermac, 1961), p. 39.

doctrine of parliamentary sovereignty has been regarded as embodying the essential component of the British constitution, the applicability of the doctrine in the Canadian context has been controversial for two reasons. First, the Diceyan-Wade notion of parliamentary sovereignty ignores the whole process of judicial review. Secondly, and this is probably more fundamental, the Diceyan notion does not take into account the possibility that Parliament or a provincial legislature may "entrench" a given statutory provision by requiring that a particular "manner and form" be satisfied before that "entrenched" provision may be altered. "Entrenching" a provision refers to the notion that that provision may not be altered by simple majority. A "manner and form" is the requirement, other than simple majority, which must be satisfied in order to alter an "entrenched" provision. The imposition of a "manner and form" requirement in a given statute binds future Parliaments to conform to the particular "manner and form" requirement in order to amend that statute. One authority for the validity of a "manner and form" requirement is the case of *Bribery Commr. v. Ranasinghe*, [1965] A.C. 172, [1964] 2 All E.R. 785. This notion of "manner and form" as a limitation on the applicability of the Diceyan definition of parliamentary sovereignty in Canada is discussed at length in Chapter 3 of W.S. Tarnopolsky's *The Canadian Bill of Rights*.[11] Professor Tarnopolsky (as he then was), in discussing the possible entrenchment of the Canadian Bill of Rights in the Canadian constitution, makes these comments:

1) There is serious doubt among high authorities even as to the validity of Dicey's contention that the United Kingdom Parliament is sovereign in the terms he used.

2) Even if the United Kingdom Parliament could be described as being sovereign, this does not mean that in enacting legislation it can ignore the "manner and form" required by law for passing that legislation.

3) Regardless of the conclusion that is reached in viewing the United Kingdom Parliament, the Canadian Parliament could never be said to have been sovereign in the Diceyan sense, nor in the modern sense put forth by Professor Wade.

4) Even if one were to conclude that the Canadian Parliament is sovereign in the sense that it cannot be prevented from passing any legislation within its jurisdiction, it cannot ignore a "manner and form" requirement for passing valid Acts of Parliament, even if Parliament can change the "manner and form" requirement by simple statute.

5) The *Canadian Bill of Rights* could be entrenched in the B.N.A. Act by requiring that any amendments be in a specified "manner and form", and by further requiring a specified "manner and form" for amending this requirement.[12]

Indeed, the primacy provision contained in the Canadian Bill of Rights is, in itself, a "manner and form" requirement. That provision requires that all federal statutes must conform to the substantive provisions contained in the Canadian Bill of Rights unless Parliament, in enacting a statute, specifically provides that that statute shall operate notwithstanding the Canadian Bill of Rights. In effect, this primacy

---

[11]2nd ed. (Toronto: McClelland and Stewart, 1975).

[12]*Ibid.*, p. 104.

provision validly binds future Parliaments, in that in order to avoid the operation of the Canadian Bill of Rights, future Parliaments must specifically so provide. This requirement runs contrary to the Diceyan notion of parliamentary sovereignty.

The implied Bill of Rights contained in the preamble to the Constitution Act of 1867 also imports into our constitutional system the doctrine of "rule of law". Professor Dicey set out the following elements constituting his definition of "rule of law":

(1) the supremacy of regular law as opposed to the influence of arbitrary power, excluding the existence of arbitrariness, prerogative, or even of wide discretionary authority on the part of the government;

(2) equality before the law, excluding the idea of any exemption of officials or others from the duty of obedience to the law which governs other citizens;

(3) the law of the constitution is not the source but the consequence of the rights of individuals as defined and enforced by the courts.[13]

These elements of "rule of law" have been restated in terms of a modern context by Professor H. W. Jones:

(1) in a decent society it is unthinkable that government, or any officer of government, possesses arbitrary power over the person or the interests of the individual;

(2) all members of society, private persons and government officials alike, must be equally responsible before the law; and

(3) effective judicial remedies are more important than abstract constitutional declarations in securing the rights of the individual against encroachment by the state.[14]

For a fuller discussion of "rule of law" the reader may consult Chapter 4 of Tarnopolsky's *The Canadian Bill of Rights*. In addition, see the case of *Roncarelli v. Duplessis*, [1959] S.C.R. 121, 16 D.L.R. (2d) 689.

The foregoing discussion has pointed to some implied values arising out of the express provisions contained in the Constitution Act of 1867, together with some express values arising out of the whole scheme of the Act. Accordingly, despite its rather benign or sterile appearance at first glance, the Constitution Act of 1867 does in fact have a value orientation. Nonetheless, much has changed with respect to value orientation with the inclusion of an entrenched Charter of Rights. All kinds of values arise in the Canadian Charter of Rights and Freedoms, including those related to fundamental freedoms (expression, the holding of religious beliefs, and the exercise of association and peaceful assembly), mobility from province to province, protections related to the criminal justice system, egalitarianism, multiculturalism and others. Furthermore, these values have, by virtue of s. 1 of the Charter, been put in the context of what should be tolerated in a free and democratic society. Indeed, the

---

[13]Dicey, pp. 202-203, footnote 3.

[14]Jones, "The Rule of Law and the Welfare State" (1958), 58 Col. L. Rev. 149.

change of constitutional orientation from that of jurisdiction to one of content and jurisdiction represents, at the very least, a codification or perhaps a new recognition that certain values ought to be promulgated through our nation's highest law so that they are advanced in the most effective way. In institutional terms, there is yet another value recognition which flows from the entrenchment of a Charter of Rights in the Constitution. Put simply, we now recognize that in the protection and preservation of civil liberties, the notion of parliamentary sovereignty or supremacy must be subservient to the constitution. And to this end, subject to s. 33 of the Charter, we entrust our judiciary with the responsibility of ensuring that having regard to the content of laws, the Constitution reigns supreme over ordinary legislative enactment. So clearly, by virtue of the recognition and advancement of specific values and by virtue of the institutional arrangements by which we protect those values, the highest law of the land is now a much more value-oriented instrument than it was prior to April 17, 1982.

Reference will be made to convention, custom and usage, as the principal unwritten components of the Canadian constitution, in the discussion on constitutional amendment, at a later point in this chapter.

CONSTITUTIONAL BASIS OF LEGISLATIVE AUTHORITY

The most important provisions in the Constitution Act of 1867 are those provisions distributing legislative jurisdiction between the Parliament of Canada on one hand, and the provincial legislatures on the other. The two main sections of the Constitution Act of 1867 concerned with the division of powers are ss. 91 and 92, although there are other sections dealing with this as well.

Section 91 reserves exclusively to the Parliament of Canada a general grant of legislative authority, together with exclusive legislative jurisdiction in respect of various matters contained in the twenty-nine enumerations following the general grant. Similarly, s. 92 reserves to the provincial legislatures exclusive legislative authority in respect of those matters falling within the sixteen enumerations contained in s. 92. There is one exception, however, in s. 92 and that relates to s. 92(10) (a), (b) and (c) which, by operation of s. 91(29), bring certain matters within federal jurisdiction.

The relevant provisions contained in the Constitution Act of 1867 in respect of the division of powers follow:

VI. DISTRIBUTION OF LEGISLATIVE POWERS

Powers of the Parliament

91. It shall be lawful for the Queen, by and with the Advice and Consent of the Senate and House of Commons, to make Laws for the Peace, Order, and good Government of Canada, in relation to all Matters not coming within the Classes of Subjects by this Act

assigned exclusively to the Legislatures of the Provinces; and for greater Certainty, but not so as to restrict the Generality of the foregoing Terms of this Section, it is hereby declared that (notwithstanding anything in this Act) the exclusive Legislative Authority of the Parliament of Canada extends to all Matters coming within the Classes of Subjects next herein-after enumerated; that is to say, — . . .

1A. The Public Debt and Property.
2. The Regulation of Trade and Commerce.
2A. Unemployment insurance.
3. The raising of Money by any Mode or System of Taxation.
4. The borrowing of Money on the Public Credit.
5. Postal Service.
6. The Census and Statistics.
7. Militia, Military and Naval Service, and Defence.
8. The fixing of and providing for the Salaries and Allowances of Civil and other Officers of the Government of Canada.
9. Beacons, Buoys, Lighthouses, and Sable Island.
10. Navigation and Shipping.
11. Quarantine and the Establishment and Maintenance of Marine Hospitals.
12. Sea Coast and Inland Fisheries.
13. Ferries between a Province and any British or Foreign Country or between Two Provinces.
14. Currency and Coinage.
15. Banking, Incorporation of Banks, and the Issue of Paper Money.
16. Savings Banks.
17. Weights and Measures.
18. Bills of Exchange and Promissory Notes.
19. Interest.
20. Legal Tender.
21. Bankruptcy and Insolvency.
22. Patents of Invention and Discovery.
23. Copyrights.
24. Indians, and Lands reserved for the Indians.
25. Naturalization and Aliens.
26. Marriage and Divorce.
27. The Criminal Law, except the Constitution of Courts of Criminal Jurisdiction, but including the Procedure in Criminal Matters.
28. The Establishment, Maintenance, and Management of Penitentiaries.
29. Such Classes of Subjects as are expressly excepted in the Enumeration of the Classes of Subjects by this Act assigned exclusively to the Legislatures of the Provinces

And any Matter coming within any of the Classes of Subjects enumerated in this Section shall not be deemed to come within the Class of Matters of a local or private Nature comprised in the Enumeration of the Classes of Subjects by this Act assigned exclusively to the Legislatures of the Provinces.

Exclusive Powers of Provincial Legislatures

92. In each Province the Legislature may exclusively make Laws in relation to Matters coming within the Classes of Subjects next herein-after enumerated; that is to say, —

1. The Amendment from Time to Time, notwithstanding anything in this Act, of the Constitution of the Province, except as regards the Office of the Lieutenant Governor.

2. Direct Taxation within the Province in order to the raising of a Revenue for Provincial Purposes.

3. The borrowing of Money on the sole Credit of the Province.

4. The Establishment and Tenure of Provincial Offices and the Appointment and Payment of Provincial Officers.

5. The Management and Sale of the Public Lands belonging to the Province and of the Timber and Wood thereon.

6. The Establishment, Maintenance, and Management of Public and Reformatory Prisons in and for the Province.

7. The Establishment, Maintenance, and Management of Hospitals, Asylums, Charities, and Eleemosynary Institutions in and for the Province, other than Marine Hospitals.

8. Municipal Institutions in the Province.

9. Shop, Saloon, Tavern, Auctioneer, and other Licences in order to the raising of a Revenue for Provincial, Local, or Municipal Purposes.

10. Local Works and Undertakings other than such as are of the following Classes: —

a. Lines of Steam or other Ships, Railways, Canals, Telegraphs, and other Works and Undertakings connecting the Province with any other or others of the Provinces, or extending beyond the Limits of the Province:

b. Lines of Steam Ships between the Province and any British or Foreign Country:

c. Such Works as, although wholly situate within the Province, are before or after their Execution declared by the Parliament of Canada to be for the general Advantage of Canada or for the Advantage of Two or more of the Provinces.

11. The Incorporation of Companies with Provincial Objects.

12. The Solemnization of Marriage in the Province.

13. Property and Civil Rights in the Province.

14. The Administration of Justice in the Province, including the Constitution, Maintenance, and Organization of Provincial Courts, both of Civil and of Criminal Jurisdiction, and including Procedure in Civil Matters in those Courts.

15. The Imposition of Punishment by Fine, Penalty, or Imprisonment for enforcing any Law of the Province made in relation to any Matter coming within any of the Classes of Subjects enumerated in this Section.

16. Generally all Matters of a merely local or private Nature in the Province.

Education

93. In and for each Province the Legislature may exclusively make Laws in relation to Education, subject and according to the following Provisions: —

(1) Nothing in any such Law shall prejudicially affect any Right or Privilege with respect to Denominational Schools which any Class of Persons have by Law in the Province at the Union:

(2) All the Powers, Privileges, and Duties at the Union by Law conferred and imposed in Upper Canada on the Separate Schools and School Trustees of the Queen's Roman Catholic Subjects shall be and the same are hereby extended to the Dissentient Schools of the Queen's Protestant and Roman Catholic Subjects in Quebec:

(3) Where in any Province a System of Separate or Dissentient Schools exists by Law at the Union or is thereafter established by the Legislature of the Province, an Appeal shall lie to the Governor General in Council from any Act or Decision of any Provincial Authority affecting any Right or Privilege of the Protestant or Roman Catholic Minority of the Queen's Subjects in relation to Education:

(4) In case any such Provincial Law as from Time to Time seems to the Governor General in Council requisite for the due Execution of the Provisions of this Section is not made, or in case any Decision of the Governor General in Council on any Appeal under this Section is not duly executed by the proper Provincial Authority in that Behalf, then and in every such Case, and as far only as the Circumstances of each Case require, the Parliament of Canada may make remedial Laws for the due Execution of the Provisions of this Section and of any Decision of the Governor General in Council under this Section . . .

Old Age Pensions

94A. The Parliament of Canada may make laws in relation to old age pensions and supplementary benefits, including survivors' and disability benefits irrespective of age, but no such law shall affect the operation of any law present or future of a provincial legislature in relation to any such matter.

Agriculture and Immigration

95. In each Province the Legislature may make Laws in relation to Agriculture in the Province, and to Immigration into the Province; and it is hereby declared that the Parliament of Canada may from Time to Time make Laws in relation to Agriculture in all or any of the Provinces, and to Immigration into all or any of the Provinces; and any Law of the Legislature of a Province relative to Agriculture or to Immigration shall have effect in and for the Province as long and as far only as it is not repugnant to any Act of the Parliament of Canada . . .

THE THIRD SCHEDULE

Provincial Public Works and Property to be the Property of Canada

1. Canals, with Lands and Water Power connected therewith.
2. Public Harbours.
3. Lighthouses and Piers, and Sable Island.
4. Steamboats, Dredges, and public Vessels.
5. Rivers and Lake Improvements.
6. Railways and Railway Stocks, Mortgages, and other Debts due by Railway Companies.
7. Military Roads.
8. Custom Houses, Post Offices, and all other Public Buildings, except such as the Government of Canada appropriate for the Use of the Provincial Legislatures and Governments.
9. Property transferred by the Imperial Government, and known as Ordnance Property.
10. Armouries, Drill Sheds, Military Clothing, and Munitions of War, and Lands set apart for general Public Purposes.

MISCELLANEOUS PROVISIONS

109. All Lands, Mines, Minerals, and Royalties belonging to the several Provinces of Canada, Nova Scotia, and New Brunswick at the Union, and all Sums then due or payable for such Lands, Mines, Minerals, or Royalties, shall belong to the several Provinces of Ontario, Quebec, Nova Scotia, and New Brunswick in which the same are situate or arise, subject to any Trusts existing in respect thereof, and to any Interest other than that of the Province in the same . . .

121. All Articles of the Growth, Produce, or Manufacture of any one of the Provinces shall, from and after the Union, be admitted free into each of the other Provinces . . .

125. No Lands or Property belonging to Canada or any Province shall be liable to Taxation . . .

132. The Parliament and Government of Canada shall have all Powers necessary or proper for performing the Obligations of Canada or of any Province thereof, as Part of the British Empire, towards Foreign Countries, arising under Treaties between the Empire and such Foreign Countries.

133. Either the English or the French Language may be used by any Person in the Debates of the Houses of the Parliament of Canada and of the Houses of the Legislature of Quebec; and both those Languages shall be used in the respective Records and Journals of those Houses; and either of those Languages may be used by any Person or in any Pleading or Process in or issuing from any Court of Canada established under this Act, and in or from all or any of the Courts of Quebec.

The Acts of the Parliament of Canada and of the Legislature of Quebec shall be printed and published in both those Languages.

The matters contained in the pre-patriation s. 91(1) are still part of the Constitution, but they are now included in ss. 3-5 of the Charter, together with a related provision concerned with the right to vote.

It is not appropriate, in a text of this nature, to outline in detail the respective legislative jurisdictions of the Parliament of Canada and of the provincial legislatures in respect of those matters contained in the more important enumerated heads of ss. 91 and 92 of the Constitution Act of 1867. To do so properly would require a detailed analysis, not within the purport of an introductory text. However, so that the reader may appreciate the limitations placed upon the various legislative bodies in Canada, it might be appropriate to outline, in a brief and summary form, the division of legislative jurisdictions in respect of some of the more important enumerated heads.

Under the general power of Parliament, contained in s. 91 of the Constitution Act of 1867, the Parliament of Canada is given exclusive legislative authority to enact laws in respect of the peace, order and good government of Canada. The peace, order and good government clause, however, has met with various interpretations over the years. Under the emergency doctrine, Parliament may legislate, under the peace, order and good government clause, in respect of emergency situations arising out of war or famine, or conditions arising out of war or famine but which survive the termination of the period of war or famine. In addition, in one case, it was held that national intemperance was a type of emergency contemplated under the emergency doctrine. Finally, as a result of the reference case[15] concerning the constitutionality of the Anti-Inflation Act, 1974-75-76 (Can.), c. 75, certain types of economic emergencies might give rise to appropriate federal legislation. In effect, upon the application of the emergency doctrine, Parliament may encroach upon those matters falling within provincial legislative authority under the provisions contained in s. 92 of the Constitution Act of 1867.

Under the "national dimensions" doctrine, Parliament is given authority to legislate, under the peace, order and good government clause, in respect of those matters which affect the Dominion as a whole. It is difficult to rationalize the list of ad hoc matters which have been held to be within federal jurisdiction under this doctrine, but they include such matters as nuclear energy, aeronautics and the national capital region. Under this doctrine Parliament may again encroach upon those matters falling within provincial jurisdiction.

Finally, the peace, order and good government clause has been regarded as a residuary power in respect of those matters not falling within any of the specific enumerations in either s. 91 or 92. This was illustrated in the

---

[15]*Reference re Anti-Inflation Act*, [1976] 2 S.C.R. 373, 68 D.L.R. (3d) 452, 9 N.R. 541.

Hauser[16] case, where the residuary power was invoked to justify federal narcotics legislation, but it was suggested in that case that residual matters are only those which did not exist at Confederation. It was even suggested by some judges that residual matters must also be in the nature of emergencies, although that notion was not in accord with the view of the majority.

Generally speaking, under s. 91(2) of the Constitution Act of 1867, the Parliament of Canada has exclusive legislative jurisdiction over the regulation of international and extraprovincial trade. The provinces, on the other hand, possess exclusive jurisdiction over purely intraprovincial trade. However, this distinction has become somewhat blurred in recent cases as a result of an application by the courts of a "functional" or "flow of trade" analysis. Under a functional analysis, the courts often ask to what extent it is possible to sever an apparently intraprovincial operation, functionally speaking, from the whole of an extraprovincial operation. Recent cases leave some doubt as to what truly remains "intraprovincial trade" in view of the modern, highly interrelated economics of the various trading jurisdictions. (See, for example, the *C.I.G.O.L.*[17] and *Central Canada Potash*[18] cases). The Supreme Court of Canada has also recently explored the notion of a general trade and commerce power (see the *Labatt's*[19] case).

The Parliament of Canada, under s. 91(27) of the Constitution Act of 1867, is granted exclusive legislative jurisdiction in respect of criminal law and procedure, although not in respect of the constitution of courts of criminal jurisdiction. A key issue, therefore, is the domain of criminal law. Criminal law has been defined in many ways and most often in a very wide sense to include subject matters which, by their very nature, fall within the domain of criminal jurisprudence. These matters, generally, are contained in legislation promoting public peace, order, security, health or morality. In other words, the court examines an impugned statute and asks, in terms of its operational effects, whether that statute was enacted with a view to a public purpose which can support it as being in relation to criminal law. To support the legislation as a valid exercise of criminal law, the ordinary, though not exclusive, object of that law must be directed at public peace, order, security, health or morality.

---

[16]*R. v. Hauser*, [1979] 1 S.C.R. 984, [1979] 5 W.W.R. 1, 8 C.R. (3d) 89, 98 D.L.R. (3d) 193, 46 C.C.C. (2d) 481, 26 N.R. 541, 16 A.R. 91.

[17]*Can. Indust. Gas & Oil Ltd. v. Sask.*, [1978] 2 S.C.R. 545, [1977] 6 W.W.R. 607, 80 D.L.R. (3d) 449, 18 N.R. 107.

[18]*Central Can. Potash Co. v. Sask.*, [1979] 1 S.C.R. 42, [1978] 6 W.W.R. 400, 6 C.C.L.T. 265, 88 D.L.R. (3d) 609, 23 N.R. 481.

[19]*Labatt Breweries of Can. Ltd. v. A.G. Can.* (1979), 9 B.L.R. 181, 30 N.R. 496 (S.C.C.).

On the other hand, the provinces can legislate in respect of purely regulatory matters as well as those matters referred to as "quasi-criminal" in nature. A quasi-criminal matter is one which is enacted with a view to suppressing conditions which are calculated to foster the development of crime. A quasi-criminal provincial statute is constitutionally permissible. However, a province cannot, under the guise or colour of quasi-criminal legislation, legislate matters which are truly criminal in nature and thus fall under s. 91(27).

Federal jurisdiction over radio, television, cable and pay television and other similar forms of communication, including satellite communication, as well as federal jurisdiction over interprovincial railway and trucking operations, are derived from the exceptions contained in s. 92(10)(a) of the Constitution Act of 1867.

The Parliament of Canada has jurisdiction in respect of both direct and indirect taxation, while the provincial jurisdiction is limited to direct taxation within the province for provincial purposes. One major difficulty is the categorization of taxes as either direct or indirect.

The foregoing is only a sampling of the various enumerations in ss. 91 and 92, and the discussion under each of these enumerations is very limited, given the scope of this text. However, one can appreciate the limitations which legislators must accept on both the federal and provincial levels, given both the express provisions contained in the Constitution Act of 1867 along with the limitations arising out of the interpretation by the courts of those express provisions.

The division of legislative jurisdiction in ss. 91 and 92 of the Constitution Act of 1867 has given rise to what has been referred to as the "watertight compartment theory". By this theory, the doctrine of exclusivity has created two watertight legislative compartments. Accordingly there is a certain constitutional rigidity in Canada which must be surmounted by various means. First, the courts have allowed the notion of permissible interdelegation. While it is not constitutionally permissible for Parliament, for example, to pass a law delegating its exclusive legislative jurisdiction in respect of a given matter to the legislative assembly of a province, it can, nonetheless, delegate part of its exclusive legislative jurisdiction to a subordinate agency of a provincial legislature. Secondly, flexibility has been achieved through agreements reached at federal-provincial conferences which subsequently form the basis of a mutually agreed-upon legislative scheme. These agreements include conditional grants or grants-in-aid which tie certain conditions to the provision of funds from the federal government to the province. These conditions usually relate to how these funds are to be spent. Thus, even though the money is to be spent with respect to a matter within provincial jurisdiction, the tying of conditions gives the federal government some say as to the exercise of a matter normally within provincial jurisdiction. In recent years, equalization payments have played a major role in federal/ provincial fiscal arrangements. Indeed, equalization has become constitutionally entrenched as a separate Part of the Canada Act of 1982.

Another device to provide flexibility in the constitution is the amending formula. Certain portions of the Constitution Act of 1867 used to be amendable by an Act of the Parliament of Canada according to the provision contained in the old s. 91(1). This power of amendment allowed Parliament to unilaterally amend only those matters which fell purely within federal jurisdiction. Section 91(1) was a 1949 amendment to the Constitution Act of 1867, enacted as a complement to s. 92(1), which allowed the provincial legislature to unilaterally amend only those matters which fell purely within provincial jurisdiction. However, there were other matters which could only be amended, through the application of certain conventional rules and procedures, by an Act of the Parliament of Great Britain. These matters were set out in s. 91(1) of the Constitution Act of 1867:

> . . . matters coming within the classes of subjects by this Act assigned exclusively to the Legislatures of the provinces, or as regards rights or privileges by this or any other Constitutional Act granted or secured to the Legislature or the Government of a province, or to any class of persons with respect to schools or as regards the use of the English or the French language or as regards the requirements that there shall be a session of the Parliament of Canada at least once each year, and that no House of Commons shall continue for more than five years from the day of the return of the Writs for choosing the House: Provided, however, that a House of Commons may in time of real or apprehended war, invasion or insurrection be continued by the Parliament of Canada if such continuation is not opposed by the votes of more than one-third of the members of such House.

The conventional rules and procedures under which an amendment affecting any of the above matters would be effected were thought to be as follows:

> The first general principle that emerges in the foregoing resume is that although an enactment by the United Kingdom is necessary to amend the British North America Act, such action is taken only upon formal request from Canada. No Act of the United Kingdom Parliament affecting Canada is therefore passed unless it is requested and consented to by Canada. Conversely, every amendment requested by Canada in the past has been enacted.

> The second general principle is that the sanction of Parliament is required for a request to the British Parliament for an amendment to the British North America Act. This principle was established early in the history of Canada's constitutional amendments, and has not been violated since 1895. The procedure invariably is to seek amendments by a joint Address of the Canadian House of Commons and Senate to the Crown.

> The third general principle is that no amendment to Canada's Constitution will be made by the British Parliament merely upon the request of a Canadian province. A number of attempts to secure such amendments have been made, but none has been successful. The first such attempt was made as early as 1868, by a province which was at that time dissatisfied with the terms of Confederation. This was followed by other attempts in 1869, 1874, and 1887. The British Government refused in all cases to act on provincial government representations on the grounds that it should not intervene in the affairs of Canada except at the request of the federal government representing all of Canada.

The fourth general principle is that the Canadian Parliament will not request an amendment directly affecting federal-provincial relationships without prior consultation and agreement with the provinces. This principle did not emerge as early as others but since 1907, and particularly since 1930, has gained increasing recognition and acceptance. The nature and the degree of provincial participation in the amending process, however, have not lent themselves to easy definition.

There have been five instances — in 1907, 1940, 1951, 1960, and 1964 — of federal consultation with all provinces on matters of direct concern to all of them. There has been only one instance up to the present time in which an amendment was sought after consultation with only those provinces directly affected by it. This was the amendment of 1930, which transferred to the Western provinces natural resources that had been under the control of the federal government since their admission to Confederation. There have been ten instances [in 1871, 1875, 1886, 1895, 1915, 1916, 1943, 1946, 1949 and 1949(2nd Sess.)] of amendments to the Constitution without prior consultation with the provinces on matters that the federal government considered were of exclusive federal concern. In the last four of these, one or two provinces protested that federal-provincial consultations should have taken place prior to action by Parliament.[20]

As indicated earlier, as part of the events leading up to the enactment of the Canada Act by the U.K. Parliament, the question arose as to whether the Parliament of Canada could unilaterally request, by Resolution of both Houses of Parliament, that Her Majesty place before the U.K. Parliament the new constitutional package. This issue was litigated through the courts, including a final determination of the matter by the Supreme Court of Canada (all of which occurred prior to obtaining the agreement of nine of the provinces and the federal government to make the request to the U.K. Parliament). As a result, the case raised the issue as to whether essentially political questions should be dealt with as legal matters. Indeed, the concern expressed by some of the twenty-two judges who heard the case in Manitoba, Quebec, Newfoundland and in the Supreme Court of Canada was that while this concern may be real, it does not take into account a recognition that in most constitutional cases the matters come before the court as a result of some political disagreement.

In any event, the issue which came before the courts was simply whether the Parliament of Canada had jurisdiction to unilaterally make the request to the Queen in the United Kingdom. That, in turn, raised the issues as to what were the various rules regarding the amending of the Constitution and, secondly, as to what was the status of convention in Canadian constitutional law. Ultimately, the Supreme Court of Canada concluded that in view of the fact that the new constitutional package contained an entrenched Charter of Rights which, in turn, contained provisions that directly affected the power of Parliament and the provincial legislatures to pass laws in respect of matters within their respective jurisdictions, the new package did therefore directly affect federal/provincial relations. Given that conclusion, the question remained as to whether Parliament nonetheless had the authority to unilaterally make

---

[20]*The Amendment of the Constitution of Canada* 4-7 (1965), A White Paper issued by the Honourable Guy Favreau, Minister of Justice.

the request to the United Kingdom. The Supreme Court held that, strictly speaking, there was no legal bar to the Parliament of Canada doing this. However, it also held that there was a convention to the effect that if an amendment to the Constitution directly affected federal/provincial relations, that is to say the division of legislative jurisdiction, then the consent of not all, but a substantial number, of the provinces must be obtained before Parliament could proceed with the proposed amendment. Accordingly, the Supreme Court of Canada held that the unilateral request of the Parliament of Canada to Her Majesty in the United Kingdom to place the new constitutional package before the U.K. Parliament was proper in a strict legal sense, but improper in a conventional sense. Subsequent to this decision, the consent of a substantial number of the provinces was obtained and the Resolution was enacted by Parliament, satisfying both the legal and conventional requirements under the old B.N.A. Act as interpreted by the Supreme Court of Canada.

The case raises two important points concerning the role of convention in our constitutional law. The first point relates to the establishment of a convention. Clearly, conventions are customs or traditions or usages which, through the passage of time and consistency of application, have hardened or crystallized into conventions. Also, as a result of the above case, it is clear that a convention can never become a law, that is, a custom or usage can become a convention, but a convention cannot become law. The difficult question that remains, therefore, is how to know when custom or usage has, in fact, crystallized into convention. Clearly, this would be determined by the courts in each instance depending upon the individual circumstances. The second point relates to the status of convention in our legal system. It is now clear that a convention is not enforceable by a court. In the case of a government disobeying a convention, the only remedy or sanction is by way of political consequence. For example, with respect to the new constitutional package, the pronouncement by the Supreme Court of Canada that the federal government's plans were legally correct but conventionally incorrect served, no doubt, in part to motivate the federal government and the provincial governments to conduct one final effort at political compromise which, in fact, led to a final agreement.

The new Constitution does contain a comprehensive amending formula. The general rule is that a matter which directly affects federal/provincial relations can be amended by consent of the federal government and two-thirds of the provinces, provided those provinces constituting the two-thirds contain 50 per cent of the population of Canada. There are special amendment procedures relating to special matters, some of which require unanimity for amendment. Interestingly, one of those special matters relates to the composition of the Supreme Court of Canada. As a result of those provisions in ss. 41 and 42 of the Constitution Act of 1982, in effect, the Supreme Court of Canada is given constitutional status, notwithstanding the fact that the Supreme Court of Canada is constituted under an ordinary statute of Parliament. In effect, the Constitution Act has elevated the Supreme Court of Canada to constitutional status.

Accordingly, the devices of federal/provincial negotiations (and the resulting agreements), interdelegation, and amendment have provided for some flexibility in our constitution.

As indicated earlier, the main heads of legislative jurisdiction in ss. 91 and 92 have been subject to various interpretations at various stages of our history. Generally, the notion of a strong central government was emasculated by interpretations of the Judicial Committee of the Privy Council in the 1920's and 1930's. However, stronger federal legislative authority has been restored by the Supreme Court of Canada since it became the final court of appeal for all criminal and civil matters in 1949.

CONSTITUTIONAL BASIS OF JUDICIAL AUTHORITY

The constitutional basis of judicial authority in Canada is provided for in ss. 96 to 101 of the Constitution Act of 1867. These sections are set out as follows:

VIII. JUDICATURE

96. The Governor General shall appoint the Judges of the Superior, District, and County Courts in each Province, except those of the Courts of Probate in Nova Scotia and New Brunswick.

97. Until the laws relative to Property and Civil Rights in Ontario, Nova Scotia, and New Brunswick, and the Procedure of the Courts in those Provinces, are made uniform, the Judges of the Courts of those Provinces appointed by the Governor General shall be selected from the respective Bars of those Provinces.

98. The Judges of the Courts of Quebec shall be selected from the Bar of that Province.

99. (1) Subject to subsection (2) of this section, the judges of the superior courts shall hold office during good behaviour, but shall be removable by the Governor General on address of the Senate and House of Commons.

(2) A judge of a superior court, whether appointed before or after the coming into force of this section, shall cease to hold office upon attaining the age of seventy-five years, or upon the coming into force of this section if at that time he has already attained that age.

100. The Salaries, Allowances, and Pensions of the Judges of the Superior, District, and County Courts (except the Courts of Probate in Nova Scotia and New Brunswick), and of the Admiralty Courts in Cases where the Judges thereof are for the Time being paid by Salary, shall be fixed and provided by the Parliament of Canada.

101. The Parliament of Canada may, notwithstanding anything in this Act, from Time to Time provide for the Constitution, Maintenance, and Organization of a General Court of Appeal for Canada, and for the Establishment of any additional Courts for the better Administration of the Laws of Canada.

Section 92(14) of the Constitution Act of 1867 provides an additional basis of judicial authority:

92. In each Province the Legislature may exclusively make Laws in relation to Matters coming within the Classes of Subjects next herein-after enumerated; that is to say . . .

14. The Administration of Justice in the Province, including the Constitution, Maintenance, and Organization of Provincial Courts, both of Civil and of Criminal Jurisdiction, and including Procedure in Civil Matters in those Courts.

The above provisions may be summarized in the following way:

The Parliament of Canada is granted legislative competence to enact laws providing for the establishment of certain courts and tribunals under the provisions of s. 101 of the Constitution Act of 1867. The various provincial legislatures are given authority to enact laws to provide for the establishment of certain provincial courts and tribunals under the provisions of s. 92(14) of the Constitution Act of 1867 (read together with the exclusion of federal jurisdiction to do so in s. 91(27) of the Constitution Act of 1867).

There are essentially three provisions of the Constitution Act of 1867 providing for the appointment of judges. First, s. 101 gives Parliament authority to enact laws establishing certain federal courts and tribunals and, by implication, also gives Parliament authority to pass legislation respecting the appointment of judges to these courts, the salaries of these judges, their tenure of office and their removal. Secondly, ss. 96 to 100 provide for, among other things, the federal appointment of judges to serve on county or district, and superior courts established by the province under the provisions of s. 92(14). And thirdly, s. 92(14) provides for, by implication, the appointment of judges at the provincial level to serve on provincial courts established under s. 92(14). In summary then, the Constitution Act of 1867 provides for:

1. Federal courts and tribunals constituted under federal legislation enacted pursuant to legislative authority granted Parliament under s. 101 of the Constitution Act of 1867, with federally appointed judges pursuant to this same section.

2. Provincial courts constituted under provincial legislation enacted pursuant to legislative authority granted under s. 92(14) of the Constitution Act of 1867, with federally appointed judges pursuant to the provisions contained in ss. 96 to 100 of the Constitution Act of 1867.

3. Provincial courts constituted under provincial legislation enacted pursuant to legislative authority granted under s. 92(14) of the Constitution Act of 1867, with provincially appointed judges pursuant to the provisions contained in this same section.

A more detailed description of the judiciary in Canada is set out in the chart below.

The foregoing is reviewed again in Chapter 9, together with a discussion on the process of appointment of judges.

LEVEL OF COURT	NAME OF COURT	ENABLING STATUTE ESTABLISHING COURT	APPOINTING AUTHORITY	SALARY	TENURE OF OFFICE	RETIREMENT
Federal	Supreme Court of Canada	Supreme Court Act (enacted pursuant to s. 101 of the Constitution Act)	The Governor in Council (i.e., Minister of Justice)	Set by the Judges Act	During good behaviour (pursuant to the Supreme Court Act and provisions in the Judges Act)	75 (pursuant to the Supreme Court Act)
Federal	Federal Court of Canada	Federal Court Act (enacted pursuant to s. 101 of the Constitution Act)	The Governor in Council (i.e., Minister of Justice)	Set by the Judges Act	During good behaviour (pursuant to the Federal Court Act and provisions in the Judges Act)	75 (pursuant to the Federal Court Act)
Federal	Federal Administrative Tribunals	Various enabling statutes (enacted pursuant to s. 101 of the Constitution Act)	See various enabling statutes	See various enabling statutes	See various enabling statutes	See various enabling statutes
Provincial	Court of Appeal, Court of Queen's Bench, or a single Supreme Court (Appellate and Trial Divisions)	Judicature Act (pursuant to s. 92 (14) of the Constitution Act)	The Governor General pursuant to s. 96 of the Constitution Act (i.e., Minister of Justice)	Set in the Judges Act (pursuant to s. 100 of the Constitution Act)	Pursuant to s. 99 of the Constitution Act during good behaviour (and subject to additional provisions in the Judges Act)	75 (pursuant to s. 99 (2) of the Constitution Act)
Provincial	District or County Court	District Court Act (pursuant to s. 92(14) of the Constitution Act)	The Governor General pursuant to s. 96 of the Constitution Act (i.e., Minister of Justice)	Set in the Judges Act (pursuant to s. 100 of the Constitution Act)	During good behaviour (pursuant to the Judges Act)	70 (pursuant to the Judges Act)
Provincial	Provincial Courts	Varies from province to province but a common formulation might be a single court with various divisions (criminal, family, juvenile and small claims) or might be two or more courts as constituted by various statutes.	See various enabling statutes	Set in particular enabling statutes	Set in particular enabling statutes	Set in particular enabling statutes which vary from province to province; in most provinces at age 70
Provincial	Provincial Administrative Tribunals	Various enabling statutes	Pursuant to various enabling statutes	Pursuant to various enabling statutes	Pursuant to various enabling statutes	Pursuant to various enabling statutes

CONSTITUTIONAL PROCEDURE

At one time, the final court of appeal in all civil and criminal cases was the Judicial Committee of the Privy Council. Then, after certain amendments to the Criminal Code and after a series of cases,[21] the Supreme Court of Canada became the final court of appeal in all criminal cases. However, civil cases could still be appealed to the Judicial Committee of the Privy Council. Finally, in 1949, the Supreme Court of Canada became the final court of appeal for all civil and criminal cases.[22] The jurisdiction of the Supreme Court of Canada is set out in the Supreme Court Act, R.S.C. 1970, c. S-19. This Act was amended significantly in 1975 to abolish the prevailing civil monetary jurisdiction with the result that now the Supreme Court is able to choose the cases it regards as raising matters of national importance or important issues of law, and to decide only those cases. The criminal appeal jurisdiction, however, remains unchanged. The effect of this amendment will strengthen the authority of the Supreme Court in adjudicating matters of legal and national importance. Commenting on the specific consequences arising out of this amendment, the Chief Justice of Canada remarked that the new system increased the quality of the court's work and created a marked reduction in the backlog that existed prior to the 1975 amendment, with the result that the court is now permitted to sit in a full bench of nine judges for at least two-thirds of all appeals.[23]

How does a constitutional case arise? Often it can arise in the course of private litigation. Also there is the possibility of a reference under the provisions of a provincial Constitutional Questions Act or a reference under the provisions of the federal Supreme Court Act. As a result of the application of *Thorson v. A.G. Can.*[24] a taxpayer now has the locus standi to challenge the constitutionality of a public statute where the issue sought to be raised is a justiciable one, where all members of the public alike are affected by the legislation and no person or class of persons has any particular or special interest in the matter, and where the legislation is not regulatory in nature but is declaratory and directory and creates no offences and imposes no penalties, but does involve the expenditure of public money by creating an administrative structure which oversees the implementation of the legislation. It is doubtful that in the federal system it is a necessary precondition to a private individual initiating proceedings on his own to test the constitutional validity of federal

---

[21]*Br. Coal Corp. v. R.*, [1935] A.C. 500, [1935] 2 W.W.R. 564, 64 C.C.C. 145, [1935] 3 D.L.R. 401 (P.C.); *Nadan v. R.*, [1926] A.C. 482, [1926] 1 W.W.R. 801, 45 C.C.C. 221, [1926] 2 D.L.R. 177 (P.C.).

[22]*A.G. Ont. v. A.G. Can.*, [1947] A.C. 127, [1947] 1 W.W.R. 305, [1947] 1 D.L.R. 801 (P.C.).

[23]See the Globe & Mail, 3rd February 1977.

[24][1975] 1 S.C.R. 138, 43 D.L.R. (3d) 1, 1 N.R. 225.

legislation, that he first request the federal Attorney General to commence such proceedings, since in such a system the Attorney General is the officer of the government who is obliged to enforce the legislation.

These conditions were somewhat relaxed in *McNeil v. N.S. Bd. of Censors*,[25] where the Supreme Court of Canada held that the distinction between a regulatory statute and a declaratory statute was not

> a distinction that could be controlling, especially in the light of the reserve of discretion in the Court, and more especially because a word or the term "regulatory" is not a term of art, not one susceptible of an invariable meaning which would in all cases serve to distinguish those in which standing to a taxpayer or citizen would be granted and those in which it would not.

Moreover, the Chief Justice held that a challenge to a regulatory statute is permissible, in the discretion of the court, if the provisions contained in the regulatory statute strike at the members of the general public as the central aspect of the regulatory statute.

More recently, in the *Borowski* case,[26] a challenge to the abortion provisions contained in the Criminal Code on the basis of their alleged non-conformity to the provisions of the Canadian Bill of Rights, the Supreme Court of Canada relaxed the above rules of standing even further. Speaking for the majority, Mr. Justice Martland stated as follows:

> [T]o establish status as a plaintiff in a suit seeking a declaration that legislation is invalid, if there is a serious issue as to its invalidity, a person need only to show that he is affected by it directly or that he has a genuine interest as a citizen in the validity of the legislation and that there is no other reasonable and effective manner in which the issue may be brought before the court.

As a result of the above decisions, particularly in light of the *Borowski* case, it is probable that under s. 52(1) of the Constitution Act of 1982, there is a wide latitude for the average citizen to come forth and challenge the constitutionality of public statutes on the basis of their non-conformity to the provisions contained in the Canadian Charter of Rights and Freedoms. The reader will recall that s. 52(1) says that the Constitution of Canada (including the Canadian Charter of Rights and Freedoms) is the supreme law of Canada and any law that is inconsistent with the Constitution is of no force and effect to the extent of the inconsistency. As such, with the above line of cases relating to standing requirements, it is suggested by many that s. 52(1) will become the vehicle by which the average citizen has access to the courts to chal-

---

[25][1976] 2 S.C.R. 265, 32 C.R.N.S. 376 at 379, 55 D.L.R. (3d) 632, 12 N.S.R. (2d) 85, 5 N.R. 43.
[26]*Borowski v. Min. of Justice*, [1982] 1 W.W.R. 97 at 117, 24 C.R. (3d) 352, 31 N.R. 331 (S.C.C.).

lenge the constitutionality of legislation which contains provisions contrary to the Canadian Charter of Rights and Freedoms.

Under the provisions of various statutes, there are requirements that notice be given to the appropriate Attorney General and to the federal Minister of Justice before a challenged statute may be declared unconstitutional. Under these provisions, the person receiving notice has a right to intervene and a right to be heard. In addition, often third parties, usually governments, but on occasion labour unions, trade associations and private interest groups, apply to the court to intervene and make representations in a case in which they are not directly interested. These interventions are often allowed, solely in the discretion of the court, and, in the case of provincial governments, are rarely refused.

The whole process of constitutional decision-making, according to Professor Barry Strayer in his treatise *Judicial Review of Legislation in Canada*,[27] is somewhat different from the process of simple statutory interpretation. The process engaged in by the courts in constitutional cases is, rather, one of "constitutional adjudication". Special doctrines of interpretation such as the aspect, ancillary or necessarily incidental, and trenching doctrines are employed. But in determining the constitutionality of an impugned statute the court must still address itself to the central question as to the intent of the legislature in enacting that statute. In this connection, Professor Strayer argues for broadened rules of evidence so as to permit more evidence to be adduced in connection with the legislative history of an impugned statute in order to determine the intent of the legislature in enacting that statute.

At present, the rule of evidence in respect of legislative history is a narrow and restrictive one (see Chapter 11). However, Professor Strayer argues for the admissibility of evidence in order to determine what he refers to as "legislative facts". That is, in deciding constitutional cases, the court ought to be aware of general facts concerning the economic, social and political context of legislation. In order to ascertain these facts, Professor Strayer then argues for the admissibility of statements made by members of legislative bodies, reports of legislative committees and Royal Commissions, direct evidence, and other types of evidence now excluded under the existing rule concerning the admissibility of legislative history.

The thrust of Dr. Strayer's thesis emphasizes, as Professor Cheffins maintains, that constitutional law cannot be isolated, as can the law of trust, for example, from political, economic and social reality. Students of constitutional law must regard this discipline as all-encompassing; it

---

[27]University of Toronto Press, 1968.

cannot be compartmentalized and insulated from the realities of the other components which define modern Canadian society.

This view has been recognized judicially. For example, in the *Anti-Inflation*[28] case, referred to earlier, the courts took into account all sorts of extrinsic evidence, including the effect of severe inflation and recession on the value of the Canadian dollar on international money markets. There are several other examples in cases decided over the past few years which, consistent with Dr. Strayer's thesis, have permitted the use of extrinsic evidence in the constitutional law area. This will become increasingly important in the making of judicial determinations under the Canadian Charter of Rights and Freedoms. For example, s. 1 of the Charter, the so-called "limitations" clause, provides that every right in the Charter is guaranteed subject only to such reasonable limits prescribed by law as can be demonstrably justified in a free and democratic society. The use of the term "demonstrably" invites, one might argue, the increased use of either judicial notice and/or extrinsic evidence. There are other examples as well and these were referred to at an earlier point in this chapter.[29] Clearly, in view of the expanded role of the judiciary under a regime of entrenched rights, together with a broader standing requirement than previously existed, courts will no longer be constrained, at least in constitutional cases, by strict, narrow evidentiary rules that might have worked a hardship on the judicial decision-making process in the past.

There has always been debate as to whether the law of civil liberties falls within the domain of constitutional law. Several years ago the only issue concerning civil liberties was not whether legislation was bad or evil, but rather whether the legislative body enacting the given piece of legislation had the constitutional authority to do so. But then there were many instances in which the courts invoked the constitutional division of powers in order to declare ultra vires a statute containing provisions tending to derogate from notions of egalitarianism and individual liberty. Now, with the entrenchment of the Canadian Charter of Rights and Freedoms in the Constitution, civil liberties are clearly constitutional concerns. Notwithstanding this, the reader should be aware of the many developments in the area of the law of civil liberties in the past quarter century.

In 1960, the Canadian Bill of Rights was enacted. Essentially, the Canadian Bill of Rights is a statutory code of conduct to which all other federal statutes must conform. These statutory guidelines ensure that no federal statutes violate certain protected human rights set out in the Canadian Bill of Rights, unless a federal statute specifically states that it

---

[28]*Reference re Anti-Inflation Act*, [1976] 2 S.C.R. 373, 68 D.L.R. (3d) 452, 9 N.R. 541.
[29]See the section dealing with the Significance of Entrenchment, *supra*.

shall operate notwithstanding the Canadian Bill of Rights (see earlier discussion).

The provisions of the Canadian Bill of Rights are still relevant in view of the provision contained in s. 26 of the Charter which states that the "guarantee in this Charter of certain rights and freedoms shall not be construed as denying the existence of any other rights or freedoms that exist in Canada". As such, the Canadian Bill of Rights continues in force.

Some of the provisions of the Canadian Bill of Rights are set out as follows:

The Parliament of Canada, affirming that the Canadian Nation is founded upon principles that acknowledge the supremacy of God, the dignity and worth of the human person and the position of the family in a society of free men and free institutions;

Affirming also that men and institutions remain free only when freedom is founded upon respect for moral and spiritual values and the rule of law;

And being desirous of enshrining these principles and the human rights and fundamental freedoms derived from them, in a Bill of Rights which shall reflect the respect of Parliament for its constitutional authority and which shall ensure the protection of these rights and freedoms in Canada:

Therefore Her Majesty, by and with the advice and consent of the Senate and House of Commons of Canada, enacts as follows:

1. It is hereby recognized and declared that in Canada there have existed and shall continue to exist without discrimination by reason of race, national origin, colour, religion or sex, the following human rights and fundamental freedoms, namely,

(a) the right of the individual to life, liberty, security of the person and enjoyment of property, and the right not to be deprived thereof except by due process of law;

(b) the right of the individual to equality before the law and the protection of the law;

(c) freedom of religion;

(d) freedom of speech;

(e) freedom of assembly and association; and

(f) freedom of the press.

2. Every law of Canada shall, unless it is expressly declared by an Act of the Parliament of Canada that it shall operate notwithstanding the *Canadian Bill of Rights*, be so construed and applied as not to abrogate, abridge or infringe or to authorize the abrogation, abridgment or infringement of any of the rights or freedoms herein recognized and declared, and in particular, no law of Canada shall be construed or applied so as to

(a) authorize or effect the arbitrary detention, imprisonment or exile of any person;

(b) impose or authorize the imposition of cruel and unusual treatment or punishment;

(c) deprive a person who has been arrested or detained
(i) of the right to be informed promptly of the reason for his arrest or detention,
(ii) of the right to retain and instruct counsel without delay, or
(iii) of the remedy by way of habeas corpus for the determination of the validity of his detention and for his release if the detention is not lawful;

(d) authorize a court, tribunal, commission, board or other authority to compel a person to give evidence if he is denied counsel, protection against self crimination or other constitutional safeguards;

(e) deprive a person of the right to a fair hearing in accordance with the principles of fundamental justice for the determination of his rights and obligations;

(f) deprive a person charged with a criminal offence of the right to be presumed innocent until proved guilty according to law in a fair and public hearing by an independent and impartial tribunal, or of the right to reasonable bail without just cause; or

(g) deprive a person of the right to the assistance of an interpreter in any proceedings in which he is involved or in which he is a party or a witness, before a court, commission, board or other tribunal, if he does not understand or speak the language in which such proceedings are conducted.

It is interesting to note that some rights contained in the Canadian Bill of Rights are not contained in the Canadian Charter of Rights and Freedoms while others are contained in the Charter and not in the Bill. It appeared to the legal profession in 1960 that the enactment of the Canadian Bill of Rights heralded a new era in the development of the law of civil liberties in Canada. To the legal profession in 1983, however, the 1960 enactment does not have the importance that many thought it would.

The status of the Canadian Bill of Rights in 1983 is not entirely clear. Most lawyers cannot reconcile the decisions of the Supreme Court of Canada in *R. v. Drybones*,[30] *A.G. Can. v. Lavell*,[31] and *A.G. Can. v. Canard*.[32] One thing is clear, however, and that is that the spirit, if not the substance of *Drybones* has been significantly whittled down since it was rendered. Some experts do not regard this as the death of the Canadian Bill of Rights as a viable instrument in ensuring the preservation of the political, egalitarian and legal civil liberties of Canadians, but rather they regard recent cases as merely growing pains in the development of the law of civil liberties in Canada. Many experts continually point to the American experience, arguing that it took the American judiciary almost two hundred years to develop the law of civil liberties whereas the Canadian experience is limited to merely twenty-three years and we are perhaps expecting too much to happen too quickly. ·

In view of the entrenchment of the Canadian Charter of Rights and Freedoms in the Canadian constitution the issue is somewhat moot, but the experience of the Canadian Bill of Rights remains relevant insofar as it might serve as a predictor of judicial attitudes in the protection of civil liberties. On the other hand, one might expect what may be described as judicial "activism" in the preservation of civil liberties given that we are now entering a new era where civil liberties have become constitutionally entrenched in the highest law of the land.

In addition to the Bill of Rights, there have been other developments in the law of civil liberties during the past quarter century. All the

[30][1970] S.C.R. 282, 71 W.W.R. 161, 10 C.R.N.S. 334, [1970] 3 C.C.C. 355, 9 D.L.R. (3d) 473.
[31][1974] S.C.R. 1349, 23 C.R.N.S. 197, 11 R.F.L. 333, 38 D.L.R. (3d) 481.
[32][1976] 1 S.C.R. 170, [1975] 3 W.W.R. 1, 52 D.L.R. (3d) 548, 4 N.R. 91.

provinces and the federal government have enacted anti-discrimination legislation. While a Bill of Rights is a statutory code of conduct to which all other statutes must conform, anti-discrimination legislation is concerned with protection against private discriminatory conduct. This, too, is an area covered by ss. 15 and 28 of the Canadian Charter of Rights and Freedoms, and, like the Canadian Bill of Rights, by virtue of s. 26 of the Charter, those provincial and federal anti-discrimination laws continue in force.

In addition to the above, there is other legislation directed at providing protection and ensuring preservation of our civil liberties. For example, the institution of ombudsman has now been established in most provinces. Indeed, the first International Conference of Ombudsmen was held in Edmonton in 1976 and a second in Jerusalem in 1980. Somewhat akin to the function served by the office of the ombudsman is the current legislative development ensuring the protection of privacy and providing for freedom of information, including the federal Access to Information Act enacted in June of 1982.[33]

Accordingly, the reader can appreciate that the law of civil liberties in Canada is a dynamic and developing area in which legislation, at all levels of government, is presently under consideration. It will provide protection for the individual in the face of private discrimination, large, impersonal modern bureaucracy and, generally, against legislation violating fundamental human liberties. This will be particularly so in view of the entrenchment of the Charter of Rights in the new Constitution.

The law of civil liberties cannot properly be the subject of a detailed discussion in a treatise of this nature; however, the reader should appreciate the extent to which the law is presently responding to issues of this nature. For further discussion of these issues, the reader might consult the various works cited in the bibliography at the end of this chapter.

The whole field of Canadian constitutional law forms the major substructure of the Canadian legal and political system and it cannot be given proper treatment in merely a single chapter. However, it is hoped that the reader will appreciate the constitutional basis underlying the distribution of legislative authority as well as the constitutional basis underlying the creation of courts and the appointment of judges in Canada.

At the time of this writing, there is still much concern in Canada in connection with proposals for substantial changes in the distribution of legislative power, and to some extent, the situation presently is in a state of flux. That fact, taken together with the commencement of a new era characterized by an entrenched Charter of Rights, makes the study of Canadian constitutional law a dynamic and exciting exercise.

---

[33]This Act came into force on 1st July 1983.

SELECTED BIBLIOGRAPHY OF ARTICLES AND TREATISES
ON THE CONSTITUTIONAL BASIS
OF JUDICIAL AND LEGISLATIVE AUTHORITY IN CANADA

ARTICLES

Abel, A.S., "Constitutional Charter for Canada" (1978), 28 U.T.L.J. 265.

Abel, "Re Official Languages Act: A Comment" (1974), 20 McGill L.J. 595.

Abel, "The Neglected Logic of 91 and 92" (1969), 19 U. of T. L.J. 487.

Abel, "The Role of the Supreme Court in Private Law Cases" (1965), 4 Alta. L. Rev. 39.

Abel, "What Peace, Order and Good Government?" (1968), 7 Western Ont. L. Rev. 1.

Acorn, "The Background" (Constitutional Law Problems in Canadian Oil and Gas Legislation) (1964), 3 Alta. L. Rev. 367.

Alexander, "A Constitutional Strait Jacket for Canada" (1965), 43 Can. Bar Rev. 262.

Atkey, "The Role of the Provinces in International Affairs" (1971), 26 Int. J. 249.

Auburn, F.M., "The Canadian Bill of Rights and Discriminatory Statutes" (1970), 86 L.Q.R. 306.

Ballem, "Constitutional Validity of Provincial Oil and Gas Legislation" (1963), 41 Can. Bar Rev. 199.

Beaudoin, G.-A., "Le bilinguisme et la Constitution" (1973), 4 R. Gen. 321.

Beaudoin, G.-A., "La Cour suprême et la protection des droits fondamentaux" (1975), 53 Can. Bar Rev. 675.

Beaudoin, G.-A., "Linguistic Rights in Canada" in *The Practice of Freedom*, McDonald, R. St. J. and Humphrey, J.P. (eds.). Toronto: Butterworths, 1979.

Beckton, C.F., "A.G. for Canada v. Claire Dupond: The Right to Assemble in Canada?" (1979), 5 Dalhousie L.J. 169.

Beetz, J., "Le contrôle juridicionnel du pouvoir législatif et les droits de l'homme dans la Constitution du Canada" (1958), 18 R. du B. 361.

Berger, S., "Application of the Cruel and Unusual Punishment Clause Under the Canadian Bill of Rights" (1978), 24 McGill L.J. 161.

Bracken, G., "Federal Law Relating to Search and Seizure" (1974), 23 U.N.B.L.J. 53.

Brent, "The Right to Religious Education and the Constitutional Status of Denominational Schools" (1976), 40 Sask. L. Rev. 239.

Brun, H., "La Charte des droits et libertés de la personne: domaine d'application" (1977), 37 R. du B. 179.

Brun, H. and Tremblay, G., "Les langues officielles au Canada" (1979), 20 C. de D. 69.

Caron, M., "Le Code civil québécois: instrument de protection des droits et libertés de la personne?" (1978), 56 Can. Bar Rev. 197.

Carr, "Division of Legislative Powers under the British North America Act — The Case for Fully Concurrent Powers" (1971), 4 Man. L.J. 297.

Cline, E. and Finley, M.J., "Whither the Implied Bill of Rights?" (1980-81), 45 Sask. L. Rev. 137.

Cohen, S.A., "Controlling the Trial Process: the Judge and the Conduct of the Trial" (1977), 36 C.R.N.S. 15.

Conklin, W.E., "Constitutional Ideology, Language Rights and Political Disunity in Canada" (1979), 28 U.N.B.L.J. 39.

Crommelin, "Jurisdiction over Onshore Oil and Gas in Canada" (1975), 10 U.B.C.L. Rev. 86.

Diefenbaker, J.G., "A Half-Century Encounter with Civil Liberties" (1972-73), 5 Man. L.J. 255.

Driedger, "Statute of Westminster and Constitutional Amendments" (1968), 11 Can. Bar J. 348.

Driedger, "The Search for an Amending Formula" (1967), 10 Can. Bar J. 524.

Favreau, "Constitutional Amendment in a Canadian Canada" (1966-67), 12 McGill L.J. 384.

Gibson, D., "Charter or Chimera: A Comment on the Proposed Canadian Charter of Rights and Freedoms" (1979), 9 Man. L.J. 363.

Gibson, "Constitutional Amendment and the Implied Bill of Rights" (1966-67), 12 McGill L.J. 497.

Gibson, "Constitutional Jurisdiction Over Environmental Management in Canada" (1973), 23 U. of T. L.J. 54.

Gibson, "Constitutional Law" (1967), 2 Man. L.J. 283.

Gibson, "Constitutional Law — Federalizing the Judiciary" (1966), 44 Can. Bar Rev. 674.

Gibson, "Interjurisdictional Immunity in Canadian Federalism" (1969), 47 Can. Bar Rev. 40.

Gibson, "The Constitutional Context of Canadian Water Planning" (1969), 7 Alta. L. Rev. 71.

Hanssen, "The Federal Declaratory Power Under the British North America Act: With an Appendix" (1968), 8 Man. L.J. 87.

Head, "The Canadian Offshore Minerals Reference: The Application of International Law to a Federal Constitution" (1968), 18 U. of T. L.J. 131.

Head, "The Legal Clamour over Canadian Off-shore Minerals" (1967), 5 Alta. L. Rev. 312.

Hogg, P.W., "Constitutional Power Over Language", [1978] L.S.U.C. Special Lectures 229.

Hogg and Grover, "The Constitutionality of the Competition Bill" (1976), 1 Can. Bus. L.J. 197.

Janisch, H.N., "What is Law?" (1977), 55 Can. Bar Rev. 576.

Kaiser, "Constitutional Aspects of the Regulation of Canadian Computer Technology" (1971), Queen's L.J. 97.

Katz, "Constitutional Problems of a Unified Family Court System" (1974), 6 Man. L.J. 211.

Kovach, "An Assessment of the Merits of Newfoundland's Claim to Offshore Mineral Resources" (1975), 23 Chitty's L.J. 18.

Krauss, M., "Interpretation de lois — historie législative" (1980), 58 Can. Bar. Rev. 756.

La Forest, "The Labour Conventions Case Revisited" (1974), 12 Can. Year Book Int. L. 137.

Lang, "The Machinery of Constitutional Change and Amendments" (1966), Can. Bar Papers 159.

Laskin, "Amendment of the Constitution" (1963), 15 U. of T. L.J. 190.

Laskin, "Amendment of the Constitution: Applying the Fulton-Favreau Formula" (1965), 11 McGill L.J. 2.

Laskin, "Occupying the Field: Paramountcy in Penal Legislation" (1963), 41 Can. Bar Rev. 234.

Laskin, "The Canadian Constitution After the First Century, Part I" (1967), 45 Can. Bar Rev. 395.

Lederman, "The Concurrent Operation of Federal and Provincial Laws in Canada" (1962-63), 9 McGill L.J. 185.

Lederman, "Unity and Diversity in Canadian Federalism: Ideals and Methods of Moderation" (1976), 14 Alta. L. Rev. 34.

Leon, J.S., "Cruel and Unusual Punishment: Sociological Jurisprudence and the Canadian Bill of Rights" (1978), 36 U.T. Fac. L. Rev. 222.

Lyon, "The Central Fallacy of Canadian Constitutional Law" (1976), 22 McGill L.J. 40.

Lysyk, "The Unique Constitutional Position of the Canadian Indian" (1967), 45 Can. Bar Rev. 513.

McConnell, W.H., "Unreasonable Searches and Seizures: a 'Fourth Amendment' for Canada" (1980), 11 R.D.U.S. 155.

McDonald, "Constitutional Aspects of Canadian Anti-Combines Law Enforcement" (1969), 47 Can. Bar Rev. 161.

MacKenzie, "Planning of the B.N.A. Act" (1974), 6 Ottawa L. Rev. 332.

McNairn, "Aeronautics and the Constitution" (1971), 49 Can. Bar Rev. 411.

McNairn, "Transportation, Communication and the Constitution: The Scope of Federal Jurisdiction" (1969), 47 Can. Bar Rev. 355.

MacPherson, J.C., "Developments in Constitutional Law: The 1978-79 Term" (1980), 1 Supreme Court L. Rev. 77.

MacPherson, J.C., "Developments in Constitutional Law: The 1979-80 Term" (1981), 2 Supreme Court L. Rev. 49.

McWhinney, "Techniques of Constitutional Interpretation" (1967), 5 Col. I. Dr. Comp. 67.

Mallory, "The B.N.A. Act: Constitutional Adaptation and Social Change" (1967), 2 Thémis 127.

Martin, "Newfoundland's Case on Offshore Minerals, A Brief" (1975), 7 Ottawa L. Rev. 34.

Marx, "Language Rights in the Canadian Constitution" (1967), 2 Thémis 239.

Morin, "A Constitutional Court for Canada" (1965), 43 Can. Bar Rev. 545.

Morris, "Canadian Federalism and International Law" (1974), Can. Persp. 55.

Morris, "The Treaty-Making Power: A Canadian Dilemma" (1967), 45 Can. Bar Rev. 478.

Mullan, "Standing After McNeil" (1976), 8 Ottawa L. Rev. 32.

Nadin-Davis R.P., "Comment: Civil Liberties — Right to Counsel" (1980), 58 Can. Bar Rev. 686.

Proulx, D., "Egalité et discrimination dans la Charte des droits et libertés de la personne: étude comparative" (1980), 10 R.D.U.S. 381.

Proulx, D., "La suprématie des droits et libertés de la personne et la question constitutionnelle au Canada" (1981), 12 R. Gen. 413.

Richardson and Quigley, "The Resources Industry, Foreign Ownership and Constitutional Methods of Control" (1975), 39 Sask. L. Rev. 92.

Russell, "Constitutional Reform of the Canadian Judiciary" (1969), 7 Alta. L. Rev. 103.

Sanders, D., "Aboriginal Peoples and the Constitution" (1981), 19 Alta. L. Rev. 410.

Schmeiser, D.A., "The Case Against Entrenchment of a Canadian Bill of Rights" (1973), 1 Dalhousie L.J. 15.

Schmeiser, D.A., "The Entrenchment of a Bill of Rights" (1981), 19 Alta. L. Rev. 375.

Scott and Lederman, "A Memorandum Concerning Housing, Urban Development and the Constitution of Canada" (1972), 12 Plan. Can. 33.

Scott, "Canadian Federalism: The Legal Perspective" (1967), 5 Alta. L. Rev. 262.

Smiley, "Candian Federalism and the Spending Power: Is Constitutional Restriction Necessary?" (1969), 17 Can. Tax J. 467.

Strayer, "Amendment of the Canadian Constitution: Why the Fulton-Favreau Formula?" (1966), 1 Can. Legal Studies 119.

Strayer, "The Flexibility of the B.N.A. Act" (1969), Agenda 197.

Tarnopolsky, W.S., "Just Desserts or Cruel and Unusual Treatment or Punishment? Where Do We Look for Guidance?" (1978), 10 Ottawa L. Rev. 1.

Tarnopolsky, W.S., "The Canadian Bill of Rights from Diefenbaker to Drybones" (1971), 17 McGill L.J. 437.

Tarnopolsky, "The Effectiveness of Constitutional Guarantees and other Governmental Declarations on Human Rights and Fundamental Freedoms" (1967), 5 Col. I, Dr. Comp. 117.

Tarnopolsky, W.S., "The Historical and Constitutional Context of the Proposed Canadian Charter of Rights and Freedoms" (1981), 44 Law and Contemporary Problems 169.

Tarnopolsky, W.S., "The Supreme Court and Civil Liberties" (1976), 14 Alta. L. Rev. 58.

Taylor, M.R., "The Status of Individual Rights and Freedoms under the Constitution Act, 1981" (1982), 40 Advocate 119.

Thompson, "Implications of Constitutional Change for the Oil and Gas Industry" (1969), 17 Alta. L. Rev. 369.

Trudeau, "Constitutional Reform and Individual Freedoms" (1969), 8 Western Ont. L. Rev. 1.

Trudeau, P.E., "Les Droits de l'homme et la suprématie parlementaire" in Les Droits de l'homme, le féderalisme et les minoritiés (Gotlieb, A., ed.), Toronto: Institut canadien des affaires internationales, 1970.

Weiler, "Supreme Court of Canada and Canadian Federalism" (1973), 11 Osgoode Hall L.J. 225.

TREATISES

Abel, A.S., Toward a Constitutional Charter for Canada. Toronto: U. of T. Press, 1980.

Beaudoin, G.-A., Essais sur la Constitution. Ottawa: Editions de l'Université d'Ottawa, 1979.

Beck, J.M., The Shaping of Canadian Federalism: Central Authority or Provincial Right? Copp Clark Publishing Company, 1971.

Berger, T., Fragile Freedoms. Toronto: Clarke Irwin, 1981.

Browne, G.P., Documents on the Confederation of British North America. Toronto: McClelland and Stewart, 1969.

Cheffins, R.I. and R.N. Tucker, The Constitutional Process in Canada, 2nd ed. McGraw-Hill Ryerson, 1976.

Chevrette, F. and Marx, H., Droit Constitutionel: notes et jurisprudence. Montreal: Les Presses de l'Université de Montréal, 1982.

Clements, W.H.P., *The Law of the Canadian Constitution*, 3rd ed. Toronto: Carswell, 1916.

Cook, R., *Canada and the French-Canadian Question*. Macmillan of Canada, 1966.

Creighton, D.G., C.P. Stacey, P.B. Waite, W. Ullmann, A.G. Bailey and G.F.G. Stanley, *Confederation*. University of Toronto Press, 1967.

Crepeau, P.A. and C.B. Macpherson, eds. *The Future of Canadian Federalism*. University of Toronto Press, 1965.

Dawson, R.M. and W.F. Dawson, *Democratic Government in Canada*, 4th ed. rev. by N.M. Ward. University of Toronto Press, 1971.

Dawson, R.M., *The Government of Canada*, 5th ed. rev. by N.M. Ward. University of Toronto Press, 1970.

de Smith, S.A., *Constitutional and Administrative Law*. Harmondsworth: Penguin, 1971.

de Smith, S.A., *Judicial Review of Adminsitrative Action*, 3rd ed. London: Stevens, 1973.

Dicey, A.V., *Introduction to the Study of the Constitution*, 10th ed. by E.C.S. Wade. London:Macmillan, 1961.

Doerr, A. and Carrier, M., *Women and the Constitution in Canada*. Ottawa: Can. Advisory Council on the Status of Women, 1981.

Gall, G., ed., *Civil Liberties in Canada*. Toronto: Butterworths, 1982.

Heuston, R.F.V., *Essays on Constitutional Law*, 2nd ed. London: Stevens, 1964.

Hockin, T.A., *Government in Canada*. McGraw-Hill Ryerson, 1976.

Hogg, P.W., *Constitutional Law of Canada*. Toronto: Carswell, 1977.

Holdsworth, Sir Wm., *A History of English Law*, 7th ed. by A.L. Goodhart and H.G. Hanbury, Vols. I and II. London: Methuen, 1956.

Jennings, Sir W. Ivor, *The Law and the Constitution*, 5th ed. University of London Press, 1959.

Kallen, E., *Ethnicity and Human Rights in Canada*. Toronto: Gage Publishing, 1982.

Kelsen, H., *General Theory of Law and the State*. Harvard University Press, 1949.

Kennedy, W.P.M., *Essays in Constitutional Law*. Oxford, London, 1934.

La Forest, G.V., *The Allocation of Taxing Power under the Canadian Constitution*, Canadian Tax Foundation, April 1967.

La Forest, G.V., *Disallowance and Reservation of Provincial Legislation*. Ottawa: Department of Justice, 1955.

La Forest, G.V., *Natural Resources: Public Property Under the Canadian Constitution*. University of Toronto Press, 1969.

Laskin, B., *Canadian Constitutional Law: Cases, Text and Notes on Distribution of Legislative Power*, 4th ed. rev. by A.S. Able and J. Laskin, Toronto: Carswell, 1975.

Lederman, W.R., *The Courts and the Canadian Constitution*. McClelland and Stewart, 1967.

Lefroy, A.H.F., *Canada's Federal System*. Toronto: Carswell, 1913.

Lyon, J.N. and R.G. Atkey, *Canadian Constitutional Law in a Modern Perspective*. University of Toronto Press, 1970.

MacKinnon, F., *The Crown in Canada*. Glenbow-Alberta Institute, McClelland and Stewart West, 1976.

Mackintosh, W.A., *The Economic Background of Dominion-Provincial Relations*. McClelland and Stewart, 1964.

Mallory, J.R., *The Structure of Canadian Government*. Macmillan of Canada, 1971.

Marshall, G., *Constitutional Theory*. Oxford: Clarendon, 1971.

Marshall, G., *Parliamentary Sovereignty and the Commonwealth*. Oxford: Clarendon, 1957.

Marshall, G. and C.G. Moodie, *Some Problems of the Constitution*. Rev. 4th ed. London: Hutchinson, 1967.

McRuer Report, *Royal Commission of Inquiry into Civil Rights*. Queen's Printer, Toronto: Report No. 1, Vols. I-III, 1968; Report No. 2 Vol. IV, 1969; Report No. 3, Vol. V, 1971.

McWhinney, E., *Judicial Review*, 4th ed. University of Toronto Press, 1968.

Meekison, J.P., *Canadian Federalism: Myth or Reality*, 2nd ed. London: Methuen, 1971.

Mitchell, J.D.N., *Constitutional Law*, 2nd ed. Edinburgh: W. Green, 1968.

Molgat, Senator G.L. and M. MacGuigan, *Constitution of Canada — Final Report of Special Joint Committee of the Senate and of the House of Commons*. Information Canada, Ottawa, 1972.

Ontario Advisory Committee on Confederation: Background Papers and Reports, Vol. I. Queen's Printer of Ontario, 1967.

Ontario Advisory Committee on Confederation: Background Papers and Reports, Vol. II. Queen's Printer of Ontario, 1970.

Ouellet, F., L.A.H. Smith, D.G. Creighton and W.H. Parker, *Constitutionalism and Nationalism in Lower Canada*. University of Toronto Press, 1969.

Report of the Royal Commission on *Bilingualsim and Biculturalism*, vols. I-IV. Queen's Printer, Ottawa, 1967-1970.

Report of the Royal Commission of Inquiry on *Constitutional Problems* (Tremblay Report). Quebec, 1956.

Report of the Royal Commission on *Dominion-Provincial Relations* (Rowell-Sirois Report). Canada, 1940.

Report of the Special Joint Committee of the Senate and House of Commons on *The Constitution of Canada*. Queen's Printer, Ottawa, 1972.

Riddell, W.R., *The Constitution of Canada*. New Haven, Conn.: Yale University Press, 1917.

Roberston S., *Courts and the Media*. Toronto: Butterworths, 1981.

Russell, P.H., *Leading Constitutional Decisions* 2nd ed. Toronto: McClelland and Stewart, 1973.

Sawer, G., *Modern Federalism*. Smithers and Benellie.

Schmeiser, D.A., *Civil Liberties in Canada*. Oxford, London, 1964.

Scott, F.R., *The Canadian Constitution and Human Rights*. Toronto: Canadian Broadcasting Corporation, 1959.

Scott, F.R., *Civil Liberties in Canada*. University of Toronto Press, 1959.

Secretary's Report on *The Constitutional Review 1968-1971* by the Canadian Intergovernmental Conference Secretariat. Information Canada, Ottawa. 1974.

Sharp, M., *Federalism and International Conferences on Education*. A Supplement to Federalism and International Relations. Queen's Printer, Ottawa, 1968.

Smiley, D.V., *Canada in Question: Federalism in the Seventies*, 2nd ed. McGraw-Hill Ryerson, 1976.

Smiley, D.V., *Constitutional Adaptation and Canadian Federalism Since 1945*. Information Canada, Ottawa, 1970.

Smith, A., *The Commerce Power in Canada and the United States*. Butterworths, 1963.

Stanley, M. *Short History of the Canadian Constitution*. Ryerson, 1969.

Strayer, B.L., *Judicial Review of Legislation in Canada*. University of Toronto Press, 1968.

Tarnopolsky, W.S., *Discrimination and the Law in Canada*. Toronto: DeBoo, 1982.

Tarnopolsky, W.S., ed., *Some Civil Liberties Issues of the Seventies*. Toronto: Carswell, 1975.

Tarnopolsky, W.S., *The Canadian Bill of Rights*. Toronto: Carswell, 1966.

Tarnopolsky and Beaudoin, eds., *Canadian Charter of Rights and Freedoms: Commentary*. Toronto: Carswell, 1982.

Tarnopolsky, Wright, Beaudoin and Cody-Rice, *Newspapers and the Law, Les quotidiens et la loi*, annexed to the Kent Report. Ottawa: Supply and Services, 1981.

Trudeau, P.E., *A Canadian Charter of Human Rights*. Queen's Printer, Ottawa, 1968.

Trudeau, P.E., *Charte canadienne des Droits de l'homme*. Ottawa: Queen's Printer, 1968.

Varcoe, F.P., *The Constitution of Canada*. Toronto: Carswell, 1965.

Waite, P.B., *The Confederation Debates in the Province of Canada/1865*. McClelland and Stewart, 1965.

Waite, P.B., *The Life and Times of Confederation, 1865-1867,* "Politics, Newspapers and the Union of British North America". University of Toronto Press, 1962.

Weiler, P., *In the Last Resort. A Critical Study of the Supreme Court of Canada.* Toronto: Carswell/Methuen, 1974.

Wheare, K.C., *The Constitutional Structure of the Commonwealth.* Oxford, 1960.

Wheare, K.C., *Federal Government,* 4th ed. Oxford, 1963.

Wheare, K.C., *The Statute of Westminster and Dominion Status,* 5th ed. Oxford, 1953.

Whyte, J.D., and W.R. Lederman, *Canadian Constitutional Law — Cases, Notes and Materials on the Distribution and Limitations of Legislative Powers Under the Constitution of Canada.* Toronto: Butterworths, 1975.

6

THE INSTITUTIONS: THE ROLE OF COURTS IN CANADA

INTRODUCTION

An inquiry into the role of courts in Canada necessarily involves an inquiry into the role and function of judges. That inquiry, however, is the subject of a major discussion in Chapter 9. Judges sit in various different courts; the hierarchy of courts within the Canadian judiciary is also made the subject of two discussions in this treatise. In the preceding chapter, we directed our attention to the constitutional basis of judicial authority in Canada; in the following chapter, we will be examining that same hierarchy in terms of the various functions of the different courts at the various levels. Accordingly, the purpose of this chapter is to bridge the gap between our knowledge of the constitutional basis for the establishment of courts in Canada and the later discussions (in Chapters 7 and 9) of the functions of the various courts and the role of the judge in exercising those functions. This chapter will discuss, by way of a general introduction, the role and function of courts in Canada.

THE ATMOSPHERE OF THE COURTS

There are, essentially, two features which describe the atmosphere in Canadian courts. The first feature is a custom or convention that the proceedings are to be held openly and in public. The second feature is that proceedings are to be conducted in an atmosphere of decorum and dignity commensurate with the seriousness or importance of the work engaged in by our courts.

1. THE OPEN COURT

A legal philosopher, Jeremy Bentham, once said:

> In the darkness of secrecy, sinister interest and evil in every shape have full swing. Only in proportion as publicity has place can any of the checks applicable to judicial injustice operate. Where there is no publicity there is no justice. Publicity is the very soul of justice. It is the keenest spur to exertion and the sheerest of all guards against improbity. It keeps the judge himself while trying under trial. The security of securities is publicity.[1]

---

[1] Quoted from the Ontario Law Reform Commission, "Report on Administration of Ontario Courts", Part I, 1973, p. 205.

The view espoused above reflects a tradition of our Anglo-Canadian legal system. That tradition, of course, arose out of a sad and perverse chapter in our legal history, associated with the proceedings of the Star Chamber, and similar expressions of manifest injustice and unfairness throughout our legal history. In short, the scrutiny and vigilance which arise out of the publicity of proceedings held in our courts are regarded as essential in ensuring the preservation of justice and in ensuring public acceptance, confidence and credibility in our courts as vital institutions in society.

Notwithstanding the foregoing, however, there are instances where the desire for publicity conflicts with the responsibility of our courts to provide for the protection of the rights of certain classes of persons appearing before the courts. For example, proceedings of the juvenile court are held in camera. Proceedings are closed to the public for reason that the philosophy underlying the Juvenile Delinquents Act, R.S.C. 1970, c. J-3, dictates that it is the court's responsibility, upon a finding of delinquency, not only to protect the public, but also to effect a disposition in the best interests of the child. As a result, in order to undertake the latter responsibility, it is felt that it is in the best interests of the child to hold the proceedings under the Juvenile Delinquents Act in private.[2]

There are other instances in the law in which our parliamentarians have felt it advisable that the proceedings of courts be held in camera. For example, under the Criminal Code, R.S.C. 1970, c. C-34, upon an application by counsel for an accused person at a preliminary inquiry, the judge must order that the proceedings of that preliminary inquiry, excepting only the disposition at the end of the inquiry, not be publicized until there is, subsequently, a conviction at trial. Another example of a prohibition on publication arises out of amendments a few years ago to the former rape (now sexual assault and aggravated sexual assault) sections of the Criminal Code. Under these amendments, publication of the name of the complainant or victim of the rape is banned. One should, however, draw a distinction between the departures from the principle of the open court contained in the instances described above. In juvenile proceedings, the entire matter is held in private, while in respect of the two examples under the Criminal Code set out above, the proceedings are still held in public and anyone may enter the court; however, there is a ban on publication.[3] This distinction aside, the common denominator

---

[2]The new Young Offenders Act, 1980-81-82-83 (Can.), c. 110, which is not yet in force, also contains similar provisions.

[3]In addition to the preceding examples, s. 576.1 (as enacted by 1972, c. 13, s. 49) of the Criminal Code provides:

"576.1(1) Where permission to separate is given to members of a jury under subsection 576(1), no information regarding any portion of the trial at which the jury is not present shall be published, after the permission is granted, in any newspaper or broadcast before the jury retires to consider its verdict.

linking all of these examples is a desire on the part of our legislators (and, by implication, on the part of our courts) that the rights of certain classes of persons appearing before the courts be protected. It is a question of balancing the protections arising out of the concept of the open court, including the desire for publicity and the public's right to know, with the protection of the rights of certain classes of private individuals appearing before the courts, including the harm that would come to those persons in the event of publicity. Nonetheless, the occasions which require a derogation from the concept of the open court are rare because both traditionally and in the present, that balance is strongly tilted towards the desire to conduct proceedings openly and in public.[4]

Notwithstanding this, one might consider the remarks of Dr. Max Wyman, a former president of the University of Alberta and a commissioner on the Kirby Commission studying the lower courts in the province of Alberta:

> I began to wonder what had happened to Jeremy Bentham's *security of securities*, and why our open courts do not seem to apply any checks to the appearance of judicial injustice. The names of people, not charged with any offence, are often bandied about in those open courts, and the news media have the power to disseminate to the world, in a matter of hours, serious innuendos concerning people who have no defence. I've begun to wonder whether those open courts, as they have now come to be, may be destroying more lives than they save . . . I began to wonder what safeguards were being taken to guard innocent people, wrongly accused of crime, from suffering such stigma. It seems to me that the open court, with the attendant publicity, is an open invitation to all and sundry to jump to the wrong conclusion.
>
> If the presumption of innocence is to mean anything in our system of law, the privacy of people should be guarded up to, and until, an actual conviction takes place. Does the public really have a right to know that people have been accused of crimes even when adjudication later deems them to be innocent of those crimes? I think not.
>
> The confusion that now reigns in those open courts has now become so great that some people answer to the wrong name, and plead guilty to the wrong charges, and it takes months to discover and rectify situations like this. Indeed, I now see none of the benefits that Bentham so clearly saw for those open courts. Although I hardly advocate a return to the Star Chamber, I do advocate a serious re-examination of the proper role an open court should play in our scheme of things. If the purpose of an open court is to protect the accused, then the accused should have an unprejudiced choice as to whether he or she wants to have his or her case heard in an open court.[5]

"(2) Every one who fails to comply with subsection (1) is guilty of an offence punishable on summary conviction.

"(3) In this section, 'newspaper' has the same meaning as it has in sections 262 to 281 by virtue of section 261."

[4]For a discussion of the American position on similar issues, see U.S. News & World Report, 14th August 1978.

[5]Comments on the Criminal Law and the Legal Process, May 1975. Those readers who are interested in a more detailed examination of the relationship between the press as an institution in society, on one hand, and the law and the Canadian legal system, on the other hand, including the application of the fundamental notion of freedom of the press, may consult the following four treatises: Kesterton, *The Law and the Press in Canada* (Toronto:

There is an inherent power vested in all judges to generally supervise and control the proceedings in their courts which allows a judge to close his courtroom to the press and/or public if there is a legitimate reason for doing so. Occasionally this is done where the evidence assumes a particularly salacious character. This whole question concerning the relationship between the open court and freedom of the press, and the desire in certain circumstances either to hold proceedings in camera or to order, upon pain of a citation of contempt of court, a ban on publication was, in fact, the subject of controversy a few years ago. In an Ontario case, a trial judge ordered a ban on the publication of the evidence adduced at trial of a criminal matter, without more than the vaguest of reasons for doing so. This subsequently gave rise to editorial condemnation. In addition, one often reads of the fate which awaits, upon imprisonment, persons convicted of sexually related crimes, especially those committed on children. In order to protect the lives of those individuals, some persons have suggested that there be a restriction on the publication of their names at trial.

The issue of the open court has recently been the subject of considerable litigation. For example, in R. v. N., [1980] 1 W.W.R. 68, 15 B.C.L.R. 218, 10 C.R. (3d) 68, 48 C.C.C. (2d) 97, 11 R.F.L. (2d) 45, 102 D.L.R. (3d) 417, the British Columbia Court of Appeal held that a Juvenile Court Judge has the discretion under s. 12(1) of the Juvenile Delinquents Act to permit the members of the public to attend at the trial of a child charged with a delinquency. Section 12(1) provides as follows:

12. (1) The trials of children shall take place without publicity and separately and apart from the trials of other accused persons, and at suitable times to be designated and appointed for that purpose.

(2) Such trials may be held in the private office of the judge or in some other private room in the court house or municipal building, or in the detention home, or if no such room or place is available, then in the ordinary court room, but when held in the ordinary court room an interval of half an hour shall be allowed to elapse between the close of the trial or examination of any adult and the beginning of the trial of a child.

(3) No report of a delinquency committed, or said to have been committed, by a child, or of the trial or other disposition of a charge against a child, or of a charge against an adult brought in the juvenile court under section 33 or under section 35, in which the name of the child or of the child's parent or guardian or of any school or institution that the child is alleged to have been attending or of which the child is alleged to have been an inmate is disclosed, or in which the identity of the child is otherwise indicated, shall without the special leave of the court, be published in any newspaper or other publication.

(4) Subsection (3) applies to all newspapers and other publications published anywhere in Canada, whether or not this Act is otherwise in force in the place of publication.

McClelland and Stewart, Carleton Library Series, 1976); Adam (ed.), *Journalism, Communication and the Law* (Scarborough: Prentice-Hall of Canada Ltd., 1976); Beckton, *Law and the Media* (Toronto: Carswell, 1982) and Robertson, *Courts and the Media* (Toronto: Butterworths, 1981).

Essentially, the Court of Appeal held that the words "without publicity" in the above section do not mean "in camera". Accordingly, the Juvenile Court Judge has the discretion to allow members of the public to attend juvenile proceedings.[6]

More recently, there have been a number of similar cases arising out of the provisions contained in the new Canadian Charter of Rights and Freedoms. Some newspapers have raised the issue in connection with s. 2 of the Charter, which provides that

> [e]veryone has the following fundamental freedoms: . . .
>
> (b) freedom of . . . expression, including freedom of the press and other media of communication . . .

In addition, s. 11 provides that

> [a]ny person charged with an offence has the right . . .
>
> (d) to be presumed innocent until proven guilty according to law in a fair and public hearing . . .

It should be noted that, unlike s. 2, the benefit of this section is restricted to persons charged with criminal offences.

Although the scope of these sections has not as yet been defined by the Supreme Court of Canada, they have been considered by some other courts. For a sense of how the courts are reacting to these sections specifically, and to the new Charter generally, see the following cases: *Re S.D.A.* (1982), 28 R.F.L. (2d) 121 (B.C. Prov. Ct.); *A.G.N.S. v. McIntyre* (1982), 132 D.L.R. (3d) 385, 49 N.S.R. (2d) 609, 67 A.P.R. 199 (S.C.C.); *R. v. B.; Edmonton Journal v. A.G. Alta.,* Alta. Q.B., Dea J., 7th January 1983, [1983] A.W.L.D. 183, [1983] W.D.F.L. 320; *Malartic Hygrade Gold Mines (Que.) Ltd. v. R. in Right of Que.* (1982), 16 A.C.W.S. (2d) 498 (Que. S.C.); *R. v. B. (C.R.)* (1982), 30 C.R. (3d) 80 (Ont. H.C.); *R. v. Banville* (1982), 30 C.R. (3d) 59, 69 C.C.C. (2d) 520, 141 D.L.R. (3d) 36, 41 N.B.R. (2d) 114, 107 A.P.R. 114 (Prov. Ct.); *R. v. Collins,* Ont. Co. Ct., Hogg Co. Ct. J., 14th December 1982 (not yet reported); *R. v. Gallant*

---

[6]For some other instances over the past few years where this issue has arisen, see the following newspaper reports:

1. Unprecedented ban on reporting of evidence *and* decision at bail hearing of child charged with murder — see Edmonton Journal, 5th August 1981.

2. Rejection of a defence request to exclude press from guilty plea concerning a sexual offence committed by an adult on a juvenile — see Edmonton Journal, 13th April 1981.

3. Similar issues were recently considered by the Supreme Court of the United States — see Newsweek Magazine, 27th August 1979 and U.S. News & World Report, 20th August 1979.

4. A Provincial Judge orders a ban on the reporting of a bawdy house trial, including the identification of those witnesses who had "paid for sex" — see Edmonton Journal, 29th August 1979. The order is subsequently upheld by a Supreme Court Judge — see Edmonton Journal, 29th September 1979. But it was later overruled by a Court of Appeal decision — see Edmonton Journal, 29th October 1979.

(1982), 38 O.R. (2d) 788, 70 C.C.C. (2d) 213, 2 C.R.R. 144 (Prov. Ct.); *R. v. J.* (1982), 37 O.R. (2d) 173, 68 C.C.C. (2d) 285, 137 D.L.R. (3d) 671, 1 C.R.R. 202 (Prov. Ct.); *R. v. L'Esperance* (1982), 8 W.C.B. 352 (Que. Sess. Ct.); *Southam Inc. v. R.* (1982), 70 C.C.C. (2d) 257, 141 D.L.R. (3d) 341 (Ont. H.C.).

In order to protect against any improprieties on the part of the press, including any abuses in relation to press coverage of judicial proceedings, several so-called "press councils" have been established throughout Canada. These press councils are essentially bodies which conduct a form of self-regulation arising out of complaints against participating newspapers.[7]

Finally, Dr. Wyman is not alone, in his views set out above, in expressing a desire that a re-examination of the concept of the open court be conducted. For example, the executive director of the Alberta Council on Aging recently made these remarks:

> . . . the council maintains the media, especially the printed media, "doesn't realize the implications of what they are printing."
>
> Printing the names, ages and addresses "is a form of persecution and a violation of human rights as these people have no say in having this information published" . . . The council is calling on all editors and publishers to review stories of violent crimes and think about the consequences before releasing names, ages, and addresses . . . The council is not questioning the freedom of the press but their prerogative to infringe on human rights.[8]

---

[7]See, for example, "A Report on the Alberta Press Council", Edmonton Journal, 20th December 1976. Virtually every daily (and some weekly) newspapers now belong to a provincial press council. In addition, many newspapers have a form of self-regulation in the form of an "ombudsman" to whom people can complain. While this may be helpful, the individual serving in this capacity is not in reality an ombudsman for he lacks independence from his employer/newspaper.

See also Macdonald and Russell, *Journalists' Attitudes Towards the Police and the Judiciary* (Toronto: Canadian Daily Newspaper Publishers Association, 1978); Parker, *Collision Course? Free Press and the Courts*, from a symposium of lawyers and journalists at Osgoode Hall Law School (Toronto: Ryerson Polytechnical Institute, 1966); LaMarsh, "Abuse of Power by the Media" (1979), Lectures L.S.U.C. 651; Atkey, "Freedom of Information: The Problem of Confidentiality in the Administrative Process" (1980), 18 U.W.O.L. Rev. 153.

The move towards promoting continued self-regulation on the part of the newspapers has been particularly heightened since the report of the Kent Royal Commission on Newspapers was released in 1982. The Commission recommended, among other things, the enactment of a Newspaper Act to control the monopolistic and oligopolistic practices of the large newspaper chains. At the time of this writing the federal government has agreed to proceed on this recommendation, notwithstanding the newspaper industry's claims that a Newspaper Act would constitute an infringement of the freedom of the press.

[8]The Edmonton Journal, 18th December 1976. In the United States, the use of so-called "gag orders" by the courts arouses far more concern, reaction, and editorial criticism than that arising out of the employment of similar restrictions on publicity in Canada.

Accordingly, at least in respect of the criminal law, the notion of the freedom of the press and the concept of the open court are not without some current challenge. However, these criticisms notwithstanding, the concept of the open court, including the associated publicity which arises therefrom, represents essentially a fundamental protection afforded to those persons appearing in proceedings before our courts which defines an essential feature of the atmosphere surrounding the conduct of proceedings in Canadian courts.

2. DIGNITY AND DECORUM

The television and motion picture portrayal of American courts that is familiar to many lay persons is certainly not applicable to Canadian courts. Although Canadian courts perhaps do not conduct their proceedings with the same strictness and formality exercised by their British counterparts, nonetheless there exists an air of formality in Canadian courts. Judges are addressed in certain formal ways and the manner in which counsel addresses the court depends, in turn, upon the particular level of the judiciary occupied by that court. Judges are often gowned and, depending upon the level of the judiciary and the nature of the proceedings, counsel are also gowned.

While some may argue that these formalities constitute a certain stuffiness, if not elitism, on the part of judges and lawyers, the counter argument is more persuasive. This argument holds that by conforming to certain formalities, the court achieves the prestige it deserves, given the important function it exercises in society. Arising out of this prestige, the proceedings before our courts will then be conducted in an atmosphere of dignity and decorum. This is not to say that Canadian courts are humourless institutions. On the contrary, many members of the legal profession in Canada are able to relate many anecdotes arising out of experiences in Canadian courts. The notions of dignity and decorum, however, are designed to serve essentially two fundamental objectives. The first is that, in order to ensure that the objectives of fairness and justice are achieved, proceedings should never stoop to a level of frivolity. Secondly, in regarding judicial proceedings as a search for truth and justice, Canadian judges and lawyers strongly adhere to the notion that this search ought not to be conducted in an atmosphere of showmanship, dramatics, flamboyance or sensationalism. In short, an atmosphere of dignity and decorum is regarded as best suited to the search for truth and, ultimately, the attainment of justice.[9] That is why, at least in respect of proceedings in Canadian courts, the American television and

---

[9] Recently, two Ontario judges warned lawyers and members of the public that they would not proceed in divorce cases unless those who appeared before them were properly dressed. For an analysis of those pronouncements, see the article appearing in The Edmonton Sun, 1st February 1982.

motion picture image of court proceedings is generally inaccurate. That is also why, in defining the nature of the atmosphere surrounding Canadian courts, one must add to the concept of the open court the additional notions of dignity and decorum.

3. TELEVISION IN THE COURTROOM

Probably the most dramatic development over the past few years in connection with the issues of openness and dignity and decorum in our courts relates to the use of television in the courts. Television has now been allowed in some U.S. courts for a number of years.[10]

In Canada, the Supreme Court of Canada allowed television cameras to be present during the historic pronouncement of its decision on the unilateral patriation of the Canadian constitution, and in Ontario there has been some significant work done on an experimental basis in connection with television in the courtrooms.[11] However, while on the one hand, it might be argued that television provides an openness in court proceedings readily available to all, on the other hand, it is arguable that television in the courtroom could have the effect of detracting from the dignity and decorum to which we have become accustomed.

Clearly, the progress of this development should depend on a careful assessment of the current experiments involving the use of television in our courts with a view to achieving a balance between the desire to attain openness and the desire to protect the important notions of dignity and decorum from the dangers of sensationalism.

THE FUNCTION OF COURTS IN CANADA

Generally speaking, the role of our courts is to provide a fair and just resolution of the various problems and conflicts that are brought before them. The attainment of justice, through the instrumentality of fair and impartial proceedings, defines the essential nature of the function of our system of courts in Canada. Indeed, if all the lawyers in Canada were canvassed as to what views, if any, they all had in common, probably only one view would emerge: that procedural fairness is essential in the quest for justice.

In terms of resolving particular disputes before the courts, one must view the role of the courts (and, by implication, the role of judges) in

---

[10]For a brief discussion of the American position, see U.S. News & World Report, 9th February 1981.

[11]In particular, one might refer to the Ontario experiment and the related study thereof conducted by the Radio Television News Directors Association of Canada (R.T.N.D.A.). This study, entitled *Electronic Public Access to Court: A Proposal for its Implementation Today,* was submitted on November 18, 1982. It was prepared by the R.T.N.D.A. Special Committee on Electronic Public Access (Mr. Con Stevenson (CKOC) Chairman; Mr. Craig Armstrong (CBC - Toronto); Mr. Gordon Haines (CIJY-TV); and Mr. Daniel Henry (CBC, Legal Counsel)). This report presents an excellent argument in favour of television cameras in the courtroom.

terms of providing objective arbitration of particular disputes. However, that definition by itself would probably be insufficient. One would, in addition, have to examine the nature of the process of objective arbitration. Essentially, that process is an exercise in the search for truth. Upon the discovery of the truth, through an application of our rules of procedure and rules of evidence, the courts then exercise a decision-making jurisdiction, after which the appropriate disposition is made.

Broadly speaking, however, there is one final component necessary in order to define the role of courts in the Canadian legal system. That final component is, essentially, the method by which the courts conduct the foregoing search for truth. And that method is in the nature of an application of the rules of procedure and evidence in the context of an adversarial system. In short, our system of judicial decision-making is based on the assumption that the search for truth is best conducted in the context of an adversarial system. Moreover, in resolving particular disputes, it is through the instrumentality of that system that our courts ensure fairness and the attainment of just results.

Mr. Justice Antonio Lamer, a former Chairman of the Law Reform Commission of Canada and now a Justice of the Supreme Court of Canada, described the role and function of our courts as providing a "conflict resolution service". In addition, our courts exercise a second-ary function: namely the provision of a forum for the dramatic reaffirma-tion of transgressed societal values. Mr. Justice Lamer referred to this as the "dramatization function". Moreover, he indicated that both the conflict resolution and dramatization functions share the following essen-tial characteristics:

1. Adjudicative
2. Authoritative
3. Adversarial
4. Visible, mandatory, official and presided over by a judicial officer
5. Applies predetermined, objective norms

Finally, Mr. Justice Lamer described the role exercised by administra-tive tribunals as arbitrative in nature, possessing the same essential characteristics as listed above.[12]

ARBITRATION AND ADJUDICATION IN THE CONTEXT OF AN ADVERSARIAL SYSTEM

In order to understand the process of judicial decision-making utilized by our courts in resolving disputes, it is necessary first to characterize the process of "adjudication" and, secondly, to examine the nature of the "adversarial system".

---

[12]"Are We Over-judicialized", address delivered to the Canadian Institute for the Adminis-tration of Justice, 18th February 1977.

Professor Paul Weiler made these remarks concerning the above in a significant article on the process of judicial decision-making:

> The first characteristic of "adjudication" is that it has the function of settling disputes (between private individuals or groups, or the government and the individual). These disputes are not future-oriented debates over general policy questions, although, as we shall see, the latter can enter into the final resolution of the problem. Rather, the disputes which are necessary to set the process of adjudication in motion involve "controversies" arising out of a particular line of conduct which causes a collision of specific interests. There is no *logical* or *factual* necessity about this proposition. There can be exceptions and the question of defining the limits of the adjudicative function can be difficult and debatable in the marginal areas.
>
> The legal problems presented to adjudication can be at least several degrees removed from a purely private and concrete dispute. At the other extreme is the decision of a court, completely on its own motion, to issue a statement establishing or changing an existing rule of law, with no argument of counsel at all. This is rare, but not unheard of, as is shown by the recent example of the House of Lords overruling the *London Street Tramways* rule of the inviolability of its own precedents. Much more common is the use by the court of an opinion disposing of a particular dispute to issue general statements about the law that are not absolutely "necessary" for the decision. Intermediate between these two is the case of the advisory opinion, where the court is asked for its opinion on the constitutional legality of proposed legislation.[13]

In addition, Professor Weiler points out that, on occasion, the function of courts is to exercise a role which is different from adjudication. In this connnection, he refers to the process of "mediation".

> Not all modes of settling specific, concrete, "private" disputes can be characterized as adjudication, though. Another possible technique is that of "mediation". Essentially, this process is designed to induce an agreement of the parties as to the specific type of settlement which is preferable in the interests of each at the time of settlement. By contrast, adjudication results in an authoritative settlement which is imposed on one (or both) of the parties whatever be his attitude toward it. Not all authoritative settlements can be properly attributed to adjudication, especially those which purport to be nothing more than the fiat of one who wields "legitimated power" because of his position in a hierarchical system (nor, by the way, those that proceed from chance, as the throw of the dice). Although this conclusion might be obvious, it has an interesting corollary for the exercise by the decision-maker of a type of managerial or discretionary function. Why this type of forward-looking disposition of the problem (which shifts values between the parties in the light of society's best future interests) is inconsistent with adjudication can only be seen by considering the "adversary" nature of the latter.[14]

Finally, Professor Weiler characterizes the adversarial process in the following way:

> An adversary process is one which satisfies, more or less, this factual description: as a prelude to the dispute being solved, the interested parties have the opportunity of adducing evidence (or proof) and making arguments to a disinterested and impartial arbiter who decides the case on the basis of this evidence and these arguments. This is

---

[13]"Two Models of Judicial Decision-Making" (1968), 46 Can. Bar Rev. 406 at 410.
[14]*Ibid.*, pp. 411-412.

by contrast with the public processes of decision by "legitimated power" and "mediation-agreement", where the guaranteed private modes of participation are voting and negotiation respectively. Adjudication is distinctive because it guarantees to each of the parties who are affected the right to prepare for themselves the representations on the basis of which their dispute is to be resolved.

This is the minimum descriptive content of adjudication as an adversary institution.[15]

EFFECTIVENESS OF OUR SYSTEM OF COURTS — THE IMPORTANCE OF SCRUTINY AND RESPONSIVENESS

However one defines the adversarial system, and the process by which the courts conduct their arbitrative and adjudicative functions, the key issue is whether the Canadian model, in fact, "works". Indeed, the search for a definition or a universal description of the Canadian model of judicial decision-making is more or less in the nature of an academic exercise, because, first, among judges themselves, there is no uniformity of opinion as to their role and function, and secondly, because a definition is unimportant; what is important is whether our system "works".

For a judicial system to "work", it must be able to successfully achieve the objectives of that system. In Canada, it is doubtful that members of the legal profession, including both judges and lawyers, as well as members of the public at large, share a uniformity of opinion as to what these objectives are. However, at the very least, most Canadians would presumably agree that as a fundamental objective of the Canadian legal system, our courts must entertain a search for truth, and that that search for truth must be conducted in a manner and with the result that might, broadly speaking, be characterized as the dispensation of justice. In turn, the dispensation of justice must not only be directed at those persons appearing before our courts, but also at the same time it must be directed to the best interests of society at large. This rather broad and generic description of the fundamental objectives underlying the process of judicial decision-making in Canada is set out to assist in the answering of that basic, but vitally important, question raised above. Does the Canadian legal system "work"? In other words, is our system successful in achieving the fundamental objectives set out above?

Clearly, no system can be perfect. It is important, however, to ensure that those persons who are involved with the Canadian legal system, namely, judges, lawyers, law reformers, law teachers, legislators, the press and members of the public at large, always strive for the achievement of perfection. Moreover, those persons ought to subject the Canadian legal system to continual scrutiny, periodic review and, where advisable, necessary reform. Continual scrutiny of the Canadian legal

---

[15]*Ibid.*, p. 412.

system by all those connected with it probably provides the best safe-guard in ensuring that the legal system successfully achieves its fundamental objectives.

Generally speaking, most observers would agree that our legal system is successful in achieving its basic objectives. However, in order to ensure that our legal system maintains its effectiveness in accomplishing these objectives, and in order to maintain its integrity as a vital institution in Canadian society, the legal system must not fall prey to two dangers. Judges, lawyers and judicial administrators should not react negatively to the scrutiny suggested above. Indeed, they must themselves take an active part in the conduct of that scrutiny. For example, the chief judges and chief justices of the various benches in several provinces have recently taken an active role in reducing the problem of a large backlog of cases. On the theory that justice delayed is justice denied, these chief judges and chief justices have, often upon their own initiative, taken the necessary measures in order to solve or, at the very least, reduce this particular problem. And indeed, many of these chief judges and chief justices have been quite successful in reducing the backlog.[16]

However, scrutiny of the legal system is not, in itself, sufficient. It is also important for our courts to be responsive to suggestions of possible reform, where those suggestions are well founded and necessary. In order to be responsive, it is necessary that our courts regard themselves as ultimately responsible to society at large. Because our judges occupy a special and unique position in society, there is always the danger that our courts might become somewhat isolated; with isolation, these institutions might also lose touch with the community at large.[17] However, this isolation will not occur if the members of the Canadian judiciary regard our system of courts as not merely components of our legal system, but

---

[16]One current issue of some controversy relates to whether the function of judicial administration should remain in the hands of the chief judge or chief justice of every bench in Canada, or alternatively, whether that function should reside in the hands of professionally trained court administrators. Generally speaking, the response of the courts to this suggestion of reform has been somewhat negative. The reason, however, does not relate to any notion of responsiveness or lack thereof, but rather, is related to a serious and fundamental concern on the part of our courts. Specifically, that concern is that a withdrawal of the judicial administrative function into the hands of a civil servant might effectively do harm to the notion of judicial independence. Given the importance of judicial independence from government, the argument against a withdrawal of the judicial administrative function to specialized personnel is a compelling one. However, the controversy still continues. See Watson, "The Judge and Court Administration" in Linden (ed.), *The Canadian Judiciary* (Osgoode Hall, 1977), p. 163; Millar & Baar, *Judicial Administration in Canada* (Kingston: McGill-Queen's University Press, 1981); and Deschênes C.J., *Masters in Their Own House* (Ottawa: Canadian Judicial Council, 1982).

[17]Some degree of isolation is, however, necessary. For a further consideration of the constraints of judicial life, see the discussion on the role of the judge set out in Chapter 9.

rather as vital institutions mandated by society to ultimately serve society. With this notion in mind, our courts will possess a character of responsiveness.

Through the instrumentality of scrutiny and responsiveness, the Canadian legal system can continue to be successful in achieving its fundamental objectives and to enjoy the collective trust vested in it by the society at large. Our courts will remain the beneficiaries of the reputation of integrity they have earned, and will continue to command the confidence of all persons in society.[18]

CANADIAN COURTS AS INSTITUTIONS IN SOCIETY

In the above section of this chapter, reference was made to two important notions. First, it was suggested that our courts are not only components of the legal system, but also they are, at the same time, vital and independent institutions in society at large. Secondly, it was also suggested that in order for our courts to effectively achieve their fundamental objectives, they must possess the confidence and trust of the members of society. In order to enjoy this confidence and trust, our courts must possess a reputation of the highest integrity.

The importance of the first notion relates to the role and responsibility of courts in society. Society must regard our system of courts and the courts must regard themselves as mandated by society, concerned with the interests of society, and as ultimately responsible and accountable to society. The importance of the second notion relates to fundamental considerations of power and authority. Persons in authority are only able to exercise power over those that they govern, without force, if they enjoy the trust and confidence of those that they govern. This is true of the relationship between parent and child, teacher and student, employer and employee, politician and constituent, and others. It is also true of our courts in relation to all members of society, whose lives and affairs our courts govern. In order to gain that trust our courts must be regarded by all as singularly vital and independent institutions possessing the utmost of integrity. Traditionally, our courts have always enjoyed the prestige they deserve, largely owing to the nature of the important functions that they exercise. In addition, our courts have earned an added measure of integrity through their just exercise of the judicial decision-making process. Built into that decision-making process are certain devices which ensure the preservation of the integrity of our courts. The most important device is the power of the court to find a

---

[18]For some recent journalistic reflections on our courts, see the following sources: (1) On the Supreme Court of Canada — see Maclean's Magazine, 12th February 1979; and (2) On the Canadian legal system, generally, see "Justice in the 1980's", a four-part series appearing in the Toronto Star, 8th-11th February 1982.

person in contempt of court in certain circumstances. This power is, essentially, the method by which our courts ensure the respect of those persons appearing before them.[19] The engendering of respect in this way contributes to the maintenance of the integrity of our courts as vital institutions in society.

CONCLUSION

If one were to list the three most important institutions in society, that list would contain, broadly speaking, our legislative bodies, our bureaucracies and our courts. But if one were to ask upon which of these institutions we must rely in the event of disputes between legislative bodies, between a citizen and the bureaucracy, and between citizen and citizen, the answer would, of course, be our courts. Our system of courts is not only a fundamental component of the Canadian legal system; it is also an important and independent institution within society. Indeed, given the special importance in the event of disputes arising between the other major institutions in society, our system of courts must be regarded as no less than an essential structural component of society itself.

In this chapter, we have examined the Canadian system of courts on a somewhat general level. In the next chapter, we will examine the hierarchy of the various courts in Canada and discuss the specific functions exercised by each of those courts.

---

[19]There is, in law, more than one type of contempt; and, in addition, there is more than one type of circumstance in which a person could be found in contempt. With respect to the latter, a person need not appear in court to be in contempt of court. For example, the reader might recall the so-called "judges affair", where a cabinet minister was found guilty of contempt of court arising out of intemperate criticism by the cabinet minister of a decision in a case, adjudicated following an investigation conducted by his department. Also, a violation of the terms of certain types of orders issued by a court constitute a contempt of court. For example, the violation of a prohibition order under the Combines Investigation Act, R.S.C. 1970, c. C-23, is, essentially, in the nature of a contempt of court.

7

HIERARCHY OF
FEDERAL AND PROVINCIAL COURTS
AND DIVISION OF RESPONSIBILITY

Thus far, we have examined Canadian courts as vital components of the Canadian legal system and of Canadian society. We have entertained a discussion as to the constitutional basis of judicial authority in Canada, and examined the judiciary in terms of its functions, broadly defined. The present chapter will concern itself with the particular functions exercised by courts at various levels of the judiciary. It is important to realize at the outset that the specific courts each exercise specific functions. While it is true that Canadian courts, generally speaking, exercise a common function (a function characterized in the last chapter as being in the nature of arbitration and/or adjudication), this common function must be defined in terms of specific jurisdictions, depending upon the particular stratum occupied by a given court in the judicial hierarchy. The jurisdictional variations among the various courts relate to distinctions based upon differing monetary jurisdictions, or to jurisdictional limitations based upon various specific areas of the law or to other considerations.

One important consideration, however, is a constitutional limitation imposed upon certain provincial courts. More specifically, those courts constituted by provincial statute with judges provincially appointed cannot, constitutionally, exercise the same or similar functions as those exercised by courts which are constituted by provincial statutes with judges federally appointed. The latter courts are often referred to as "s. 96 courts". These courts are governed by the provisions set out in ss. 96 to 100 of the Constitution Act of 1867. Those provisions were set out earlier in Chapter 5; among other things, they provide for the federal appointment of judges in these particular types of provincially constituted courts.

Specifically, the s. 96 courts are the courts of superior jurisdiction in a province (namely, the supreme court of a province, including both the appellate and trial divisions, and both of those courts in those provinces where the two divisions are constituted as separate courts) and the county or district courts of a province.[1]

On occasion, a provincially constituted court with judges provincially appointed, or a provincially constituted administrative tribunal with a hearing officer provincially appointed, will hear and adjudicate a given matter which arguably falls within the domain of a county or district, or superior court of a province. In this event, the decision of the judge or the hearing officer may be challenged on the basis that the court or tribunal had no jurisdiction to hear the matter, in that such a court or tribunal was exercising a function normally reserved to s. 96 courts. As a result of various constitutional challenges on this basis, the jurisprudence has provided several tests to assist in the determination as to whether a particular function exercised by a court is a s. 96 function.[2]

In addition to the above constitutional limitation, the specific functions to be exercised by courts at various levels must be determined by reference to two sources. Often the statute establishing a given court will set out the specific functions reserved for that court. In addition, various other statutes within a jurisdiction might also dictate the functions

---

[1]The county or district courts in several provinces have been merged or amalgamated in recent years with the superior courts of trial jurisdiction. This has occurred recently in Alberta, Saskatchewan, and New Brunswick, and is about to occur in Manitoba. Where a province has retained an intermediate s. 96 court, with some exception, e.g. Newfoundland, it is designated as a county, rather than district, court.

[2]For a discussion of the various tests enunciated by the courts in determining whether a given matter is reserved to a s. 96 court, see the following leading cases: *Reference re Adoption Act*, [1938] S.C.R. 398, 71 C.C.C. 110, [1938] 3 D.L.R. 497; *L.R.B. of Sask. v. John East Iron Works Ltd.*, [1948] 2 W.W.R. 1055, [1949] A.C. 134, [1948] 4 D.L.R. 673 (P.C.); *Dupont v. Inglis*, [1958] S.C.R. 535, 14 D.L.R. (2d) 417; *Concerned Citizens of B.C. v. Capital Reg. Dist.*, [1980] 6 W.W.R. 193, affirmed [1981] 1 W.W.R. 359, 25 B.C.L.R. 273, 118 D.L.R. (3d) 257 (C.A.); *Reference re Residential Tenancies Act*, [1981] 1 S.C.R. 714, 123 D.L.R. (3d) 554, 37 N.R. 158; *A.G.N.S. v. Gillis* (1980), 39 N.S.R. (2d) 97, 71 A.P.R. 97 (C.A.); *Jones v. Bd. of Trustees of Edmonton Catholic School Dist. 7*, [1977] 2 S.C.R. 872, [1976] 6 W.W.R. 336, 1 M.P.L.R. 112, 70 D.L.R. (3d) 1, 11 N.R. 280, 1 A.R. 100; *Crevier v. A.G. Que.*, [1981] 2 S.C.R. 220, 127 D.L.R. (3d) 1, 38 N.R. 541; *Seminary of Chicoutimi v. A.G. Que.*, [1973] S.C.R. 681; *C.B.C. v. Cordeau*, [1979] 2 S.C.R. 618, 14 C.P.C. 60, 48 C.C.C. (2d) 289, 101 D.L.R. (3d) 24, 28 N.R. 541 (*sub nom. C.B.C. v. Que. Police Comm.*); *Reference re S. 6 of the Family Relations Act, 1978*, [1980] 6 W.W.R. 737, 18 R.F.L. (2d) 17, 23 B.C.L.R. 152, 116 D.L.R. (3d) 221, varied in part [1982] 1 S.C.R. 62, [1982] 3 W.W.R. 1, 26 R.F.L. (2d) 113, 36 B.C.L.R. 1, 40 N.R. 206 (*sub nom. Polglase v. Polglase*); *Tomko v. L.R.B. (N.S.)*, [1977] 1 S.C.R. 112, 76 C.L.L.C. 14,005, 69 D.L.R. (3d) 250, 14 N.S.R. (2d) 191, 7 N.R. 317, 10 N.R. 35; *Pepita v. Doukas*, [1980] 1 W.W.R. 240, 16 B.C.L.R. 120, 101 D.L.R. (3d) 577 (C.A.); *Re C.U.P.E. and Guelph Gen. Hosp.* (1978), 22 O.R. (2d) 348, 13 C.P.C. 206, 93 D.L.R. (3d) 359 (H.C.); *Mississauga v. Peel*, [1979] 2 S.C.R. 244, 9 M.P.L.R. 81, 97 D.L.R. (3d) 439, 26 N.R. 200, 9 O.M.B.R. 129; *Reference re Proposed Legislation Concerning Leased Premises and Tenancy Agreements* (1978), 89 D.L.R. (3d) 460 (Alta. C.A.); *Re Constitutional Questions Act*, [1978] 6 W.W.R. 152, 7 R.P.R. 104, 11 A.R. 451 (C.A.); *Re Miramichi Lumber Co.* (1977), 83 D.L.R. (3d) 545, 20 N.B.R. (2d) 35, 34 A.P.R. 35 (C.A.); *A.G. Que. v. Farrah*, [1978] 2 S.C.R. 638, 86 D.L.R. (3d) 161, 21 N.R. 595.

reserved for a given court. For example, the Federal Court has particular matters reserved to its trial and appellate divisions by virtue of the provisions contained in the Federal Court Act, R.S.C. 1970, c. 10 (2nd Supp.), and various other federal statutes. A more striking example may be found in connection with the superior court of a province. For instance, the supreme court of a province might be given authority to adjudicate particular matters under the provisions of the enabling statute which establishes that court. In addition many particular statutes, both federal and provincial, assign specific functions to the supreme court of every province. Moreover, the Judicature Act and the rules of court or the rules of practice, which are essentially regulations under the Judicature Act, also assign specific functions to the supreme court. Therefore one must look not only to the enabling statute, but also to all of the regular statutes of both Parliament and the provincial legislature, including, in particular, the Judicature Act of the province and the rules of practice or rules of court, in order to define the jurisdiction of the supreme court of a province.

Prior to studying the various functions assigned to the specific courts, it is useful to know the names of the various courts and where they fall within the judicial hierarchy. Accordingly, set out below is a diagrammatic representation of all the major courts within the Canadian judicial hierarchy. It is not exhaustive; some minor courts at the municipal level, for example, are not included, and there is no mention of administrative tribunals at either the federal or provincial level. The chart is intended to apply to all of the provinces of Canada, but there are, in reality, significant differences from province to province, some of which are contained in notations in the chart. The reader should appreciate that the court system within a particular province may differ from the general model described below.

CHART 1

THE SYSTEM OF COURTS IN CANADA GENERALLY

A. *Federal Courts — Courts constituted under federal statutes with judges federally appointed.*

Supreme Court of Canada	**Federal Court of Canada**
— The Chief Justice of the Supreme Court is also the Chief Justice of Canada — Eight Puisne Justices	— Appellate Division — Trial Division

B. *Provincial Courts — Courts constituted under provincial statutes with judges federally appointed.*

Courts of Superior Jurisdiction of a Province
or the
Supreme Court of a Province

Apellate Division
— This court is often referred to as the Court of Appeal of the province
— The Chief Justice of the Appellate Division is also the Chief Justice of the province

---

Trial Division
— In some provinces, such as Manitoba, for example, the two divisions here are separate courts constituted by separate statutes, with the trial court known as the Court of Queen's Bench
— Often this court is simply referred to as the Supreme Court of the province
— The Chief Justice of this court is properly referred to as the Chief Justice of the Trial Division

Note: In the province of Ontario, there is a further subdivision with the creation of the Divisional Court. The Divisional Court has an administrative law jurisdiction in respect of the granting of prerogative remedies. In addition, in December of 1976, the Supreme Court of Ontario was further subdivided to create a family law division.

County or District Courts

— In certain circumstances, the District or County Court judges exercise the jurisdiction of local judges of the Supreme Court of a province

Surrogate Courts

— Usually, judges of the County or District Court serve in the capacity of Surrogate Court Judges

---

Note: As indicated elsewhere, many of the provinces have or are about to merge their county or district courts with their superior courts. The result of such an amalgamation is the elimination of an intermediate court of trial jurisdiction with judges who are federally appointed.

C. *Provincial Courts — Courts constituted under provincial statutes with judges provincially appointed.*

Provincial Courts

Juvenile Court	Family Court	Provincial Court (Criminal Jurisdiction)	Small Claims Court

Note: In some provinces, by the operation of various enabling statutes, two or more of the above courts are combined into a single court, with various divisions. For example, in Ontario the Provincial Court is divided into Family and Criminal Divisions, whereas the Small Claims Court is established under a separate statute. Alternatively, some provinces provide concurrent jurisdiction for judges serving on one or more of the above courts to deal with matters arising in another of the above courts. For example, in Alberta, under the Provincial Court Act, R.S.A. 1980, c. P-20, a judge of the Provincial Court has jurisdiction to sit in either, some or all of the criminal, small claims, family or juvenile divisions.

Because, as indicated earlier, one must look to so many different sources in defining the jurisdiction of particular courts, it is difficult to describe, at least in respect of provincially constituted courts across Canada, the specific functions of those courts. However, the various provincially constituted courts do share certain functions which are common from province to province. Of course, federally constituted courts exercise the same functions uniformly throughout all provinces.

Set out below are several diagrammatic representations defining the functions assigned to each of these courts. On occasion, reference is made in the following diagrams, by way of example, to specific functions assigned to particular courts in the provinces of Ontario, Quebec and Alberta. With the possible exception of the province of Quebec, the various functions described are exercised by similar courts in all provinces. One major difference is, however, the manner in which a particular province constitutes particular courts. For example one province may constitute its courts of superior jurisdiction with trial and appellate divisions, while another province may establish two separate courts with two enabling statutes. Or, as in the case of Ontario, a province may create a third division of its superior court (namely, in this example, the Divisional Court). One province may constitute its provincial court with criminal, small claims, family and juvenile divisions, while another constitutes those courts as separate entities established under separate enabling statutes. Also, the monetary jurisdictions of the various courts of civil jurisdiction may differ from province to province. Accordingly, the following charts are not intended to be exhaustive, as that would require a detailed examination of all the various statutes which assign particular functions to various courts in all provinces. Rather, they are intended to provide the reader with an appreciation of the types of matters dealt with by the various courts, at all levels of the judiciary, including especially the particular types of matters reserved for s. 96 courts under the Canadian constitution.

From an examination of the following diagrams, one should appreciate the diversity of matters which come before our courts. Judges must decide cases arising out of a multitude of areas of human concern reflected in the many specialized areas of the law. Accordingly, a judge must be thoroughly cognizant of the many areas of the law over which he is given jurisdiction.

CHART 2

SUPREME COURT OF CANADA

— The Supreme Court of Canada is the highest court in Canada
— Nine justices: one Chief Justice, who also serves as the Chief Justice of Canada, and eight Puisne Justices

(a) *Criminal Cases*
— Adjudicates appeals from the provincial courts of appeal in respect of the following matters:
   (i) indictable offences where an acquittal has been set aside or where there has been a dissenting judgment on a point of law
   (ii) (prior to abolition) capital murder convictions, as of right
   (iii) questions of law for both summary convictions and indictable offences, if leave to appeal is first granted

(b) *Civil Cases*
— Appeals heard under a 1975 amendment to the Supreme Court Act only if leave is given on any matter of public importance or on an important issue of law or of mixed law and fact
— Cases no longer have to involve a sum of money exceeding a set amount

(c) *Reference Jurisdiction*
— Can also give opinions on constitutional and other matters which involve:
   (a) the interpretation of the Constitution Act
   (b) the interpretation of federal or provincial legislatures
   (c) the powers (jurisdiction) of Parliament or the provincial legislatures
   (d) any matter which is referred to the Supreme Court under the provisions contained in the Supreme Court Act, R.S.C. 1970, c. S-19.

NOTE: Some of the more important provisions of the Supreme Court Act are set out in Appendix A to this chapter.

CHART 3

FEDERAL COURT OF CANADA

> — Fourteen federally appointed judges
> — One Chief Justice

Appellate Division
— Hears appeals from the Trial Division of the Federal Court
— Adjudicates applications to renew and set aside decisions of federal boards, commissions or other tribunals, only on specific grounds
— Determines questions of law, jurisdiction or practice referred by federal boards, commissions or other tribunals
— Adjudicates appeals under various federal Acts other than the Income Tax Act, the Estate Tax Act and the Canadian Citizenship Act

Trial Division
— Exclusive jurisdiction:
    (a)   to hear applications for writs in relation to anyone in the Canadian Armed Forces stationed outside Canada
    (b)   to grant equitable relief against any federal board, commission or other tribunal
    (c)   to hear matters of copyright, trademark, industrial design and patents of invention
— Original jurisdiction and, unless otherwise provided, exclusive jurisdiction in claims against the Crown
— Residuary jurisdiction:
    (a)   where no other Canadian court has jurisdiction
    (b)   in matters of Federal Court jurisdiction not specifically assigned to the Federal Court, Appeal Division
— Shares concurrent jurisdiction with other courts over:
    (a)   bills of exchange and promissory notes
    (b)   aeronautics
    (c)   interprovincial works and undertakings
    (d)   claims by the Crown or Attorneys General
    (e)   actions against an officer or servant of the Crown for acts or omissions committed in carrying out his duty
    (f)   admiralty
— Also adjudicates:
    (a)   federal-provincial or interprovincial disputes where legislatures agree
    (b)   citizenship appeals
    (c)   appeals under the Income Tax Act or the Estate Tax Act

CHART 4

THE SUPERIOR OR SUPREME COURTS OF A PROVINCE

Appellate Division or Court of Appeal
— Appeals from Surrogate Court over a given monetary amount
— Adoption appeals from a District or County Court
— Family matter appeals from the Supreme Court, Trial Division
— Civil matter appeals from District or County Court and Supreme Court, Trial Division
— Appeals of criminal cases
— Applications for new trials
— All questions or issues of law

Trial Division or Court of Queen's Bench
— This court has almost unlimited scope
— Indictable offences under s. 427 of the Criminal Code
— Indictable offences by election
— Appeals of summary conviction offences by way of stated case
— Appeals from Juvenile Courts
— Appeals of permanent wardship from District Court
— All civil matters over a given monetary amount
— Divorces, judicial separations and guardianships
— Appeals from Family Court
— Administrative law jurisdiction in respect of applications to review and set aside decisions of provincial boards, commissions, etc.

CHART 5

COUNTY OR DISTRICT COURTS

— Indictable offences by election (with a judge alone or a judge and jury now)
— Appeals of summary conviction offences (see s. 755 of the Criminal Code)
— All civil matters within a given monetary jurisdiction
— All appeals from Small Claims Court
— Cases involving permanent wardship or adoption
— Appeals from the Family Court

SURROGATE COURTS

— Cases are adjudicated by District or County Court Judges
— Testamentary matters and causes
— Issues and revokes grants of probate and administration
— Appoints, controls or removes guardians

CHART 6

PROVINCIAL COURTS

Juvenile Court

— The judges for this court are appointed from any judges in the province
— Jurisdiction covers cases involving the Child Welfare Act, neglected children and juvenile delinquency

---

Family Court

— Provincial Court Judges
— Deserted wives and children, maintenance, custody
— Some offences under the Criminal Code (for example, assault of a spouse or a child)

Provincial Court (Criminal Division)

— all summary conviction offences
— Indictable offences under s. 483 of the Criminal Code
— Indictable offences by election
— All preliminary hearings
— Breaches of provincial Acts

Small Claims Court

— Statutory and monetary jurisdiction differs for each province
— For example, in Alberta the Small Claims Court:
    (a)   Is part of the Provincial Court
    (b)   Handles claims for debt not exceeding $1,000 and for damages not exceeding $1,000 and for counterclaims for the same amounts
    (c)   Does not have jurisdiction in cases involving title to land, devise, bequest or limitation, malicious prosecution, false imprisonment, defamation, criminal conversation, seduction or breach of promise of marriage, replevin, action against a magistrate, or the recovery of taxes
— By contrast, in Ontario
    (a)   Small Claims Court is independent from other provincial courts
    (b)   Claims not exceeding $1,000
    (c)   Replevin not exceeding $1,000 except where the matter involves title to land, toll, custom or franchise
— In both Ontario and Alberta, although the parties may be represented by lawyers they need not be.
— In Quebec:
    (a)   Claims may not exceed $1,000
    (b)   Parties must appear in person without the representation of a lawyer; if a party is ill or otherwise unable to appear he may appoint a friend or relative to speak for him

CHART 7

Quebec Court System[3]

Court of Appeal
— Provincial court constituted under provincial statutes
— Judges federally appointed
— This court has jurisdiction to hear both civil and criminal cases on appeal

Superior Court
— Provincial court constituted under provincial statutes
— Judges federally appointed
— This court has some civil jurisdiction
— Adjudicates appeals under Pt. XXIV of the Criminal Code

Provincial Court
— Provincial court constituted under provincial statutes
— Judges provincially appointed
— Formally known as the Magistrate's Court
— Jurisdiction in civil matters, penal statutes (both federal and provincial) and criminal matters (arts. 54, 55, 56 and 57 of the Code of Civil Procedure)

Court of the Sessions of the Peace
— Provincial court constituted under provincial statutes
— Judges provincially appointed
— Looks after both federal and provincial penal matters and some criminal matters as well
— Very similar to the District Court

Social Welfare Court
— Provincial court constituted under provincial statutes
— Judges provincially appointed
— Adjudicates cases involving juvenile delinquents, adoption, infringements of by-laws by children under 18, admission of children to youth protection schools, and general family matters such as neglect
— Arbitrates in family disputes

Municipal Court
— Provincial court constituted under provincial statutes
— Judges provincially appointed

Small Claims Court
— Provincial court constituted under provincial statutes
— Judges provincially appointed
— Claims must not exceed $1,000
— Parties must appear in person without the representation of a lawyer, and if they are ill or otherwise unable to appear they may appoint a friend or a relative to speak for them

Court of Justices of the Peace
— Provincial court constituted under provincial statutes
— Judges provincially appointed
— Jurisdiction of justices of the peace
— Looks after the issuance of warrants and the enforcement of municipal by-laws

From the foregoing, one can appreciate not only the expertise required of judges in hearing a wide variety of matters, covering virtually all areas of the law, but also the complexity of the model of judicial decision-making discussed earlier. It is not enough to describe the role of courts in Canada as, essentially, adjudicative and/or abritrative. This general characterization must be broadened if our model of the judicial decision-making process is to accurately describe the role of our courts in exercising the specific functions assigned to them. More important, however, than a search for a broader definition is the question whether our courts are successfully applying this basic model to real-life circumstances. In fact, judges do effectively adapt the basic adjudicative/arbitration model of judicial decision-making in order to resolve the particular matters before our courts.

In summary, the processes of objective adjudication and arbitration cannot be divorced from the context in which they are conducted. In this connection, one should appreciate that these processes are conducted in the context of a flexible and adaptable adversarial system. That is why the Canadian legal system is able to effectively exercise the various specific functions assigned to it and, by doing so, successfully achieve its institutional objectives.

This is an important point in our examination of the Canadian legal system: we have progressed from a consideration of the Canadian legal system as an abstract entity containing various institutions with somewhat generically described functions, to an appreciation of the legal system as a highly structured complex. This complex contains a matrix of institutions, exercising specifically assigned functions, and charged with the resolution of real and highly specific problems, covering virtually all aspects of human life and human affairs. With that juncture in mind, let us now consider the role of judges and lawyers in the Canadian legal system.

---

[3]For a summary of the Ontario court system, in chart form, see the Toronto Star, 8th August 1982. For a summary of the Alberta court system, see "Courts in Alberta", a booklet prepared by the Department of the Attorney General of Alberta in September 1979. In respect of the Quebec court system, see also Chapter 8.

APPENDIX A

THE SUPREME COURT OF CANADA

For detailed study of the Supreme Court of Canada see Weiler, *In the Last Resort* (Carswell/Methuen, 1974). Set out below are some of the key sections of the Supreme Court Act, R.S.C. 1970, c. S-19. The legislative jurisdiction of Parliament to establish a supreme court is set out in s. 101 of the Constitution Act of 1867. Pursuant to that jurisdiction, Parliament established the Supreme Court of Canada in 1875.[4] Also, particular attention should be directed to the amendment in 1974-75-76, c. 18, s. 5, to the Supreme Court Act, contained in s. 41(1) of the Act, set out below.

For those who wish to engage in a study of the development of the Supreme Court of Canada as the final court of appeal in respect of all criminal and civil matters, see the following three cases: *Nadan v. R.,* [1926] A.C. 482, [1926] 1 W.W.R. 801, 45 C.C.C. 221, [1926] 2 D.L.R. 177 (P.C.); *Br. Coal Corp. v. R.,* [1935] A.C. 500, [1935] 2 W.W.R. 564, 64 C.C.C. 145, [1935] 3 D.L.R. 401 (P.C.); *A.G. Ont. v. A.G. Can.,* [1947] 1 W.W.R. 305, [1947] A.C. 127, [1947] 1 D.L.R. 801.

THE SUPREME COURT ACT[5]

4. The Supreme court shall consist of a chief justice to be called the Chief Justice of Canada, and eight puisne judges, who shall be appointed by the Governor in Council by letters patent under the Great Seal.

5. Any person may be appointed a judge who is or has been a judge of a superior court of any of the provinces in Canada, or a barrister or advocate of at least ten years standing at the bar of any of the provinces.

6. At least three of the judges shall be appointed from among the judges of the Court of Appeal, or the Superior Court, or the barristers or advocates of the Province of Quebec . . .

9. (1) Subject to subsection (2), the judges hold office during good behavior, but are removable by the Governor General on address of the Senate and House of Commons.

---

[4]On the occasion of the 100th anniversary of that event, the Canadian Bar Review published a special two-part series to commemorate the anniversary: see (1975), 53 Can. Bar. Rev. 459 and 649. In addition, the Canadian Association of Law Teachers made that anniversary the subject of its deliberations at its annual meeting, held in Edmonton in June of 1975. The papers delivered at that meeting are set out in a special edition of the Alberta Law Review: see (1976), 14 Alta. L. Rev. 1.

[5]The Constitution Act of 1982, in a sense, entrenches the Supreme Court of Canada as part of our constitutional fabric. The Supreme Court Act was enacted as an ordinary statute of the Parliament of Canada and could have been repealed at will by Parliament, although many regarded the Supreme Court Act as quasi-constitutional legislation and therefore politically inexpedient to repeal. Now, however, by virtue of ss. 41 and 42 of the Constitution Act of 1982, the unanimous consent of the Parliament of Canada and the legislatures of all of the provinces is required in order to amend the Supreme Court Act to effect a change in the composition of the Supreme Court of Canada. This requirement, in effect, "constitutionalizes" the Supreme Court of Canada.

(2)   A judge ceases to hold office upon attaining the age of seventy-five years . . .

22.   All persons who are barristers or advocates in any of the provinces of Canada may practise as barristers, advocates and counsel in the Supreme Court.

23.   All persons who are attorneys or solicitors of the superior courts in any of the provinces of Canada may practise as attorneys, solicitors and proctors in the Supreme Court . . .

25.   Any five of the judges of the Supreme Court shall constitute a quorum and may lawfully hold the Court . . .

28.   (1)   No judge against whose judgment an appeal is brought, or who took part in the trial of the cause or matter, or in the hearing in a court below, shall sit or take part in the hearing of or adjudication upon the proceedings in the Supreme Court.

(2)   In any cause or matter in which a judge is unable to sit or take part in consequence of this section, any four of the other judges of the Supreme Court constitute a quorum and may lawfully hold the Court.

29.   Any four judges constitute a quorum and may lawfully hold the Court in cases where the parties consent to be heard before a court so composed . . .

35.   The Supreme Court shall have, hold and exercise an appellate, civil and criminal jurisdiction within and throughout Canada . . .

37.   An appeal lies to the Supreme Court from an opinion pronounced by the highest court of final resort in a province on any matter referred to it for hearing and consideration by the lieutenant governor in council of that province whenever it has been by the statutes of that province declared that such opinion is to be deemed a judgment of the highest court of final resort and that an appeal lies therefrom as from a judgment in an action.

38.   Subject to sections 40 and 44, an appeal to the Supreme Court lies with leave of the highest court of final resort in a province from a final judgment of that court where, in the opinion of that court, the question involved in the appeal is one that ought to be submitted to the Supreme Court for decision . . .

41.   (1)   Subject to subsection (3), an appeal lies to the Supreme Court from any final or other judgment of the highest court of final resort in a province, or a judge thereof, in which judgment can be had in the particular case sought to be appealed to the Supreme Court, whether or not leave to appeal to the Supreme Court has been refused by any other court, where, with respect to the particular case sought to be appealed, the Supreme Court is of the opinion that any question involved therein is, by reason of its public importance or the importance of any issue of law or any issue of mixed law and fact involved in such question, one that ought to be decided by the Supreme Court or is, for any other reason, of such a nature or significance as to warrant decision by it, and leave to appeal from such judgment is accordingly granted by the Supreme Court . . .

References by Governor in Council

55.   (1)   Important questions of law or fact concerning

(a)   the interpretation of the *Constitution Acts;*

(b)   the constitutionality or interpretation of any federal or provincial legislation;

(c) the appellate jurisdiction as to educational matters, by the *Constitution Act, 1867,* or by any other Act or law vested in the Governor in Council;

(d) the powers of the Parliament of Canada, or of the legislatures of the provinces, or of the respective governments thereof, whether or not the particular power in question has been or is proposed to be exercised; or

(e) any other matter, whether or not in the opinion of the Court *ejusdem generis* with the foregoing enumerations, with reference to which the Governor in Council sees fit to submit any such question;

may be referred by the governor in Council to the Supreme Court for hearing and consideration; and any question concerning any of the matters aforesaid, so referred by the Governor in Council, shall be conclusively deemed to be an important question.

(2) Where a reference is made to the Court under subsection (1) it is the duty of the Court to hear and consider it, and to answer each question so referred; and the Court shall certify to the Governor in Council, for his information, its opinion upon each such question, with the reasons for each answer; and the opinion shall be pronounced in like manner as in the case of a judgment upon an appeal to the Court; and any judge who differs from the opinion of the majority shall in like manner certify his opinion and his reasons.

(3) Where the question relates to the constitutional validity of any Act that has heretofore been or is hereafter passed by the legislature of any province, or of any provision in any such Act, or in case, for any reason, the government of any province has any special interest in any such question, the attorney general of the province shall be notified of the hearing, in order that he may be heard if he thinks fit.

(4) The Court has power to direct that any persons interested, or, where there is a class of persons interested, any one or more persons as representatives of such class, shall be notified of the hearing upon any reference under this section, and such persons are entitled to be heard thereon.

(5) The Court may, in its discretion, request any counsel to argue the case as to any interest that is affected and as to which counsel does not appear, and the reasonable expenses thereby occasioned may be paid by the Minister of Finance out of any moneys appropriated by Parliament for expenses of litigation.

References by Senate or House of Commons

56. The Court, or any two of the judges thereof, shall examine and report upon any private bill or petition for a private bill presented to the Senate or House of Commons, and referred to the Court under any rules or orders made by the Senate or House of Commons.

APPENDIX B

THE COURT SYSTEM OF THE UNITED STATES

By way of comparison, it is interesting to examine the United States court system. In the United States there are basically two court systems, one at the state level and the other at the federal level. The state courts concern themselves with matters falling within state jurisdiction under the American Constitution, while the federal courts concern themselves with matters falling within federal jurisdiction under the American Constitution. With respect to the former, the highest court of appeal is the state Court of Appeal. With respect to the latter, the highest court of appeal is the Supreme Court of the United States. With one exception, one cannot appeal from the decision of a state Court of Appeal to a federal court. The exception relates to the raising of a constitutional matter in the course of proceedings in the state courts. If a constitutional matter is raised, an appeal lies from the state Court of Appeal to courts within the federal court system. Ultimately, this might lead to an appeal to the Supreme Court of the United States.

A summary of the hierarchy of the courts in the dual court system of the United States is set out below:

ORGANIZATION OF UNITED STATES COURT SYSTEM

A. *Federal Courts*[6]

    1. Supreme Court of the United States
    2. Circuit Courts of Appeal
    3. United States District Courts

B. *State Courts*

    1. Appellate courts
       (a) Intermediate courts
       (b) Courts of last resort
    2. Trial courts of general jurisdiction
    3. Courts of special and limited jurisdiction

The reader should appreciate two fundamental distinctions between the American and Canadian court systems. First, the Canadian courts are derived, essentially, from the British system. (See the discussion on

---

[6]Jurisdiction of federal courts
  1. Matters relating to citizenship
  2. Federal matters:
    (a) violation of federal statutes
    (b) constitutional issues
  3. Matters falling within the original jurisdiction of the Supreme Court.

this subject in the Hamlyn Lectures, delivered by Chief Justice Laskin, referred to in Chapter 4.) Secondly, as indicated above, the Canadian court system is unified, while the American court system consists of two separate systems of courts.[7]

---

[7]For a recent observation on the work of the Supreme Court of the United States, see Zion, "The Supreme Court: A Decade of Constitutional Revision", in The New York Times Magazine, 11th and 18th November 1979. In addition, see the rather controversial book on the Supreme Court of the United States by Woodword and Armstrong, *The Brethren: Inside the Supreme Court* (New York: Simon and Schuster, 1979); and see also various commentaries written in connection with that publication, especially the cover story in Newsweek Magazine, 10th December 1979; The New York Times Book Review, 16th December 1979; and the articles appearing in Time Magazine, 17th December 1979, U.S. News & World Report, 17th December 1979, Maclean's Magazine, 21st January 1980, and Time Magazine, 10th March 1980. for other accounts of the work of the Supreme Court of the United States, see the cover story in U.S. News & World Report, 26th March 1979, and the articles appearing in Time Magazine, 5th November 1979, Newsweek Magazine, 22nd September 1980, Time Magazine, 10th November 1980, and Saturday Review, December 1979. For a brief discussion of how the U.S. Supreme Court has recently dealt with some specific issues, see Newsweek Magazine, 9th October 1978 and Time Magazine, 17th September 1979.

8

THE QUEBEC LEGAL SYSTEM

INTRODUCTION

The other parts of this book show that the Canadian legal system belongs to the great family of the common law, with the remarkable exception of the Province of Quebec. This province, in fact, uses a mixed system: its public law derives from the common law, while its private (civil) law has its roots in Romano-German juridical ground. This particularism is a result of the colonial history of North America, whose possession and domination was long disputed by the two great powers of the time: Great Britain and France.

Their legal systems, brought over to America, survived and now co-exist in Quebec. The two systems are characterized by fundamental differences. Professor Friedman thus describes them.

> The contrast between the attitude of these two groups or systems has been often and vividly portrayed, as one between logical and empirical methods, between deductive and inductive thinking, between the rule of reason and the rule of experience.[1]

We must not, however, place undue emphasis on these differences, since each basic legal system is inspired by the same constitutional principles and has its legal source and application in identical political institutions. Furthermore, each system is interpreted by similar judicial institutions.[2]

INTRODUCTION AND PRESERVATION OF FRENCH CIVIL LAW IN THE PROVINCE OF QUEBEC

1. INTRODUCTION OF FRENCH LAW IN NOUVELLE-FRANCE

The Canadian territory was a French possession and colony from 1534 to 1760. Its customs and institutions, its social and political organization as well as its legal system were therefore French. Although during the seventeenth century Nouvelle-France constituted little more than a commercial venture for the imperial metropolis, as early as 1627 La

---

[1]Friedman, "Stare Decisis at Common Law and under the Civil Code of Québec" (1953), 31 Can. Bar Rev. 723 at 724.

[2]The Supreme Court of Canada comprises 6 members from the Common Law provinces and 3 from the Civil Law Province of Québec and constitutes in regard to both systems of law the highest tribunal.

Compagnie des cent associés assumed, by royal decree, responsibility for law and order within the colony. In 1647, the King created the Conseil souverain: it included the Governor General, the Governor of Montreal and, pending the nomination of a bishop for Québec, the Superior of the Jesuits. After 1648, the Conseil included two people's representatives, elected for three years. This gave to Nouvelle-France its first judicial institution, as the Conseil was the tribunal of first instance. There was a right of appeal to the Governor General.

In 1663, the colony was only 2500 strong when Louis XIV dissolved La Compagnie des cent associés and granted full executive, legislative, and judicial powers to the Conseil souverain. He thus made Nouvelle-France largely autonomous vis-à-vis the metropolis. In such circumstances, one may ask what kind of legal system existed in this territory. France was then a land of common law or "droit coutumier": during the sixteenth century, more than 360 general or local customs had been counted. The same variety of law prevailed in the Canadian colony until 1664, when the Edit établissant la compagnie des Indes occidentales (An Act establishing the Company of the West Indies) introduced a single system: La coutume de la prévôté et vicomté de Paris. This custom had been compiled in 1510 and was later revised in 1680: it comprised 16 titles and 362 articles of law. It contained sections on goods and property, real and personal actions, prescription, execution of judgments, matrimonial regimes, gifts and estates. French authors such as Dumoulin, Ferrière and Pothier had already commented on the interpretation of the custom. In matters of obligations, contracts, tutorships and curatorships, the principles of Roman law were applied. Canon law governed family matters such as marriage and filiation. These were the three sources of the "common" law in Nouvelle-France.

The system of real property was based on the rules of the seigniorial regime, a quasi-feudal regime. As to the statutory law, it was composed of royal edicts (i.e., before 1663, the ordinances of the Parlement de Paris, and from 1663 to 1763, those of the Conseil souverain, and the edicts and regulations of the Governor General and the Intendant).

Therefore, when the British conquest of 1760 took place, Nouvelle-France enjoyed a complete political, social and judicial organization which made it practically autonomous; it possessed a unified and exclusive legal system which, joined to its specific language, religion and culture, made it a true nation.

2. THE BRITISH CONQUEST

On September 8, 1760, with the capitulation of Montreal, the inhabitants of Nouvelle-France became subjects of the King of England[3].

---

[3]The Capitulation of Montreal, Art. 41.

Constitutionally, a provisional regime was installed: the country was under military rule, under General Amherst, until 1763. As to the legal system, criminal matters followed the rules of martial law, while in civil matters French law continued to apply "until the King's pleasure be known."[4]. On this subject, General Amherst wrote, on September 23, 1760: "As to disputes which may arise between the inhabitants, I should wish they may be settled between them according to their laws."[5] It is noteworthy that the judgments and orders of the tribunals were pronounced in French, unless both parties were English-speaking.

Such an arrangement reflected the general policy of Great Britain towards the establishment of the English legal system in its colonies. The technique employed to legally bind a colony to the metropolis varied according to the circumstances.[6] Blackstone writes in his *Commentaries on the Laws of England:*

> . . . our most distant plantations in America and elsewhere are also in some respect subject to the English laws. Plantations on colonies, in distant countries, are either such where the lands are claimed by right of occupancy only, by finding them desert and uncultivated and peopling them from the mother country; or where, when already cultivated, they have been either gained by conquest, or ceded to us by treaties. And both these rights are founded upon the law of nature, or at least upon that of nations. But there is a difference between these two species of colonies, with respect to the law by which they are bound. For it hath been held that if an uninhabited country be discovered and planted by English subjects, all the English laws there in being, which are the birthright of every subject, are immediately there in force. . .

> But in conquered or ceded countries, that have already laws of their own, the King may indeed alter and change those laws; but till he does actually change them, the ancient laws of the country remain, unless such as are against the law of God, as in the case of an infidel country.[7]

3. THE TREATY OF PARIS AND THE ROYAL PROCLAMATION OF 1763

On February 10, 1763, France and Great Britain concluded the Treaty of Paris, whereby, inter alia, France ceded to Great Britain its colonies of Canada and Acadia, and its territories east of the Mississippi. While the document provided that the French inhabitants of America would keep their liberty of religion "to such extent as allowed by the laws of Great Britain", it remained silent concerning the legal system applicable to the ceded territory. This matter was to remain unsettled until George III's Royal Proclamation of October 7, 1763, enforced on 18th August

---

[4]*Ibid.*, art. 42.

[5]Placart d'Amherst, cited in Lionel Groulx, *Histoire du Canada Français*, Title III, Ed. Action nationale (1952), p. 21.

[6]*Ibid.*, pp. 43-45.

[7]Introduction, Section IV.

1764, which gave Québec its first constitution under British rule.[8] This edict stipulates, inter alia:

(1) the establishment of a civil government;[9]

(2) the right to hold general elections in order to constitute a legislative assembly "so soon as the state and circumstances of the said colonies will admit thereof ";

(3) the power of this new legislative body to make laws "for the public peace, welfare and good government of the said colonies and for the people and inhabitants thereof, as near as may be agreeable to the laws of England, and under such regulation and restrictions as are used in other colonies"; and

(4) the power given to the Governor of creating courts of justice (of first and second instance) "for hearing and determining all causes, as well Criminal as Civil, according to Law and Equity, and as near as may be agreeable to the Laws of England".

The very text of the Proclamation is a clear statement of intention to carry out first and foremost a colonial policy: it was meant in fact to favor a quick and massive English immigration. The imposed legal system, while offering security to the newly arriving British settlers, provided first a means of unification of the Canadian society and secondly constituted a policy of assimilation of the French population. While the latter was allowed to keep its freedom of religion[10], it nonetheless found itself immersed in a foreign legal system. This system upset the basis of its patrimonial security, for example by transforming the rules of property and estate law. It provided a judicial organization available without distinction to all subjects of the King, but which applied exclusively the rules of English law and allowed English barristers only before the courts. This distressed the French, and Governor Murray therefore softened the rigours of the transition by creating an inferior tribunal, the Court of Common Pleas. Only the French had access to it, since it was provided that it would apply French laws until the population had become familiar with the English laws; the Court had jurisdiction over proceedings commenced before October 1, 1764; in addition, French lawyers were allowed to plead before it.

There were varied reactions to the new system: the French community, with the approval of Governor Murray and later on of Governor Carleton and certain British jurists, petitioned the King for:[11]

---

[8]The English jurist Lord Mansfield had indeed qualified the proclamation "The Imperial Constitution of Canada".

[9]Under the authority of Governor James Murray.

[10]The King had even authorized the constitution of a Catholic archdiocese.

[11]See inter alia: Letter from Carleton to Shelburne (20th December 1777); petition of the Canadians (1770); petition of the Canadians (1773).

(1) The maintenance of the laws and customs of the land to the extent that they did not conflict with the general well-being of the colony;

(2) A French-speaking judiciary;

(3) The right to act as jurors;[12]

(4) The proclamation of new laws in French;

(5) The abolition of legal and political ostracism based on religion.[13]

Governor Carleton ordered a group of Canadian jurists[14] to compile the French laws in force in the colony before the conquest. This was published in 1772 and confirmed the applicability of such a legal system.

4. THE QUEBEC ACT, 1774

The second Canadian constitution was the result not only of these demands but also of the failure of the general policy of 1763. The Quebec Act, an imperial law, received the royal sanction on June 22, 1774. This law abrogated not only the Royal Proclamation of 1763 but also all Canadian Legislative work since the conquest. Moreover, it re-established French civil law as well as civil procedure in force in the colony before its cession. The English criminal law and procedure would continue to apply. Freedom of religion was maintained and the Catholic clergy was allowed to collect tithes. Moreover, the social hierarchy based on the seigniorial land system was maintained.

This legislation clearly displeased the English population, since it threatened the policy of homogeneity of race and religion and since it disrupted uniformity of laws within the Empire. However, the "instructions to Carleton" of January 3, 1775, regarding the application of this law should have reassured and satisfied them, since the instructions provided that the new legislative council should bear in mind, when legislating to constitute the law courts, that judgments in matters of obligations, contracts and civil torts would be based in part, if not entirely, on the rules of English law. An attempt at unification was therefore made, but Governor Carleton ignored it.

---

[12]In England Catholics were traditionally refused this function.

[13]English law provided that the persons appointed to political and judicial functions were required to take the oath of the Test (prescribed by the Test Act of 1673) swearing that they were of the Anglican faith.

[14]François-Joseph Cugnet, M. Jacrau, Chartier de Lotbinière, et al.

5. THE CONSTITUTIONAL ACT OF 1791

The Constitutional Act of 1791, by separating Canada into two autonomous regions, accentuated a cultural and legal cleavage: Upper Canada, with a predominantly Anglo-Saxon population, adopted the common law system, while Lower Canada, with its predominantly French population, kept its civil law system.

6. THE ACT OF UNION AND THE B.N.A. ACT

Neither the Act of Union of 1840 nor the British North America Act[15] in fact questioned the principles incorporated in the Québec Act. As a result, the British never wholly established uniform laws within their Canadian colony.

THE CODIFICATION

The legal history of French Canada shows that if the civil law was naturally introduced with the settling of Nouvelle-France, its preservation after the English conquest was maintained only after an intense political struggle between two opposing wills: the will to preserve the cultural identity of the minority by saving and maintaining its familial, social and economic system, against the will to unify the structures and rules of a new national entity by ensuring the predominance of the institutions of the majority. A rather chaotic course of events had brought about the application of French private law, first on a voluntary basis for the French-speaking population only, and thereafter on an imposed basis for all of the inhabitants of Lower Canada (the Province of Quebec).

By the early part of the nineteenth century, the substantive contents of the civil law[16] had considerably deteriorated, compared to what they had been at the time of the conquest. There were many reasons for this: the deficiencies and sometimes the complete absence of legal education in the province; the aging of the sources of civil law and its rupture from its legal family ties; its isolation in a common law environment; its borrowings from a different system of principles and traditions; the impact of new legislation which was strange to it, such as the laws of the imperial parliament and the statutes of the Legislative Council. Lord Durham's report in 1839 described the system thus:

---

[15] Art. 92(13) grants the provinces exclusive jurisdiction in matters of property and civil rights. It is to be noted that by s. 129, French law was to remain in force in the Province of Quebec for as long as the legislative assembly did not legislate on a given subject.

[16] See *supra*, Section 1.

The law of the Province and the administration of justice are, in fact, a patch-work of the results of the interference, at different times, of different legislative powers, each proceeding on utterly different and generally incomplete views and each utterly regardless of the other. The law itself is a mass of incoherent and conflicting laws, part French, part English, and with the line between each very confusedly drawn.

A reform was imperative if this system of law was to survive. In order to correct and affirm the law of Québec, codification, a method familiar to the Romano-German family of law, was considered. Experiments in codification had recently given favourable results in France. On June 10, 1857, a bill which had been tabled by Georges-Etienne Cartier was adopted and sanctioned. It was entitled "an Act to provide for the codification of the laws of Lower Canada relative to civil matters and procedure" (1857 (Can.), c. 43). This law provided for the nomination of three commissioners who were lawyers from Lower Canada[17] and of two bilingual secretaries with legal training.[18] Sections 4 and 5 of this law described the object of the exercise:

Art. 4. The said Commissioners shall reduce into one code, to be called the Civil code of Lower Canada, those provisions of the laws of Lower Canada which relate to civil matters and are of a general and permanent character, whether they relate to commercial cases or to those of any other nature; but they shall not include in this code, any of the laws relating to Seigniorial or feodal tenure.

Art. 5. The said Commissioners shall reduce into another code, to be called the Code of Civil Procedure of Lower Canada, those provisions of the laws of Lower Canada which relate to procedure in civil matters and cases, and are of a general and permanent character.

Since this task contemplated mainly the form of the law and not its substance, the Commissioners only had to transcribe the rules of law in existence at the time. Regarding form, the Napoleonic Code, or the French Civil Code, was the prime source of inspiration. To reformulate and restructure Quebec law as it existed without, however, copying the French law, the Commissioners also used the Napoleonic Code, applying a technique of analogy.[19]

"A Bill respecting the Civil Code of Lower Canada" accompanied by the Commissioners' report was tabled before the legislature on January 31, 1865. This Bill became law on August 1, 1866.[20] The Civil Code abrogated all laws then in force, in those cases "in which there is a provision herein having expressly or impliedly that effect; in which such

---

[17] Honourable Justice R.E. Caron (Court of Queen's Bench), Honourable Justice C.D. Day (Superior Court) and Honorable Justice A.M. Morin (Superior Court) were appointed.

[18] Me J.V. Baudry and Me T.K. Ramsay were appointed.

[19] Great similarities exist between the French and Quebec civil codes since they flow from the same legal sources: La Coutume de Paris, Roman Law and Canon Law.

[20] 29 Vict., c. 41.

laws are contrary to or inconsistent with any provision herein contained; in which express provision is herein made upon the particular matter to which such laws relate."[21]

The Code of Civil Procedure, strongly influenced by the French Code de Procédure Civile and by the Code of Civil Procedure of Louisana,[22] came into force on June 28, 1867.

These codes had multiple results. First, the codes were bilingual: the English and French versions were official and could be interpreted one by the other, without one having priority over the other. Secondly, the English minority of the Province of Quebec was henceforth integrated into a credible and structured legal system. Thirdly, the codification dissipated the constant threat to the preservation and survival of the Quebec civil law. Finally, the codification brought Quebec law closer to its family origin, the Romano-German family of law, a dominant feature of which was its written system of law.

THE ROMANO-GERMAN FAMILY OF LAW

When it adopted its Civil Code and the Code of Civil Procedure, Quebec was taking part in the vast movement of codification, which, during the nineteenth and twentieth centuries, involved most of the countries of the Romano-German family of law.[23] Such a movement was not fortuitous: it resulted from the characteristics of this legal system.

To better understand the relation between codification and the system, it is perhaps in order to define codification:

Codification is the process of converting the law of a country, or a part of it, into a code, whether that law consists of statutes, or case-law, or customs, or of all three.[24]

Codification: Process of collecting and arranging the laws of a country or state into a code, i.e. into a complex system of positive law, scientifically ordered and promulgated by legislative authority.[25]

It follows that codification involves not only the collection of laws but also their arrangement into a coherent system. Thus it contributes to the

---

[21]Art. 2712 C.C.

[22]One must remember that Louisiana, before being ceded by Napoleon Bonaparte to the United States in 1803, was a French territory under the same legal system as that of Nouvelle-France.

[23]René David, *Les grands systèmes de droit contemporains*, Précis Dalloz, 7th ed., France (1978), No. 83, p. 111. This family of law is worldwide; Continental and Occidental Europe (the Ancient Roman Empire), Latin America, a large portion of Africa, the Middle East, Japan, Indonesia etc. Colonization and codification have contributed to this expansion.

[24]Rapalje and Lawrence's *Law Dictionary*, Vol. 1, U.S.A. (1883), p. 222.

[25]Black's *Law Dictionary*, 4th ed., U.S.A. (1951), p. 324.

structuring of the law. The question may be posed whether the techniques of codification could be applied in the common law system, where each decision may become a rule of law and where the general rule is what remains after all exceptions are accounted for. The answer must be in the negative, since the basis of codification rests upon a different concept of the rule of law. Within the Romano-German family, the rule of law, instead of being the direct solution to a specific case, stands above specific applications: it is the expression of a general standard which attempts to cover as many situations as possible. For example, in Quebec law, the entire tort system is covered by the following single section of the Civil Code:

> **Art. 1053 C.C.**: Every person capable of discerning right from wrong is responsible for the damage caused by his fault to another, whether by positive act, imprudence, neglect or want of skill.

Whether a claim results from an automobile accident, a dispute between neighbours, professional negligence, the contamination of cattle by pollution of their source of water, s. 1053 C.C. is the applicable rule of law.

Within the codified system, the rule of law, as opposed to the common law, is characterized by its generality; it stands somewhere between the absolute principle and the solution of a specific case. Therein lies the main difference. In England, the law was an element of political unification; the development of the common law was closely tied to the growth of the authority of the Crown and the centralization of the Royal Courts.[26] The Romano-German family developed within one common culture, without any political objective: its legal system was initially conceived in the universities. During the Renaissance, the schools of "haut-savoir" were inspired by humanistic ideals: jurists mingled with philosophers and theologians. The general trend was to integrate science and morality into an idealistic view of the human being and of society. This included the law. As a result, the Roman law, on which the scholars had first based their research, was discarded in favor of "natural law": elaborating a legal system was the occasion for creating a model of social organization. Thus, in the Romano-German family, the law is more often expressed in concepts and principles than in modes of application: it is a rational construction, stressing logic and conciseness rather than pragmatism. Codification illustrates the jurists' frame of mind within this family of law: ideally, by simply reading a Code, a citizen could not only acquaint himself with the law but also receive moral and social values designed to motivate his behaviour.

Appendices A and B partially reproduce the tables of contents of the two Quebec codes. Appendix A is a synopsis of the "jus comune" of

---

[26]David, *supra*, note 23, No. 28, at p. 40.

Quebec law (the equivalent of Anglo-Canadian common law): one can readily observe the easy accessibility offered by this method. Appendix B also reveals at a glance the complete procedural sequence of any given litigation, from the jurisdiction of the court to the institution of action and the execution of a judgment. Quebec law has naturally reached a degree of sophistication which, in practice, makes it hardly accessible to the layman, but the objective of simplicity remains.

From this fundamental conceptual distinction between the systems, other distinctions follow concerning, for example, the hierarchy of the sources of law and the roles of judges and lawyers, which we will presently consider.

THE SOURCES OF LAW

All countries of the Romano-German family divide the law into categories; thus, we find the basic distinction between public and private law. This is particularly true in Quebec, where rules of French source are applied in private law whereas rules of English source are applied in public law. The comments which follow therefore apply only to the private law of Quebec.

The Romano-German system is almost entirely a system of written law. Its primary source is therefore legislation, the other sources being subsidiary. The rules are relatively general. Basic laws are couched in precise and even technical terms, as intelligible as possible to the layman. The order of importance of laws is as follows: at the highest level, we find the constitution and constitutional laws, followed by treaties, codes, laws, regulations, decrees, and finally, orders in council.

Contrary to the common law system, the second source of law is doctrine. The reason is found in the academic origin of the Romano-German family. The role of doctrine can be defined as follows:

> The doctrine does not consider its role as to simply express or to structure, as much as possible, the various elements supplied by practical experience. It feels it must, from the mass of daily experience, resulting from various events and emergencies often decided without too clear guiding principles, formulate the rule of law which hence might be the inspiration of judges and practitioners.[27]

In theory, therefore, doctrine results from an effort of reflection which not only encourages the evolution of the law but also allows it to remain consistent with renewed fundamental values. In practice, however, doctrine is mostly a commentary on jurisprudence.

Jurisprudence is a source which is gaining in importance. There is little difference, all proportions being considered, in quantity and qual-

---

[27]*Ibid.*, No. 70, p. 93.

ity of judicial reports between the common law and Quebec civil law systems. However, the techniques of judicial analysis are somewhat different, as is pointed out in the chapters concerning the role of judges and the doctrine of "stare decisis".

Finally, until 1866, custom and usage formed the body of Quebec law. This was abolished to all practical purposes by the codification. They may still be referred to in the absence of other rules to interpret ambiguous contracts, on a basis of equity.

It is to be noted that in Quebec laws, as in the laws of all countries of the Romano-German family, the concept of equity is unknown. Professor David gives the following explanation:

> The characteristic flexibility of the concepts of the Romano-German family includes equity as an integral part of the system so that it is not felt that specific rules or autonomous jurisdictions of equity are required to correct or supplement the system of juridical solutions.[28]

This has not prevented the legislator from introducing in Québec certain "equitable remedies" such as private or public injunctions.[29]

THE ROLE OF QUEBEC JUDGES — THE DOCTRINE OF "STARE DECISIS"

1. JUDICIAL ORGANIZATION

The Canadian constitution (the B.N.A. Act under its new name of "The Constitution Act, 1867") provides Quebec with the same judicial organization and appointments as the other provinces.[30] The high courts, in Quebec, consist of the Superior Court, which is the court of general jurisdiction, and the Court of Appeal.

An outline of the judicial hierarchy is as follows:

COURT OF APPEAL

Jurisdiction: general appeal jurisdiction over Superior Courts and all Provincial Courts

---

[28]*Ibid.*, No. 113, p. 151.

[29]Code of Civil Procedure, ss. 751 *et seq.* There are some who hold the view that even without legislation, the Quebec courts could have used these very practical remedies by relying exclusively on the inherent powers of the Superior Court. This power is obviously based on the common law.

[30]We refer the reader to Chapters 5, 6 and 7.

SUPERIOR COURTS

Jurisdiction: civil from $10,000 up, criminal jury trials, family and bankruptcy

PROVINCIAL COURTS

Provincial Court: civil up to $10,000

Small Claims Court: civil up to $1,000

Court of the Sessions of the Peace: criminal without jury.

Labour Court: Labour

Municipal Court: some criminal summary convictions and municipal by-laws

Judges of the Superior Courts are federally appointed, under s. 96 of The Constitution Act.

The Province of Quebec appoints the judges of its Provincial Courts (see Chapter 6, Chart 7). It also has many administrative bodies, such as Boards and Commissions, exercising judicial or quasi-judicial functions.

Excepting the Court of Appeal, the Provincial Courts and other administrative bodies exercising judicial or quasi-judicial functions are subject to the superintending and reforming power of the Superior Court. This reforming power is often substantially checked by statutory "privative clauses".

Judges are appointed among those members of the Quebec Bar having a civil law education and at least ten years standing.[31]

Our English type of judicial organization is not identical to that of the countries of the Romano-German family of law. In those countries, as here, the structure is hierarchical; however, in many of them, the Supreme Court either exercises a final appeal jurisdiction, as does the Supreme Court of Canada, or exercises only a power to quash, without adjudicating on the merits of cases.[32] As to the appointment of judges, the Romano-German system differs from the Canadian system; in the former, judges are chosen not from practitioners, but from jurists who have trained especially to become judges and have graduated from a School for Magistrates. They are therefore career judges. Another distinctive trait is in the form of decisions. In countries of the Romano-German

---

[31]As will be seen later, it is possible in Quebec to receive legal training in civil law and additionally in common law.

[32]La Cour de cassation is a court of last resort: its role essentially consists in upholding or quashing the decision of a lower court and returning the case to another court of the same level in order that a new decision be rendered. Such is the system in France and Italy.

family as well as in Canada, judicial decisions must be motivated[33], but their style and form may vary from the technique of "seeing" and "considering"[34] to that of an essay pure and simple.[35] In the former countries, judgments are often rendered per curiam when the bench is formed of several judges: there are no dissenting opinions or minority judgments. In Quebec, the Code of Civil Procedure stipulates that judgments must be signed and must mention dissenting opinions.[36] Thus the law of Quebec in this aspect differs from its own source.

2. THE ROLE OF JUDGES AND CASES, OR "JURISPRUDENCE", IN THE ROMANO-GERMAN SYSTEM

The Romano-German system gives priority to legislation over doctrine or jurisprudence. This affects the judge's role: it consists essentially in applying the written law and, subsidiarily, in interpreting it when it is ambiguous.

In other words, the code, as interpreted by the Courts, is the Supreme law.[37]

Judges are not makers of law.[38] As Justice Mignault comments:

Let me insist on this last observation that the civil law is a logical system, for from this it follows that the determination of controversies before the courts must proceed upon legal principles. The Court is not bound to hunt up a case supporting the legal principle relied on, but it suffices that its decision conforms to the dictates of reason as embodied in the maxims and principles of the Civil law, or as taught by the jurists who have written on law.[39]

In the Romano-German system, this specific approach to law, its structure and the role attributed to the judiciary, sets aside the rule of precedent or "stare decisis":[40]

---

[33]In Quebec, this obligation is found in s. 519 of the Code of Civil Procedure: "[I]t (the judgment) must moreover set out reasons for judgment, unless it refers to written opinions that the judges have filed in the record."

[34]Notably in France, Belgium, Spain and Portugal. It is to be noted that this technique was often utilized by certain Quebec judges.

[35]Notably in Germany, Greece, Italy, Switzerland and Sweden.

[36]Section 519, Code of Civil Procedure: "every judgment must contain . . . the names of the judges who heard the case, with mention of those who did not share the opinion of the majority;"

[37]Mignault, *The Authority of Decided Cases* (1925), 3 Can. Bar Rev. 1 at 14.

[38]However, certain notions, such as enrichment without cause and abuse of right, found in the civil law, result exclusively from jurisprudence and have become rules of law. Examples remain very rare.

[39]See *supra*, note 37, at p. 20.

[40]As it is described in Chapter 10.

There is no doubt that the doctrine of "stare decisis" or of the binding effect of judicial decisions, is a doctrine peculiar to the common law, and is fully recognized in all countries where the common law has been introduced. Perhaps it is natural that it should be so, for the whole body of the common law, as well as of equity, is made up of such decisions. It is otherwise in Civil law countries, for they, or at least the greater part of them, a conspicuous exception being South Africa, have enacted complete codes wherein is consigned, or supposed to be, the whole "corpus juris civilis."[41]

In theory, "stare decisis" does not exist in civil law. French and Quebecois authors share this view. Thus, Planiol:

In theory, judicial interpretation is free; each tribunal may adopt the solution which seems to it the best and most fair; it is bound neither by the decisions it has previously rendered in similar cases nor by the decisions of another tribunal, even a higher one. Thus, the trial courts may, on some disputed questions, hold contrary views to those of their appeal courts, but their decisions are greatly exposed to be reviewed in appeal.[42]

Also Mignault:

Apart from the case decided, it (the decision) has no authority and binds no one; it neither binds third parties nor the very court which has rendered it. If another case arises, similar on all points but distinct, the court seized of this case is free to follow its prior interpretation or to express a different one.[43]

In the Romano-German system, jurisprudence is a secondary source of law. In view of what has been said above, one may ask what purpose it serves. In fact, it serves two purposes.

The first is a persuasive one, similar to precedent, where the position taken by a superior court on a given subject is set and consistent.[44] Mignault thus defines jurisprudence:

Of course, in France, a single judgment is not a binding authority even on the court which has pronounced it; on the contrary, a series of judgments may be accepted as conclusive, taking then the name of "jurisprudence" . . .[45]

The actual risk run by a judge who does not follow jurisprudence is the probability of being reversed in appeal.

The second purpose of jurisprudence is to stimulate the development of the law. Although the codes are supposedly complete, situations occur where the rule of law has never been applied. Regardless of the

---

[41]See *supra*, note 37, at p. 1.

[42]*Traité Elémentaire de Droit Civil*, 5th ed. (1950), No. 128, p. 740.

[43]*Traité de Droit Civil Canadien* (1895), vol. 1, p. 111.

[44]Louis Baudoin, *Le Droit Civil de la Province de Québec*, Wilson & Lafleur (ed.) (1953), pp. 92 *et seq.*

[45]See *supra*, note 37, at p. 11.

case, a judge cannot abstain from deciding.[46] In such a circumstance, the court would simply, on general principles of law, proceed by deduction or by analogy in order to arrive at a satisfactory solution, being mindful not to commit legal heresy.

> But it is not all, for the Courts may draw from a rule enacted in a code certain deductions which are not expressed therein or, by analogy, they may apply an article of the code to cases which the article does not mention. In this way, the law is developed and this development is obviously of very great importance, for the distinctive merit of a code is its brevity, and its purpose is not to provide for every possible contingency, but to lay down certain general rules whereby, and especially by their natural and logical development, the infinite variety of controversies may be decided conformably to legal principles.[47]

This view, which prevails in countries of codified law, allows changes in jurisprudence to take place without the risks or uncertainties which would arise in common law countries, because such changes do not affect the basis of the system.

One might think that, codified laws being more accessible, this would bring about greater predictability and security in legal relations. It is unfortunately not the case, as the codes give the courts a greater freedom of interpretation.

3. THE ROLE OF JUDGES AND JURISPRUDENCE IN THE QUEBEC SYSTEM

Since the organization of the judiciary in Quebec follows the English model, its structure is similar to that of the other Canadian provinces.

Quebec law partakes of both systems, the Romano-German concerning private law and the common law with respect to public law. This context creates a phenomenon of mutual influence which somewhat affects the legal culture. By attaching undue importance to jurisprudence and the doctrine of "stare decisis", Quebec jurists and judges have turned away from their original juridical sources. Mignault thus comments on this situation:

> This being the case and in view of our close relationship with the two systems (let me speak now as a Québec lawyer), our civil law being French, our commercial law partly English and partly French, our procedure and mode of conducting trial a mixture of the two, and our criminal law entirely English — it is natural that insofar as the authority of decided cases is concerned, we should be nearer to the English than to the French system.[48]

---

[46]Section 11 of the Quebec Civil Code reads as follows: "a judge cannot refuse to adjudicate under pretext of the silence, obscurity or insufficiency of the law". Section 4 of the French Civil Code is similar.

[47]See *supra*, note 37, at p. 2.

[48]*Ibid.*, p. 11.

This attitude results from the strong influence of the common law approach and technique,[49] from the technique of judgment writing, and also from the obvious desire of Quebecers to preserve their law. In the latter case, the rule of precedent has the advantage of ensuring uniformity of interpretation of the law and thus of confirming basic principles.

Professor Friedman makes an interesting résumé of the state of Quebec law on the question of "stare decisis";

In conclusion, the position of stare decisis in the civil law of Québec may be summarized as follows:

(1) Stare decisis is accepted in all its rigour in so far as the decisions of the Supreme Court of Canada on the Québec civil law are concerned.

(2) As regards the Québec Court of Queen's Bench (appeal side) and the lower Québec courts, they overrule themselves or depart from the judgments of a higher court in the hierarchy on very exceptional occasions. The acceptance of the French doctrine that the text of the code, as distinct from any judicial or non-judicial commentary, is supreme authority enables them to do so. The record shows that such departures are rare.

(3) On the other hand, the theoretical liberty to depart from precedent is countered by the strong traditionalism of the Québec courts, which makes them look to the established doctrine and precedent of the civil law with an orthodoxy far stricter than that practised by French courts.

(4) The Québec technique of individual judgments, which is that of the common-law courts, brings in its train the complexities of the common-law doctrine of stare decisis, and the oblique methods of disregarding precedent which have been analyzed in regard to the common law.

(5) In its total practical effect, the Québec doctrine and practice of precedent is remarkably close to that of the common law. The latter is not nearly as absolute in its obedience to precedent as is commonly supposed, while the Québec courts are generally most reluctant to depart from precedent.[50]

It may therefore safely be said that the Quebec courts, like the other Canadian courts, feel bound by the decisions of the Judicial Committee of the Privy Council and by those of the Supreme Court of Canada. In the same manner, the lower courts in Quebec feel bound by the decisions of their courts of appeal.

LEGAL EDUCATION

Six universities, five of which are francophone, provide legal education for Quebec lawyers. In Quebec, they are: l'Université de Montréal, l'Université du Québec à Montréal, l'Université Laval and l'Université

---

[49]It must be remembered that the majority of the judges of the Supreme Court of Canada have a common law education.

[50]Friedman, *Stare decisis at common law and under the Civil Code of Québec* (1953), 31 Can. Bar Rev. 723 at 746-47.

de Sherbrooke; the anglophone university is McGill. In Ontario, there is l'Université d'Ottawa. All of these universities, including l'Université d'Ottawa, provide education in civil law. In addition, McGill and Ottawa offer education in common law. The Quebec Bar accepts exclusively candidates educated in civil law. Common law students must register with one of the law societies of a Canadian common law province. It is also possible for a civil law graduate to graduate in common law after one additional year of studies at McGill or Ottawa.

After obtaining his degree in civil law, the student must attend the professional school of the Quebec Bar or of the Chambre des Notaires. The Order of Notaries is another distinctive trait of the Romano-German family. Notaries can, to a degree, be compared to solicitors in the common law countries, but certain differences exist. For example, the documents notaries write (mostly contracts) constitute authentic documentary proof. Thus their simple production in evidence is proof of their legality and of their contents. Moreover, the Civil Code provides that certain contracts must be notarized to be valid. They are the so-called formal contracts: such are hypothecs and marriage contracts.

In the professional schools, the student follows academic training for eight months and must pass six examinations, after which he articles for six months with a lawyer (notaries are dispensed from articling). Once these stages are completed, the student is admissible to become a member in good standing of the Bar.

APPENDIX A
CIVIL CODE

I BOOK FIRST
   Of persons

II BOOK SECOND
   Of property, of ownership
   and its different modifications

III BOOK THIRD
   Of the acquisition and exercise
   of rights of property

   1. Of successions

   2. Of gifts inter vivos and by will

3. Of obligations
    a)   of contracts
    b)   of quasi-contracts
    c)   of offences and quasi-offences
    d)   of obligations which result from the
         operation of law solely
         of the object of obligations
         of the effects of obligations
    e)   of different kinds of obligations
    f)   of the extinction of obligations
    g)   of proof

4. Of marriage covenants and of the effect
    of marriage upon the property of the consorts

5. Of sale

6. Of exchange

7. Of lease and hire

8. Of mandate

9. Of loan

10. Of deposit

11. Of partnership

12. Of life rents

13. Of transaction

14. Of gaming contracts and debts

15. Of suretyship

16. Of pledge

17. Of privileges and hypothecs

18. Of registration of real rights

19. Of prescription

IV BOOK FOURTH
    Commercial Law

APPENDIX B
CODE OF CIVIL PROCEDURE

I BOOK ONE
General provisions

1. Introductory provisions

2. The Courts

3. Rules applicable to all actions

II BOOK TWO
Ordinary procedure in Courts
of first instance

1. Institution of action and appearance

2. Contestation of the action

3. Default to appear and default to plead

4. Incidental proceedings

5. Proof and hearing

6. Decision upon a question of law: declaratory
   judgment on motion

7. Judgment

III BOOK THREE
Remedies against judgments

1. Revocation of judgment

2. Appeal

IV BOOK FOUR
Execution of judgments

1. Voluntary execution

2. Compulsory execution

V BOOK FIVE
Special proceedings, such as seizure before
judgment and injunction
Extraordinary recourses, such as certiorari,
mandamus and habeas corpus

9

THE ROLE OF JUDGES AND LAWYERS

INTRODUCTION

No matter how well-designed the system of law and no matter how appropriate the institutions created to function within that system, its effective application depends upon the efforts of those who man the institutions. Basically, those persons who man the legal system and the institutions contained in that system fall within one of the following categories:

1. Lawyers (serving in the separate and unique functions of barristers and solicitors, law reformers, teachers and many related vocations);

2. Judges (at various levels within the judicial system with various responsibilities in accordance with the governing statute setting out the jurisdiction of the court over which they preside);

3. Specialized administrative personnel, some of whom assist lawyers and some of whom assist judges; and

4. Staff of the various departments, agencies, boards and commissions of government at all levels, which bodies are responsible for the various aspects of the administration of justice.

Obviously, the key persons in our legal system are the judge and the lawyer, but, as indicated above, there are others. The lawyer is often assisted by paralegal personnel such as professional title searchers, law clerks (many of whom are now trained in special courses at the community college or technical school level), legal secretaries and others.[1] Also, judges (that is, courts) are assisted by court clerks, court reporters, registrars and others. Finally, both lawyers and judges are assisted by external government agencies, including such personnel as official guardians, public trustees and the like.

All of these people share the responsibility of ensuring the efficient functioning of the institutions within the legal system. Therefore, they must work co-operatively one with the other to ensure the fair, just and

---

[1] For a discussion of paralegal training in Canada, see Thompson, *How to Become a Lawyer in Canada* (Edmonton: Acorn Books, 1979) and Taman, "The Emerging Legal Paraprofessionals", in Slayton and Trebilcock (eds.), *The Professions and Public Policy* (Toronto: University of Toronto Press, 1978).

efficient administration of justice. In addition, they must work co-operatively with those manning other institutions in society. For example, accountants and medical professionals are often called upon in the course of the lawyer's or judge's conduct of his everyday responsibilities.

We must focus our attention on judges and lawyers, for it is they who are specifically trained and best understand the nature and purpose of our legal system and it is they who play the most dramatic and significant role in ensuring the effective functioning of that system. Historically, the training of lawyers was conducted entirely on an apprenticeship basis; now, in Canada, legal training is a very formalized and institutionalized process. In the past many judges were not trained as lawyers; although presently in Canada there are still some judges who are not lawyers, their number is small and dwindling. They sit exclusively on lower court benches and all new appointments reflect the conventional wisdom that members of the judiciary should properly be members of the legal profession. Most judges are appointed from the ranks of senior practising lawyers, although some are now being appointed from the ranks of legal academicians. The latter kind of appointment, although fairly common in the United States, was, until recently, relatively infrequent in Canada. The training of lawyers and the appointment of judges will be discussed, among other things, in the topics set out below.

LAWYERS

1. TRAINING OF LAWYERS

Dr. Max Wyman, former Chairman of the Alberta Human Rights Commission, a member of the Kirby Commission of Inquiry, and a former President of the University of Alberta, made these remarks on the objectives of legal education in an address to a class of first-year law students:

> Although I have no knowledge of the curriculum of the Faculty of Law, I would hope that it would make new students of law not mechanics of the law. To spend an inordinate amount of time teaching how to draft wills or transfer titles is not, in my opinion, a justified use of university time. You can learn such matters faster and better in actual practice in a law office. To teach you, by the case law approach, how to search legal literature for the perfect defence of a client may be justified, but that will not make you students of the law.
>
> To be students of the law you must be prepared to study some of the big ideas of the law, and big ideas do exist in abundance in the literature of the law. You must be prepared to examine critically the present purpose and scope of the law, and to decide whether that purpose and scope is still consistent with social mores of our time. Indeed as students of the law, you must be prepared to challenge the statements of your teachers, always demanding an understanding of what they say, always demanding a proof of what they say. If you are content to regurgitate that which you are taught, then you must become a legal mechanic, not legal scholars.[2]

---

[2] An address to the Faculty of Law, University of Alberta, 3rd to 7th November 1975.

Generally speaking, a prospective lawyer must (with some exceptions) undertake successful studies at the undergraduate level at a Canadian university. Most law schools admit students who have performed well in a general Bachelor's Degree program. Some universities, however, admit law students with two years or less of undergraduate training. Some students enter law possessing graduate degrees in all sorts of fields, in the humanities, social sciences, and the natural sciences, while others are already trained in other professions such as engineering and medicine. Some students return to law school after many years in business and industry. Because of the large number of applicants and the limited number of first-year places, obviously no student automatically obtains admission; he or she has to perform well in competition with all other applicants. Once admitted, a student is required to take three years of full-time academic study in a faculty of law. In Canada, as of the date of this writing, there are no night programs and there is only one part-time program leading to a law degree,[3] although there has been discussion of such training. In contrast, in the United States, many such programs are accredited.[4]

Upon graduation, a student is required to serve a one-year period of articles of clerkship under a practising member of the bar of that province. This period provides the graduating law student with an opportunity to learn from an experienced practitioner many of the techniques and procedures not included in the academic courses given at law school.[5] Upon completing his term of articles in, and the bar admission course of a particular province, the student becomes a member of the Law Society of that particular province.[6] Generally, a student who graduates from a law school in a common law province of Canada may, after serving his period of articles in and successfully completing the bar admission course of another common law province, be called to the bar of, (that is,

---

[3]The one program to date is that offered at the College of Law at the University of Saskatchewan in Saskatoon.

[4]For a further discussion of legal education in Canada, see Thompson, *How to Become a Lawyer in Canada* (Edmonton: Acorn Books Ltd., 1979); the Hon. Mr. Justice R.J. Matas, Admission and Education Committee of the Law Society of Manitoba and The Council of the Faculty of Law of the University of Manitoba, "Report of the Special Committee on Legal Education" (1979), and the subsequent article, the Hon. Mr. Justice R.J. Matas, "Legal Education in the Wake of the 60's" (1979), 44 Sask. L. Rev. 63. See also the Bibliography on "Legal Education in Canada", appended to this chapter.

[5]Apparently, many new lawyers are unhappy with various aspects of their training. See the Financial Post, 31st January 1981.

[6]The Law Society of Upper Canada recently instituted a Practice Advisory Service which is designed, among other things, to advise and assist new or inexperienced lawyers on the opening or administration of a law practice. Also in Ontario, several lawyers recently established a "Mentor Program", the first of its kind in North America, where junior members of the criminal bar are teamed up with senior members in order to provide a system or network for informal advice. See Maclean's Magazine, 20th July 1981.

become a member of) the Law Society of that other province. This transferability does not as readily exist between the common law provinces and the province of Quebec for the reason that the province of Quebec has a civil law system requiring different formal legal training in university.

There are other ways of becoming eligible for membership in the law society of another province and these derive from the statute governing the legal profession in that province. A fairly common method for the lawyer who has been a practising member of one province for a number of years is to successfully complete transfer examinations set by the law society of the province to which he or she wishes to transfer. The eligibility to write these exams is often based on a minimum number of years of practise in the former province. The successful transferee is not then precluded from retaining his membership in the province from which he or she is transferring; many lawyers are members of more than one law society. Also, lawyers from one province will appear before the court of another province on an occasional or ad hoc basis for a particular case without being formally enrolled as a member of the bar of that province. However, the general and most common method of entering the legal profession is, after earning a Bachelor of Laws degree, to serve a period of articles in a particular province and then pass the bar admission course of that province.

Once a student is called to the bar of a particular province, he becomes in Canada a barrister, solicitor and notary public. Unlike the United Kingdom, where a person practises as either a barrister or solicitor but not both, there is no legally sanctioned distinction in Canada and therefore a practising lawyer may perform as a barrister and/or a solicitor. Generally speaking, the functional distinction is that a barrister articulates a client's case in a court of law in the course of litigation, whereas a solicitor performs more or less technical procedures such as drafting of agreements and wills and other types of work generally referred to as "office" or "desk" work.[7]

2. CAREERS OPEN TO LAWYERS

Upon graduation, the new barrister and solicitor need not enter into the practice of law. In the United States, it is estimated that just over 50 per cent of the lawyers practice law. In Canada, historically, and this is essentially true today, most law school graduates want to become mem-

---

[7]The usual designation on a lawyer's letterhead and business card is that of "barrister and solicitor". A Calgary law firm whose members restricted their practice to court work designated themselves as "barristers at law". This was disallowed by the Law Society of Alberta for the reason that the designation implied specialization which was not then, as it is not now, formally recognized by the Law Society. See St. John's Report, 30th March 1979.

bers of the bar and practise their chosen profession. However, following the trend in the United States, and in response to a more crowded marketplace, many lawyers are entertaining the idea of using their law degrees for other related vocations. Thus it is somewhat misleading to refer to a single "career in law" as such. Legal training affords an individual the opportunity to engage in many careers, and often a lawyer changes from one "career" to another during the course of his or her working life. Set out below is a summary of the various opportunities available to the new graduating lawyer.

A career in law can mean, as it does to most persons, the day-to-day practice of law. In this capacity the lawyer interacts directly with clients to accomplish one or both of two objectives. One is to order and regulate the affairs of his clients, be they individual or corporate clients. This is the practice of preventive law in order to ensure that the client's affairs are conducted in accordance with the rules set down by statutes and various other sources. The other is to articulate a client's case in a court of law if the client is accused of committing a criminal offence or sued in a civil action.

One recent development in respect of private practice is the movement toward accredited specialization in a given area of the law. Although this has not yet been formally structured, two studies (one by the Law Society of Upper Canada and the other by the Law Society of Alberta) have recommended movement in this direction. Some provincial law societies have permitted lawyers to publicly advertise that they restrict their practices to certain specialized areas, although this is far removed from a true system of accredited specialization.[8] The Canadian Bar Association has recently undertaken a major study of specialization.[9]

Many lawyers are employed in government service at both the provincial and federal levels acting as government advisors, conducting legal research, drafting legislation and serving as counsel in litigation matters involving the government.

All of the provinces and the federal government have law reform commissions which conduct detailed studies into areas of the law that may require reform and submit reports containing their recommendations to their respective legislatures. Lawyers who enjoy in-depth legal research may find employment with a law reform commission challenging.

Many lawyers work in the business world, whether as lawyers in corporate legal departments or as businessmen using their legal training indirectly.

---

[8]See A.G. Can. v. Law Soc. of B.C.; Jabour v. Law Soc. of B.C., [1982] 5 W.W.R. 289, 37 B.C.L.R. 145, 19 B.L.R. 234, 137 D.L.R. (3d) 1, 66 C.P.R. (2d) 1, 43 N.R. 451 (S.C.C.).
[9]See the National, March 1983, p. 4.

Opportunities are available to lawyers in the teaching profession. Teaching law to law students in the various faculties of law in Canada, or to paralegals or legal secretaries in the various Community Colleges provides a rewarding career to those who wish to interact with students and at the same time conduct scholarly legal research.

It is becoming less unusual to find lawyers who are also members of other professional associations. For example, there are many persons in Canada who hold both law and medical degrees, and these persons often act as coroners or engage in advisory work for the government or for private industry in connection with medico-legal matters.

In short, law is truly a multi-faceted profession and legal training affords a person an opportunity to engage in all sorts of professional opportunities.

The reader can appreciate that generally the role of the lawyer is difficult to define, and depends essentially upon how legal training has been utilized upon graduation.

One current concern relates to the number of lawyers who are entering the profession. The existing bar is concerned, as can be expected, with marketplace economics. Indeed, the proliferation of lawyers is so great that, for example, in Alberta, the average number of years of practice experience since graduation is approximately 4 or 5 years. In Ontario, the Law Society of Upper Canada recently established a Special Committee on Numbers of Lawyers to consider this issue, and it reported to convocation (i.e., the "Benchers" or legislative body of the society in general meeting) that

(1) given existing economic circumstances, more lawyers are engaged in private practice than are needed;

(2) the Law Society should not place arbitrary limits on the number of persons entering the profession;

(3) the law schools should review the number of persons entering first year of their law programmes; and

(4) members of the public considering a legal career should be educated as to the economic difficulties facing practitioners.[10]

---

[10]See Law Society of Upper Canada, Communiqué No. 130, 27th January 1983. For reaction to the above conclusions, see the Financial Post, 12th March 1983 and the editorial appearing in the Edmonton Journal, 7th February 1983. For some further discussion on the "oversupply" of lawyers, see the Toronto Star, 13th March 1983, p. A16, and, generally, with respect to the "oversupply" of professionals, including lawyers, the column written by J. McArthur appearing in the Toronto Star, 10th March 1983.

The "oversupply" of lawyers has led to competition among lawyers in the marketplace both in Canada and the United States. See the Toronto Star, 10th June 1979 and the Edmonton Journal, 12th June 1979 (in connection with a so-called "price-cutting war" in

3. THE LAWYER-CLIENT RELATIONSHIP

Let us now direct our attention to the practising lawyer. In this capacity, he has two responsibilities. First, he must articulate and advance the best interests of his client; it is often said that he must be the champion of his client's interests. This is particularly important in the field of criminal law where an accused client faces a prosecutor possessing access to all the powerful investigatory machinery of the state. The lawyer must consider his client's interests as paramount and his client must be able to rely on the assumption that his lawyer will do so. This basic mutual understanding will undoubtedly foster the confidence and trust that must underly the lawyer-client relationship. In order to preserve and protect this confidence, the law has recognized a special and unique privilege with respect to communications between a lawyer and his client. The common law provides that communication, written or oral, flowing from a client to his lawyer is privileged, that is, it may not be disclosed by the lawyer in a court of law or to a tribunal or otherwise unless and until such time as the client waives this privilege. The privilege will not exist in the event that any communication between a client and his lawyer involves criminal conduct by the lawyer himself. The important point is that this privilege is vital to the confidential and trusting relationship between a client and solicitor and is recognized nowhere else in the common law. For example, contrary to popular belief, there is no privilege at common law between a doctor and his patient even when the doctor is a psychiatrist, nor is there privilege between a priest and his parishioners or between a journalist and his confidential sources. However, in various states in the United States and in some provinces in Canada these other "privileges" have been created by statutes. For example, in the province of Newfoundland a privilege between priest and penitent has been created by statute.

The law's recognition of the need for a vital and trusting relationship between a lawyer and his client through the rule relating to privilege is consistent with the notion that the lawyer's essential responsibility is to protect and to articulate the interests of his client.

4. THE LAWYER'S ROLE AS AN OFFICER OF THE COURT

The lawyer's second responsibility is to act at all times as an officer of the court. In taking his oath as a member of the bar of a particular province, the lawyer promises to serve the judicial system at all times as an officer of the court. In serving as an officer of the court, the lawyer

---

Ontario); Newsweek Magazine, 26th February 1979 (in connection with cut-rate divorce); Time Magazine, 9th October 1978 (in connection with supermarketing legal services); Consumer Reports, September 1979 (for advice on paying less for a lawyer); the New York Times, 26th August 1979 (on marketing legal services in large, multibranch firms); the Edmonton Sun, 18th December 1981 (on "bargain-basement" divorce fees).

must always consider the public good and must work to preserve the integrity of a free and democratic society. He must protect, preserve and respect the institutions within the legal system, and he has a special obligation to ensure that unfairness and injustice do not occur in a court of law. This means, for example, that he must advance the case law, both in support of and against his client's position, so that a judge can adjudicate a particular dispute with a full knowledge of the relevant law. Likewise, the Crown prosecutor in a criminal trial, as an officer of the court, must strive to ascertain the truth as he seeks to prove the case against the accused. Once the truth is ascertained, it is up to the judge to register a conviction against or an acquittal in favour of the accused.

There is no question that the dictates of our system require that a lawyer exercise a special role in society as an officer of the court placing the interests of justice and fairness ahead of the narrower interests of his particular client. However, at the same time, the lawyer must regard his client's interests as vital. This often leads to a dilemma. Accordingly, codes of ethics have been established to permit lawyers to resolve these difficult situations. We will now examine the relevant codes of ethics governing the behaviour of lawyers in Canada. Lord MacMillan once said:

> The code of honour of the Bar is at once its most cherished possession and the most valued safe-guard of the public. In the discharge of his office the advocate has a duty to his client, a duty to his opponent, a duty to the Court, a duty to the State, and a duty to himself. To maintain a perfect poise amidst the various and somewhat conflicting claims is no easy feat.

The pull of these "conflicting claims" referred to by Lord MacMillan is perhaps more severe on the Canadian lawyer in view of the fact that several codes of ethics govern his or her professional conduct.

5. STANDARDS OF CONDUCT REQUIRED OF LAWYERS

To begin with, the legal profession in every province is governed by provincial statute. This statute generally defines the standard of conduct required of a barrister and solicitor in the province and, in the event that this standard is not met, it outlines the methods of disciplining the lawyer whose conduct has fallen short of the standard. But it would be misleading to conclude that a lawyer must conform only to the particular standard set out in the statute in a given jurisdiction without reference to any other codes of ethics. If a lawyer's conduct meets the statutory standard of conduct governing the profession in a given province, he will likely not be disciplined, but at the same time, he may very well fall short of other standards set out in more extensive codes of ethics. For example, in the province of Alberta, in addition to the statutory standard which must be met to avoid being disciplined, a lawyer must also conform to the canons of ethics established by the Benchers of the Law Society.

These canons set out the various duties that the lawyer has to the state, to the court, to his fellow lawyer, and to himself. In Alberta, for example, under the Legal Profession Act, R.S.A. 1980, c. L-9, a lawyer may be disciplined if his behaviour is "conduct unbecoming" a barrister or solicitor. It may or may not be that the violation of a particular canon of ethics constitutes "conduct unbecoming" a barrister or solicitor. Under a 1981 amendment to the Legal Professional Act, R.S.A. 1980, c. L-9, a member or student member of the Law Society may be disciplined for any act or conduct which "is incompatible with the best interests of the public or the members of the Society, or . . . tends to harm the standing of the legal profession generally . . . whether or not that act or conduct is disgraceful or dishonourable and whether or not that act or conduct relates to the practice of law". See the Legal Profession Amendment Act, 1981 (Alta.), c. 53, s. 47. In any event, a lawyer must not only ensure that his conduct is such that it is "becoming" a barrister or solicitor, but he must also ensure that all the detailed canons of ethics are followed. In addition to the statute governing the legal profession in each province as well as the detailed canons of ethics, the various provincial law societies have issued specific rulings in order to provide guidance to the members of the profession in particular areas of ethical uncertainty. In addition to all of the foregoing, recently the Canadian Bar Association has established its Code of Professional Conduct. Many law societies in Canada are considering adopting the Canadian Bar Association Code in their respective canons of legal ethics.[11] Until this is done, the Canadian Bar Association Code of Professional Conduct is strictly not binding on lawyers; however, it provides some basic guidelines to which lawyers should properly conform. An abbreviated form is set out below.

I. The lawyer must discharge his duties to his client, the court, members of the public and his fellow members of the profession with integrity.

II. a) The lawyer owes a duty to his client to be competent to perform the legal services which the lawyer undertakes on his behalf.

b) The lawyer should serve his client in a conscientious, diligent and efficient manner and he should provide a quality of service at least equal to that which lawyers generally would expect of a competent lawyer in a like situation.

III. The lawyer must be both candid and honest when advising his client.

IV. The lawyer has a duty to hold in strict confidence all information acquired in the course of the professional relationship concerning the business and affairs of his client, and he should not divulge any such information unless he is expressly or impliedly authorized by his client or required by law to do so.

---

[11] As of the date of this writing, eight provincial law societies have adopted the Canadian Bar Association Code, with certain modifications necessitated by their own enabling legislation. With respect to Quebec, see its Professional Code, R.S.Q. 1977, c. C-26. See also the B.C. Barristers and Solicitors Act, R.S.B.C. 1979, c. 26, (replacing the earlier Legal Professions Act). Section 1 of the new Act specifically includes a definition of "conduct unbecoming".

V. The lawyer must not advise or represent both sides of a dispute and, save after adequate disclosure and with the consent of the client or prospective client concerned, he should not act or continue to act in a matter when there is or there is likely to be a conflicting interest. A conflicting interest is one which would be likely to affect adversely the judgment of the lawyer on behalf of or his loyalty to a client or prospective client or which the lawyer might be prompted to prefer to the interests of a client or prospective client.

VI. The lawyer who engages in another profession, business or occupation concurrently with the practice of law must not allow such outside interest to jeopardize his professional integrity, independence or competence.

VII. The lawyer owes a duty to his client to observe all relevant rules and laws regarding the preservation and safekeeping of the property of the client entrusted to him. Where there are no such rules or laws or the lawyer is in any doubt, he should take the same care of such property as a careful and prudent man would take of his own property of like description.

VIII. When acting as an advocate the lawyer must, while treating the tribunal with courtesy and respect, represent his client resolutely, honourably and within the limits of the law.

IX. The lawyer who holds public office should in the discharge of his official duties adhere to standards of conduct as high as those which this Code requires of a lawyer in the practice of law.

X. The lawyer should not

a) stipulate for, charge or accept any fee which is not fully-disclosed, fair and reasonable;

b) appropriate any funds of his client held in trust or otherwise under his control for or on account of his fees without the express authority of his client, except as permitted by the Rules of his Governing Body.

XI. The lawyer owes a duty to his client not to withdraw his services except for good cause and upon notice appropriate in the circumstances.

XII. The lawyer should encourage public respect for and try to improve the administration of justice.

XIII. Lawyers should make legal services available to the public in an efficient and convenient manner which will command respect and confidence and by means which are compatible with the integrity, independence and effectiveness of the profession.

XIV. The lawyer should assist in maintaining the integrity of the profession and should participate in its activities.

XV. The lawyer should assist in preventing the unauthorized practice of law.

XVI. The lawyer's conduct towards other lawyers should be characterized by courtesy and good faith.

XVII. The lawyer should observe the rules of professional conduct set out in this Code in the spirit as well as in the letter.

The law society established by the provincial statute governing the legal profession in that province is responsible for such matters as:

1. Administering the affairs of the legal profession in that province;

2. Establishing standards for admission to the bar;

3. Setting and collecting annual fees;

4. Arranging errors and omissions insurance;

5. Legal aid;

6. Disciplining of lawyers.

Generally these disciplinary obligations are discharged by the governing body within each law society, usually called the benchers of the law society. Depending upon the particular provisions in the governing statute, the benchers usually establish a discipline committee to investigate an allegation of misconduct on the part of a particular lawyer, hold a hearing if necessary, and depending on the findings, discipline the lawyer accordingly. This formula is basically followed in each province, although there are some differences.

Discipline can take many forms, including everything from frequent auditing of a lawyer's accounts to fining or suspending him. The ultimate sanction is disbarment, where a lawyer is struck from the rolls of the particular law society and is prohibited from engaging in the practice of law. While the governing act generally provides the possibility of reinstatement after a number of years, upon disbarment a person is no longer a member of the legal profession. The most difficult determination throughout this process is whether the lawyer's conduct has amounted to a disciplinary offence. While the governing statute generally defines the standard of conduct that is expected of a lawyer, this is usually couched in general words that provide little guidance as to what in a specific instance constitutes a disciplinary impropriety. To determine this, the body of precedent established in Canada must be examined.

Whether a lawyer's incompetence constitutes a disciplinary offence is a currently controversial issue. Generally speaking, incompetence has not been held to be conduct unbecoming a barrister and solicitor or professional misconduct.[12] The conventional wisdom has been that a client's remedy against an incompetent lawyer is a negligence suit for damages.[13] However, there are several indications that it will soon

---

[12]One should consider the recent case of *Lockhart v. MacDonald* (1979), 38 N.S.R. (2d) 671, 69 A.P.R. 671, varied 42 N.S.R. (2d) 29, 77 A.P.R. 29, 118 D.L.R. (3d) 397, which was varied 44 N.S.R. (2d) 261, 83 A.P.R. 261, 118 D.L.R. (3d) 397 at 420, leave to appeal to S.C.C. refused 118 D.L.R. (3d) 397n, 35 N.R. 265n (S.C.C.), where, at trial, it was held that a solicitor without specialized training was not competent to provide financial advice. The court held that the acceptance of a retainer constituted an undertaking by the solicitor that he was competent to perform the services for which he was retained. On appeal, it was held that the solicitor need only demonstrate skill, care and competency in providing a service for his client — he is not obliged to guarantee results. But, in Alberta, see s. 47(3) of the Legal Profession Amendment Act, 1981 (Alta.), c. 53, where, for the first time, it is provided that "conduct deserving of sanction includes incompetently carrying on the practice of law and incompetently carrying out duties or oblibations undertaken by a member or a student-at-law in his capacity as a member or student-at-law".

[13]See two recent cases, *Banks v. Reid* (1977), 18 O.R. (2d) 148, 4 C.C.L.T. 1, 81 D.L.R. (3d) 730, reversing 6 O.R. (2d) 404, 53 D.L.R. (3d) 27 (C.A.), and *Demarco v. Ungaro* (1979), 21 O.R. (2d) 673, 8 C.C.L.T. 207, 95 D.L.R. (3d) 385.

become a ground for discipline. First, there are a few cases where gross incompetence has been held to be conduct unbecoming or professional misconduct. For example, a case to which the reader might refer is the case of *Baron v. F.*[14] where it was held to be "good cause" to justify suspension of a member if that the member was guilty of a series of acts of gross negligence which taken together would bring the legal profession into disrepute. Secondly, the Canadian Bar Association Code of Profession conduct contains a provision that a lawyer owes a duty to his client to be competent. Thirdly, reference may be made to recent amendments to the Legal Profession Act of Alberta (see footnote 12, supra). Fourthly, reference may be made to the Legal Profession Act of the province of Saskatchewan, R.S.S. 1978, c. L-10, where gross negligence is specifically recognized as a ground for discipline.

In view of these indicators it is probably reasonable to conclude that incompetence will be recognized as a legitimate ground for discipline, which is a significant departure from the present situation.[15]

Mark M. Orkin in his treatise on *Legal Ethics*[16] indicates that the charging of exorbitant fees might constitute "conduct unbecoming"; however, the Canadian Bar Association Code suggests that there must be some element of fraud or dishonesty involved before such overcharging will constitute a disciplinary offence. Reference may be made to the case of *German v. Law Soc. of Alta.*, [1974] 5 W.W.R. 217, 45 D.L.R. (3d) 535 (Alta. C.A.), in which a similar issue is raised.[17] In some jurisdictions (such as Ontario) the charging of fees on a contingency basis constitutes a breach of ethics, while in other jurisdictions (such as Alberta) such charging is permissible.

The Canadian Bar Association Code provides that a lawyer cannot represent both sides in a dispute and should not act where there is or is likely to be a conflict of interest. That general statement is clarified, of course, by particular rulings of the various provincial law societies. For

---

[14][1945] 4 D.L.R. 525 (Law Soc. of B.C.). This case was considered in *Midgley v. Law Soc. of Alta.* (1980), 12 Alta. L.R. (2d) 35 (Q.B.) (re *in camera* hearing). The *Midgley* case was discussed in the Alberta Report, 21st December 1979 and the Globe and Mail, 13th February 1980. See also remarks by Mr. Midgley in his column in the Edmonton Sun, 11th January 1981.

[15]See W.H. Hurlburt, "Incompetent Service, and Professional Responsibility" (1980), 18 Alta. L. Rev. 146. See also Federation of Law Societies of Canada, Canadian Bar Association and the Canadian Institute for the Administration of Justice, *The Legal Profession and Quality of Service* (Report and Materials on the Conference on Quality of Legal Services) (1979), and the *Further Report and Proposals* regarding the same conference (1981).

[16]*Legal Ethics: A Study of Professional Conduct* (1957).

[17]This case was applied in another case involving the medical profession. See *Ringrose v. College of Physicians and Surgeons (Alta.) (No. 2)*, [1978] 2 W.W.R. 534, 83 D.L.R. (3d) 680, 8 A.R. 113 (C.A.).

example, it is a common ruling in several jurisdictions that a lawyer can only act for both the vendor and purchaser in a real estate transaction provided that he inform both parties in advance that he is doing so, receives the consent of both parties, and ceases to act in the event that a conflict of interest arises which cannot be resolved. Orkin points out that a lawyer's failure to disclose a personal interest in a client's action constitutes a serious disciplinary offence. Also, a lawyer who acts against a former client in the same or similar matter in which he previously represented that client has a conflict of interest for which he may be disciplined. Finally, although there are constraints upon a lawyer entering into a contract with a client in which the lawyer may receive a benefit, there is no absolute rule which prohibits a lawyer from contracting with his clients: *Shumiatcher v. Law Soc. of Sask.* (1967), 58 W.W.R. 465, 60 D.L.R. (2d) 318, leave to appeal to S.C.C. refused 61 D.L.R. (2d) 520 (Sask. C.A.).

One of the major complaints of members of the public against the legal profession is that lawyers do not sufficiently inform their clients as to the progress of their work. A lawyer does, however, owe a duty to his client to keep him informed, and this includes responding to reasonable requests for information. It is irresponsible and unethical for a lawyer to fail to respond to a telephone call from his client, to fail to keep an appointment, or to fail to meet work deadlines anticipated by his client, to refuse to answer written communications, or generally, to not report on the progress and completion of his work. The intentional concealment of material facts from a client or the false representation to a client about the progress of an action constitute grounds for disbarment. In addition, provincial law society rulings and the Canadian Bar Association Code of Professional Conduct indicate that it is "conduct unbecoming" to disclose confidential information or to use it for one's own purposes.

The rules concerning the withdrawal of services are not easy ones to define, although at least some of them are fairly clear. For example, a lawyer owes a duty to an accused person whom he represents to continue to represent him through to the end of his trial. However, as indicated in the Canadian Bar Association Code, counsel can withdraw for good cause provided he has given his client appropriate notice, and indeed, in certain circumstances he must withdraw.

A lawyer has certain duties which he must perform as an officer of the court and failure to carry out these duties will usually render the lawyer liable to being disciplined, usually by disbarment. The following is a list set out in Orkin's *Legal Ethics* of such transgressions constituting disciplinary offences.

1. Deliberately deceiving or misleading the Court
2. Refusing to answer interrogatories
3. Abuse of the judicial process
4. Writing abusive and improper letters to the Court

   5. Perjury
   6. Forging jurat to an affidavit
   7. Falsely representing his instructions
   8. Wilfully acting without authority
   9. Permitting client to swear a false affidavit
  10. Using an affidavit which is false to his own knowledge
  11. Making false statements in an affidavit of costs
  12. Falsely representing that an injunction has been granted
  13. Tampering with a witness
  14. Impersonation to obtain payment of moneys out of Court
  15. Securing witness of the adverse side to keep out of the way at trial
  16. Assisting a criminal to escape the country
  17. Procuring release of a prisoner by. bribe
  18. Falsifying or forging a writ or a deed
  19. Suppressing an affidavit
  20. Subornation of perjury
  21. Arranging sham bail
  22. Indemnifying a person putting up bail
  23. Tampering with the jury
  24. Avoiding service of an Order of the Master requiring a lawyer to pay over money
  25. Advising a client to sue a person when the suit is clearly vexatious
  26. Being intoxicated in Court
  27. Failing to comply with an Order of the Court although only if made against the lawyer in his professional capacity
  28. Refusing to assist the Court
  29. Aiding client to obtain fraudulent discharge of bankruptcy
  30. Wrongfully running up costs
  31. Taking unnecessary steps

In addition to the above, the Canadian Bar Association Code indicates that a lawyer should not appear before a judge with whom he or his associates have a business or personal relationship, nor should a lawyer, of course, attempt to influence a court's decision by bribery. The latter conduct would inevitably lead to disbarment.

The Canadian Bar Association Report makes certain comments in connection with a lawyer's conduct of advocacy in a court. For example, a lawyer should not waive his client's rights without the informed consent of his client; in civil matters, a lawyer may not resort to technical arguments for the purpose of delaying or harassing the opposite side; in criminal matters, however, a lawyer may place a greater reliance on technical arguments; if a fair and reasonable settlement can be effected, a lawyer has a responsibility to advise his client to settle; in a criminal trial, under the appropriate circumstances, it is permissible for a lawyer to advise his client to plead guilty to a lesser and included offence; if a lawyer is rude, disruptive, provocative or in any other way conducts himself in court so as to be in contempt of court, this naturally would be grounds for discipline. The lawyer must assist the court by revealing the law he has researched on a particular point, whether it is in favour of or opposed to his client's position. (However, failure to do so, which constitutes a disciplinary offence, would probably not lead to the ultimate sanction of disbarment.)

Orkin points out that a lawyer owes the same obligation towards the discipline committee of his provincial law society as he does to the court. This is given statutory recognition in, for example, the Legal Profession Act of the province of Alberta, where it is "conduct unbecoming" for a lawyer to refuse to co-operate with the discipline committee. Similarly, there have been some disbarments recently as a result of a lawyer's failure to reply to letters from his provincial law society. There is no doubt that such a failure constitutes "conduct unbecoming" and, in fact, represents a serious breach of professional responsibility.

Generally speaking, lawyers have certain professional responsibilities to their colleagues in the legal fraternity. Rulings of the various provincial law societies indicate that a lawyer is expected to reply promptly to communications from his fellow lawyer; however, to use an Alberta example, the wording of this ruling, to the effect that it would be "at the very least discourteous" to fail to reply promptly, would seem to indicate that although this might be "conduct unbecoming" it would most likely not warrant disbarment. The Canadian Bar Association Code indicates that a lawyer is generally expected to deal courteously and fairly with a fellow lawyer and not to indulge in sharp practice. Both the Canadian Bar Association Report and various rulings of the provincial law societies indicate that the tape recording of a communication with another lawyer without his consent is forbidden (and, indeed, it might be the subject of criminal liability under recent amendments to the Criminal Code). The above sources also indicate that it is unethical to communicate on a matter directly with a person represented by counsel without that counsel's consent. Also, of great importance, the Canadian Bar Association Report and the various rulings of the respective provincial law societies indicate that it is a lawyer's duty to report any misconduct on the part of his fellow lawyer. For example, an Alberta ruling indicates that "it is proper and desirable for any member to report such incidents". However, the mild language in which the ruling is phrased suggests that the failure to report such a lawyer might not in every case result in discipline; however, no doubt a failure to report a matter regarding a shortage of trust funds or a serious breach of an undertaking made by a fellow lawyer would constitute "conduct unbecoming".

It is generally considered that the legal profession, because of its position in society and its special knowledge, is under a responsibility to carry out legal reform. Indeed, lawyers and judges have accepted this responsibility and play key roles in changing the law. At the same time, the Canadian Bar Association Report also indicates that it is the lawyer's duty to maintain respect for the legal system as it presently exists. In short, criticism must be reasonable and bona fide. The lawyer must disclose whether, in making criticism, he is acting for a particular client or speaking on his own behalf or speaking in the public interest. A lawyer need not believe in the cause he espouses if he is acting for a client, but if he is acting in the public interest he must truly believe in the validity of the cause.

Similarly, writing in a 1967 edition of the Law Society Gazette, the editor offered the view that a lawyer can only use legal means to change the system. Accordingly, and this is buttressed by the Canadian Bar Association Report, civil disobedience by a lawyer is not permissible.[18] The lawyer cannot counsel, assist or engage in activities against the law. However, as Professor Mark MacGuigan (at the time of this writing the Minister of Justice of Canada) indicates in another edition of the Law Society Gazette, a breach of a statute, especially a minor regulatory statute, would not, however, lead to disbarment. On the other hand, in yet another article appearing in the Law Society Gazette, it was suggested that there may be a positive duty to act against an unjust law. This latter view is definitely not held by most lawyers and is most certainly in error. Along similar lines, reference may be made to the case of *Martin v. Law Soc. of B.C.*, [1950] 3 D.L.R. 173 (B.C. C.A.), in which a person was held to be ineligible for admission to the bar of British Columbia because he was a member of the Communist Party and such membership indicated an implicit advocacy for the overthrow of government. While Orkin goes further and suggests that such membership would be grounds for disbarment, there are some lawyers in Canada who do possess similar political views and are not, in fact, nor likely will be, the subject of disciplinary action.

Regarding a lawyer's personal life: it is not professional misconduct to be a co-respondent in a divorce action; it is, however, according to certain rulings issued by some provincial law societies "conduct unbecoming" for a lawyer not to meet his financial obligations.

The Canadian Bar Association Report indicates that a lawyer should help prevent the practice of law by unauthorized persons,[19] and to this end there are rulings of various provincial law societies to the effect that it is "conduct unbecoming" to split fees with unqualified persons.

In respect of legal aid, the Canadian Bar Association Report indicates that a lawyer can decline employment except where he has been assigned by the court to act as counsel. But he should, at the same time, try to

---

[18]See *Midgley v. Law Soc. of Alta.* (1980), 12 Alta. L.R. (2d) 35 (Q.B.).
[19]See *R. v. Nicholson*, (1979), 8 Alta. L.R. (2d) 299, 14 A.R. 450, 46 C.C.C. (2d) 230, reversing 5 Alta. L.R. (2d) 98, 12 A.R. 595 (C.A.), where an accused incorporated several companies for the public for a fee. The accused did not represent himself as a lawyer, nor did he provide legal advice; he merely filled out the required forms. He was convicted at trial but on appeal the conviction was quashed. The court held that the accused only performed clerical work and that such work cannot be said to be reserved to the legal profession.

prevent a situation in which a person would have no representation, and he should not refuse a brief because a client's cause is unpopular or because he believes the person to be guilty.

One area of difficulty relates to the lawyer's outside interests. And, by outside interests, one is referring to other employment (in business, for example), public office and public appearances. The Canadian Bar Association Report indicates that a lawyer's outside interests should not affect his professional judgment in dealing with his clients. If his outside interests are not related to his practice of law, there is usually no problem unless the outside interests tend to bring the profession into disrepute. Moreover, as Orkin indicates, there are some types of outside activities which can lead to disbarment, and these would include the renting of premises as a brothel (see *Re Weare*, [1893] 2 Q.B. 439), acting as a bookmaker, and other dubious outside enterprises.

Some rulings of the provincial law societies indicate that it is a disciplinary offence to carry on any business which makes it difficult for a client to know whether the lawyer is acting as a lawyer or is acting in another capacity. However, to use an Alberta ruling as an example, the wording is again expressed in mild language to the effect that it is "most undesirable" to do so and, therefore, although it is a disciplinary offence to do so, a violation of this ruling is probably not a ground for disbarment. With respect to this rule, the Canadian Bar Association Report indicates that a lawyer must indicate the capacity in which he is acting, especially if he also serves as an accountant, engineer, merchant, land developer, building contractor, real estate, insurance or financial agent, broker, financier, property manager or public relations advisor.

Both the Canadian Bar Association Report and various rulings of the provincial law societies indicate that in the event a lawyer holds public office his official duties are paramount, and if there is a conflict a client should not be accepted or, in the case of an existing client, the lawyer should end the relationship with that client. Moreover, the Canadian Bar Association Report adds that the lawyer holding public office in a given body should not appear before that official body in a professional capacity.

Both the Canadian Bar Association Report and various provincial law society rulings indicate that a lawyer cannot solicit appearances on television, radio or other public forum in his professional capacity or use such appearances for advertisement or engage in any appearance that might bring the legal profession into disrepute. For example, a ruling of the Law Society of Alberta indicates that a lawyer can appear in his personal and private capacity if the reason for his appearance is not related to his professional capacity. It was held in one case to be "conduct unbecoming" for a lawyer to carry on a regular radio broadcast, not for reason of the conducting of the broadcast itself, but for its particular style and type. In that case, the offender was reprimanded and ordered to cease the broadcasts. The decision gives the impression that if the lawyer had refused to comply, he would have been disbarred. Reference may be made to the case of *Merchant v. Benchers of Law Society of Sask.*, [1972] 4 W.W.R. 663, 25 D.L.R. (3d) 708, reversed [1973] 2 W.W.R. 109, 32 D.L.R. (3d) 178 (Sask. C.A.).

In examining the various governing statutes, most provinces use the words "professional misconduct" or "conduct unbecoming" a barrister or solicitor as the grounds for discipline. When the given provincial statute, however, contains only the expression "conduct unbecoming", then it appears that these words both encompass "conduct unbecoming" as well as "professional misconduct", as these two phrases are used in provinces containing the two-fold standard. Generally speaking, the term "professional misconduct" is concerned with indiscretions committed while exercising professional duties and the term "conduct unbecoming" relates to non-professional misconduct, which nonetheless harms the reputation of the legal profession. Reference should also be made to the new formulation in the Alberta Legal Profession Act where the test becomes one of conduct "incompatible with the best interests of the public" or which "tends to harm the standing of the legal profession". See the discussion appearing earlier in this chapter and an article reviewing the disciplinary role of the Law Society of Alberta in the Alberta Report, 9th May 1983.

However, the particular behaviour which falls under either or both of the above formulas is more difficult to define. Some assistance has been rendered by legal writers such as Mark M. Orkin, who in his treatise *Legal Ethics* has divided the disciplinary offences into various categories. Also, the statute governing the legal profession in a province may contain provisions that specifically define what constitutes "conduct unbecoming". For example in the Legal Profession Act of Alberta, it is conduct unbecoming a barrister or solicitor to fail to co-operate with an investigating committee inquiring into a lawyer's conduct, to have been convicted of an indictable offence, and to fail to given an accounting to a client when directed to do so by the Secretary of the Discipline Committee. However, such conduct will not necessarily lead to disbarment. For example, whether the commission of a criminal offence gives rise to discipline depends on several factors. At common law, prima facie, conviction of a criminal offence was a ground for discipline. However, disbarment was not mandatory: the nature of the crime was usually considered. Orkin suggests that the test was whether the offence imported the notion of disgrace of character rendering a person unfit for an honourable profession. However, it is of interest to note that a recent amendment to the Legal Profession Act in Alberta states that conduct may be "unbecoming" whether or not the conduct is disgraceful or dishonourable. Therefore, in at least the province of Alberta, the statutory standard may be more rigid than Orkin's suggested common law standard. It would seem to be immaterial whether such conduct is committed in the course of a lawyer's private conduct or in his professional capacity. Obviously it is a more serious matter if such an offence is committed in the latter capacity. Reference may be made to the case of *Prescott v. Law Soc. of B.C.*, [1971] 4 W.W.R. 433, 19 D.L.R. (3d) 446 (B.C. C.A.), wherein a lawyer was disbarred for committing an offence contrary to the Income Tax Act, R.S.C. 1952, c. 148. Although he did not attempt to evade the law, he was found guilty of gross negligence in keeping accounts. In this case, it was held to be immaterial that the particular offence was not committed within the lawyer's professional capacity. With respect to the nature of the crime, criminal offences involving fraud or dishonesty, by their very nature, generally lead to disciplinary action and often disbarment. Examples of such offences include bribery, forgery, perjury, making false affidavits, embezzlement, theft, obtaining money or goods by false pretenses, and several others. In addition, a conviction for obstructing justice would almost certainly be a ground for disbarment, whether committed in the course of a lawyer's professional or private capacity, since its very nature is such as to bring the legal profession into disrepute.

Conviction for an offence involving immoral conduct or moral turpitude would constitute conduct unbecoming but would probably not lead to the ultimate sanction of disbarment.

There is some behaviour often, but not necessarily, leading to conviction for a criminal offence involving fraud or dishonesty for which, it can be said with assurance, disciplinary action will take the form of disbarment. Such conduct includes a lawyer's misusing funds that he holds in trust for his clients, misappropriating clients' funds, failing to apply clients' funds as directed, obtaining money from clients for fictitious disbursements, and falsely stating that disbursements have been paid. A ruling of the Law Society of Alberta stating that failure to give a client an accounting when he demands it will constitute conduct unbecoming and a prescription in the Canadian Bar Association Code of Professional Conduct that a lawyer has a duty to keep his clients' property safe would indicate that even less serious such behaviour would nevertheless render a lawyer liable to severe disciplinary sanctions.

In addition to all of the foregoing, Orkin lists some specific types of conduct which are grounds for disbarment:

1. Making a false recital in a deed
2. Subornation of perjury in a witness
3. Attempted subornation of a jury
4. Assisting a client to obtain a fraudulent discharge in insolvency
5. Permitting a client to make a false affidavit
6. Accepting a transfer of property in fraud of transferor's creditors
7. Advising how improperly to defeat a garnishee order
8. Assisting a criminal to escape from the country

9. Obtaining the release of a prisoner by a bribe
10. Advising collusion in a divorce case (see *Dicks v. Dicks*, [1949] 2 W.W.R. 866 (B.C.))
11. Maintenance and champerty
12. Bribery
13. Compelling a client to sign an agreement giving the lawyer a share of property recovered on prosecution
14. Canvassing for business
15. Abusing position as commissioner for oath to obtain retainer
16. Acting as a solicitor while under suspension
17. Acting without a practising certificate
18. Holding out as a solicitor before admission to practice
19. Malicious conduct
20. Failing to supervise staff properly so that they were able to defraud the public
21. Employing a person of known bad character without supervision
22. Assisting a creditor to obtain an undue preference
23. Passing worthless cheques
24. Giving offensive or improper letters
25. Giving false references
26. Making untrue statements to procure a passport for another person
27. Permitting a client to suppress a will
28. Antedating deed to defraud creditors or income tax authorities or to avoid judgments
29. Forging a signature to a mortgage
30. Making a false income tax return

Professional responsibility, including professional ethics, is a vast and extremely important topic which must be studied in even more depth, in order to truly understand the role of the lawyer in our legal system.[20] Accordingly, for a greater understanding of the ethical requirements of the legal profession and of professional responsibility in general, the following sources might be helpful:

1. Orkin, *Legal Ethics*
2. Arthurs, *Casebook on the Legal Profession*

---

[20]The public perception of lawyers is often not good. According to the Consumers Association of Canada, lawyers head the list of professionals most frequently complained about. See the Edmonton Journal, 27th February 1980. The questions of competence, ethics, and, indeed, "caring" frequently arise. With respect to "caring", see the Financial Post, 20th June 1981. With respect to competence and ethics, see U.S. News & World Report, 1st December 1980 ("Lawyers Giving Public a Raw Deal"); the Toronto Star, 26th January 1981 ("Lawyers Who Stoop to Fraud Eroding Faith in the Profession"); the Financial Post, 6th June 1981 ("Lawyers Probe Origins of Legal Incompetence"); U.S. News & World Report, 11th May 1981 ("Why Lawyers are in the Doghouse"); Newsweek Magazine, 11th December 1981 ("Lawyers on Trial"); the Edmonton Journal, 3rd February 1979 ("Incompetent Alberta Lawyers May Face Action from Peers"); Harper's Magazine, October 1978 ("Ontario Moves to Stamp Out Lawyers' Errors"); the Toronto Star, 11th March 1979 ("Feel Your Lawyer's Blundered? Now, Finally, You Can Sue Him"); Time Magazine, 10th April 1978 ("Those #*X&!!! Lawyers"); U.S. News & World Report, 26th February 1979 ("Putting the Spotlight on Lawyers' Misdeeds"); and the Edmonton Journal, 29th January 1982 ("Critics Call Lawyers Greedy and Arrogant"). See also the Edmonton Journal, 10th August 1978 and 14th January 1982, where U.S. Chief Justice Warren Burger is very critical of recent law school graduates. See also the Edmonton Journal, 16th April 1979 and Time Magazine, 8th December 1980.

3. Law Society of Upper Canada, *Professional Conduct Handbook*
4. Boulton, *A Guide to Conduct and Etiquette at the Bar* (U.K.)
5. Freedman, *Lawyers' Ethics in an Adversary System* (U.S.)
6. American Bar Association, *Code of Professional Responsibility and Commentary*
7. American Bar Association, *Draft Model Rules of Professional Conduct,* May 1981
8. *American Lawyers Code of Conduct,* June 1980 (Discussion paper)
9. Laud, *Lectures on Professional Conduct and Etiquette* (U.K.)
10. Council of Law Society, *A Guide to Professional Conduct,* 1974 (U.K.)
11. Disney *et al., Lawyers* (Australia)
12. Pirsig & Kirwin, *Professional Responsibility* (U.S.)
13. Kaufman, *Problems in Professional Responsibility* (U.S.)
14. Hazard, *Ethics in the Practice of Law* (U.S.)
15. Galston, *Professional Responsibility of the Lawyer* (U.S.)

There is, of course, no mandatory retirement age for members of the legal profession, although there is provision in the enabling statutes governing the provincial law societies for resignation from the law societies. The danger that an unsuspecting public is without protection against a lawyer who has become mentally incapacitated, senile, ill, infirm[21] or addicted to alcohol or drugs is only partially allayed by the availability of an action in negligence for damages. Thus, some law societies in Canada are presently considering making such incapacity or infirmity a ground for disciplinary sanction.

THE MODERN LAWYER

Today's lawyer faces new challenges. The proliferation of laws has meant that he or she[22] is encouraged to specialize. The growing number of lawyers has created a highly competitive marketplace. For some this

---

[21]See discussion by G. Parker on "Disability as a Form of Incompetence" in *The Legal Profession and Quality of Service, supra,* note 15, at p. 505. Recently, in Manitoba, this problem has been addressed by the creation of both Standards and Discipline Committees of the Law Society of Manitoba. In the case of incompetence or infirmity, the matter would be dealt with by the Standards Committee with a view to assisting the lawyer through remedial or therapeutic measures, while in the case of traditional disciplinary concerns, the matter would be dealt with by the Discipline Committee. These changes followed the recommendations of the Law Society of Manitoba Report on Competency (otherwise known as the Matas report).

[22]A growing number of women are entering the legal profession. Forty to fifty per cent of the students in all first year law school classes are female. See the Globe and Mail, 15th May 1980, on "Women Lawyers".

has led to unemployment.[23] Others have been prompted to try new methods of attracting clients: some now advertise the areas to which they have restricted their practice;[24] others depict or describe their practices in unconventional ways;[25] some are practising in new locales, i.e., supermarkets or department stores; some are reaching out to different segments of the community through "storefront" practices.[26] To increase the range of legal services that can be offered, a large established Toronto law firm has attempted to break new ground by opening a so-called "branch office" in Calgary. The Law Society of Alberta reacted by passing a regulation disallowing this type of operation, the validity of which is presently being challenged in the courts.[27] The "public image" of the profession could be improved upon.[28] The misbehaviour and incompetence of a few has severely affected the professional reputation of all members of the profession.[29] One by-product of this is that malpractice insurance rates have increased.[30] In Alberta, as a result of two very serious cases of defalcation, special levies have had to be assessed for two years in a row in order to restore the Law Society's Assurance Fund.

---

[23]See the Canadian Bar Association, *Economic Survey of Canadian Law Firms* (1980). See also the Edmonton Journal, 17th November 1981 and the New York Times, 6th August 1978.

[24]For Canadian commentary on advertising by lawyers, see the Vancouver Sun, 18th September 1979; the Calgary Herald, 19th December 1978; the Edmonton Journal, 6th February 1979, 5th September 1979 and the editorial of 4th June 1979; and the Globe and Mail, 15th May 1978. For a discussion of the American position on advertising by lawyers, see the New York Times, 26th November 1978 and 3rd August 1980, Time Magazine, 21st August 1978 and the Edmonton Journal, 14th December 1978.

[25]For example, Vancouver lawyer Jack James established "The Law Shoppe" — see the Edmonton Journal, 21st February 1980 and 3rd February 1981. An American lawyer founded a chain of legal service centres called the "Law People" — see the Edmonton Journal, 22nd May 1979. Another example is the "Dial-A-Law" service operated by the Calgary Legal Guidance Public Service Project sponsored by the Alberta Branch of the Canadian Bar Association and the Law Society of Alberta. See earlier discussion of the *Jabour* case and a description of Mr. Jabour's Neighbourhood Legal Clinic in Maclean's Magazine, 19th February 1979.

[26]See, for example, Hoffman, "Lawyers for the Poor: Why Not the Best?", in New York Magazine, 14th May 1979, and the articles in Newsweek Magazine 9th October 1978, 14th January 1980, and 6th April 1981.

[27]See *Black v. Law Soc. of Alta.*, [1983] 3 W.W.R. 7 (Alta. Q.B.); for a discussion of the background to this case, see the Financial Post, 20th March 1983.

[28]See the Toronto Star, 9th February 1982 ("Lawyers Worry About Future of Profession"). On "How to Challenge Your Lawyer's Bill", see the Financial Post, 10th January 1981 and on the procedure to launch complaints against lawyers, see the Edmonton Journal, 31st January to 2nd February 1980.

[29]See Today Magazine, 19th July 1980, and J. Anderson, "How to Choose the Right Lawyer", in Reader's Digest, December 1980. See also "Know Your Lawyer", a pamphlet prepared by the Law Society of Alberta and the Alberta Branch of the Canadian Bar Association.

[30]See the Edmonton Journal, 29th October 1979.

However, the modern lawyer continues to do well financially[31] (in some cases attracting considerable notoriety from such financial success)[32] and to maintain a highly visible profile.[33]

(As an aside, changes in the financing of legal services should be noted. One new development is the growth of prepaid legal service plans[34] which often form part of the benefits sought in collective bargaining.[35] Another older development, legal aid, began in the mid-1960's and is now established in every province.)[36]

The practice of law continues to be a satisfying profession, but in view of the new challenges being faced it has become an increasingly stressful occupation. For an interesting discussion on lawyers and stress, see Maclean's Magazine, 29th January 1979.

For a discussion of other aspects of the professional life of the modern lawyer, readers should consult the extensive bibliography appended to this chapter.[37]

---

[31]See Canadian Bar Association, *Economic Survey of Canadian Law Firms, supra.* For a discussion of this report, see the Financial Post, 22nd November 1980.

[32]The counsel to the Krever Royal Commission on Confidentiality of Health Records billed the Ontario government more than $200,000 for his work over 15 months. This attracted some controversy. See the Toronto Star, 27th June 1979. See also Goulden, *The Million Dollar Lawyers* (New York: Putnam, 1979); Time Magazine, 27th July 1981; and the New York Times, 3rd August, 1979.

[33]See M. Ryval, "The Defender", in Quest Magazine, 1981; "The New High Rollers: Canada's Celebrity Lawyers" in Maclean's Magazine, 17th September 1979; J. Battan, *Lawyers* (Toronto: MacMillan, 1979); and K. Auletta, "Don't Mess with Roy Cohn: The Legal Executioner", in Esquire Magazine, 5th December 1978.

[34]This is also briefly discussed in Chapter 12.

[35]See L. Wilson and C. Wydnzynski, "Prepaid Legal Services: Legal Representation for the Canadian Middle Class" (1978), 28 U. of T.L.J. 25. See also the Globe and Mail, 5th May 1979 and 26th May 1980, Time Magazine, 4th September 1978 and the Financial Post, 11th November 1978, 10th February 1979, and 6th March 1982.

[36]See the Globe and Mail, 4th May 1978 and 18th October 1979; the Toronto Star, 3rd May 1978, and the Calgary Albertan, 16th August 1979.

[37]For a discussion of lawyers as lobbyists, see G. Gall (1977), 15 Alta. L. Rev. 400; and see U.S. News & World Report, 10th March 1980 ("Washington Lawyers: Rise of the Power Brokers"); for a discussion of the large number of lawyers, the modern law student and professors, the work done at major law reviews, bar exams, recent hiring practices of major law firms, and recent new publications for lawyers, all in the context of the U.S. judiciary system, see, respectively, the New York Times, 1st April 1979, 4th November 1979 and 13th May 1980, Time Magazine, 25th February 1980, Newsweek Magazine, 1st December 1980 and Time Magazine 26th February 1979. For a discussion of the draft of the new American Bar Association Code of Professional Responsibilities, see the New York Times 7th January 1980.

Some concluding remarks on the role of the lawyer will follow the discussion of the role of the judge.[38]

JUDGES

The role of the judge does not lend itself to simple definition. A consideration of the fundamental role that a judge plays within our legal system pertains, of course, to a judge exercising his power as judge. However, there is a related capacity arising out of the prestige and status of the judiciary in our system, and that is the judge acting in a special capacity off the bench. For example, judges are often appointed members of Royal Commissions of Inquiry, tribunals, and other such bodies. These commissions of inquiry usually deal with ad hoc matters of national or provincial importance. A discussion of judges serving in other capacities will be raised at a later point in this chapter.

The role of the judge depends, to some extent, upon the particular bench on which he or she sits. The courts in the various jurisdictions are all governed by different enabling statutes. These statutes set out the judge's power and the nature of the matters over which the judge has jurisdiction. Thus, the role of one judge may be somewhat different than that of another by virtue of the different enabling statutes. However, these differences are often minor and, they do not preclude a more generic description of the judicial function in Canada. (The constitutional basis for judicial authority in Canada, including the legal structural basis for the various enabling statutes under which our courts are established, is set out in Chapter 5.)

Generally speaking, the role of the judge[39] within the Canadian legal system may be defined as that of an arbiter in resolving particular disputes. Disputes of a factual nature are determined by trial judges; disputes relating to the interpretation of a point of law are determined by judges having appellate jurisdiction.

To take this definition one step further, the role of the judge as arbiter in resolving particular disputes is carried out objectively, on the basis of evidence adduced through the workings of the adversarial system. The

---

[38]See bibliography appended to this chapter on the "Role of the Lawyer" in Canada. For a comparative analysis, see, in respect of the United Kingdom, R. Hazell (ed.), *The Bar on Trial* (London: Quartet Books, 1978), and, in respect of the United States, F. Rodell, *Woe Unto You, Lawyers!* (New York: Berkeley, 1980) (originally published in 1939), and J.C. Goulden, *The Million Dollar Lawyers* (New York: G.P. Putnam's Sons, 1978). (The same author wrote *The Superlawyer*, published in 1972.)

[39]For a biographical sketch of certain judges, see, for example, Deslauriers, *La Cour Superieure du Quebec et ses juges 1849 — 1er janvier 1980* (Quebec: Imprimerie Provinciale Inc., 1980); Vaughan, "Emmett M. Hall: A Profile of the Judicial Temperament" (1977), 15 O.H.L.J. 306; and Stubbs, "The First Juvenile Court Judge: Hon. T. Mayre Daly, R.C." (1979), 10 Man. L.J. 1.

essential nature of the adversarial system is that the judge acts as the objective decision-maker in the face of opposing interests, with each interest arguing and articulating the merits of its position. In contrast, the inquisitorial, or continental European, judge takes carriage of the proceedings and is ultimately responsible for the ascertainment of truth within the court. The system in Canada is founded on the belief that through an adversarial contest the truth will eventually emerge. The European system on the other hand is premised on the belief that only through an activist role on the part of the judge will the truth be ascertained.

Any attempt at providing a more detailed description of the role of the judge in the Canadian legal system must take into account that judges themselves do not share the same belief as to their role.[40]

Consider the following extract of comments made by the Chief Justice of the Quebec Superior Court concerning the role of the judge. (This passage is taken from the Toronto Globe & Mail, 30th October 1974).

Judges Should Be Legislators, Quebec Chief Justice Argues

A two-month-old controversy over how far judges can go in replacing the lawmakers surfaced again here yesterday in a meticulously documented speech by Chief Justice Jules Deschênes of the Quebec Superior Court.

Chief Justice Deschênes told a Chamber of Commerce meeting that on paper the legislative, executive and judicial sections of Government are distinct but in practice they overlap, and when the lawmakers don't pass laws that are in keeping with "changing social conditions" it is up to the judges to exercise their "legislative power" and change the law to suit the times.

Yesterday, Chief Justice Deschênes tried to explain to his audience of businessmen why judges should legislate at times.

He cited more than 40 cases in which courts changed the law or overruled provincial or federal laws they decided didn't apply any longer or were wrong.

These included:

The 1970 Drybones case in which the Supreme Court of Canada decided that the Indian Act section forbidding Indians' being drunk on reserves was inoperative because it didn't apply equally to all Canadians;

---

[40]Reference may be made to two special editions of the Canadian Bar Review published in commemoration of the 100th anniversary of the establishment of the Supreme Court of Canada. These two editions appear in volume 53 of the Canadian Bar Review and are cited as (1975), 53 Can. Bar Rev. 459, and (1975), 53 Can. Bar Rev. 649. In addition, also celebrating the Centenary of the Supreme Court of Canada, a special edition of the Alberta Law Review was published. That edition is cited as (1976), 14 Alta. L. Rev. 1. A major study of the Supreme Court of Canada is contained in Paul Weiler's treatise entitled *In the Last Resort* (Toronto: Carswell, 1974). For the little known information on ad hoc Supreme Court Justices, see Boult, "Ad Hoc Judges of the Supreme Court of Canada" (1978), 25 Chitty's L.J. 289. See the detailed description of the study conducted at the University of Alberta in 1976 appearing in the first edition in this book. Work is currently in progress in respect of two studies conducted under the auspices of the Canadian Institute for the Administration of Justice, namely the "Study of the Alberta Judiciary" and the research relating to the "Role of the Chief Justice and Chief Judge in Canada."

The 1959 Roncarelli case in which the Supreme Court said the Quebec Government had acted wrongly by revoking a man's license because he was a Jehovah's Witness;

The 1973 Manitoba Egg War case in which the court said a provincial law impeded interprovincial commerce.

He said there had been 1972 judicial interpretations of Canada's constitution since Confederation.

He said that judges have "opened new roads and widened perspectives on the law as they sought modern solutions compatible with changing conditions in our society."

Chief Justice Deschênes said provincial labor laws are undergoing a "mini-revolution" in the courts because of recent court decisions. "Jurisprudence has more surprises in store for the citizens of our country."

"The first role" of judges, he said, "is to apply the law as it exists and this is the task to which they put most of their efforts. More often than not, there is no doubt in the law . . . However, sometimes the evolution of thinking or morals tends to create an imbalance between the law and the facts.

"That's when the courts must take on, with a reflected audacity, the heavy burden of adapting the law to the new social realities which show up."

He said that if a judge were there only to apply the law he would be reduced to a robot.

"The defenders of such a view would become its victims and soon be among its most virulent critics."

Consider also the following sample of the views expressed by some Alberta judges as to the role of the judge in the Canadian legal system:[41]

(1) As far as the legislative role of the judges is concerned . . . I emphatically state that the function of a judge is not that of the law maker. The problem with this whole area of course is one of connotation and semantics. There can be no question that in the day to day functioning of judges they will contribute considerably to the growth and development of law. It is also true that in our constitutional system there is a fair amount of overlapping between the functions of the executive, the legislature and the judiciary. It is important to recognize that the lines dividing the three branches of government are rather gray and broad, but I think it is equally important to emphasize the paramount function of each branch of government and that each should be vigilant in minimizing its interference with the others' responsibility.

Basically I am of the view that there should be as much certainty in the law as possible. In other words the citizen at any given time should know where he stands in his relationships with his fellow citizen and with the state. If laws are changed without notice then the position of the citizen is rendered uncertain. For that reason I feel that generally the law should not change except by the action of the legislature. The problem with laws being changed by judges is that the change occurs without notice to the public. Secondly, I feel that even in a democratic system as highly developed as our own the citizen has a rather limited opportunity to control the law. That opportunity is of course expressed by the fact that the legislature is accountable to the voter. There is no similar accountability between the judiciary and the public and it is therefore my view that the judiciary must be very careful to keep its law making role within the limits set by the existing rules of

---

[41]This sample is taken from a 1976 study conducted at the University of Alberta. For more details concerning that study, see the first edition of this book.

law. I therefore of course feel that the doctrine of stare decisis is a doctrine essential to the proper functioning of our judicial system. If that doctrine is taken away from the judicial system then each judge becomes a law unto himself and the citizen is no longer subject to the rule of the law but is in danger of being subject to the rule of the man.

(2) The judge is to apply the law fairly as it is enacted. Without this, the law is unknown not only to the practicing lawyer but to the judges and the public and jockeying for a particular judge would be a large part of the court work of barristers. No judge, applying the law as it is, becomes a robot, but at least he should know in fact what it is, and if he should err, the appeal courts will give guidance in their judgment.

(3) . . . should exercise an essentially interpretative process . . . one should apply the laws as enacted and be guided accordingly, and this does not mean that we necessarily agree to all of them.

(4) All human societies have one characteristic in common and that is that the struggle for power therein is an ongoing phenomenon. The great achievement of liberal democratic societies was that they domesticated that struggle and brought it within constitutional confines. In our system government power is diffused amongst the judicial, executive and legislative branches of government out of a wholesome recognition of the fact that no person and no group can be trusted with too much power. It is only by continuing to recognize such self-evident truths and by continuing to preserve such a division of power that individual liberty can be maintained.

It therefore follows that judges have no right to invade the legislature function. They cannot be trusted with absolute or excessive power any more than any other group in society. The judge's role is to interpret the law and not to make it. I realize of course that in the course of interpreting the law a judge may incidentally also be said to be making law on occasion. It is impossible to place the three government functions into watertight compartments. There is necessarily some overlapping but it is important that each branch of government recognize its limitations and not endeavour to assume the role of another.

(5) The notion that a judge should legislate in the real sense is a destructive one. [The courts would become] an oligarchy of dictators, imposing their ideas about the shape of society upon the ordinary citizen. [This would be a] gross abuse of judges' powers [and would result in] a lack of public respect for the impartiality of the courts . . . A judge who adopts an activist role respecting social questions becomes a protaganist, and loses his capacity as an arbiter. A judge, however, can adapt law to new realities as a proper judicial function. The courts must take cognizance of changes in conditions in applying the rules.

(6) I believe that, as judges, we are an arm of government and in the execution of our duties we should not transgress the role of the legislator or the administrator. If the rule of law is to have any validity, legislating should be done by legislators and judges should restrict themselves to interpreting legislation and applying the common law, previous judicial interpretations and common sense to the facts before them for the purpose of reaching a decision. I believe that a judge can be innovative in his approach to the interpretation, and that in his interpretation he can reflect changing social values, but he should not go to the extent of usurping the function of the legislature. In summary, I feel that judges should exercise an essentially interpretive function.

(7) Lord Atkin said in *United Australia Ltd. v. Barclays Bank Ltd.*, [1941] A.C. at 29, [1940] 4 All E.R. 20, quoted approvingly by Milvain C.J.T.D. in *McGee v. Waldern and Cunningham*, [1971] 4 W.W.R. 684 at 693, 4 R.F.L. 17 (Alta.):

"When these ghosts of the past stand in the path of justice clanking their medieval chains the proper course for the Judge is to pass through them undeterred."

(8) My view is that it is not the judge's function to make laws. That is up to the legislatures and Parliament . . . The fact is, however, that the judge has frequently to interpret any given piece of legislation in the light of changed conditions and circumstances which may or may not have existed at the time the legislation was enacted, and to that extent a judge may be thought to be making the law . . . It is to be borne in mind that the very nature of the common law is that it is a growing thing, it has to adapt itself to changing times and to different environments, but I do not think a judge should consider himself as a lawmaker.

(9) I cannot agree, however, that judges should have the power to, in effect, determine the public pulse, and as a consequence of this determination override clear statutory provision. The judge must function within the framework of the law. Responsibility for determining when changes in law are appropriate must rest with the legislative authority.

(10) [A judge should stay out of the political and social arena for the reason that he doesn't have the] facility to canvass public opinion nor to properly assess it . . . [However, he should not be in an] ivory tower [impervious to social change].

(11) Certainly in some new areas where the law can be applied or extended logically to fit a new situation a judge is in fact "making" new law. But it is only really a logical extension of an existing principle to fit a new set of facts and not breaking new legislative ground.

(12) The role of the judge in our legal system is to formulate the law and to keep in pace with the times. That naturally involves formulating law which is in accordance with the needs of society today. In other words, what one might have thought fifty years ago on any subject might not be applicable at all today and if a judge were to apply the law in that sense we would soon have chaos, and to apply the law a judge would be reduced to a robot. His function of course is to decide judicially in the light of existing conditions which involves many changes from time to time, and in my thinking a good judge must be in tune with the times . . . The law is an amorphous body of principles and the judge's function is most important because he must, in reaching his judgment, keep in mind the widened perspectives on the law as Chief Justice Deschenes mentions, compatible with changing conditions in our society.

(13) A judge's role is primarily to interpret and apply the law . . . I see no impropriety in saying I don't like the law, so long as I apply it and enforce it (which it is my duty to do). We recall that Mr. Justice Sissons of the Northwest Territories in one case refused to enforce a law with which he did not agree. I would not be surprised that in the long view, and in these fast-changing times, and with the prospect of new young judges "tempered in the crucible of change", the old attitude of interpreting the law but not criticizing it will be "bent if not broken".

But whether the judge sees himself as lawmaker or law interpreter, it is of paramount importance that he or she, for purposes of credibility and public acceptance, ensure that the court is an arena where the interests of justice are served by searching for the truth in an atmosphere of fairness, dignity and decorum.[42]

---

[42]See also Cecil, *The English Judge* (London: Arrow Books, 1979); and Lord Denning, *The Discipline of Law* (London: Butterworths, 1979). For a further discussion of the Canadian judiciary as reported in the press, see the Edmonton Journal, 13th December 1977, 16th November 1979, 15th August 1980, 14th July 1980 and the Globe and Mail, 16th January 1980, 12th January 1981 and 29th June 1981. See especially the Edmonton Journal, 24th January 1981 and the feature in the Toronto Star, 10th February 1982, as part of its series on "Justice in the 80's". See also the Toronto Star, 10th February 1982.

There will be some discussions later in this chapter on legal and other constraints imposed upon judges. Essentially, these constraints are imposed to ensure impartiality on the part of the judge, to promote public acceptance and credibility of our courts and the judicial system and most importantly, to guarantee that the search for truth will be conducted in a fair and dignified manner. Ultimately, if the judicial process operates successfully, the search for truth will become synonymous with the achievement of justice.

Because judges play such an important role in our legal system, it is necessary to examine how they are appointed and what conduct is expected of them during their tenure of office. Although the constitutional basis for the appointment of judges is discussed in Chapter 5 of this book, a brief review is set out below.

1. THE APPOINTMENT OF JUDGES

(a) Constitutional Basis

The relevant provisions of the Constitution Act of 1867 are set out below:

VII. JUDICATURE

96. The Governor General shall appoint the Judges of the Superior, District, and County Courts in each Province, except those of the Courts of Probate in Nova Scotia and New Brunswick.

97. Until the Laws relative to Property and Civil Rights in Ontario, Nova Scotia, and New Brunswick, and the Procedure of the Courts in those Provinces, are made uniform, the Judges of the Courts of those Provinces appointed by the Governor General shall be selected from the respective Bars of those Provinces.

98. The Judges of the Courts of Quebec shall be selected from the Bar of that Province.

99. (1) Subject to subsection (2) of this section, the judges of the superior courts shall hold office during good behaviour, but shall be removable by the Governor General on address of the Senate and House of Commons.

(2) A judge of a superior court, whether appointed before or after the coming into force of this section, shall cease to hold office upon attaining the age of seventy-five years, or upon the coming into force of this section if at that time he has already attained that age.

100. The Salaries, Allowances, and Pensions of the Judges of the Superior, District and County Courts (except the Courts of Probate in Nova Scotia and New Brunswick), and of the Admiralty Courts in Cases where the Judges thereof are for the Time being paid by Salary, shall be fixed and provided by the Parliament of Canada.

101. The Parliament of Canada may, notwithstanding anything in this Act, from Time to Time provide for the Constitution, Maintenance, and Organization of a General Court of Appeal for Canada, and for the Establishment of any additional Courts for the better Administration of the Laws of Canada.

Exclusive Powers of Provincial Legislatures

92. . . .

4. The Establishment and Tenure of Provincial Offices and the Appointment and Payment of Provincial Officers.

14. The Administration of Justice in the Province, including the Constitution, Maintenance, and Organization of Provincial Courts, both of Civil and of Criminal Jurisdiction, and including Procedure in Civil Matters in those Courts.

It is important to realize that there is no provision in the Constitution Act of 1867 establishing a specific court in Canada. What the Constitution Act of 1867 does provide is as follows:

(i) Federal Courts and Tribunals

The Parliament of Canada is granted legislative competence to enact laws providing for the establishment of certain courts and tribunals under the provisions of s. 101 of the Constitution Act of 1867.

(ii) Provincial Courts and Tribunals

The various provincial legislatures are given authority to enact laws to provide for certain provincial courts and tribunals under the provisions of s. 92(14) of the Constitution Act of 1867. (This section must be read together with the exclusion of federal jurisdiction to do so in s. 91(27) of the Constitution Act of 1867.)

(iii) Provisions in the Constitution Act of 1867 Regarding the Appointment of Judges

There are three sets of provisions of the Constitution Act of 1867 regarding the appointment of judges. First, s. 101 gives Parliament the authority to enact laws establishing certain federal courts and tribunals and, by implication, also gives Parliament the authority to pass legislation respecting the appointment of judges for these courts, their salaries, tenure of office and removal from office. Secondly, ss. 96 to 100 provide for the appointment of the judges of the superior, district and county courts in each province, and their salaries and pensions. And thirdly, s. 92(14) of the Constitution Act of 1867 authorizes by implication the appointment of judges at the provincial level to serve on provincial courts established under that section.

Thus, in Canada, the judiciary presides over three types of courts:

(1) Federal courts constituted under federal legislation enacted pursuant to s. 101 of the Constitution Act of 1867, with federally appointed judges.

(2) Provincial courts constituted by provincial legislation enacted pursuant to s. 92(14) of the Constitution Act of 1867, with federally

appointed judges under the provisions of ss. 96 to 100 of the Constitution Act of 1867.

(3) Provincial courts constituted under provincial legislation enacted pursuant to s. 92(14) of the Constitution Act of 1867 with provincially appointed judges.

(b) The Process of Appointment

Essentially, there are eleven, not one, processes of appointment. First, there is the single federal process of appointment of justices to the Supreme Court of Canada, to courts of superior jurisdiction in the provinces, and to county and district courts in the provinces. In addition, each of the ten provinces has its own process of appointment of provincial judges to the provincial courts. As a result, there may be no uniformity in these processes.

The process of judicial appointment has always been surrounded with secrecy. This perpetuated the belief held by many that political considerations were paramount as factors in appointing judges. Many held (and indeed many still do hold) the view that to become a judge it is beneficial to have had a political affiliation with the party in power which is making the judicial appointment. This is, of course, impossible to ascertain with any certainty. However, owing to recent public disclosures at the federal level, there is good reason to believe that if there ever was a political component in the appointment process, that component has now substantially been removed. These disclosures are as follows. First, in February 1976, at a conference sponsored jointly by the Canadian Institute for the Administration of Justice and the Annual Lecture Series of Osgoode Hall Law School of York University, an address was made to the conference by a Special Assistant to the Minister of Justice of Canada. This address, for the first time, put on public record previously undisclosed details concerning the process of appointment.[43] Secondly, in a feature article appearing in the Toronto Star, dated 17th April 1976, similar disclosures were made as to the federal process of appointment (including, in addition, a discussion of the appointing process for provincially appointed judges in the province of Ontario). This article is set out, in part, as follows:

> Nearly every judge on the bench vividly remembers the day, while he was still practising law, that his secretary buzzed on his intercom to tell him the federal justice minister — or the provincial attorney-general — was calling him.
>
> Those first calls revolve around a single question: Would the lawyer accept appointments to, for example, the trial division of the Supreme Court? If he says yes, the minister thanks him and says he'll be in touch. He usually — but not always — will be.

---

[43]The proceedings of that conference were recently published in a treatise entitled *The Canadian Judiciary*, edited by Allen M. Linden (now Mr. Justice Linden) (Toronto: Osgoode Hall Law School, York University, 1976).

If the lawyer gets the second call, it will come any time from a week to a month later. This time, the minister tells him his appointment will be announced within a few days or, occasionally, within a few hours. He thanks the lawyer for agreeing to serve.

Lawyers sometimes turn down the opportunity in the first phone call. They are seldom asked again . . .

Picking the men and women to fill the vacancies involves a talent search that is both endless and increasingly meticulous.

The pressures that make it this way include the law's growing complexity, the relentless expansion of caseloads and the belief of governments that appointing the best people is really the only way to restore the public's shrunken respect for the courts. One result of all this is that the bench is rarely used any more as a reward for faithful political cronies of dubious ability.

Instead, the federal justice department — whose approach is roughly duplicated by the provinces — actively encourages lawyers, judges, members of Parliament, law school deans and private citizens to send in the names of lawyers they think would make good candidates.

Sometimes, a lawyer who wants to be a judge will ask his colleagues to write the minister and propose his name. During one month in mid-1975, former justice minister Otto Lang got 69 letters on behalf of one lawyer. (He still hasn't been appointed).

It used to be regarded as bad form to be openly eager for the job but Ottawa recently passed the word that there would be nothing wrong with a lawyer writing in to say he'd take the post if it was offered.

Every name seriously put forward is checked. Lawyers and judges across the nation are growing accustomed to phone calls from the Ottawa office of Ed Ratushny, special ministerial adviser on judicial appointments, asking about an individual's integrity, temperament, personal and work habits, professional competence and ability to get along with other people.

Says Ratushny: "Assurances are given in relation to the absolute confidentiality of any comments which are made. Indeed, the comments, which are taken down by hand, are given to the minister in exactly the same form. They are not dictated or transcribed and no one other than the minister has access to them.

"If specific problems are suggested, more detailed inquiries are made to determine whether they are confirmed or prove not to be substantial."

The inquiries have to be exhaustive because the stated qualifications for selection are so general. About the only requirement for the provincial criminal bench is a law degree. The federal courts, however, are restricted to lawyers with at least 10 years in practice — which the government insists is the reason it hasn't picked more women, who began enrolling in law schools in large numbers only within the last five or six years.

Once candidates have been decided upon, the federal and provincial procedures differ.

Ottawa submits the names to the Canadian Bar Association's national judiciary committee, which assesses them as either "well qualified," "qualified" or "not qualified." Neither Justice Minister Ron Basford nor his predecessor, Otto Lang, appointed anyone turned down by the organized bar.

The Ontario attorney-general sends the name of his candidates to the Judicial Council, whose seven members include chief Justice George Gale of Ontario and Chief Justice Willard Estey of the Ontario Supreme Court's trial division. Only one nominee rejected by the council ever made it to the bench — and that was more than six years ago.

Where do the successful appointees come from? Most are lawyers in private practice. In the four years he was federal justice minister, John Turner named 111 judges. Two were promoted from one bench to the next. Eleven others included a law professor, crown attorneys, an official from his own department, a member of Parliament and a lawyer who worked for Canadian National Railways.

Otto Lang, Turner's successor, named 161 federal judges and all but 22 were lawyers in private practice. The average age of the newcomers under both ministries was 48, but several were in their mid-30s.

Until Turner's appointment to the justice portfolio in 1968, only two women had ever reached the federal bench in Canada. Turner added three; Lang, five, and Justice Minister Ron Basford so far has picked two more.

When all the checks and reports and votes are in — and favourable — the candidate gets the second phone call. Between his acceptance and his swearing-in, he must unload his law practice by finding colleagues willing to take on his unfinished cases. He must resign his company directorships and other business connections . . .

At their installations, federal judges "do solemnly and sincerely promise and swear that I will duly and faithfully, and to the best of my skill and knowledge, execute the powers and trust reposed in me . . . so help me God."[44]

Probably the most difficult question for the appointing authority is determining what qualifications should be sought in the potential judicial appointee. Anthony Lewis, a journalist, stated in an article appearing in the New York Times dated 20th October 1974 that "the character of any country's judges is one test of its civilization". In that article, entitled "What Makes a Good Judge", he compares the British and American methods of appointing judges. He makes reference to the American Bar Association's Committee on the Federal Judiciary and compares its function with that of the Lord Chancellor who chooses High Court judges in England from approximately 2,000 practising barristers. The writer indicates, having regard to the American model, that

in the last twenty years . . . [the American Bar Association Committee] has won for itself a weighty role in the scrutinizing of Federal judicial appointments. The conservative history of the A.B.A. raised some doubts about that role, but on the whole the committee has satisfied most observers that it takes a non-ideological view of nominees based on a not too narrowly professional judgment of their qualities. For example, the committee insists on trial experience for lawyers picked as trial judges. But it might give warm approval to the choice of a law teacher for the Court of Appeals, where his reflective qualities would be more appropriate.

Again, referring to the American experience, the journalist makes reference to "a visionary model" of what constitutes a good judge. In particular, he refers to the views of Judge Learned Hand. Specifically, he states as follows:

---

[44]For some earlier disclosures along similar lines see the remarks of Professor Ed Ratushny in "Le pouvoir judiciare en 1984" (1974), 5 Revue Générale De Droit 389, and the remarks of G.M. Stirling, Q.C., in "A Symposium on the Appointment, Discipline and Removal of Judges" (1973), 11 Alta. L. Rev. 279 at 285. See also an article by Columnist Geoffrey Stevens appearing in the Globe and Mail, 16th March 1974.

Learned Hand, who sat as a district judge and then for decades as a revered member of the Court of Appeals for the Second Circuit, made the most ringing statement of the large view that a judge ought to bring to interpreting the Constitution. He should, Judge Hand said "have at least a bowing acquaintance with Acton and Maitland, with Thucydides, Gibbon and Carlyle, with Homer, Dante, Shakespeare and Milton, and Machiavelli, Montaigne and Rabelais, with Plato, Bacon, Hume and Kant . . . For in such matters everything turns upon the spirit in which he approaches the questions before him. The words he must construe are empty vessels into which he can pour nearly anything he will. Men do not gather figs off thistles, nor supple institutions from judges whose outlook is limited by parish or class."

That glorious statement, visionary even as to Supreme Court appointments, has to be read against other realities so far as lower Federal courts are concerned. Their judges simply must have the technical training, the legal interest and experience to get through enormous volumes of often highly complicated work.

Generally speaking, most people would regard honesty, fairness, patience and intelligence as the types of qualities that a judge should have. Age is also an important consideration. The appointing authority must balance the advantages and disadvantages of appointing a judge at a young age. At the provincial court level for example, the advantage is that the judge is more attuned to the problems faced by younger persons who represent most of the individuals who appear before him; on the other hand, remaining on the same bench for a number of years until the age of retirement may have a stultifying effect. A second disadvantage of an early appointment is the relative lack of experience up to the date of appointment. It is interesting to note that at the joint meeting of the Canadian Institute for the Administration of Justice and the Annual Lecture Series of Osgoode Hall Law School of York University held in February of 1976, the Special Assistant to the Minister of Justice of Canada indicated that at least in respect of federal appointments, one of the primary attributes sought in a prospective judge is the ability to listen. Undoubtedly, such an attribute includes more than the mere ability to hear evidence, in addition, it includes the patience to hear an argument through to its end and the intellectual capability to understand the complexities of a given position.

Unfortunately, no matter how carefully the process of appointment is conducted there will be members of the judiciary who will conduct themselves in less than an acceptable manner. One of the most important, but difficult, issues for resolution by the appropriate authorities is whether a judge ought to be removed from office or impeached.

2. REMOVAL OF JUDGES

(a) Retirement

Federally appointed judges may remain in office until the age of retirement. That age, for judges serving on the Supreme Court of Canada and the Federal Court of Canada, is seventy-five years, pursuant to provisions contained, respectively, in the Supreme Court Act, R.S.C.

1970, c. S-19, and the Federal Court Act, R.S.C. 1970, c. 10 (2nd Supp.). For judges serving on courts of superior jurisdiction in the provinces, the age of compulsory retirement is seventy-five years, pursuant to s. 99(2) of the Constitution Act of 1867. Judges serving on the county or district court benches are compulsorily retired at the age of seventy years, pursuant to s. 26 of the Judges Act, R.S.C. 1970, c. J-1. Finally, judges serving on provincial court benches are compulsorily retired in accordance with the provisions contained in the enabling provincial statutes establishing those courts. Usually, these statutes provide for compulsory retirement at age seventy.

(b) Standards of "Good Behaviour"

Aside from mandatory retirement, the only other limitation on a judge's tenure of office is the requirement that he must conduct himself in such a manner as to constitute good behaviour. There is no test common to all courts as to what constitutes good behaviour and, therefore, it is necessary to consult the various enabling statutes. Judges of the Supreme Court of Canada and the Federal Court of Canada, pursuant to the provisions contained, respectively, in the Supreme Court Act and the Federal Court Act, hold office during "good behaviour". Judges serving on courts of superior jursidiction in the provinces, by virtue of the provision contained in s. 99(1) of the Constitution Act of 1867, also hold office during "good behaviour". This provision was derived from s. 7 of the Act of Settlement of 1701. Judges of the county or district courts, pursuant to the provision contained in s. 34 of the Judges Act, also hold office during "good behaviour".

In addition to the foregoing, reference should be made to ss. 39 to 43 of the Judges Act. These provisions,[45] enacted in 1971 created the Canadian Judicial Council. The function of the Council is set out in s. 39(2):

(2) The objects of the Council are to promote efficiency and uniformity, and to improve the quality of judicial service, in superior and county courts.

(2.1) In furtherance of its objects, the Council may

(a)   establish from time to time a conference of chief justices;
(b)   establish from time to time seminars for the continuing education of judges; and
(c)   subject to section 40, make the inquiries and the investigation of complaints or allegations described in that section.

More specifically, at the request of the Minister of Justice of Canada or the Attorney General of a province, the Council conducts inquiries, under the provisions contained in s. 40, to determine whether a judge of a superior, district or county court should be removed from office. Under s. 40, the Council may recommend to the Minister of Justice of

---

[45]1970-71-72 (Can.), c. 55, s. 11, amended by 1974-75-76 (Can.), c. 48, s. 17, and by 1976-77 (Can.), c. 25, s. 15.

Canada that a judge should be removed from office. The particular grounds to support such a recommendation are set out in s. 41(2) of the Act:

(2) Where, in the opinion of the Council, the judge in respect of whom an inquiry or investigation has been made, has become incapacitated or disabled from the due execution of his office by reason of

    (a)   age or infirmity,
    (b)   having been guilty of misconduct,
    (c)   having failed in the due execution of his office, or
    (d)   having been placed, by his conduct or otherwise, in a position incompatible with the due execution of his office,

the Council, in its report to the Minister of Justice of Canada under subsection (1), may recommend that the judge be removed from office and that he cease to be paid any further salary.

The effect of this amendment to the Judges Act is to provide some scope or definition as to what constitutes "good behaviour". The provisions of s. 41(2) are probably not exhaustive in delimiting the bounds of what does not constitute "good behaviour", but they do provide at least some guidelines in applying this broadly worded standard. (Other grounds might include incompetence and non-judicial misbehaviour.) Moreover, the provisions of ss. 39 to 43 provide a mechanism for determining whether removal from office is warranted. Together, these provisions add greater precision to the removal procedure of federally appointed judges in Canada.

Finally, the standard of conduct expected of judges serving on provincial court benches is set out in the various provincial enabling statutes. In addition, a mechanism has been established in most provinces providing for an investigation, hearing, and other procedures before a removal is effected. It will therefore be necessary for the reader to refer to the various provincial enabling statutes in order to ascertain the specific details of the removal procedure in a given province. Consider, for example, the following commentary reported in the Globe and Mail, 26th February 1977:

The Ontario Judicial Council is hindered in its task of hearing complaints against provincial judges because it is not empowered to discipline a jurist, Attorney-General Roy McMurtry said yesterday.

The council, made up of Ontario's four senior jurists and the treasurer of the Law Society of Upper Canada, was created by the Provincial Courts Act in 1968. Under the statute, its proceedings are secret.

Mr. McMurtry said if plans proceed to reorganize the administration of the courts, the council would receive the disciplinary powers. Reorganization plans set out by Mr. McMurtry in a draft document last fall would transfer formal control of the courts from his ministry to the judicial council.

Under the existing setup, the council meets once a month to hear complaints against judges. Although it does not impose discipline, it can recommend action to the Attorney-General.

For a further discussion of proposed reform of the Ontario Council see the Globe and Mail, 30th December 1976.[46] Also, for a description of the British Columbia Judicial Council see the Globe and Mail, 31st December 1976.[47]

In determining what constitutes "good behaviour" during which a judge may serve in office, it is interesting to note at the outset that no superior court judge in Canada has ever been removed under the provision contained in s. 99 of the Constitution Act of 1867. However, there have been four attempts at removal:

(1) 1868 — petition for removal of Mr. Justice Aime Lafontaine of the Quebec Superior Court. A select committee reported on the matter, but the report was not printed.

(2) 1874 — petition against Mr. Justice T.J.L. Loranger of the Supreme Court of Quebec. The matter went to a select committee in 1877 and after the inquiry, no further action was taken.

(3) 1874 — petition against Chief Justice E.B. Wood of Manitoba. There was a motion for appointment of a select committee, but before any action was taken, the Chief Justice died.

(4) 1966-67 — inquiry into the conduct of Mr. Justice Leo Landreville of the Supreme Court of Ontario by a Royal Commission consisting of Mr. Justice Ivan C. Rand, formerly of the Supreme Court of Canada. After considering the Rand report a joint committee recommended removal. However Mr. Justice Landreville resigned while Parliament was preparing for his removal by joint address.

County court judges, who also hold office during "good behaviour", are also removable for "misbehaviour, or for incapacity or inability to perform [their] duties properly by reason of age or infirmity". Pursuant to these provisions, four county court judges have been removed:

(1) 1915 — His Honour Judge C.R. Fitch of the District Court of Rainy River, Ontario.

---

[46]See Greene, "Judicial Independence and Professional Autonomy: A Discussion of Two Rationales for Judicial Involvement in Court Administration", a paper prepared for the Annual Meeting of the Canadian Political Science Association in Ottawa, June 9, 1982; and, McCormick, "Judicial Councils for Provincial Judges in Canada: A Survey of the Experience of the Five Western Provinces", a paper delivered for the Annual Meeting of the Canadian Political Science Association in Montreal, June 1980.

[47]Recently, a B.C. Provincial Court Judge was suspended after soliciting a prostitute but was reinstated after a period of convalescence in connection with a related alcohol abuse problem. See the Edmonton Journal, 11th November 1978. On the question of secrecy and the impeachment process, see the Edmonton Journal, 8th, 9th and 10th January 1981.

(2) 1928 — His Honour Judge H.F. Maulson of the County Court of the Northern Judicial District of Manitoba.[48]

(3) 1933 — His Honour Judge Lewis St. George Stubbs, Senior Judge of the County Court of the Eastern District of Manitoba. Judge Stubbs was removed for criticizing the actions of superior court judges, for publishing a pamphlet criticizing officers of the Crown, and for addressing an accused with defamatory language.

(4) 1933 — His Honour Judge L.H. Martell was removed for issuing dishonoured cheques and for drunkenness.

The review machinery of the Canadian Judicial Council was put into operation for the first time in respect of His Honour Judge William A. Sheppard, an Ontario County Court Judge. The judge was found in contempt of court for disobeying an order made in the course of a matrimonial dispute with his former wife. However, before the Canadian Judicial Council met to consider this matter, he resigned: see the Toronto Star, 11th December 1976, and the Globe and Mail, 29th January 1977.

Provincially, two Ontario magistrates were subject to removal for misbehaviour. In the first case, Magistrate Frederick Bannon was found guilty of such gross misbehaviour as to make himself totally unfit for his office. This finding arose out of an inquiry held by Mr. Justice Campbell Grant, a commissioner appointed for that purpose. Magistrate Bannon had discussed, with a criminal, cases pending before him, and aided the criminal by giving him information as to bail matters and as to which judges should try certain cases. The criminal then sold this information. Although the judge knew of the criminal's whereabouts when a warrant was out for his arrest he did not report it. He dealt with him in real estate and fraudulently obtained money for the criminal. Magistrate Bannon, however, resigned before the investigation took place.

In the second case, Judge Lucien Kurata was found unfit for office in an inquiry held by Mr. Justice Donald Keith for attempting to solicit sexual gratification from a prostitute scheduled to appear before him and from a policewoman whom he believed to be a prostitute awaiting trial, and for falsely testifying as to these incidents.

The most recent case involves Ottawa Judge Harry Williams, who had invited a prostitute from an escort agency to visit him in his chambers.

---

[48]The first two removals were brought to the author's attention by Chief Judge Alan R. Philp (as he then was) of the Manitoba County Court. Chief Judge Philp (now Mr. Justice Philp of the Manitoba Court of Appeal) prepared a paper entitled "Judicial Conduct: Independence and Integrity — Discipline and Removal", for the County and District Court Annual Seminar sponsored by the Canadian Judicial Council, 1977, and revised in 1978. His assistance is greatly appreciated. See also the Research Project prepared by Kowalishin, "The Removal of Federally-Appointed Judges in Canada", C.I.A.J., 1975.

One of the key issues in this case was whether the hearing ordered by the Ontario Judicial Council and conducted by Mr. Justice Sydney Robins should be held in private or in public. Mr. Justice Robins recommended Judge Williams' removal from office, and this was effected by Act of the Ontario Legislature.[49]

Often, a judge will resign from office in anticipation of the invocation of the impeachment process. This occurred recently in Alberta with respect to a District Court Judge who suffered from kleptomania, in Ontario with respect to a County Court Judge for reasons not publicly advanced, and in British Columbia with respect to two superior court justices, one convicted for a second time of impaired driving,[50] and the other allegedly involved in a morals impropriety.

On occasion, the impeachment process is begun but does not lead to removal. The most dramatic recent example of this is the Canadian Judicial Council's investigation of Mr. Justice Thomas Berger prompted by certain remarks that he made relating to the political events surrounding the "patriation" of the "new" constitution. The Council concluded that the public expression of political views in the nature of those made by Mr. Justice Berger constituted an "indiscretion", but that they were not a "basis for a recommendation that he be removed from office". On the basis of this recommendation, no further action was taken.[51]

However, several months later, Mr. Justice Berger somewhat surprisingly tendered his resignation as a judge. Consider the following account of his resignation as reported in the Globe and Mail, 29th April 1983.

> Thomas Berger has resigned as a judge of the B.C. Supreme Court because of a disagreement with Bora Laskin, Chief Justice of the Supreme Court of Canada, over whether judges should ever speak out on political issues.
>
> Announcing he will leave the bench on August 27, Mr. Justice Berger said he could not accept the recent ruling by the Canadian Judicial Council and the Chief Justice that it was improper for judges to speak out on political issues or on their work on royal commissions.
>
> Judge Berger said he agrees that judges should not discuss their inquiries into alleged wrongful acts, but he said there are rare occasions when members of the bench should speak out on matters of public interest.
>
> Judge Berger was faulted by a fellow judge and excoriated by Prime Minister Pierre Trudeau last year for criticizing the constitutional accord reached in November, 1981,

---

[49]See Government of Ontario, *Report of the Commission of Inquiry into the Conduct of Provincial Judge Harry J. Williams* (1978). This report also appears in (1978), 12 L.S.U.C. Gazette 161. See also the Globe and Mail, 16th December 1977.

[50]See the Edmonton Journal, 12th May 1981.

[51]See the Globe and Mail, 4th September 1982, and the Edmonton Journal, 3rd September 1982. See also the C.B.A. National, May, 1983. A somewhat similar issue recently arose in respect of a Chief Justice who, while a Judge but prior to being appointed a Chief Justice, signed an anti-abortion petition which was subsequently published. See the Edmonton Journal, 17th May 1983.

by nine premiers and the Federal Government. In speeches and in an article published by the Globe and Mail, the B.C. Judge had condemned the absence from the new Constitution and Charter of Rights of native rights guarantees and a veto for Quebec.

The council, composed of the country's 27 Chief Justices, said last June that Judge Berger's comments had been indiscreet. Many interpreted the ruling, the first of its kind in Canadian history, as a reprimand.

Chief Justice Laskin, head of the council, reinforced the ruling when he said in a rare public speech last September that judges do not have the right to speak out on political issues. He said judges must not only be impartial but must appear to be impartial.

"A judge has no freedom of speech to address political issues which have nothing to do with his judicial duty", the Chief Justice said.

In an obvious reference to the incident involving Judge Berger, he said that any judge who feels so strongly that he must speak out "is best advised to resign from the bench."

In his letter of resignation this week to federal Justice Minister Mark MacGuigan, Judge Berger said: "On rare occasions a judge may have an obligation to speak out on human rights and fundamental freedoms . . . this is in keeping with Canadian experience . . .

"I have conducted three royal commissions while on the bench. This is work in which Canadian judges have been engaged since Confederation. Chief Justice Laskin, in his speech to the Canadian Bar Association, . . . deprecated judges undertaking such tasks.

"Furthermore, he and the council take the view that, once the work of the commission is completed, a judge may not discuss its work in public.

"This is a sound rule in relation to inquiries into alleged wrongful acts. But . . . I and others (such as Mr. Justice Emmett Hall) have felt at liberty to discuss the work of our commissions, not in a partisan way but as a means of informing the bar, university audiences, and others about matters of public interest.

"I do not think that my concept of judge as public servant . . . entails any erosion of public confidence in the independence of the judiciary."

Consider also the reaction of key officials and others, as also reported in the Globe and Mail, of the same date:

Justice Minister Mark MacGuigan said yesterday he has no qualms about accepting the resignation of Mr. Justice Thomas Berger of the B.C. Supreme Court . . .

"In the light of the new Charter of Rights and Freedoms, I think it's especially important judges recognize (it is) much more important than ever before to avoid engaging themselves in controversial subjects which may well come before them on the bench," the minister said.

Mr. MacGuigan also said he was unhappy that Judge Berger made public his letter of resignation now although he plans to remain a judge until August 27. "This could engender a further controversy around a sitting judge."

Earlier, a leading human rights lawyer said the Government should refuse to accept the resignation of Judge Berger until there has been more debate on the propriety of judges speaking out on public issues.

"I would like to see Justice Minister MacGuigan request Mr. Justice Berger to defer that resignation until such time as there can be a parliamentary and public determination of what ought to be the ground rules for judges," Alan Borovoy, general counsel for the Canadian Civil Liberties Association, said in a telephone interview from Toronto.

Mr. Borovoy said he favors allowing judges, in certain circumstances, to speak out on public issues. The matter is so important and fundamental to society that Parliament and the public at large should help determine the rules for judges, rather than leave it to the Canadian Judicial Council, he said.

Conservate Senator Jacques Flynn, a former federal justice minister, said yesterday that judges should, on occasion, feel free to speak out on public issues, provided they are not being asked to render decisions on those questions.

Senator Flynn, now Opposition leader in the Senate, said that on a matter as important as the Constitution "as long as a judge doesn't have to render a judgment on a particular question . . . it seems to me that he would be entitled to comment.

". . . in this particular case, I would not have considered it out of place for a judge to express something like that" . . .

Much has been written concerning Mr. Justice Berger's colourful career, including the controversial review of his judicial status by the Canadian Judicial Council and his subsequent resignation. In respect of the latter, see, for example, the editorial reactions of the Globe and Mail (29th April 1983) and the Edmonton Journal (30th April 1983).

It was suggested by R. MacGregor Dawson in his treatise *The Government of Canada* that "good behaviour" includes all but "deliberate wrong-doing". He further suggests that "a judge may be stupid", often in error on the law, lazy and neglectful and somewhat biased, without threat of removal. He suggests that "bribery, gross partiality and criminal proclivities" are the only examples of misbehaviour. Nonetheless, the standards required of good behaviour seem to have been raised with the Landreville affair. Mr. Justice Landreville was found to be unfit for office in that:

(1) He failed to remove suspicion of impropriety in receiving 7,500 shares of stock without consideration;

(2) He showed gross contempt before the Securities Commission of Ontario in giving evidence; and

(3) He failed to show his innocence surrounding the dealing of a franchise to supply natural gas to Sudbury.

It is important to note that the transaction took place before Mr. Justice Landreville was appointed to the bench and that it was recognized that Mr. Justice Landreville's conduct in exercising his judicial duties did not constitute misbehaviour. Mr. Justice Rand suggests that the test to be applied in considering a judge's behaviour is as follows:

Would the conduct, fairly determined in the light of all circumstances, lead such persons to attribute such a defect of moral character that the discharge of the duties of the office thereafter would be suspect? Has it destroyed unquestioning confidence of uprightness, of moral integrity, of honesty in decision, the elements of public honour?[52]

Mr. Justice Rand also suggests other conduct which would not constitute good behaviour:

---

[52]Commission of Inquiry into the dealings of the Honourable Mr. Justice Leo A. Landreville with Northern Ontario Gas Limited, 1966. The Federal Court of Canada (Trial Division) a decade later criticized the proceedings of this Royal Commission. See *Landreville v. R.*, [1977] 2 F.C. 726, 75 D.L.R. (3d) 380. See also the Globe and Mail report on this decision, 12th April 1977.

Persistent neglect of duty, persistent incapacity arising from drink or similar causes, deliberate refusal to accept and apply unquestioned rules of law to the detriment of suitors; following a life of profligacy . . .[53]

Lastly, in order to better understand what constitutes "good behaviour", consider the following summary of cases of removal for reason of misbehaviour. These cases all arose in various non-Canadian jurisdictions.

English and Welsh

Many of the following cases are set out in Henry Cecil, *Tipping the Scales*, Hutchinson & Co., London, 1964, and Andrew Dewar Gibb, *Judicial Corruption in the U.K.*, W. Green & Son, Edinborough, 1957.

1. Two Lord Chancellors have been impeached:
   1620 — Lord Bacon, for accepting gifts from suitors.
   1725 — Lord Macclesfield, for appointing people to the office of Chancery Master in exchange for money, knowing such money came from suitors' funds paid into court.

2. 1865 — Lord Chancellor Westbury was investigated on charges of arranging the resignations of two legal officials so he could substitute his relatives. He subsequently resigned.

   After the enactment of the Act of Settlement of 1701 providing for security of tenure only during good behaviour, complaints have been made to Parliament against seventeen high court judges. Of these, nine were English, one was Welsh and seven were Irish.

3. 1721 — Baron Page, for alleged bribery of electors. This attempt at impeachment was narrowly defeated.

4. 1813, 1816 — Lord Ellenborough, for, on a first charge, writing down evidence not fair to the accused. It was held that this was not a ground for impeachment as it was not done deliberately. A second charge, for alleged "partiality, misrepresentation, injustice and oppression" was held to be not founded. During the trial it was often said there had to be not only evidence of misconduct but also evidence of a corrupt mind or improper motive. Moreover, the tendering of a personal opinion to a jury as to the guilt or innocence of an accused is not misconduct.

5. 1821 — Mr. Justice Best, for fining a man five times during the course of the trial. It was held not to be misconduct and was justified to stop blasphemy in court.

6. 1825-1826 — Mr. Kenrick (Welsh), on a first charge, for allegedly trying to have someone prosecuted for theft so the accused would forfeit his house and Mr. Kenrick could then buy it. It was held that

---

[53]*Ibid.*

the allegation was not proved, but it was also held that a judge's private conduct could provide grounds for removal. On a second charge, for refusing to grant a search warrant but issuing a note instead. He later demanded that the note be given back and had it forcibly taken. For this he was liable for damages. However, while such conduct was held to be discreditable it was not serious enough to require removal. It was also held that being obstinate and irritable is not enough for removal. In this case, the judge eventually resigned.

7. 1843 — Lord Abinger, for using the bench for purposes of making political speeches. The motion for removal was defeated as there was no evidence of badness of heart or corrupt intent.

8. 1867 — Lord Chief Baron Kelly, for allegedly pledging the truth of a statement for purposes of deceiving a committee. It was held to be completely unfounded.

9. 1906 — Mr. Justice Grantham, for allegedly deciding two identical cases in completely opposite ways for political reasons. In this case, it was held that there must be some moral defect. Although the judge's behaviour was discreditable, his conduct was not sufficient for removal.

10. 1924 — Mr. Justice McCardie, for speaking in court against the government's action on a particular issue. It was held that although judges should not speak on political matters, this conduct was not a moral delinquency justifying removal.

Irish

1. 1830 — Sir Jonah Barrington was removed for using court money for his own purposes.

2. Mr. Justice Fox resigned after he had called members of the jury names because he disagreed with their verdict.

3. Mr. Justice Johnson was found guilty of libelling high-ranking officials and he subsequently resigned.

General

1. It is recognized that, at common law, an office held during good behaviour could be forfeited for: (a) misconduct in office; (b) neglect of duties; (c) the acceptance of an incompatible office; or (d) conviction for a serious crime. (See B. Shartel, "Federal Judges — Appointment, Supervision and Removal" (1929-30), 28 Mic. L. Rev. 870 at 901.)

2. (a) It is the opinion of some that misbehaviour does not include incapacity or incompetence. (See Webster, *The Judiciary: The Report*

of a Justice Sub-Committee, Stevens & Sons, London, 1972, pp. 58-59, and Shartel, *supra*, at p. 904.)

(b)   Others believe incapacity by reason of health is misbehaviour. (See Cecil, *Tipping the Scales, supra*, at p. 144.)

3. To constitute misbehaviour, it appears there must be some element of moral blame which almost seems to be in the nature of a mens rea requirement (see Cecil, *Tipping the Scales, supra*, at p. 144).

United States

Generally, an analysis of the term "good behaviour" based on United States[54] authorities is not particularly helpful in understanding the term as it is used in Canada. The United States constitutional position is such that its federal judges hold office during good behaviour but are impeachable for treason, bribery, and other high crimes and misdemeanours. This has led some to believe that misbehaviour must be in the nature of treason, bribery, and other high crimes and misdemeanours. (See, for example, Preble Stolz, "Disciplining Federal Judges: Is Impeachment Hopeless?" (1969), 57 Cal. L.R. 659 at 663.) However, others have recognized certain distinctions in defining misbehaviour. For example, one suggestion is that misbehaviour includes insanity, disability (including senility), alcoholism, ignorance, sustained neglect of duty and conduct less serious than high crimes and misdemeanours. (See, for example, Raoul Berger, "Impeachment of Judges and Good Behaviour Tenure" (1970), 79 Yale L.J. 1475 at 1529.) Similarly, it is conceded that less than good behaviour could include misconduct off the bench although not amounting to the commission of a crime. (See P. Kurland, "The Appointment and Disappointment of Supreme Court Justices", [1972] Law and the Social Order 183 at 228.)[55]

On balance, however, it appears to be the general consensus that, as the term is used in the United States Constitution, it must amount to "misconduct in judicial capacity or abusing judicial power". (See, for example, Kurland, at p. 228, and John D. Feerick, "Impeaching Federal

---

[54]For a further discussion of the American judiciary, see, for example, Newsweek Magazine, 12th February 1979, 25th June 1979, 15th June 1981, and 19th April 1982; Time Magazine, 11th December 1978, 22nd January 1979, the cover story of 20th August 1979, 5th May 1980 and 21st December 1981; U.S. News & World Report, 4th and 18th June 1979, 5th November 1979, 22nd December 1980, and 19th January 1981; Maclean's Magazine, 15th January 1979; and the New York Times 15th May 1980, 10th August 1980, 27th July 1979, 7th May 1978, 26th November 1978, 5th May 1979 and 22nd April 1979. For some instances of judicial misfeasances in the U.S., see the Edmonton Sun, 12th June 1980, 29th January 1981, 3rd June 1980, and 12th May 1982. And for some "unbelievable" advice for U.S. judges, see the Edmonton Journal, 30th December 1980.

[55]See Stolz, *Judging Judges: The Investigation of Rose Bind and the California Supreme Court* (New York: The Free Press, 1981).

Judges: A Study of the Constitutional Provisions'' (1970-71), 39 Fordham L.R. 1 at 57.)

The process of impeachment and removal in the United States involves, essentially, two steps. First, the judge must be charged and impeached by simple majority before the House of Representatives. Then he is tried before the Senate, and if convicted by a two-thirds vote of the members of Senate, he is removed from office. This is not altogether dissimilar from the Canadian requirement for the removal of federally appointed judges by joint address of the House of Commons and the Senate.

Since 1796, fifty-five federal judges have been charged before the House of Representatives. Of these thirty-three were charged with "treason, bribery or other high crimes and misdemeanours". Of the fifty-five only four were found guilty and removed by the Senate. However, during the course of the proceedings, twenty-two resigned.

The grounds for the removal of the four convicted judges are as follows:

(1) Blasphemy and drunkenness (Pickering — 1803).

(2) Treason for joining the Confederacy (Humphreys — 1862).

(3) Accepting bribes (Archibald — 1912).

(4) Accepting bribes, kickbacks, income tax evasion (Ritter — 1936).

In addition, four other judges were impeached but were acquitted by the Senate. The grounds upon which these judges were impeached are set out as follows:

(1) Being "tyrannical, overbearing and oppressive" (Chase — 1804).

(2) Abuse of contempt power (Peck — 1831).

(3) Defrauding the government and bribery (Swayne — 1904).

(4) Being influenced in judicial appointments (Louderbach — 1932).

Subsequent to the impeachment of Pickering in 1803, it is interesting to note that drunkenness alone has been considered as insufficient to justify removal. In addition, misconduct in court, such as being rude, tyrannical, and irritable, which does not amount to the commission of a crime, is not impeachable conduct. Nor may a judge's decisions be grounds for removal.

On only two occasions has a judge been charged in connection with private activities:

(1) Accepting a job as commissioner of major league baseball (Landis — 1921). In this case, the House refused to even report on the matter.

(2) Alleged conflict of interest by reason of writing publicly on political subjects (Douglas — 1970). It was held that there was no evidence to support this charge.

Finally, other charges have included treason, bribery and financial irregularity, favouritism, practising law while on the bench, and appointing unqualified trustees and receivers.

(c) Conclusions

A student of the judiciary in Canada must be aware of some serious concerns.[56] It can be argued that the standard of "good behaviour" required of judges before the removal provisions become operative is not particularly stringent. That is, it takes a very dramatic malfeasance before the removal provisions are brought into force. Perhaps the removal provisions ought to be tightened, and indeed they were, to some extent, by the 1971 amendment to the Judges Act. Alternatively, one might argue that, owing to the Canadian experience to date and the dictates of tradition, the present system is quite satisfactory.

Although a judge must retire at age seventy-five, he may be quite capable of adjudicating beyond that age. By forced retirement his expertise and experience are lost. On the other hand it is possibly not too uncommon for some judges who become sick and infirm before the age of retirement to insist on maintaining their position.[57]

This, however, has probably been remedied, in respect of federally appointed judges, by the 1971 amendment to the Judges Act, discussed in some detail earlier. In addition, similar provisions are contained in provincial enabling statutes in respect of provincially appointed judges.

3. INDEPENDENCE OF THE JUDICIARY

The effect of such removal provisions is to provide the judiciary with security of tenure, and this in turn is directed at achieving an independent judiciary. In addition, there are special statutory constraints imposed on judges during their tenure of office (and, to a lesser extent, after their tenure of office) setting them apart from the average citizen or the average lawyer. These constraints have been established, essentially, for two purposes. The first is to ensure and provide for a special integrity on the part of the judiciary as an institution in society. The second is to bolster this integrity by providing for judicial independence, which is vital to the impartial and objective role that a judge must play. The

---

[56]For a somewhat critical evaluation of the Canadian judiciary, see Martin, "Criticising the Judges" (1982), 28 McGill L.J. 1.

[57]See, for example, the case of a senile judge who was suspended by the California Commission on Judicial Performance, reported in Newsweek Magazine, 24th January 1977. See also a report in the New York Times, 28th November 1976.

judiciary must function as an independent arm of the body politic. While it is true that judges are appointed by politicians and are removable by politicians, the removal is intentionally made difficult so that a judge can objectively decide cases without fear of government retribution. Security of tenure is vital to the effective operation of the judiciary, particularly in respect of those cases in which government is either directly or indirectly concerned.

One corollary of the foregoing is that a judge, in deciding a case, should not be influenced by external sources. Indeed, a judge should not even be approached by an external source in connection with a case that he must decide. This rather fundamental principle was brought into the public eye early in 1976 in the so-called "judges affair", wherein a federal cabinet minister was alleged to have criticized a decision of a court conducting a trial under the Combines Investigation Act, R.S.C. 1970, c. C-23. In particular, the cabinet minister said "I find this judgment completely unacceptable. I think it is a silly decision. I just cannot understand how a judge who is sane could give such a verdict. It is a complete shock and I find it a complete disgrace." As a result of these remarks, the cabinet minister was subsequently convicted of contempt and required to issue a "full, complete, and unreserved apology" to the court, serve a three-month probationary period, and pay costs of $500. On appeal, the requirement for an apology was dispensed with, the probationary period was annulled and the $500 in costs was converted to a $500 fine. In the course of these events, a second cabinet minister interceded on behalf of the cabinet minister convicted of contempt by telephoning the judge before whom the contempt citation was to be heard and making representations on behalf of the minister charged. This so-called "judges affair", created a substantial amount of public furor, including demands that the particular cabinet minister involved resign. It represents a recent instance where political intrusion upon an independent judiciary was not tolerated.[58] Whether the political imposition on the judiciary accomplished anything or even to what extent it constituted an imposition was irrelevant. The public debate reflected the notion that even the appearance of an imposition is contrary to the notion of an independent judiciary and is not permissible.

The independence of the judiciary is more than an ideal to be strived for, and it is more than merely a concept derived from history and

---

[58]A similar situation arose in 1980 in British Columbia. For a full account, see the Vancouver Sun, 20th March 1980. Another example involves a federal cabinet minister phoning a provincial court judge on behalf of a man about to be sentenced by that judge. See the Edmonton Journal, 9th September 1978, and the Globe and Mail, 8th September 1979. In yet another example, an Ontario cabinet minister phoned an assistant crown attorney on behalf of a constituent. See the Globe and Mail, 9th November 1978, 9th and 16th December 1978; the Toronto Star, 10th September 1978; and the Edmonton Journal, 11th and 13th September 1978.

tradition. The independence of the judiciary has a technical meaning defined in terms of the security of tenure provided for judges and the special constraints imposed upon judges. Constitutionally, our political system is based upon three branches of government — executive, legislative and judicial. Unlike the United States, there is some overlap in the executive and legislative branches of government in Canada; nonetheless, there is a rigid demarcation between the judicial and other branches of government. One could argue that, however, even this is not so since judges are appointed by the executive branch of government and are removable, at least in respect of federally appointed judges, by a joint address of the two federal legislative bodies. Furthermore, the governing statutes constituting the various courts are, of course, enacted by the legislative branch.

Recently, some four Ontario Provincial Court Judges held, in four separate cases, that they had no jurisdiction to hear cases for reason that they lacked independence. The Canadian Charter of Rights and Freedoms provides in s. 11:

Any person charged with an offence has the right . . .

(d) to be presumed innocent until proven guilty according to law in a fair and public hearing by an independent and impartial tribunal . . .

Essentially, the argument advanced was that since a provincial court judge is appointed, paid, pensioned etc. by the Attorney General of a province and since in criminal cases one of the parties to a prosecution, the Crown Prosecutor, is also appointed, paid, pensioned etc. by the same Attorney General of the province, then it follows that the judge lacks independence. This argument was accepted by four provincial judges in the so-called "judges' revolt". On appeal to the Ontario Court of Appeal a panel of five judges rejected the argument. The case, however, as of the date of publication, is on appeal to the Supreme Court of Canada.

As an aside, it is interesting to note that this is the same section of the Charter that is being used to advance some of the arguments in favour of the open court. While the media has recently advanced similar arguments under s. 2(b) of the Charter in connection with "freedom of the press", accused persons, particularly juveniles, have argued that s. 11(d) protects their right to an open hearing, without the attendant fetters on publication of the proceedings. In any event, returning to the issue of judicial independence and s. 11(d) of the Charter, the matter presumably will ultimately be decided by the highest court of the land. For a further description of this so-called "judges' revolt" in Ontario, see the Canadian Lawyer, April 1983.

Much has been written and said about the independence of the judiciary. Consider, for example, the following from Professor R. MacGregor

Dawson's classic treatise on Canadian political science entitled *The Government of Canada* concerning the independence of the judiciary:

> The judge must be made independent of most of the restraints, checks, and punishments which are usually called into play against other public officials. He is thus protected against the operation of some of the most potent weapons which a democracy has at its command: he received almost complete protection against criticism; he is given civil and criminal immunity for acts committed in the discharge of his duties; he cannot be removed from office for any ordinary offence, but only for misbehaviour of a flagrant kind; and he can never be removed simply because his decisions happen to be disliked by the Cabinet, the Parliament, or the people. Such independence is unquestionably dangerous, and if this freedom and power were indiscriminately granted the results would certainly prove to be disastrous. The desired protection is found by picking with especial care the men who are to be entrusted with these responsibilities, and then paradoxically heaping more privileges upon them to stimulate their sense of moral responsibility which has been removed. The judge is placed in a position where he had nothing to lose by doing what is right and little to gain by doing what is wrong; and there is therefore every reason to hope that his best efforts will be devoted to the conscientious performance of his duty.

> The judge will thus usually begin with the twin assets of character and ability, and these become the foundation on which the indirect appeals are based. He is paid a substantial salary, which not only removes some of the obvious temptations, but frees him from financial distractions. The importance of his office is continually stressed; his own rectitude and sense of fairness are invariably assumed; the dignity of the court and the respect accorded his office are rarely, if ever, challenged; his social position is always assured. These efforts to accentuate the eminence of the office are made infinitely more effective by the fortunate habit which the legal profession has for the judiciary and its ingrained habit of regarding a seat on the Bench as the crown of a legal career. Thus some of the very men who build up the tradition may be induced to accept judgeships a few years later, influenced to a material degree by the tradition which they themselves have helped to create. Not the least important result of this prestige is its effect on the public, who have come to accept it — and with some justification — at its face value, and who see in judicial independence a greater promise of justice than could be obtained through the application of ordinary political sanctions.[59]

Consider also the following extract taken from a classic article on the independence of the judiciary written by Professor W. R. Lederman of Queen's University, a noted Canadian constitutional scholar. The author traces the historical basis of the independent judiciary, discusses the relevant sections of the Constitution Act of 1867 (ss. 96 to 101) and then concludes as follows:

> But, it may be asked, how is it that all these fine results follow from the conditions of judicial independence studied in this article? Many of these conditions are negative ones, making the judge irresponsible, or non-accountable, in office and preventing his removal except in the most extreme circumstances. As Dr. R. MacGregor Dawson shows [in the above extract], the answer is that the conditions of judicial independence, negative though most of them are, will stimulate any person of moral integrity to do his best. Given learning and ability as well as a conscience, this will be a very effective best. Political irresponsibility in these circumstances generates moral responsibility and conscientious effort. And thus, if care has been taken with the appointment in the first place, the conditions of judicial independence will justify themselves . . .

---

[59]2nd ed. (Toronto: University of Toronto Press, 1954).

It is quite clear then that the success of our system of judicial independence rests upon the appointment of well-qualified persons to judicial office, and the question of how best to ensure this arises. The writer considers that responsibility and power in this respect should remain with the federal Cabinet, in particular with the Prime Minister and the Minister of Justice. They must answer eventually to the national Parliament for the quality of judicial appointments, and this is the proper constitutional reflection of the vital interest all citizens have in the proper administration of justice. No doubt official or voluntary association of the legal profession may play a valuable advisory role at times, but the real power of appointment should rest where it is now, at the highest level of political responsibility. Nevertheless, the professional contribution is a vital one, the impartiality and effectiveness of judges depending in important measure on the education, traditions, experience and autonomy of the legal profession from which they are drawn. Hence the main contribution that lawyers as a whole can make to the quality of the bench is to be true to their own standards as members of a learned profession.[60]

Readers who wish to engage in further study of this vital topic may consult the bibliography of materials set out at the end of this chapter. We will now turn our attention to those special constraints imposed upon judges in order to promote and advance the integrity of the judiciary as a vital institution in society and to ensure the preservation of the concept of the independence of the judiciary.

(a) Special Standards in Public and Private Life

When a lawyer becomes a judge his whole world, that is, both his public and private life, changes. In public, he must always exercise the requisite dignity and decorum commensurate with his office. Nowhere is it written that a judge cannot write a letter to the editor of a newspaper taking a position in a political controversy. However, tradition dictates that this shall not be done. There are many other instances where tradition has imposed constraints on the public and private conduct of judges. These traditions, which are really no more than conventions of judicial behaviour, also dictate, to some extent, for example, how a judge spends his recreational hours, or where a judge eats. But perhaps, more accurately, these conventions dictate how a judge should not spend his recreational hours and what establishments he should not enter. Judges must exercise restraint in language and must never consume excessive liquor in public. The dictates of tradition require the

---

[60]"The Independence of the Judiciary" (1956), 34 Can. Bar Rev. 1139 at 1178. See also the papers delivered to the meetings organized by the Canadian Judges Conference on Judge's Day at the Canadian Bar Association over the past few years. These included a paper by Professor B. Elman entitled "The Independence of the Judiciary" delivered in Calgary in 1979. Of great importance, see the definitive work, in the contemporary Canadian context, by Chief Justice Deschênes, *Masters in Their Own House* (Ottawa: Canadian Judicial Council, 1981). See the Financial Post, 7th November 1981. Work on this topic is now being conducted at the international level by the International Commission of Jurists, the International Bar Association, and other interested organizations. See, for example, the Chairman's Report at the 19th Biennial Conference, New Delhi, India, 17th-23rd October 1982.

greatest restraint, the greatest propriety and the greatest decorum from the members of our judiciary. We expect our judges to be almost superhuman in wisdom, in propriety, in decorum and in humanity. There is probably no other group in society which must fulfil this standard of public expectation and, at the same time, accept so many constraints.

Perhaps a better appreciation of the circumstances in which a new judge finds himself might be gained from a brief article which appeared in the New York Times dated 15th August 1976. That article, quoted in its entirety, is set out as follows:

ON TOP, A LONELY JUDGE

Supreme Court Justice Lewis F. Powell Jr. has provided, through an interview, an unusual glimpse of life at the judicial top. The necessity for judicial impartiality has forced him to curtail many old friendships formed during almost 40 years in private practice. He also regrets the impact his position has had on the law careers of two of his children, both of whom resent, he says, being identified as the children of a Supreme Court Justice. But he still finds the work at the Court intellectually stimulating. "All of the negatives are out-weighed," he said, "by the feeling of privilege at the opportunity to be at the Court."

Indeed, Bora Laskin, the Chief Justice of Canada, recently remarked "half facetiously" that "when you become a judge, you lose half of your freedom and when you become a chief justice, you almost lose the other half."

A judge is a public figure and, as a result, he is subject to the glare of publicity that public figures must inevitably face. For example, a county court judge in the province of Ontario was personally involved in a matrimonial dispute which involved a quarrel over a property settlement. Not every matrimonial dispute is reported on the front page of the local newspaper; this one was. Moreover, what might constitute folly or silly behaviour on the part of most persons becomes scandal if it involves a judge. Society has come to expect a very high standard of behaviour on the part of judges and that standard of behaviour is enforced through public scrutiny.

In addition, as discussed earlier, judges are limited in the extent to which they may make public remarks. First, a judge may not make any remarks in respect of any case which is "sub judice", that is, he may not make any comments concerning an ongoing case, at least not before a decision has been rendered. This constraint applies equally to both the presiding judge and other judges as well. Secondly, where a judge makes certain comments in connection with a case which has already been decided, his remarks must be very tactfully expressed and within the bounds of propriety. Because of this requirement, most judges choose not to make any public remarks in connection with particular cases decided.

However, there do not seem to be any constraints on a judge against making remarks in an anecdotal manner concerning his experiences on the bench. In fact, if there were constraints of this nature, a tradition of many after-dinner speeches at bar association meetings would be lost. Nor are there any constraints upon a judge in making public remarks concerning reform of the law and the administration of justice generally. However, it is very unwise and imprudent for a judge to extend his remarks into the political realm, suggesting, for example, that judicial reform and changes in the administration of justice would best be accomplished by the political action of a given party. In other words, a judge may say, for example, that the law concerning ownership of the matrimonial home upon dissolution of marriage ought to be changed by the legislature, but he ought not to remark that one party or another is more likely to implement this change. This whole issue, of course, came to the public's attention in respect of the *Berger* matter, discussed earlier.

(b) Special Legal Constraints Imposed on Judges

(i) Right to Vote

Under the various municipal, provincial and federal election Acts, certain judges are put into the same category as inmates in penitentiaries, inasmuch as they are all disenfranchised. In addition, as indicated above, in the course of a campaign for election, there is the additional constraint imposed upon a judge that he must be reserved and reticent in expressing his support for a particular candidate or a particular party or, for that matter, a particular ideology. In other words, he must effectively remain out of the campaign and out of politics. In summary, as a non-participant in the campaign and as a disenfranchised citizen, a judge can take no part in the electoral process.

(ii) Law Society Membership

Certain judges must resign their membership in their respective provincial law societies upon appointment to the bench. If a judge happens to be a bencher of a law society, he must naturally, with his resignation from the law society, also resign as a bencher. Once he retires from the bench (and this, of course, refers to full retirement, including retirement from a supernumerary position), he must reapply to the law society for reinstatement before he can then engage in the practice of law.

(iii) Private Practice and Private Concerns

A newly appointed judge must immediately wind up the practice of law in which he was professionally engaged. The interim period from the time his appointment is confirmed until the time that he is officially sworn in as a member of the bench is usually reserved for this purpose. He may not, during this period, act for his clients, except to the extent necessary to ensure that their files are transferred to other lawyers.

Furthermore, as a judge, he should not hear a case in which a former client is involved.

In winding up his former practice, the newly appointed judge must also terminate his partnership or his association with his former firm. Changes must be made in the nature of the relationship that he has with the lawyers with whom he was engaged in practice and with lawyers in general. Of course, long and meaningful relationships need not be terminated upon an appointment to the bench. However, there is at least some alteration in the nature of that relationship upon the appointment. It is difficult to define how this relationship is modified. Perhaps it might best be expressed as permitting a judge to maintain comity among his colleagues in the legal profession but to do so in a somewhat more reserved and distant posture than existed prior to his appointment.

Often, a lawyer is engaged in other private concerns which may or may not have arisen as a result of his membership in the legal profession. In any event, private business enterprises must be terminated upon appointment, corporate directorships must be resigned, and generally the new judge must sever all points of contact that may have existed between him and the business world. Indeed, ss. 36 and 37 of the federal Judges Act expressly provide that a judge must do so. Those sections are as follows:

36. No judge shall, either directly or indirectly, as director or manager of any corporation, company or firm, or in any other manner whatever, for himself or others, engage in any occupation or business other than his judicial duties, but every judge shall devote himself exclusively to his judicial duties, except that a district judge in Admiralty may continue to perform the duties of a public office under Her Majesty in right of Canada or of a province held by him at the time of his appointment as district judge in Admiralty.

37. (1) No judge shall act as commissioner, arbitrator, adjudicator, referee, conciliator or mediator on any commission or on any inquiry or other proceeding unless

(a) in the case of any matter within the legislative authority of Parliament, the judge is by an Act of the Parliament of Canada expressly authorized so to act or he is thereunto appointed or so authorized by the Governor in Council; or

(b) in the case of any matter within the legislative authority of the legislature of a province, the judge is by an Act of the legislature of the province expressly authorized so to act or he is thereunto appointed or so authorized by the lieutenant governor in council of the province.

(2) Subsection (1) does not apply to judges acting as arbitrators or assessors of compensation or damages under the *Railway Act* or any other public Act, whether of general or local application, of Canada or of a province, whereby a judge is required or authorized without authority from the Governor in Council or lieutenant governor in council to assess or ascertain compensation or damages.

In addition to all of the foregoing, some of the enabling statutes contain provisions requiring the judge to assume residence within a given municipality or within a particular radius of that municipality.

In short, the law imposes special constraints, legal and otherwise, upon judges in order to ensure the preservation of the integrity of our judiciary and to ensure that our courts always remain impartial and objective and, most important, independent institutions within our society.

(c) The Judge Serving in Other Capacities

Owing to the independence of the judiciary and the resulting freedom from influences from external sources, and owing to the status and prestige that members of the judiciary have in society, governments often turn to members of the judiciary to constitute Royal Commissions of Inquiry. This, of course, presents some problems for the chief judge or chief justice of a particular bench: the docket of most courts is already overloaded and the services of every judge are needed. Notwithstanding this logistical problem, many judges serve in this special capacity. In recent years, for example, judges have served as chairmen of Royal Commissions of Inquiry in respect of such matters as the investigation into the management of one of our national airlines, an examination of the implications of pipeline construction on the integrity of northern life and environment, and the investigation into the causes of an airplane crash. In addition, in recent years, the tendency has been to appoint one-man commissions. This, of course, avoids the obvious problem of dissenting opinions.

Often, with many Royal Commissions of Inquiry, the reports of the commissioners do no more than gather dust after they have been submitted to government authorities. However, although this has not been documented, it appears that probably owing to the prestige and status afforded members of the judiciary, those Royal Commissions conducted by members of the judiciary are more often acted upon. No better example of this comes to mind than the McRuer Royal Commission of Inquiry into Civil Rights in the province of Ontario where, over a number of years, many recommendations have been enacted into law.

(d) The Writing of Judgments

Judgment-writing has attracted considerable attention in recent years. For example, beginning in 1981 the Canadian Institute for the Administration of Justice embarked upon an annual programme on behalf of the Canadian Judicial Council on judgment-writing. Related issues have been voiced in recent years.[61]

(e) Personal Liability of Judges

Judges are exempt from civil liability for all acts done in their official capacity.[62] Essentially, this privilege provides an immunity for judges in

---

[61]See R. Koman, *Reasons for Judgment: A Handbook for Judges and Other Judicial Officers* (Toronto: Butterworths, 1980), and M. Taggart, "Should Canadian Lawyers be Legally Required to Give Reasoned Decisions in Civil Cases" (1983), 33 U. of T. L.J. 1.

[62]See *Floyd v. Barker* (1607), 12 Co. Rep. 23, 77 E.R. 1305.

respect of acts or omissions committed on the bench, and is usually directed at false imprisonment, defamation, and other like actions.[63] On the other hand, there is little jurisprudence suggesting the presence or lack thereof of a similar immunity in respect of criminal liability. Perhaps the closest indication that no such immunity exists is the case of *Slater v. Watts* (1911), 16 B.C.R. 36, 16 W.L.R. 234 (C.A.), where it was held that a justice of the peace was potentially liable for a civil action of assault for lashing a boy who came before him. The justice believed that the boy had attempted to entice his daughter.

In addition, readers may consult the following sources for further information on the question of judicial immunity.[64]

1. GENERAL SOURCES

Wade, H.W.R., "Administrative Law", 4th ed. Oxford: Clarendon Press, 1977, pp. 640-43.

Gray, R.J., "Private Wrongs of Public Servants" (1959), 47 California L. Rev. 303. A good analysis of the Anglo-American jurisprudence concerning the civil liability of public officers from a historical, judicial, legislative and administrative viewpoint.

Molot, Henry, L., "Administrative Bodies, Economic Loss, and Tortious Liability", Chapter 12 of *Studies in Canadian Business Law*. Comprehensive analysis of characterization of function in public officer tort liability.

Rubinstein, A., "Jurisdiction and Illegality" (Oxford: Clarendon Press, 1965), Chapter VI.

Rubenstein, A., "Liability in Tort of Judicial Officers" (1963-64), 15 U. of T.L.J. 317.

Jennings, Edward, "Tort Liability of Administrative Officers" (1936-37), 21 Minn. L. Rev. 263.

Jaffe, L., "Suits Against Governments and Officers — Damage Actions", (1963), 77 Harv. L. Rev. 209.

Feldthusen, Bruce, "Judicial Immunity: In Search of an Appropriate Limiting Formula" (1980), U.N.B.L.J. 73.

Brazier, M., "Judicial Immunity and the Independence of the Judiciary", [1976] Public Law 397.

Thompson, D., "Judicial Immunity and The Protection of Justices", (1958), 21 Mod. L. Rev. 517.

---

[63]There have been at least two recent attempts on the part of losing litigants to sue the presiding judges. One such litigant alleged that the members of the Alberta Court of Appeal who decided his case had been negligent. The Master had dismissed the claim on the basis that judicial negligence does not constitute a cause of action at common law. A similar attempt was made in Ontario a few years ago — see the Toronto Star, 26th December 1979.

[64]The author wishes to acknowledge the assistance of John Law, the Associate Director of the Legal Education Society of Alberta, for providing these sources.

Sheridan, "The Protection of Justices" (1951), 14 Mod. L. Rev. 267.
Halsbury's Laws of England 4th ed. (London: Butterworths, 1973) Vol.
   1, paras. 206-210 and paras. 213-14, at pp. 197-203.

2. CASES

Unterreiner v. Wilson et al. (1982), 40 O.R. (2d) 197 (H.C.).
Sirros v. Moore, [1975] 1 Q.B. 118, [1974] 3 All E.R. 776 (C.A.).
Foran v. Tatangello (1977), 14 O.R. (2d) 91, 73 D.L.R. (3d) 126 (H.C.).
The Marshalsea Case (1612), 10 Co. Rep. 68b, 77 E.R. 1027 (K.B.).
Houlden v. Smith (1850), 14 Q.B. 841, 117 E.R. 323.
Royal Aquarium & Summer & Winter Garden Soc. v. Parkinson, [1892] 1
   Q.B. 431 (C.A.).
O'Connor v. Waldron, [1935] A.C. 76.
O'Connor v. Isaacs, [1956] 2 Q.B. 288, [1956] 2 All E.R. 417 (C.A.).
Bradley v. Fisher (1892), 80 U.S. at 649-50.
Pierson v. Ray (1967), 87 S.C. 1213, 386 U.S. 843.

3. LEGISLATIVE PROVISIONS

See generally the Feldthusen article, *supra*, at pp. 88-91.

Therefore, it appears that judges are exempt from civil liability for all acts done in their official capacity but that this exemption probably does not extend to the commission of any criminal acts. In any event, the best protection against malfeasances on the part of judges in the course of exercising their official capacity lies in an invocation to the impeachment and removal procedures. Realistically, impeachment and removal provide the best method of remedying improper judicial conduct. In addition, the ultimate device in ensuring proper judicial conduct lies in the selection process. In short, the practice of preventive medicine, achieved through careful refinement of the selection and appointment process, is far better than the surgical upheaval that comes with impeachment and removal.

SUMMARY

Thus far, we have examined the basic foundation or substructure of the legal process in Canada. Upon that foundation, we have constructed a system which contains certain institutions. In this chapter, we have looked at the persons manning those institutions and, in particular, we have focused upon the two most important persons — the lawyer and the judge. We are now left with a completed structure and need only to make it operational in order to correctly define the legal process in Canada. To illustrate by analogy, we have now manufactured the automobile and need only to discover the nature of the fuel that will make the vehicle operational.

With only a few remaining judges presiding to date at the provincial level without formal training in law, one can generally assume that all newly appointed judges were practising lawyers before appointment.

Even this general conclusion is not without three qualifications. The first is the requirement respecting federally appointed judges that they have at least ten years' standing at the bar of any province prior to appointment. However, provincially appointed judges are not subject to this requirement. Therefore although judges are appointed from the ranks of practising lawyers, their experience in practice will vary, depending upon the appointing authority. Secondly, and this is a fairly recent phenomenon, the federal government is appointing more academics to the bench, with practice limited, in some cases for example, to service on administrative tribunals or the conduct of arbitrations. The third point, and this too is a relatively recent phenomenon, relates to the frequency, in recent years, of vertical appointments from one bench to another. Previously, most judges, at all levels, were appointed directly from the practising bar and it was very rare to witness a vertical appointment from a lower bench to a higher one. Recently, however, this has become a fairly common practice. These qualifications aside, all newly appointed judges are persons trained and experienced in the law prior to appointment. And all lawyers, prior to engaging in the practice of the law and prior to formal training in the law, are, for the most part, ambitious young persons anxious to engage in a successful career.

There is no superhuman quality in those persons who eventually assume a judicial appointment; however, we do expect superhuman qualities in the members of the judiciary. We impose special legal and ethical constraints upon them and, at the same time, we expect them to resolve difficult disputes with the wisdom of Solomon. In addition, we provide them with salaries considerably lower than those they were earning as practising members of the bar. In return, we offer them status, prestige and trust. Of these, the latter is most important. We trust them with resolving sometimes momentous issues and more often with adjudicating sensitive and emotional disputes. More important, however, we also trust them, as the ultimate arbiters, to ensure that a lawful and orderly process in resolving disputes and in determining truth replaces remedies of self-help on the streets. This same trust, to some extent, extends back to the practising lawyer. Every lawyer must not only articulate the interest of his clients to the best of his ability, but he must also act as an officer of the court, and this latter capacity provides him with a share of the trust that society reposes upon all members of the legal profession.

It is a vital feature of our liberal democratic society, in which the rule of law is supreme, that ultimate trust is placed in the legal profession to ensure that the resolution of disputes, and the search for truth, is conducted in a fair and just manner. Indeed, the imposition of this trust defines what is meant when one says that lawyers and judges occupy special positions in society. Moreover, so vital is this notion that the relationship of the legal profession, in general, and judges, in particular, to the rest of society defines an essential component of the social contract in modern society.

SELECTED BIBLIOGRAPHY
ROLE OF THE LAWYER

Arnup, "Advocacy" (1979), 13 Gazette 27.

Arthurs, "The Study of the Legal Profession in the Law School" (1970), 8 Osgoode Hall L.J. 183.

Arthurs, "Counsel, Clients and Community" (1973), 11 Osgoode Hall L.J. 437.

Arthurs and Verge, "The Future of Legal Services" (1973), 5 Can. Bar Rev. 15.

Arthurs, Willms and Taman, "The Toronto Legal Profession: An Exploratory Survey" (1971), 21 U. of T. L.J. 162.

Becker, "Professional Aristocracies and Social Change: Some Thoughts on the Profession of Law" (1974), 22 Chitty's L.J. 261.

Berlins, "Advocates of Incompetence" (1979), 13 Gazette 336.

Blakeney, "Should Lawyers Keep their Monopoly" (1973), 4 Can. Bar Assn. J. 2:23.

Bogart, "Immunity of Advocates From Suit" (1980), 29 U.N.B.L.J. 27.

Bork, "We Suddenly Feel that Law is Vulnerable" (1972), 6 Law Soc. Gazette 25.

Breitel, "Law and the Lawyers" (1981), 53 N.Y.S.B.J. 6.

Brossard, "Responsibilities of Lawyers" (1979), 13 Gazette 113.

Buchanan, D.W., "Additional Guidelines for Employment of Articling Students" (1977), 35 Advocate 250-51.

Catzman, M.A. (1978), 56 Can. Bar. Rev. 116 (case comment — *Banks v. Reid*, and *Gouzenko v. Harris*).

Christie, "The Nature of the Lawyers' Role in the Administrative Process" (1971), Lectures, L.S.U.C. 1.

Cliche, R., "Lawyers in a Changing Society" (1977), 1 Can. Community Law J. 12-17.

Cohen, "Lawyers and Learning: The Professional and Intellectual Traditions" (1961), 7 McGill L.J. 181.

Coutts, "The Public Profession of Law" (1963), 6 Can. Bar J. 101.

Cranor, C.F., "Legal Moralism Reconsidered" (1979), 89 Ethics 146, No. 2.

Davison, "Specialization . . . and Continuing Legal Education" (1980), 54 Aust. L.J. 575.

Dick, "Certification of Specialists" (1979), 37 Advocate 249.

Dorsen, "The Role of the Lawyer in America's Ghetto Society" (1972), 6 Law Society Gazette 118.

Dussault, "La juriste dans la fonction publique quebecoise" (1979), 39 R. du B. 30.

Erickson, "Legalistic and Traditional Role Expectations for Defence Counsel in Juvenile Court" (1975), 17 Can. Journal of Criminology and Corrections 78.

Esau, "Specialization and the Legal Profession" (1979), 8 Man. L.J. 255.

Evershed, "Pursuing a Learned Art . . . In a Spirit of Public Service" (1962), 20 Advocate 5.

Farris, "A Look at Tomorrow" (1971), 2 Can. Bar Assn. J. 4:4.

Farris, "Let's Kill All the Lawyers" (1972), 3 Can. Bar Assn. J. 4.

Fera, "Negligence of Solicitors" (1977), 25 Chitty's L.J. 325.

Finkelstein and Orr, "Lawyers as Businessmen See Them" (1967), 10 Can. Bar J. 243.

Finlay, "Conduct of Lawyers in the Litigious Process" (1979), Studies Civ. Proc. 15.

Finlayson, G.D., "The Legal Professional Under Attack" (1978), 12 Gazette 355.

Freedman, "The Discipline and Judicial Committees" (1977), Law Soc. Man. 145.

Gauley, "A Lawyer and his Independence in Today's Society" (1966), 31 Sask. Bar Rev. 27.

Gold, "Continuing Legal Education: A New Direction" (1975), 7 Ottawa L. Rev. 62.

Goodman, "The Lawyer in Public Life" (1971), Pitblado Lectures 129.

Guile, "Lawyer's Lumps" (1980), 38 Advocate 477.

Hall, E.M., "The Creative Role of the Lawyer" (1977), Socrates 26-28.

Hall, "Lawyers and Canadian Criminal Law in the Seventies" (1971), 5 Law Society Gazette 24.

Howland, W.G.C., "Old Fashioned Virtues and Legal Traditions" (1978) 12 Gazette 122.

Hunter, "The Law and other Professions" (1972), 3 Can. Bar Assn. J. 9.

Issalys, P., "The Professional Tribunal and the Conduct of Ethical Conduct Among Professions" (1978), 24 McGill L.J. 588.

Jarvis, "Debtors to the Profession" (1970), 4 Law Soc. Gazette 49.

Johnston, "Role of the Lawyer in our Society" (1979), 13 Gazette 119.

Killeen, G., "Your Future and the Future of Your Profession" (1978), 12 Gazette 213.

Klar, "Note on Barrister's Immunity from Suit" (1979), 7 C.C.L.T. 21.

Kutak, R.J., "Coming: The New Model Rules of Professional Conduct" (1980), 66 Amer. Bar. Assn. 47-49.

Lang, "Lawyers in an Open Society" (1972), 3 Can. Bar Assn. J. 26.

Laskin, "The Interrelationship of a University Law School and the Legal Profession" (1970), 4 Law Soc. Gazette 210.

Laskin, "The Lawyer's Responsibility in the Supervision of the Legal Order" (1971), 5 Law Soc. Gazette 63.

LeDain, "The Quest for Justice: The Role of the Profession" (1969), U.N.B.L.J. 18.

Lederman, "Canadian Legal Education in the Second Half of the Twentieth Century" (1971), 21 U. of T. L.J. 141.

Lewis, "The Lawyer's Image" (1964), 7 Can. Bar J. 210.

Macdonald, Morris and Johnston, "The New Lawyer in a Transnational World" (1975), 25 U. of T. L.J. 343.

MacIsaac, "The Age of Specialization" (1971), 2 Can. Bar Assn. J. 1:4.

Maloney, A., "Advocacy" (1978), 12 Gazete 144.

Maloney, "Role of the Independent Bar" (1979), Lect. L.S.U.C. 49.

Maloney, A., "The Role of the Lawyer in Society" (1979), 9 Man. L.J. 351-52.

Manning, "The Lawyer's Role and Other Disciplines", in Estate Planning Seminar 48 (Can. Bar Assn., Manitoba Taxation Subsection, 1970).

Marshall, "Role of the Lawyer in Developing Societies", 4 Man. L.J. 392.

Martin, "The Role and Responsibility of the Defence Advocate" (1970), 12 Cr. L.Q. 376.

Martyn, "Informed Consent in the Practice of Law" (1980), 48 Geo. Wash. L. Rev. 307.

McGillis, D., "Hanging Out Your Shingle" (1978), 2 Can. Lawyer 1:22-25.

McKelvy, "Challenge. . . Criticize. . . Question: An Address" (1973), 4 Can. Bar Assn. J. 4:1-2.

McMaster, "Law as a Profession" (1973), 31 Advocate 325.

McMurtry, R.R., "Administrative Advocacy — The Lawyer and Government" (1978), 12 Gazette 130.

McRae, D.M., "Pilot Project for the Certification of Specialists" (1977), 35 Advocate 481-86.

Megarry, "Problems of the Legal Profession" (1971), 5 Law Soc. Gazette 240.

Megarry, "Lawyers and the Public Today: Challenge and Antiphon" (1972), 1 Man. L.J. 1.

Meiselman, "Attorney Liability to Third Parties" (1981), 53 N.Y.S.B.J. 108.

Michener, "A Convocation Address" (1974), 8 Law Soc. Gazette 117.

Mignault, "The Law and the Legal Profession in the 21st Century" (1973), 5 Can. Bar Rev. 1.

Miller, "Advocate's Duty to Justice — Where Does it Belong?" (1981), 97 L.Q. Rev. 127.

Millman, "Counsellor Beware — Failure to Recognize Obvious Legal Trends" (1979), 27 Chitty's L.J. 279.

Minish (1979), 10 Man. L.J. 65.

O'Brien, "Role of the Legal Profession in Public Affairs" (1979), 13 Gazette 107.

O'Dea, "Lawyer-Client Relationship" (1980), 48 Geo. Wash. L. Rev. 693.

Ortved, W.N., "Why the Public Defender Won't Work" (1978), 12 Gazette 152.

Pattillo, "Reflections on the Law" (1970), 1 Can. Bar Assn. J.4:7.

Pitch, "Poverty Law and the Private Law Firm: An Experiment in Judicature" (1974), 22 Chitty's L.J. 60.

Radomski, "Actions Against Solicitors — Contract or Tort?" (1980), 2 Advocate's Q. 160.

Redmount, "Career Development and the Practice of Law" (1980), 5 J. Leg. Prof. 69.

Robert, P., "Le secret professionnel . . ." (1979), 39 R. du B. 472.

Robins, "Our Profession and the Winds of Change" (1972), 6 Law Soc. Gazette 137.

Robins, "Our Profession on Trial" (1973), 7 Law Soc. Gazette 1.

Ryan, "Acceptable Law in an Age of Dissent" (1971), 5 Law Soc. Gazette 73.

Sgayias, "Liability of a Lawyer for Negligence in the Conduct of Litigation" (1978), 8 Man. L.J. 661.

Sommers, "Liability of Solicitors When Recommending Settlement" (1978), 1 Advocate's Q. 361.

Speiser (1981), 67 A.B.A.J. 303.

Stinton, "Errors and Omissions Insurance" (1977), 11 Gazette 249.

Syman, "The Priest and the Lawyer" (1973), 7 Law Soc. Gazette 272.

Taman and Zemans, "The Future of Legal Services" (1973), 5 Can. Bar Rev. 32.

Thom, "Independence of the Legal Profession" (1979), 13 Gazette 173.

Thurman, "Limits to the Adversary System" (1980), 5 J. Leg. Prof. 5-19.

Turner, "The Role of Crown Counsel in Canadian Prosecution" (1962), 40 Can. Bar Rev. 439.

Turner, "Frontiers of Law and Lawyership" (1969), 12 Can. Bar J. 7.

Weiser, "Newspaperman Looks at Lawyers" (1972), 38 Man. Bar News 325.

Willis, "What I Like and What I Don't Like About Lawyers" (1970), 4 Law Soc. Gazette 52.

Wishart, "Law . . . The Great Profession" (1973), 7 Law Soc. Gazette 127.

Woodsworth, "Specialization" (1971), 20 Advocate 15.

Yarmolinsky, "The Role of the Lawyer in Today's City" (1970), 8 Osgoode Hall L.J. 393.

Yates, "The Lawyer in the Regulatory Process" (1980), 18 Alta. L. Rev. 70.

"About Our Colleagues in the Commonwealth" (1972), 6 Law Soc. Gazette 79.

Assessment of Alternative Strategies for Increasing Access to Legal Services (1980), 90 Yale L.J. 122.

"The Development of Law" (1962), 27 Sask. L. Rev. 26.

"Do You Really Want to be a Lawyer?" (1978), 32 Changing Times 45-57, No. 10.

"Law in the Space Age" (1962), 27 Sask. L. Rev. 10.

"Mental or Physical Incapacity as a Bar to the Practice of Law" (1978), J. Leg. Profession 4:219.

"Problems in Ethics and Advocacy: Panel Discussion" (1969), Lectures, L.S.U.C. 279.

"Professionals Must Change" (1970), 4 Law Soc. Gazette 60.

"The Role of the Lawyer Today and How it is Changing" (1970), 9 Western Ont. L. Rev. 150.

"The Role of the Profession in the Future Environment" (1974), Lectures, L.S.U.C. 339.

Selected Checklist of Materials on Specialization (1979), 34 Record 441-46 (May-June).

"Two Comments on A. Blakeney's Speech" (1973), 4 Can. Bar Assn. J. 2:27.

"The Wright Report and the Legal Profession" (1972), 6 Law Soc. Gazette 79.

ROLE OF THE JUDGE

Alpert, L., Atkins, B.M. and Ziller, R.C., "Becoming a Judge: The Transition From Advocate to Arbiter" (1979), 62 Judicature 325-35.

"An Address of Welcome to Fauteux and Laskin" (1970), 4 Law Soc. Gazette 99.

Bailey, F.L., with Aronson, H., *The Defense Never Rests* (New York: Stein and Day, 1971).

Batten, *In Court* (Toronto: MacMillan, 1982).

Batten, *Lawyers*, (Toronto: MacMillan, 1980).

Beetz, "Le professeur de droit et le juge" (1979), 81 R. du N. 506.

Berger, "A View from the Bench" (1974), 32 Advocate 1.

Black, "Judicial Appointments — Time for a Change" (1978), New Zealand L.J. 41-42.

Black, "The Role of an Appellate Judge" (1980), N.Z.L.J. 377.

Blacksheild, "Five Types of Judicial Decisions" (1974), 12 Osgoode Hall L.J. 537.

Boult, R. "Ad hoc Judges of the Supreme Court of Canada" (1978), 26 Chitty's L.J. 289.

Chayes, "Role of the Judge in Public Law Litigation," (1976), 89 Harv. L. Rev. 1281.

Coffin, F. *The Ways of a Judge: Reflections from the Federal Appellate Bench* (Boston: Houghton, Mifflin Co., 1980).

Coughlan, "Maxims and Suggestions for Criminal Trial Judges" (1972), 10 Alta. L. Rev. 347.

Davies, "The Role of the Judge in Contemporary Society" (1971), 5 Law Soc. Gazette 210.

Dershowitz, A.M., *The Best Defense* (New York: Random House, 1982).

Denning (Lord), *The Due Process of Law* (London: Butterworths, 1980).

Denning (Lord), *The Discipline of Law* (London: Butterworths, 1979).

De Grandpre, L.P. "From Realities to Abstractions" (1978), 9 R. Gen. 425.

Deschenes, "Justice et pouvoir" (1980), 11 R. Gen. 1:345.

Deschenes, *The Sword and the Scales* (*Les Plateaux de la Balance*) (Toronto: Butterworths, 1979).

Devlin, P., *The Judge* (Chicago: Univ. of Chicago Press, 1979).

Devlin (Lord), "Judges, Government and Politics" (1978), 41 Mod. L. Rev. 501.

Devlin (Lord), "Judges and Lawmakers" (1976), 39 Mod. L. Rev. 1.

Devitt, "Ten Commandments for the New Judge" (1979), 65 Amer. Bar. Assn. J. 574.

Dickson, The Hon. Mr. Justice B., "The Judiciary — Law Interpreters or Law-Makers" (1982), 12 Man. L.J. 1.

Dickson, "Role and Function" (1980), 14 Gazette 138.

Dion, L. "Du social, du politique et du judiciare — Pour l'autonomie du judiciare" (1978), 38 R. du B. 769.

Douglas, W.O., *The Autobiography of William O. Douglas: Go East Young Man* (New York: Random House, 1974).

Douglas, W.O. *The Court Years: 1939-1975 The Autobiography of William O. Douglas* (New York: Random House, 1980).

Feldthusen "Judicial Immunity: In Search of an Appropriate Limiting Formula" (1980), 29 U.N.B. L.J. 73.

Flango, V.E. and Ducat, C.R., "What Difference does Method of Judicial Selection Make?" (1979), 5 The Justice System J. 25-44.

Frank, *Courts on Trial* (Princeton: Princeton Univ. Press, 1949).

Franks, M.R. and Kenner, R.R., "A Proposal for a Saner Judiciary" (1977), 1 Legal Med. Q. 264.

Freedman, "Judges and the Law" (1962), 5 Can. Bar Rev. 208.

Gleeson, "Judging the Judges" (1979), 53 Aust. L.J. 338.

Griffith, J., *The Politics of the Judiciary* (Manchester: Manchester University Press, 1977).

Griffith, J. *The Politics of the Judiciary* (Glasgow: Wm. Collins Sons and Co. Ltd. 1977).

Hailsham (Lord), "Democracy and Judical Independence" (1979), 28 U.N.B.L.J. 7.

Haines, E.L., "The Judge's Role in a Changing Society" (1976), 10 Gazette 103.

Hall, "Law Reform and the Judiciary's Role" (1972), 20 Chitty's L.J. 77.

Hansard, "Election versus Selection of Judges" (1967), 15 Chitty's L.J. 251.

Hansard, "Judicial Interference" (Editorial) (1970), 18 Chitty's L.J. 71.

Henderson, G.F., "The Independence of the Judiciary" (1980), 14 Gazette 236.

Higgins & Rubin, "Judicial Discretion" (1980), 9 J. Legal Studies 129.

Johnson, S.D., "Judge's Conduct: Judicial Ethics" (1979), Tex. B.J. 42:211.

Joseph, G.S. "Advocate One Day — an Arbiter the Next" (1976), 24 Chitty's L.J. 187.

Kaminsky, M.I., "Available Compromises for Continued Judicial Selection Reform" (1979), 53 St. John's L. Rev. 466-516.

Kritzer, H.M., "Federal judges and their political environments: the influence of public opinion." (1979), 23 Amer. J. of Political Science 194-207.

Kroll, G.R., "Should There be a Right to Challenge Judges?" (1977), 35 Advocate 411.

Lang, "Judicial Appointments" (1974), 8 Law Soc. Gazette 121.

Laskin, "A Judge and His Constituencies" (1976) 7 Man. L.J. 1.

Laskin, "Judicial Integrity and the Supreme Court of Canada" (1978), 12 Gazette 116.

Laskin, "The Judge and Due Process" (1972), 1 Man. L.J. 235.

Laskin, "The Common Tie Between Judges and Law Teachers" (1972), 6 Law Soc. Gazette 147.

Laskin, "The Supreme Court of Canada" (1974), 8 Law Soc. Gazette 248.

Le Clercq, F.S., "The Constitutional Policy that Judges be Learned in the Law (U.S.)" (1980), 47 Tenn. L. Rev. 689.

Linden, A. (ed.), *The Canadian Judiciary* (Toronto: Osgoode Hall Law School, 1976).

Markey, H.T., "Needed: A Judicial Welcome for Technology: Star Wars or Stare Decisis?" (1978), 50 N.Y.S.B.J. 380.

Murphy, B., *The Brandeis/Frankfurter Connection: The Secret Political Activities of Two Supreme Court Judges* (New York: Oxford Univ. Press, 1982).

Neely, R., *How Courts Govern America* (New Haven: Yale Univ. Press, 1981).

Perkins, C.E., "The Extra-judicial Role" (1979), 3 Prov. Judges J. 3:12.

Pigeon, "The Human Element in the Judicial Process" (1970), 8 Alta. L. Rev. 301.

Robins, S.L. "The Role of the Independent Judiciary" (1979), Lectures, L.S.U.C. 23.

Robins, S.L. "Report of the Commission of Inquiry into the Conduct of Provincial Judge Harry J. Williams" (1978), 12 Gazette 161.

Saltzburg, S.A., "Unnecessarily Expanding Role of the American Trial Judge" (1978), 64 Va. L. Rev. 1.

Schmeiser, "Common Sense and the Law" (1961), 26 Sask. Bar Rev. 101.

Schmittoff, "Denning and the Contemporary Scene" (1974), 6 Man. L.J. 11.

Schwarzer, W.W., "Dealing with Incompetent Counsel — the Trial Judge's Role" (1980), 93 Harv. L. Rev. 633.

Silverman, H.W., "It's About Time: Study of the Judiciary" (1977), 25 Chitty's L.J. 19.

Silverman, "The Trial Judge: Pilot, Participant, or Umpire?" (1973), 11 Alta. L. Rev. 40.

Slatter, R., "Quality of a Judge's Experience" (1979), 65 Amer. B. Ass. J. 933-35.

Slotnick, E.E., "Federal Judicial Selection" (1979), 62 Judicature 465-510.

Southin, "Lord Denning" (1970), 5 U.B.C. L. Rev. 1

"Symposium on Appointment, Discipline and Removal of Judges" (1973), 11 Alta. L. Rev. 279.

"The Qualities of a Good Judge" (1962), 34 Man. Bar News 61.

Steel, J.B.B. "The Judge as Law Reformer" (1979), 3 Auckland Univ. L. Rev. 443.

Thom, "Judge and Company" (1974), 8 Law Soc. Gazette 237.

Tollefson, "The System of Judicial Appointments: A Collateral Issue" (1971), 21 U. of T. L.J. 162.

Tribe, L.H., "Trying California's Judges on Television: Open Government or Judicial Intimidation?" (1979), 65 Am. Bar Ass. J. 1175-1179.

Vaze, V., "Can Judges Be Law-makers?" (1978), 20 Journal of the Indian Law Institute 117-121.

Weiler, "Legal Values and Judicial Decision Making" (1970), 48 Can. Bar Rev. 1.

"Whither the Supreme Court of Canada?" (Editorial) (1973), 21 Chitty's L.J. 77.

Wishman, S., *Confessions of a Criminal Lawyer* (New York: Times Books, 1981).

Woodward & Armstrong, *The Brethren: Inside the Supreme Court* (New York: Simon and Schuster, 1979).

LEGAL EDUCATION

Arthurs, H.W., "Paradoxes of Canadian Legal Education" (1977), 3 Dal. L.J. 639-62.

Barnes, John, "The Department of Law, Carlton Univ., Ottawa" (1977), 3 Dal. L.J. 814-27.

Campbell, S., "Toward an Improved Legal Educaiton" (1978), 43 Sask. L. Rev. 81.

Consultative Group on Research and Education in Law, "Law and Learning", A Report to the Social Sciences and Humanities Research Council of Canada, (Ottawa: April 1983).

Cooke, Dr. B.F. and Taylor, J.P., "Developing Personal Awareness & Examining Values: Inter-connected Dimensions of Supervision in Clinical Legal Education" (1978), U.B.C.L. Rev. 276-94.

Fraser, F.M., "The Faculty of Law at the University of Victoria" (1977), 3 Dal. L.J. 828-36.

Fraser, "Recent Development in Legal Education — the Victoria Experience" (1979), 13 U.B.C.L. Rev. 221-39.

Fraser, J., "Legal Research" (1980), 38 Advocate 373.

Foote, "On Completion of a Legal Education" (1978), 12 Gazette 377.

Gold, "Legal Education, Law and Justice: The Clinical Experience" (1979), 44 Sask. L. Rev. 97.

Janishce, H.N., "Law & Contining Education: The Dalhousie Experience" (1977), 55 Can. Bar. Rev. 57-74.

Johnston, "Report on Legal Education in the Maritimes — Why Not a National Study?" (1977), 11 Gazette 262.

Laskin, "The Interrelationship of a University Law School and the Legal Profession" (1970), 4 Law Soc. Gazette 210.

Lederman, "Canadian Legal Education in the Second Half of the Twentieth Century" (1971), 21 U. of T.L.J. 141.

London, "Perspective on Legal Education and Admission to Practice in Manitoba" (1978), 8 Man. L.J. 553.

MacDonald, "Law Schools and Public Legal Education: The Community Law Programme at Windsor" (1979), 5 Dal. L.J. 779-90.

Macdonald, "Legal Education on the Threshold of the 1980's: Whatever Happened to the Great Ideas of the 60's" (1979), 44 Sask. L. Rev. 39.

Maczko, "The University of British Columbia Clinical Program" (1978), 36 Advocate 541.

Mazer, "Directory of Law-related Educational Activities — an Analysis", (1978), 2 Can. Community L.J. 74.

Trakman, "Canadian Law Schools" (1980), 6 Dal. L.J. 303.

Veitch and MacDonald, "Law Teachers and Their Jurisdiction" (1978), 56 Can. Bar Rev. 710.

Veitch, ''The Vocation of our Era for Legal Education'' (1979), 44 Sask. L. Rev. 21.

Woodsworth, ''What's on in Continuing Legal Education?'' (1978), 36 Advocate 35.

''Directory of Public Legal Education Services'' (1973), 3 Can. Community L.J. 69.

''Public Legal Education'' (1979), 44 Sask. L. Rev. 123 at 131 (1980), 6 Dal. L.J.

10

THE DOCTRINES OF PRECEDENT AND STARE DECISIS

INTRODUCTION

The day-to-day role of the judge in the Canadian legal system might be described as falling somewhere along a spectrum, the poles of which reflect the two opposing perceptions of a judge's function: to exercise a "quasi-legislative" role in judicial decision-making or to exercise an essentially interpretative function. The former is often described as an activist role on the part of the judiciary, where judges resolve particular matters, not in isolation, but rather in the context of social, economic and other considerations, and render decisions in such a way as to permit the law to respond to changing social conditions. Although, of course, the legislative function in Canada resides, at the federal level, in the two houses of Parliament, and at the provincial level in the various provincial legislatures, this activist notion of the judicial function suggests that the law can and should be responsive to changing times, and that this responsiveness should be effected, not only by legislative enactments, but also by judicial decisions rendered in courts of law. Those who favour this view often point to the decisions of the eminent Lord Denning in the United Kingdom and to the decisions of the Supreme Court of the United States when it was led by Chief Justice Earl Warren as two modern examples of judges exercising the judicial function according to this model.

In contrast to this model of judicial activism is the view of many judges that their role is merely interpretative: to strictly apply the law to particular facts and decide cases accordingly. Under this model, a judge is bound by precedent cases and has no discretion to modify the law in response to changing social conditions and prevailing attitudes. This view of the judicial function has been referred to, at least in respect of constitutional cases in the United States, as a strict constructionist view of the judicial function. In Canada, a recent example of this model of judicial decision-making may be found in some current cases concerning property disputes between husband and wife upon dissolution of marriage.

It is important to realize that the above definitions of the judicial function represent the extreme poles of the spectrum. Undoubtedly, most judges view their role as falling somewhere between these extremes.

As a general rule, the typical judge views his role as essentially an interpretative one, tempered, however, by the dictates of justice and fairness, together with the realization that the law, in order to gain public acceptance and credibility, must not be applied without reference to changing social conditions. However, there are limits to which a judge in deciding cases may respond to changing social conditions, limits which are defined by the dictates of certainty, predictability and consistency, and an appreciation as to where, in our system, the legislative function must properly reside.

However, to some extent, the "activist" model has been legitimized and, indeed, may become the norm as a result of the enactment of the Canadian Charter of Rights and Freedoms. The Charter clearly transfers power from Parliament and the legislatures to the Constitution as the ultimate standard against which the content of all legislation must be measured. Indirectly, it is also a transfer of power from the legislative arm of government to the judiciary, for it is the judges who have the responsibility of interpreting the constitution. Since this represents somewhat of a departure from our tradition of Parliamentary supremacy, it becomes important that our judiciary come to accept its new role.

In assessing the model of judicial decision-making that is appropriate for a particular judge, one of the key factors is how he or she regards the doctrines of precedent and stare decisis. Are they rules of law, conventions or customs now enshrined within the law, judicial attitudes, or otherwise? The characterization of these doctrines is, of course, important in defining the scope of a judge's "law-making" role.

Accordingly, this chapter will focus upon these doctrines, and through reference to the writings of legal scholars and decisions rendered in particular cases, and the results of a 1976 survey of judicial attitudes attempt to characterize these two important doctrines. Although precedent and stare decisis will be defined separately, it is artificial to consider them apart from each other, as they both form an integral part of the judicial decision-making process.

Essentially, precedent is the doctrine that requires a judge, in resolving a particular case, to follow the decision in a previous case, where the fact situations in the two cases are similar. Of course, no fact situations are ever absolutely identical. A judge may avoid the theoretical constraints imposed upon him by the doctrine of precedent by utilizing a process called "distinguishing". This permits a judge to exercise some flexibility and perhaps even creativity. Nevertheless, there may be many past cases with similar fact situations dealing with the same particular legal problem which require a judge to decide which precedent case to follow. This is particularly important when, in dealing with the same set of facts, different judges have rendered different decisions in law. In order to resolve this problem, the doctrine of stare decisis requires that a judge of a particular court must follow the previous decision of the highest court within that particular provincial jurisdiction, although he may be persuaded to differing extents by co-ordinate and higher courts outside of this provincial jurisdiction. Of course, all courts in Canada are bound by the highest court in the land, the Supreme Court of Canada.

THE OPERATION OF STARE DECISIS

The operation of the doctrine of stare decisis is best explained by reference to the English translation of the Latin phrase. "Stare decisis" literally translates as "to stand by decided matters". The phrase "stare decisis" is itself an abbreviation of the Latin phrase "stare decisis et non quieta movere" which translates as "to stand by decisions and not to disturb settled matters".

Basically, under the doctrine of stare decisis, the decision of a higher court within the same provincial jurisdiction acts as binding authority on a lower court within that same jurisdiction. The decision of a court of another jurisdiction only acts as persuasive authority. The degree of persuasiveness is dependent upon various factors, including, first, the nature of the other jurisdiction. Is the other jurisdiction a Canadian one, and if so, is it one of the nine common law jurisdictions in Canada? If the other jurisdiction is non-domestic, is it a Commonwealth jurisdiction? In short, one must determine whether there is a common legal tradition between a given jurisdiction and a foreign jurisdiction in order to determine the degree of persuasiveness to be attached to decisions rendered in that foreign jurisdiction. Second, the degree of persuasiveness is dependent upon the level of court which decided the precedent case in the other jurisdiction. The decision of the highest court that has already dealt with the particular matter would be the most persuasive. Other factors include the date of the precedent case, on the assumption that the more recent the case, the more reliable it will be as authority for a given proposition, although this is not necessarily so. And on some occasions, the judge's reputation may affect the degree of persuasiveness of the authority.

In order to explain in more detail the operation of the doctrine of stare decisis, there are five charts set out below which diagrammatically demonstrate how the doctrine operates, as it applies to each of the provincial courts in a given province and as it applies to the Supreme Court of Canada.

In examining each of the following five charts, note:

1. The degree of persuasiveness, described in the following charts, is in some cases speculative and will vary with the circumstances.

2. The binding or persuasive nature of past decisions and of collegial decisions of the same court within a given jurisdiction, as well as past and collegial decisions of the Supreme Court of Canada, is not indicated in the following charts but is discussed elsewhere in this chapter.

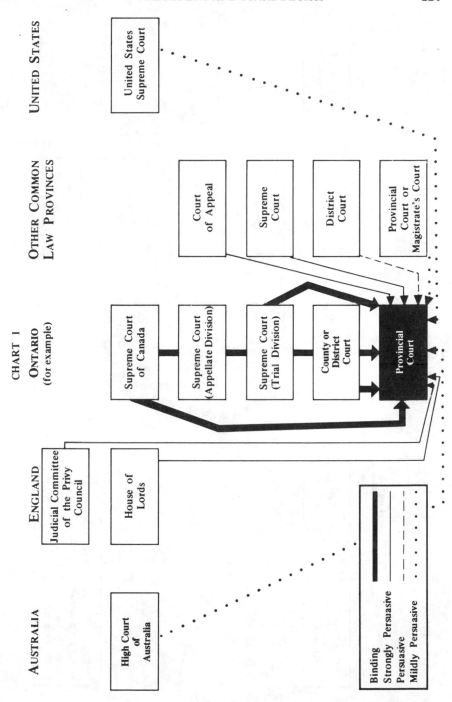

CHART 1

ONTARIO
(for example)

AUSTRALIA

ENGLAND

UNITED STATES

OTHER COMMON
LAW PROVINCES

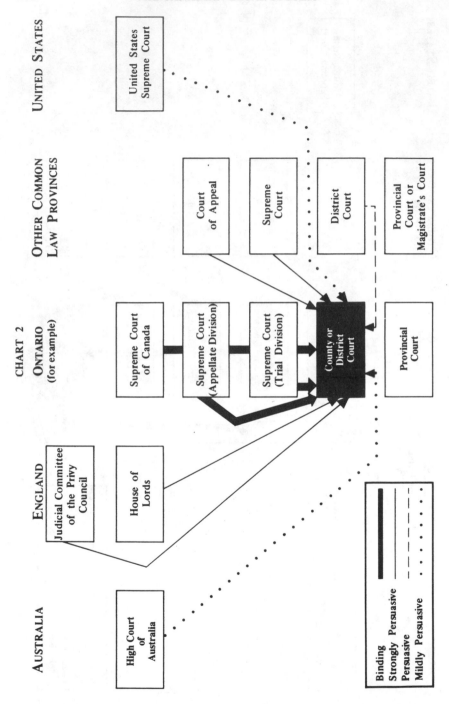

CHART 2

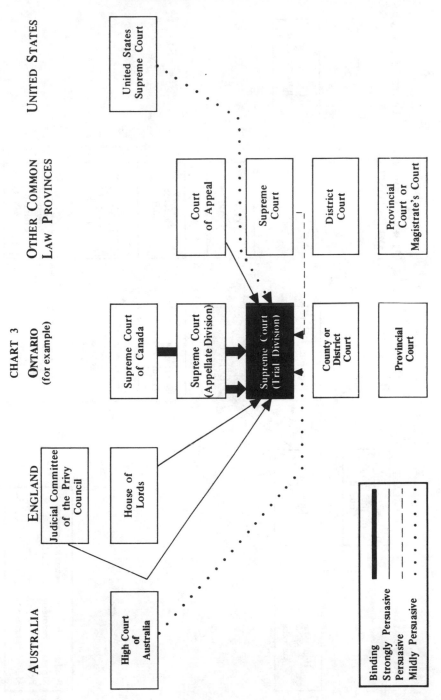

CHART 3

AUSTRALIA ENGLAND ONTARIO (for example) OTHER COMMON LAW PROVINCES UNITED STATES

High Court of Australia

Judicial Committee of the Privy Council

House of Lords

Supreme Court of Canada

Supreme Court (Appellate Division)

Supreme Court (Trial Division)

County or District Court

Provincial Court

Court of Appeal

Supreme Court

District Court

Provincial Court or Magistrate's Court

United States Supreme Court

Binding
Strongly Persuasive
Persuasive
Mildly Persuasive

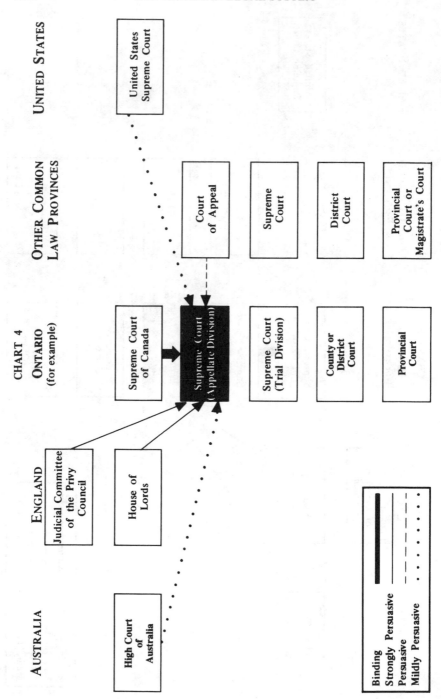

CHART 4

ONTARIO (for example)

AUSTRALIA

ENGLAND

UNITED STATES

OTHER COMMON LAW PROVINCES

United States Supreme Court

Court of Appeal

Supreme Court

District Court

Provincial Court or Magistrate's Court

Supreme Court of Canada

Supreme Court (Appellate Division)

Supreme Court (Trial Division)

County or District Court

Provincial Court

Judicial Committee of the Privy Council

House of Lords

High Court of Australia

Binding
Strongly Persuasive
Persuasive
Mildly Persuasive

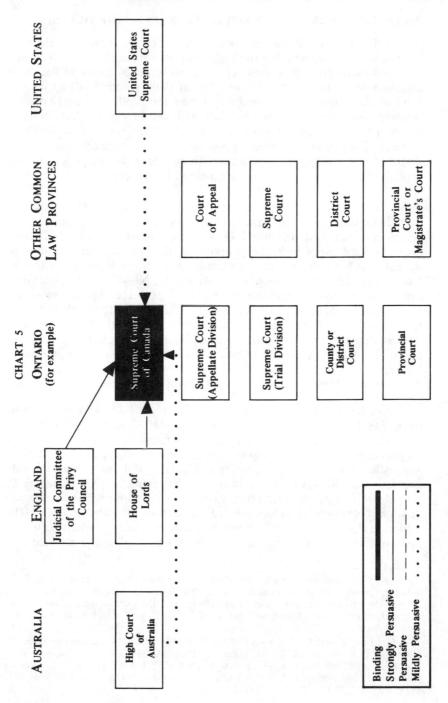

CHART 5

AUSTRALIA

ENGLAND

ONTARIO
(for example)

OTHER COMMON
LAW PROVINCES

UNITED STATES

High Court of Australia

Judicial Committee of the Privy Council

House of Lords

Supreme Court of Canada

Supreme Court (Appellate Division)

Supreme Court (Trial Division)

County or District Court

Provincial Court

Court of Appeal

Supreme Court

District Court

Provincial Court or Magistrate's Court

United States Supreme Court

Binding
Strongly Persuasive
Persuasive
Mildly Persuasive

A COMMENTARY ON THE OPERATION OF STARE DECISIS

This discussion will address four issues.[1] The first relates to the area of uncertainty as to whether the highest court within a given jurisdiction is bound by its past decisions. The second issue arises by virtue of an amendment to the Supreme Court Act in 1949, whereby all appeals to the Judicial Committee of the Privy Council in both civil and criminal matters were abolished. We are left with the residual question as to whether Canadian courts are bound by pre-1949 decisions of the Privy Council. The third issue concerns various aspects of the operation of the doctrine of stare decisis, and the fourth concerns the purposes, advantages and disadvantages of the doctrine of stare decisis.

Are the highest courts in the provinces and the Supreme Court of Canada bound by their own previous decisions? Can they reverse themselves in subsequent decisions? There is judicial authority in the following provinces supporting the proposition that the provincial court of appeal does have the power to overrule its previous decisions: Alberta, British Columbia,[2] Saskatchewan, Manitoba, New Brunswick, Prince Edward Island and Newfoundland. The Quebec Court of Appeal, however, in the tradition of the civil law system, has not committed itself to adhere to the doctrines of precedent and stare decisis and thus decisions of the highest court in that province are not binding, although they are, de facto, highly persuasive. The Ontario Court of Appeal has stated that it is bound by its previous decisions, unless those decisions were decided per incuriam. The Nova Scotia Court of Appeal has been silent to date.

As to whether the Supreme Court of Canada is bound by its previous decisions, the leading case is *Stuart v. Bank of Montreal* (1909), 41 S.C.R. 516, which held that the Supreme Court of Canada is, in law, bound by its previous decisions. However, since that time, there has been strong suggestion that either the Supreme Court is not now bound by its previous decisions, or that in future, the Supreme Court will not likely regard itself as being bound by its previous decisions. This suggestion arises out of several developments. First, as indicated above, in 1949 the Supreme Court of Canada became the final court of appeal in all criminal and civil cases by virtue of an amendment to the Supreme Court Act

---

[1] In the preparation of the second edition of this volume, the author is indebted to Dr. W. F. Bowker, the former Dean of Law at the University of Alberta and the Founding Director of the Alberta Institute of Law Research and Reform, who has taken an interest in this topic and who has kindly provided me with many cases, old and new, which serve to elucidate the many issues.

[2] See, for example, in B.C., *R. v. Yuen Yick Jun*, [1938] 2 W.W.R. 274 (see corrigenda, p. iii), [1940] 2 W.W.R. 467, 54 B.C.R. 541, 73 C.C.C. 289, [1940] 2 D.L.R. 432 (*sub nom. Ex parte Yuen Yick Jun*) (C.A.); *Bell v. Klein*, 12 W.W.R. (N.S.) 272, [1954] 4 D.L.R. 273, reversed [1955] S.C.R. 309, [1955] 2 D.L.R. 513; and *R. v. Haas*, (1962), 38 C.R. 154, 39 W.W.R. 224, 132 C.C.C. 362, 35 D.L.R. (2d) 172 (B.C. C.A.).

abolishing all appeals to the Judicial Committee of the Privy Council. Secondly, in 1966 the House of Lords issued a Practice Statement to the effect that it was no longer bound by its previous decisions. This Practice Statement must certainly have had a strongly persuasive effect on the attitude of Supreme Court of Canada. It is set out as follows:

> Their Lordships regard the use of precedent as an indispensable foundation upon which to decide what is the law and its application to individual cases. It provides at least some degree of certainty upon which individuals can rely in the conduct of their affairs, as well as a basis for orderly development of legal rules.
>
> Their Lordships nevertheless recognize that too rigid adherence to precedent may lead to injustice in a particular case and also unduly restrict the proper development of the law. They propose, therefore, to modify their present practice and, while treating former decisions of this House as normally binding, to depart from a previous decision when it appears right to do so.
>
> In this connection they will bear in mind the danger of disturbing retrospectively the basis on which contracts, settlements of property and fiscal arrangements have been entered into and also the special need for certainty as to the criminal law.
>
> This announcement is not intended to affect the use of precedent elsewhere than in this House.[3]

Thirdly, there have been several cases in which the Supreme Court of Canada has suggested, mostly in obiter, that a similar position will at some time be taken by the Supreme Court of Canada. For example, in the case of *R. v. George*, 47 C.R. 382, [1966] S.C.R. 267 at 278, [1966] 3 C.C.C. 137, 55 D.L.R. (2d) 386, Mr. Justice Cartwright (as he then was) stated in dissent as follows:

> I do not propose to enter on the question, which since 1949 has been raised from time to time by authors, whether this Court now that it has become the final Court of Appeal for Canada is, as in the case of the House of Lords, bound by its own previous decisions of law or whether as, in the case of the Judicial Committee or the Supreme Court of the United States, it is free under certain circumstances to reconsider them.

Then, in the case of *Binus v. R.*, 2 C.R.N.S. 118, [1967] S.C.R. 594 at 601, [1968] 1 C.C.C. 227, Mr. Justice Cartwright expanded on his earlier remarks:

> I do not doubt the power of this Court to depart from a previous judgment of its own but, where the earlier decision has not been made *per incuriam*, and especially in cases in which Parliament or the Legislature is free to alter the law on the point decided, I think that such a departure should be made only for compelling reasons.

The most dramatic suggestion, however, came in the case of *Harrison v. Carswell*, [1975] 6 W.W.R. 673, 25 C.C.C (2d) 186, 62 D.L.R. (3d) 68 (S.C.C.). In this case, Chief Justice Laskin stated in dissent, and probably as obiter dictum, that an issue in the case was "whether this Court must pay mechanical deference to stare decisis". He then proceeded to expand on this issue and stated as follows at p. 683:

---

[3]Practice Statement (Judicial Precedent), [1966] 1 W.L.R. 1234.

> This Court, above all others in this country, cannot be simply mechanistic about previous decisions, whatever be the respect it would pay to such decisions. What we would be doing here, if we were to say that *Regina v. Peters* (1971), 17 D.L.R. (3d) 128n (Can.), because it was so recently decided, has concluded the present case for us, would be to take merely one side of a debatable issue and say that it concludes the debate without the need to hear the other side.
>
> I do not have to call upon pronouncements of members of this Court that we are free to depart from previous decisions in order to support the pressing need to examine the present case on its merits . . . But, above all, this Court has not shown itself to be timorous in tackling important issues where it could be said, with some justification, that an important consideration was absent from an earlier judgment, even a recent one, upon which reliance was placed to foreclose examination of a similar issue in a subsequent case.

In this connection, the reader might consult a case comment related to the *Harrison* decision, written by Professors S. C. Coval and J. C. Smith of the University of British Columbia, entitled "The Supreme Court and a New Jurisprudence for Canada" (1975), 53 Can. Bar Rev. 819 at 825. In the comment the two authors make the following remarks:

> The Chief Justice focused his attention on "two areas of concern respecting the role of . . . the final Court in this country in both civil and criminal causes"; whether the Supreme Court of Canada "must pay mechanical deference to *stare decisis* and, second, whether this Court has a balancing role to play, without yielding place to the legislature". Chief Justice Laskin recognized the necessity for the law to deal with new and changing social conditions. "The present case" he states, "involves a search for an appropriate legal framework for new social facts which show up the inaptness of an old doctrine developed upon a completely different social foundation." The Chief Justice found this framework in the balancing of interest doctrine which he applied in reaching the conclusion that the right to picket as a legitimate part of the collective bargaining process outweighed the interest of the property owner or occupier in preserving the right to choose who shall come onto his property after an invitation to enter has already been extended to the public at large.

Regardless of whether the Supreme Court of Canada makes any further dramatic pronouncements as to its ability to overrule its own previous decisions, the fact that it has done so on at least four occasions[4] probably indicates that it will not, in future, regard itself as being bound by its previous decisions.

The question as to whether Canadian courts are bound by pre-1949 decisions of the Privy Council has not, as yet, been conclusively answered. Discussion has centered on whether the Supreme Court of Canada, in particular, is bound by pre-1949 decisions of the Privy Council. Chief

---

[4]See *Hill v. R.*, [1977] 1 S.C.R. 827, 23 C.C.C. (2d) 321, 58 D.L.R. (3d) 697, 6 N.R. 413; *Paquette v. R.*, [1977] 2 S.C.R. 189, 39 C.R.N.S. 257, 30 C.C.C. (2d) 417, 70 D.L.R. (3d) 129, 11 N.R. 451; *McNamara Const. (Western) Ltd. v. R.*, [1977] 2 S.C.R. 654, 75 D.L.R. (3d) 273, 13 N.R. 181 (*sub nom. Can. v. McNamara Const. (Western) Ltd.; Can. v. J. Stevenson & Assoc.*); and *Bell v. R.*, [1979] 2 S.C.R. 212, 9 M.P.L.R. 103. See also Bale, G., "Stare Decisis — The Supreme Court and Law Reform" (1978), 26 Chitty's L.J. 337, and Bale, G., "Casting Off the Mooring Ropes of Binding Precedent" (1980), 58 Can. Bar Rev. 255.

Justice Rinfret, in *Re Storgoff*, [1945] S.C.R. 526, 84 C.C.C. 1, [1945] 3 D.L.R. 673, suggested that the abolition of appeals to the Privy Council in criminal matters removed the binding character of previous Privy Council decisions in that field. The same argument could be applied to civil matters, as well, after all appeals were abolished in 1949. This was, however, a dissenting opinion and the rest of the court did not comment on the issue.

In *Negro v. Pietro's Bread Co.*, [1933] O.R. 112, [1933] 1 D.L.R. 490 (C.A.), it was held that Privy Council decisions were only binding if they arose on appeal from Canada and it was suggested in *A.G.B.C. v. Col.*, [1934] 3 D.L.R. 488 (B.C.C.A.), that Privy Council decisions were binding only if they arose on appeal from the same province. Professor Andrew Joanes, relying primarily on the *Negro* case, has concluded that the Supreme Court of Canada is bound by pre-1949 decisions of the Privy Council taken on appeal from Canada.[5] Joanes also suggests, however, that the intent of the Supreme Court Amendment Act, 1949 (2nd Sess.) (Can.), c. 37, was that pre-1949 decisions should be considered as persuasive only. W. Friedman also considers pre-1949 decisions of the Privy Council to be binding on the Supreme Court of Canada until it decides not to follow them.[6]

Another legal writer, G. R. B. Whitehead, agrees that there are no cases where the Supreme Court of Canada has not followed a Privy Council precedent, but he argues that the Supreme Court of Canada should not be bound as it has taken the place of the Privy Council and so should inherit the Privy Council's ability to overrule previous decisions.[7] The consensus in favour of the Supreme Court not being bound, therefore, seems to focus on whether the Supreme Court can overrule itself.

Notwithstanding the foregoing, in view of the changing attitudes suggested, for example, in *Harrison v. Carswell*, supra, it is very doubtful that the Supreme Court of Canada would now feel bound by pre-1949 decisions of the Privy Council. The one exception, however, might be found in the area of constitutional law and even this is not certain.

This issue was recently considered by Professor Gordon Bale in his articles "Stare Decisis — The Supreme Court and Law Reform" (1978), 26 Chitty's L.J. 337, and "Casting Off the Mooring Ropes of Binding Precedent" (1980), 58 Can. Bar Rev. 255. See also the following recent cases: *Ref. re Agricultural Products Marketing Act*, [1978] 2 S.C.R. 1198, 84

---

[5]Joanes, "Stare Decisis in the Supreme Court of Canada" (1958), 36 Can. Bar Rev. 175.

[6]Friedmann, "Stare Decisis at Common Law and under the Civil Code of Quebec" (1953), 31 Can. Bar Rev. 723 at 731.

[7]Whitehead, "The Supreme Court of Canada and the Stare Decisis Doctrine" (1967), 15 Chitty's L.J. 146.

D.L.R. (3d) 257, 19 N.R. 361; *A.V.G. Mgmt. Science Ltd. v. Barwell Dev. Ltd.*, [1979] 2 S.C.R. 43, 92 D.L.R. (3d) 289, [1979] 1 W.W.R. 330, 8 R.P.R. 1, 24 N.R. 554, and *MacDonald v. Vapour Can. Ltd.*, [1977] 2 S.C.R. 134, 22 C.P.R. (2d) 1, 7 N.R. 477, 66 D.L.R. (3d) 1. Finally, see the Foreword to Volume 1 of the Supreme Court Law Review where Chief Justice Bora Laskin states as follows:

> When appeals to the Privy Council were abolished thirty years ago, the Supreme Court became not only the final appellate Court of Canada and for Canadians. It became the Court whose decisions could not be challenged or changed, unless it be by itself or by Parliament or Provincial Legislatures in other than constitutional cases. The Court, although long adhering to *stare decisis* in respect of its own decision and those by Privy Council, has over the past few years been more receptive to re-examination of such decisions and, indeed, has overruled some decisions of its own as well as a Privy Council decision on a Canadian constitutional issue. Thus, in *Hill v. The Queen (No. 2)*, [1977] 1 S.C.R. 827, the Court overruled *Goldhar v. The Queen*, [1960] S.C.R. 60; in *Regina v. Paquette*, [1977] 2 S.C.R. 189, the Court refused to follow *Dunbar v. The King*, [1936] 4 D.L.R. 737; in *McNamara Construction (Western) Ltd. v. The Queen*, [1977] 2 S.C.R. 654 the Court overruled *Farwell v. The Queen* (1893), 22 S.C.R. 553; and in *Reference re the Agricultural Products Marketing Act* (The Egg Marketing Reference), [1978] 2 S.C.R. 1198, the Court overruled *Lower Mainland Dairy Products Sales Adjustment Committee v. Crystal Dairy Ltd.*, [1933] A.C. 178.

Other issues concerning the operation of the doctrine of stare decisis are raised in the case law. For example, the question arises as to whether a court is bound by a previous decision which was affirmed on appeal by a tie vote. There are opposing views on this issue, however. It was recently held in *R. v. Tenta*, 3 C.R.N.S. 263, 64 W.W.R. 7, [1968] 4 C.C.C. 237, 67 D.L.R. (2d) 536 (Alta. C.A.), that such a decision is binding on a lower court.

Another issue that often seems to re-emerge, relates to the question as to whether a single judge is bound by a previous decision of another judge of co-ordinate jurisdiction. Certainly, a County Court Judge in the province of Ontario, for example, is not bound by a decision of a County Court Judge in the province of British Columbia. In *Wolf v. R.*, 27 C.R.N.S. 150, [1974] 6 W.W.R. 368, [1975] 2 S.C.R. 107, 17 C.C.C. (2d) 425, 47 D.L.R. (3d) 741, it was held, in reasons written by the Chief Justice, that a provincial appellate court is not obliged, as a matter of law or of practice, to follow a decision of the appellate court of another province, unless it is persuaded that it should do so on the merits of that decision or for other independent reasons. Further, it was held that the only required uniformity among provincial appellate courts is that which results from universal conformity to decisions of the Supreme Court of Canada. In *S. v. S.* (1974), 41 D.L.R. (3d) 621, it was held by a justice of the Manitoba Queen's Bench that a decision of a court in one province interpreting a federal statute is not binding on a court of co-ordinate jurisdiction in another province. Nevertheless, such a decision should be followed, unless the judge is satisfied that the precedent decision is wrong, in order to ensure that federal statutes are interpreted uniformly throughout Canada.

In *Meurer v. McKenzie* (1977), 73 D.L.R. (3d) 477, 2 C.P.C. 109, reversed on other grounds [1978] 1 W.W.R. 114, 4 B.C.L.R. 349, 81 D.L.R. (3d) 388 (C.A.), it was held that a judge should follow a decision of a judge of a co-ordinate jurisdiction unless the validity of the prior decision has been affected by subsequent decisions, or it is shown that the judge in the earlier case made his/her decision per incuriam, or that the earlier case was a nisi prius decision given without the opportunity to fully consult the authorities. See also the case of *R. v. Kartna*, [1979] 2 M.V.R. 259 (Ont. H.C.). In *Re Ellwood Robinson Ltd. and Ohio Dev. Co.* (1975), 7 O.R. (2d) 556, it was held that an exception to the doctrine of stare decisis arises where a court of co-ordinate jurisdiction has given its judgment per incuriam, that is, without considering some aspects of the case which ought to have been considered.

Essentially, the issue is one of "comity" among judges in the same jurisdiction. In *Wallace v. Wallace* (1976), 28 R.F.L. 335, 70 D.L.R. (3d) 375 (Sask. Q.B.), one judge was reluctant to give judgment contrary to another judgment by a judge of the same court. However, in *Ex parte Guenette; Ex parte Wood* (1975), 27 C.C.C. (2d) 279 (B.C.), a judge in a later case refused to follow a judge of the same court in an earlier case where the judge in the earlier case had not had the benefit of persuasive authorities brought to his attention. In *Guenette*, it was held that where judges of the same jurisdiction differ in their interpretation of the same statute, a judge does not have to follow a previous interpretation if, for some valid reason, it was improperly determined. Some other cases which considered similar issues include: *Fickett v. Bignell*, [1977] 5 W.W.R. 599, 1 R.F.L. 269, reversed [1979] 2 W.W.R. 379 (B.C. Co. Ct.); *Re McLaughlin* (1977), 16 O.R. (2d) 375, 1 E.T.R. 181, 78 D.L.R. (3d) 275 (H.C.); and *Metro. Trust v. Latvala* (1979), 22 O.R. (2d) 680, 93 D.L.R. (3d) 688 (H.C.).

The issue arises as to whether a lower court judge in one province is bound by the decisions of an appellate court in another province. In *R. v. Constable Tpt. Ltd.*, [1967] 1 O.R. 357, [1967] 2 C.C.C. 167, 60 D.L.R. (2d) 577, a County Court Judge in the province of Ontario indicated that he felt he was bound by a prior decision of the Manitoba Court of Appeal and was not merely persuaded by it. In addition, similar views were expressed by a justice of the Supreme Court of British Columbia. In the latter case, *R. v. Simpson* (1968), 63 W.W.R. 606, 67 D.L.R. (2d) 585, the justice indicated that he was bound by a decision of another province's court of appeal "except in the most extraordinary circumstances". On the other hand, in *R. v. Beaney*, [1969] 2 O.R. 71, [1970] 1 C.C.C. 48, 4 D.L.R. (3d) 369 at 374-75, a County Court Judge in Ontario indicated that he was not bound by an appellate court in another province. In addition, the judge makes some controversial remarks concerning the operation of the doctrines of precedent and stare decisis. In particular, His Honour Judge Matheson made these comments:

Thus, unless there is competent legislation imposing on the Courts a strict rule of *stare decisis*, whether one Court is bound to decide the *rationes decidendi* of the decisions of another Court cannot be a matter of law but only of judicial attitudes and practical convenience. Just as Parliament cannot enact a law that Parliament cannot repeal, the Courts cannot be the author of a true law of *stare decisis*. A rule or law that imposes a legal obligation on a Court to follow and apply certain precedents must have its source outside that Court. This is exemplified by the ease with which the House of Lords abandoned the view — and it could therefore only have been a view, however long and jealously guarded — that it was bound by its own past decisions . . .

There is no legislative rule of law in Ontario to the effect that any Court in this Province is bound by the decisions of extra-provincial Courts, or, indeed, of any Courts . . . Within the hierarchy of appeals it would be futile for a lower Court Judge to render a decision which is inconsistent with the prior decisions of the Courts to which an immediate or ultimate appeal *from him* may be taken, for he will in all likelihood be reversed.

In *R. v. Maika* (1974), 27 C.R.N.S. 115, 17 C.C.C. (2d) 110, it was held that, in respect of criminal cases, the Court of Appeal of Ontario was bound by its previous decisions operating in favour of the subject. On the other hand, in *R. v. McInnis* (1973), 23 C.R.N.S. 152, 1 O.R. (2d) 1, 13 C.C.C. (2d) 471, it was held by the same Court that it was not bound to follow its own decisions where a prior decision was given without consideration of an applicable authority of a statutory provision. Moreover, in criminal cases, that court is not bound by its previous decisions to the same extent as in civil cases. (This perhaps represents somewhat of a departure from the previous position held by the Ontario Court of Appeal.) In *General Brake & Clutch Service Ltd. v. W. A. Scott & Sons Ltd.*, [1975] W.W.D. 158, 59 D.L.R. (3d) 741, the Manitoba Court of Appeal held that it has the power to depart from its own previous decisions. In *Re Doyle* (1976), 6 N. & P.E.I.R. 479 (Nfld.), it was held by a justice of the Trial Division that in matters of form and procedure, the trend by the courts is to place a higher value on justice than on conformity to established precedents. It has been said that the question of following precedent may be reduced to the issue of whether it is better to be wrong than consistent or vice versa.

Where a district court and a provincial court in a province have parallel jurisdiction in respect of some matters, while in other matters the district court has appellate jurisdiction, it has been held in *R. v. Cotterhill* (1977), 3 Alta. L.R. (2d) 37, that the district court's decisions in its appellate capacity were binding upon the provincial courts.

Various issues have arisen concerning the doctrine of stare decisis and the Supreme Court of Canada. When the Supreme Court of Canada states a principle of law, without reference to authorities, then the Court of Appeal from which the appeal to the Supreme Court has been launched is binding authority: see *R. v. DePagie*, [1976] 6 W.W.R. 1, 1 Alta. L.R. (2d) 30, 32 C.C.C. (2d) 89, 1 A.R. 602, leave to appeal to S.C.C. refused 32 C.C.C. (2d) 89n (S.C.C.). Where the Supreme Court of Canada decides a case on the basis of a decision of the English Court of Appeal which is subsequently overruled by the House of Lords it has been held in *Marvco Colour Research Ltd. v. Harris* (1980), 11 R.P.R. 112, 27 O.R. (2d) 686, 107 D.L.R. (3d) 632, 36 N.R. 90, affirmed 30 O.R. (2d) 162, 115 D.L.R. (3d) 512, which was reversed 26 R.P.R. 48, 141 D.L.R. (3d) 577, 45 N.R. 302 (S.C.C.), that notwithstanding the overruling by the House of Lords, a provincial superior court justice is nonetheless bound by the decision of the Supreme Court of Canada.

In *Re Ward* (1975), 20 R.F.L. 173, 9 O.R. (2d) 35, 59 D.L.R. (3d) 361, it was held that a minority decision of the Supreme Court is not binding on a lower court.

Other cases which readers may wish to consult concerning the operation of stare decisis are as follows: *R. v. Davis* (1976), 21 C.C.C. (2d) 507, 74 D.T.C. 6595 (B.C.); *R. v. Dawood*, 31 C.R.N.S. 382, [1976] 1 W.W.R. 262, 27 C.C.C. (2d) 300 (Alta. C.A.); *R. v. Dennis*, 28 C.R.N.S. 268, [1975] 2 W.W.R. 630, 22 C.C.C. (2d) 152, 56 D.L.R. (3d) 379 B.C.); *Wray v. R.*, [1974] S.C.R. 565, 10 C.C.C. (2d) 215, 33 D.L.R. (3d) 750; *R. v. Mueller* (1975), 32 C.R.N.S. 188, 29 C.C.C. (2d) 243 (Ont. C.A.); *R. v. Robertson* (1975), 29 C.R.N.S. 141, 21 C.C.C. (2d) 385 (Ont. C.A.); *Nedco Ltd. v. Clark*, 41 D.L.R. (3d) 565, reversed [1973] 6 W.W.R. 425, 43 D.L.R. (3d) 714 (Sask. C.A.); *R. v. Santeramo* (1976), 36 C.R.N.S. 1, 32 C.C.C. (2d) 35, leave to appeal to S.C.C. granted 32 C.C.C. (2d) 35n (S.C.C.); *Woloszczuk v. Onyszczak* (1976), 14 O.R. (2d) 732, 1 C.P.C. 129, 74 D.L.R. (3d) 554; *R. v. Ostridge* (1979), 22 Nfld. & P.E.I.R. 123, 58 A.P.R. 123, 2 M.V.R. 160 (P.E.I.S.C.); *Conder v. North Star Const. Co.* (1979), 17 B.C.L.R. 186, 12 R.P.R. 313, 106 D.L.R. (3d) 673 (S.C.); *R. v. Kennedy*, [1980] 4 W.W.R. 577, 6 M.V.R. 178 (Alta. Q.B.); *Reid v. Sigurdson* (1979), 32 C.B.R. (N.S.) 170, 17 B.C.L.R. 117, reversed on other grounds 37 C.B.R. (N.S.) 146, 26 B.C.L.R. 336, 118 D.L.R. (3d) 555 (C.A.); *Re A.G. B.C.; Re Diebolt*, [1980] 3 W.W.R. 193, 4 M.V.R. 167 (B.C.S.C.); *R. v. Barrett*, [1980] 4 W.W.R. 339, 15 C.R. (3d) 361, 54 C.C.C. (2d) 75, 31 A.R. 499 (C.A.); *Sellars v. R.*, [1980] 1 S.C.R. 527, 20 C.R. (3d) 381, 52 C.C.C. (2d) 345, 110 D.L.R. (3d) 629, 32 N.R. 70; *Weiss v. R.*, [1980] 5 W.W.R. 93, 19 B.C.L.R. 207, 108 D.L.R. (3d) 253 (S.C.).

Probably the best outline of the operation of the doctrine of stare decisis is the MacGuigan article, cited in the bibliography, although it should be read subject to the comments made in the more recent cases discussed above.

Essentially, the purposes and advantages of the doctrines of precedent and stare decisis are to provide in the law for:

1. certainty and predictability;

2. continuity and stability;

3. consistency; and

4. the possibility of growth: as new factual circumstances occur, this gives rise to new statements of principle.

It has also been suggested that a further advantage of these doctrines is that they contribute to the development of a case law that contains an abundance of detail as well as a practical character. Indeed, in *Woods Manufacturing Co. Ltd. v. R.*, [1951] S.C.R. 504, 67 C.R.T.C. 87, [1951] 2 D.L.R. 465 at 475, the Chief Justice of Canada made these remarks:

> It is fundamental to the due administration of justice that the authority of decisions be scrupulously respected by all Courts upon which they are binding. Without this uniform and consistent adherence the administration of justice becomes disordered, the law becomes uncertain, and the confidence of the public in it undermined. Nothing is more important than that the law as pronounced, including the interpretation by this Court of the decisions of the Judicial Committee, should be accepted and applied as our tradition requires; and even at the risk of that fallibility to which all Judges are liable, we must maintain the complete integrity of relationship between the Courts. If the rules in question are to be accorded any further examination or review, it must come from this Court or from the Judicial Committee.

It is often said that a lawyer would not be capable of rendering advice to his clients if the law lacked the predictability and certainty which arise out of the operation of the doctrine of stare decisis. However, against the desirability for certainty must be balanced the dictates of justice and fairness. Jerome Frank in his treatise *Courts on Trial* made these remarks on this balance:

> For if actually and rigorously adopted, the precedent doctrine would mean this: No matter how absurd or unwise or unjust a legal rule, once announced by a court, may turn out to be, that court must not, cannot properly, change it, but must go on endlessly applying it until the legislature, by a statute, intervenes. As the legislature often does not intervene, the precedent doctrine, as avowed by some of the courts and generally praised by the lawyers, has led to severe criticism of the legal profession by many non-lawyers . . .
>
> In sum, the doctrine of *stare decisis* seems to mean that certainty outweighs justice: Let certainty be achieved though injustice be done and the heavens fall . . .
>
> Several arguments have been advanced in support of this harsh doctrine. (1) The first is an argument of justice. Justice, it is said, requires equality of treatment. It would be intolerable, so the argument goes, if the rule that applied when Mr. Wiseman sues Mr. Simple were not applied when the same question arises subsequently in a suit of Mr. Bold against Mr. Timid . . . Only so can caprice and subjectivity be precluded. Through following precedents, courts achieve uniformity, continuity, objectivity, and, thereby equality . . . (2) A more powerful argument for *stare decisis* rests on the need for stability. Only if rules are certain and stable, it is said, can men conduct their affairs with safety. This argument assumes that most men do conduct their affairs relying on certain legal rules . . . (3) Still another argument for *stare decisis* is that without it, the "beauty and symmetry" of the legal system would be destroyed . . . (4) Another argument, seldom openly expressed but not entirely without influence, was assigned by a famous English judge, Lord Ellenborough. "If," he said, "this rule were to be changed, a lawyer who was well stored with these rules would be not better than any other man without them." . . . (5) Still another argument is the convenience of the judges . . . For a settled system is easier for judges to operate than a set of variable and mutable rules . . .

The precedent system, as I have thus far described it, seems to cause much injustice and to impede desirable social change. Yet its bark is worse than its bite. It does not really bite when a court follows a precedent which it considers just or wise; or when the judge-made rule it accepts is of neutral kind. Neither just or unjust, wise nor unwise; or when a court consults and heeds its own or other judges' earlier opinions because those opinions contain sagacious solutions of difficult problems . . . The precedent system really bites viciously only when a court, regarding a precedent as undesirable, nevertheless refuses to deviate from it.

Two further interesting and more recent commentaries along similar lines are: Hall, "Law Reform and the Judiciary's Role" (1972), 10 Osgoode Hall L. J. 399; and Freedman, "Continuity and Change — A Task of Reconciliation" (1973), 8 U.B.C.L. Rev. 209. The authors of these two articles are, respectively, a former Justice of the Supreme Court of Canada and a former Chief Justice of the province of Manitoba. In addition, other comments have been made by distinguished members of the judiciary in connection with the doctrines of precedent and stare decisis. The present Chief Justice of Canada once remarked:

It is worth remembering that for a final court consistency in decisions is merely a convenience and not a necessity. No one expects the Supreme Court to break out in a rash of reversals of previous decisions, even if it should formally dissociate itself from stare decisis . . . In my view, such dissociation, whether formally expressed or not, is imperative if the court is to develop a personality of its own.

In addition, the late eminent Mr. Justice Holmes of the Supreme Court of the United States also commented:

It is revolting to have no better reason for a rule of law than that it was so laid down in the time of Henry IV. It is still more revolting if the grounds upon which it was laid down have vanished long ago, and the rule simply persists from blind imitation of the past.

To be sure, there are certain disadvantages arising out of the operation of the doctrines of precedent and stare decisis:

1. Rigidity and inflexibility in the law;

2. The danger of illogical distinctions; and

3. The vast magnitude and complexity of detail in the common law.

DEPARTURE FROM THEORY:
THE PROCESS OF DISTINGUISHING

In order to overcome the rigidity and inflexibility inherent in a system which operates under the doctrines of precedent and stare decisis, and in order to resolve the issue as to whether justice or certainty is paramount in the event that the two are inconsistent in a particular case, the courts have utilized various devices. One such device is the process of distinguishing. Basically, distinguishing is the way by which judges can avoid the binding or persuasive nature of precedent decisions. To do so, a judge examines the material facts of the precedent case to which he must conform and the material facts of the instant case. If he finds that the precedent case has a material fact or facts absent in the instant case, or alternatively, the instant case contains a material fact or facts absent in the precedent case, he will then be in the position to deny the necessity of following the precedent case. Distinguishing cases on the basis of differences in their material facts is a somewhat subjective process in that the judge must render an opinion as to the materiality of the facts contained in both the precedent and instant cases, and sometimes to satisfy the dictates of justice and fairness in the particular case before him, a judge will make illogical distinctions. While this may serve the interests of justice in respect of the instant case, it is questionable whether illogical reasoning on the part of judges, in the long run, serves the interests of justice.

The process of distinguishing is not, however, the only way in which a judge can avoid the hardships imposed upon him under the operation of stare decisis. In addition, for example, he can characterize objectionable judicial opinions as obiter dicta, that is, he can reinterpret a precedent case so that what appears, perhaps, at first glance, to be the ratio decidendi is held to be a mere obiter comment. The ratio decidendi is the "part of the case that is said to possess authority" containing "the rule of law upon which the decision is founded".[8] On the other hand, an obiter dictum is any statement of law made by a judge that is part of a case but which does not contain the particular rule of law upon which that case is decided. A future judge, of course, is not bound by an obiter dictum; it merely has persuasive force at best.

A judge can also refuse to follow a precedent case on the basis that it was decided per incuriam, that is, he may conclude that the precedent case was decided through inadvertence. For example, he may take the position that the judge in the precedent case inadvertently did not take an important authority into consideration in rendering his decision.

Where a precedent decision is arrived at by various concurring reasons, the judge can pick and choose which reasons for judgment in the precedent case he wishes to follow. For example, often a panel of three judges will constitute the majority in a precedent decision. While all three might reach the same conclusion, they may each do so for different reasons. In examining the precedent case, a judge in an instant case can decide which reasons for judgment he wishes to follow and ignore the others.

Finally, the boldest (and probably intellectually the most honest) way in which a judge can avoid any injustice or rigidity imposed upon him under the operation of stare decisis is to take the position that a precedent case was wrongly decided and then simply ignore it.

---

[8]Williams, *Learning the Law*, 10th ed. (1969), p. 62.

JUDICIAL PERCEPTION OF THE DOCTRINES OF PRECEDENT AND STARE DECISIS: CURRENT RESEARCH

One way of determining how the doctrines of precedent and stare decisis operate is to ask sitting members of the judiciary how they regard these doctrines. Accordingly, a study, sponsored and financed by the Canadian Institute for the Administration of Justice, was conducted in the summer of 1976 at the University of Alberta. (This research is briefly mentioned in the previous chapter.)

Set out below are some of the comments received in response to this specific question posed to all judges of the province of Alberta:

Should judges, in applying the law, exercise a quasi-legislative role, as suggested by Chief Justice Deschenes [in an attached newspaper extract], in judicial decision-making, or alternatively, should judges exercise an essentially interpretative function? In this connection, I am also interested in your views as to the nature of the doctrines of precedent and stare decisis . . . how would you characterize these doctrines? Are they rules of law, conventions or customs now enshrined within the law, judicial attitudes, or otherwise?

1. . . .[precedents must be interpreted] in light of changing social conditions and values.

2. . . .[precedent and stare decisis can be characterized as] rules of law . . .[and] are needed to prevent judges from imposing their personal whims and philosophies upon society under the guise of pronouncive law.

3. Some judges are revolutionary in their thoughts and attitudes and in the law-making role of the judge, he must have some regard to precedent and should follow certainly the higher courts which are his guidelines until overruled or changed.

4. Stare decisis has become such an integral part of our law that, in my opinion, it is now a rule of law and should continue to be such . . . The doctrines of precedent and stare decisis are a fundamental part of our system of law. [There are three purposes for them: (1) they provide a basis from which lawyers can advise clients; (2) they avoid additional costs of appeals and unnecessary litigation; and (3) there is a danger that different parts of the same jurisdiction and different jurisdictions would otherwise apply different principles of law in Canada.]

5. Turning to the doctrines of precedent and stare decisis, I remember that someone once said: "I would rather be right than consistent." But precedent and stare decisis are necessary if there is to be certainty and consistency in law. Lord Reid points out in the borstal boys case that the trend is regarding the law of negligence as depending upon principle so that, when a new point emerges, one should ask not whether it is covered by authority, but whether recognized principles apply to it. The system of common law is based on precedent and on the rule that lower courts follow the rulings of appellate courts. This is necessary, but this does not mean that an appellate court cannot, for good reason, reverse itself at some future time. These, in my opinion, are rules of law.

6. [Stare decisis is, at present, a rule of law. Trial judges] are appreciative of and feel bound by decisions of other courts. [When they disagree with a superior court, it is because there is] an inclination to stretch and look for answers which meet the "justice" of the situation. [Appeal courts should not allow the law to shift too drastically and also should not have the ability to reverse themselves. The Supreme Court of Canada has, in some cases, the ability to reverse itself.]

7. [Precedent and stare decisis are subject to the process of distinguishing. They are binding rules of law.] By seeking out and finding distinctions we would of course be fulfilling a good deal more than a merely interpretative function, merely applying the law.

8. [The doctrines of precedent and stare decisis are important for certainty. An alternative would not be rule of law, but rule of man. Each judge would become a law unto himself.] As far as the legislative role of the judges is concerned . . . I emphatically state that the function of a judge is not that of the law-maker. The problem with this whole area, of course, is one of connotation and semantics. There can be no question that in the day-to-day functioning of judges they will contribute considerably to the growth and development of law. It is also true that in our constitutional system there is a fair amount of overlapping between the functions of the executive, the legislature and the judiciary. It is important to recognize that the lines dividing the three branches of government are rather grey and broad, but I think it is equally important to emphasize the paramount function of each branch of government and that each should be vigilant in minimizing its interference with the other's responsibility.

Basically, I am of the view that there should be as much certainty in the law as possible. In other words, the citizen at any given time should know where he stands in his relationships with his fellow citizen and with the state. If laws are changed without notice then the position of the citizen is rendered uncertain. For that reason I feel that generally the law should not change except by the action of the legislature. The problem with laws being changed by judges is that the change occurs without notice to the public. Secondly, I feel that even in a democratic system as highly developed as our own, the citizen has a rather limited opportunity to control the law. That opportunity is, of course, expressed by the fact that the legislature is accountable to the voter. There is no similar accountability between the judiciary and the public and it is therefore my view that the judiciary must be very careful to keep its law-making role within the limits set by the existing rules of law. I therefore, of course, feel that the doctrine of stare decisis is a doctrine essential to the proper functioning of our judicial system. If that doctrine is taken away from the judicial system, then each judge becomes a law unto himself and the citizen is no longer subject to the rule of the law but is in danger of being subject to the rule of the man . . .

9. The doctrines of precedent and stare decisis are essential to the administration of law . . .[If] some precedent or stare decisis philosophy [is not in tune with new social realities, it is the legislature, not the courts, which has the burden of adapting the law to the new realities].

10. [Precedent and stare decisis] play an important role in our courts . . . While a judge is not necessarily bound by a precedent, he is by stare decisis, i.e., a judge other than a peer.

11. Stare decisis is not a form of concrete; forever immutable . . .[The doctrine of stare decisis is the] embodiment of the desire that the law should be stable and known . . .[But it must be applied in moderation, otherwise it], when pushed to doctrinaire limits, becomes utter nonsense.

12. [Precedent is a rule of law and is binding.]

13. [The doctrines of precedent and stare decisis are hard and fast legal rules but there is always room for the device of distinguishing.]

14. I would characterize doctrines of precedent and stare decisis as conventions or customs enshrined within the law.

15. I . . . see stare decisis as tantamount to a rule of law. The force of precedent must, of course, vary from place and time, and in the absence of detailed legislative enunciation, must serve as an informative guide other than where stare decisis is in effect . . .[Both precedent and stare decisis provide for] consistency in application of the law.

16. Stare decisis is clearly a rule of law, but like our institutions it arises from custom; vis., it is enshrined because it is accepted and recognized by the populace at large . . .[A] court of last resort, [on occasion, may apply social policy to past decisions but this should not apply to provincial courts of appeal in respect of Supreme Court of Canada decisions for this would result in significant variations of law between the provinces].

17. [The role of stare decisis will probably be relaxed here as the legislature tends to lag behind social change. The House of Lords declaration in 1966 that it is not binding on itself will be a contributing factor. Also, this latitude will be particularly applicable to certain fields of law], those with social overtones [such as pornography].

18. [The quality or nature of a doctrine is irrelevant to how one labels it. Stare decisis is] useful.

In examining the above comments, it is important to realize that any conclusions reached arising out of these comments are subject to various drawbacks related to the unempirical nature of the 1976 study. Rather, the study was in the nature of a descriptive portrayal of the views of those members of the judiciary who responded to the questions posed. The survey solicited views from judges at all levels of the Alberta judiciary. In any event, set out below are some conclusions which might be reached from a study of the responses received.

First, some judges hold the view that they must slavishly adhere to the doctrines of precedent and stare decisis. Although the number of judges who subscribe to that view without qualification is small, it does represent a certain hardcore component within the Canadian judiciary. Most judges, however, strongly believe in a strict adherence to the doctrines of precedent and stare decisis but recognize that, in doing so, as one judge aptly put it, "[adherence to stare decisis] when pushed to doctrinaire limits becomes utter nonsense". Judges gave various reasons for their belief that they must follow the doctrines of precedent and stare decisis. The most common reasons advanced were those related to the notion that there must be certainty, predictability and consistency in the law. One judge, however, suggested another advantage of adherence to the doctrines in that the certainty and predictability that prevails does, as a by-product, in turn avoid additional costs of appeal and unnecessary litigation.

Secondly, while most judges did subscribe to the view that their primary judicial function is to interpret the law as it presently exists, they also suggested in their responses that in the exercise of this primary function there exists room for some judicial flexibility and creativity in order to satisfy the dictates of justice and to permit the law to be responsive to changing social conditions. In order to temper the results that would follow a strict adherence to precedent and stare decisis, most judges agreed that a resort to the process of distinguishing was the best way to inject this flexibility into the judicial function.

Thirdly, many judges expressed a sensitivity as to where the true legislative function lies. It was not uncommon for a judge to delineate the constitutional boundaries of the judicial and the legislative functions. While there might be some judges who wish to assume a "quasi-legislative" function, most chose to reserve any legislative function to the legislative bodies and to reserve to themselves a purely interpretative function. As a result, one could conclude that while the members of the judiciary appreciate the constitutional limitations on their function, nonetheless, there are some judges who proceed to utilize the doctrines of precedent and stare decisis, together with the process of distinguishing, to play an essentially "quasi-legislative" role under the guise of a purely interpretative one. The extent to which judges exercise this quasi-legislative role depends upon the extent to which an individual judge employs the process of distinguishing and other devices which give rise to judicial flexibility and creativity. This, of course, reflects the great dilemma faced by judges and the immense difficulties in sorting out the various expectations which underlie the judicial function.

As to the difficult question of categorizing the doctrines of precedent and stare decisis, there were some judges who thought it was unimportant to make such a categorization. These judges felt that it was sufficient to conclude that the doctrines of precedent and stare decisis were "useful" or "essential to the administration of justice" or "play an important part" (in our legal system) or were an "embodiment of the desire that the law should be stable". One judge described attempts at characterization "to be of limited use, much like the signs on the highway, they help, but you could get there without them". Indeed, it is possible that precise definition might have a negative effect for, if precedent and stare decisis were strictly categorized, it might not be possible to employ a device to circumvent them.

The question posed to the judges suggested that the doctrines of precedent and stare decisis might be regarded as, perhaps, rules of law, judicial attitudes, customs or conventions enshrined within the law, or otherwise. Most judges adopted one or another of these various suggested sources of the doctrines. Some, however, advanced alternatives. For example, one judge suggested that the doctrine of stare decisis was a "matter that has been determined by judicial decision". Another judge defined the doctrines in terms of their function. He suggested that, in effect, they imposed constraints in order to prevent judges from imposing their personal whims and personal philosophies. No judges, however, were as bold as His Honour Judge Matheson in the case of *R. v. Beaney, supra*, where the County Court Judge expressed the view, discussed elsewhere in this chapter, that unless there existed a statute of the legislature imposing an obligation upon a judge to follow a previous case, the doctrine of stare decisis was essentially no more than a matter of judicial attitudes and practical convenience. Although Judge Matheson may ultimately be proven correct, this strong a statement did not appear among the responses received in the survey conducted.

Yet another conclusion that might be reached is that there exists, as there existed with respect to the judicial perception as to the role of the judge, no unanimity in judicial perceptions of the doctrines of precedent and stare decisis, although there emerges a majority view. Probably the dictates of custom and convention, together with an element of judicial comity, demand universal acceptance of these doctrines. At the very least, if this conclusion is correct, it indicates how important the notion of convention is in defining an important source of law in the Canadian legal system.

As indicated earlier, the research conducted at the University of Alberta during the summer of 1976 related only to the members of the judiciary in the province of Alberta. The results from the Alberta survey are only suggestive of certain conclusions, and while many of these conclusions are probably universally accurate, unfortunately they are derived from only a small local sample. Perhaps, at some future time, a nation-wide survey of this nature might be conducted. Only then will a truly representative picture emerge as to judicial perceptions of the doctrines of precedent and stare decisis, and of the role of the judge in the Canadian legal system. In the meantime, the University of Alberta project represented a first and unprecedented step in examining the fundamental attitudes of the judiciary in conducting its day-to-day responsibilities as an essential arm of the Canadian body politic.

SELECTED BIBLIOGRAPHY
ON THE
DOCTRINES OF PRECEDENT AND STARE DECISIS

ARTICLES

Allen, "Importance of Following Precedent in the Development of Law and the Administration of Justice", 26 Mo. Bar J. 190.

Bale, "Casting Off the Mooring Ropes of Binding Precedent" (1980), 58 Can. Bar Rev. 255.

Bale, "The Quiet Revolution" (1966), 14 Chitty's L.J. 329.

Bale, "*Stare Decisis* — The Supreme Court and Law Reform" (1978), 26 Chitty's L.J. 337.

Bentil, "Court of Appeal's Adherence to its Jurisprudence", 34 New. L.J. 733.

Bernier, "L'autorité du précédent judiciaire à la Cour de Québec" (1971), 6 Thémis 535.

Birmingham, "Neutrality of Adhering to Precedent", [1971] Duke L.J. 541.

Birnbaum, "Stare Decisis versus Judicial Activism: Nothing Succeeds Like Success", 54 A.B.A.J. 482.

Boulanger, "Le précédent judiciaire dans le droit privé francais contemporain" (1961), 21 Ridu. B. 65.

Brazier, "Overruling House of Lords Criminal Cases", [1973] Crim. L.R. 98.

Calder, "Stare Decisis and the Supreme Court of Canada" (1961), 1 Western L. Rev. 36.

Cardozo, "Adherence to Precedent. The Subconscious Element in the Judicial Process" in *The Nature of the Judicial Process*. New Haven: Yale University Press, 1932.

Coval and Smith, "The Supreme Court and a New Jurisprudence for Canada — *Harrison v. Carswell*" (1975), 53 Can. Bar Rev. 819.

Cross, "Ratio Decidendi and Obiter Dictum" in *Precedent in English Law*, 2nd ed., Oxford Clarendon Press, 1968.

Cross, "Recent Developments in the Practice of Precedent — The Triumph of Common Sense", 43 Aust. L.J. 3.

Cross, "Stare Decisis in Contemporary England" (1966), 82 L.Q. Rev. 203.

Curtis, "*Stare decisis* at Common Law in Canada" (1978), 12 U.B.C.L. Rev. 1.

Deutsch, "Precedents and Adjudication", 83 Yale L.J. 153.

Dobbym, "Prospective Limitation of Constitutional Decisions on Criminal Cases", 36 Mod. L. Rev. 301.

Dworkin, "Stare Decisis in the House of Lords" (1962), 25 Mod. L. Rev. 163.

Fairchild, "Limitation of New Judge-Made Laws to Prospective Effect Only: 'Prospective Overruling' or 'Sunbursting' " (1967), 51 Marq. L. Rev. 254.

Finch, "Stare Decisis and Changing Standards in English Law" (1973), 51 Can. Bar Rev. 523.

Frank, "Illusory Precedents: The Future of Judicial Somnambulism" in Smith (ed.), *Law and the Modern Mind*, 1970.

Freedman, "Continuity and Change — A Task of Reconciliation" (1973), 8 U.B.C.L. Rev. 209.

Friedland, "Prospective and Retrospective Judicial Lawmaking" (1974), 24 U. of T. L.J. 170.

Friedmann, "Stare Decisis at Common Law and under the Civil Code of Quebec" (1953), 31 Can. Bar Rev. 723.

Freidmann, "Precedent and Legal Development" in *Legal Theory*, 5th ed., Stevens, 1967, p. 463.

Geddes, "Authority of Privy Council decisions in Australian courts" (1978), 9 Fed. L. Rev. 427.

Gibson, "*Stare Decisis* and the Action *Per Quod Servitium Amisit* — Refusing to Follow the Leader" (1980), 13 C.C.L.T. 309.

Hall, "Law Reform and the Judiciary's Role" (1972), 10 Osgoode Hall L.J. 399.

Hare, "Stare Decisis" (1970), 31 Ala. Law 273.

Hiller, Jack A., "The Law — Creative Role of Appellate Courts in the Commonwealth", 27 International and Comparative Law Quarterly 85-126 (1978).

Hirsch, "Reducing Law's Uncertainty and Complexity", 21 U.C.L.A. L. Rev. 1233.

Hubbard, "Le Processus Judiciaire Du 'Common Law' " (1968), 28 R. du B. 1.

Joanes, "Stare Decisis in the Supreme Court of Canada" (1958), 36 Can. Bar Rev. 175.

Jones, "Stare Decisis — Sovereignty — Cows and Changing Circumstances", 18 U. of T. Fac. L. Rev. 163.

Kavanagh, "Stare Decisis in the House of Lords" (1973), 5 N.Z.U. L. Rev. 323.

Kennedy, "Case and Comment" (1955), 33 Can. Bar Rev. 340.

Kennedy, "Case and Comment" (1959), 27 Can. Bar Rev. 465.

Kelman, "Force of Precedent in the Lower Courts", 14 Wayne L. Rev. 3.

Kidd, "*Stare decisis* in intermediate appellate courts: Practice in the English Court of Appeal, the Australian State Full Courts and the New Zealand Court of Appeal" (1978), 52 Aust. L.J. 274.

Landes and Posner, Legal Precedent: A Theoretical and Empirical Analysis, 19 Journal of Law and Economics 249-313 (1976).

Lang, "Is There A Ratio Dividend?" (1974), 48 Aust. L.J. 146.

Langbein, "Modern Jurisprudence in the House of Lords: The Passing of the London Tramways", 53 Cornell L.R. 807.

Lapres, "Stare Decisis — Binding Effect of Decisions of House of Lords on Lower Courts" (1974), 52 Can. Bar Rev. 128.

Lawlor, "Axioms of Fact Polarization and Fact Ranking — Their Role in Stare Decisis" (1969), 14 U. of T. L. Rev. 703.

Leach, "Revisionism in the House of Lords: The Bastion of Rigid Stare Decisis Falls" (1967), 80 Harvard L. Rev. 197.

Llewellyn, "The Two-Faced Doctrine" in *The Bramblebush*, 1930, p. 66.

Lyon, "Drybones and Stare Decisis" (1971), 17 McGill L.J. 594.

MacGuigan, "Precedent and Policy in the Supreme Court" (1967), 45 Can. Bar Rev. 627.

MacIntyre, "The Use of American Cases in Canadian Courts", 2 U.B.C.L. Rev. 478.

Marshall, "Binding Effect of Decisions of the Judicial Committee of the Privy Council" (1968), 17 Int. and Comp. L.Q. 743.

Mitchell, "The Role of Courts in Public Policy-Making: A Personal View" (1975), 33 U. of T. Fac. L. Rev. 1.

Moran, "Stare Decisis in an Era of Judicial Activism: One State's Answer" (1969), U. Tel. L. Rev. 51.

Murphy, "Legal Quality of Judicial Decisions", 7 Duquesne L. Rev. 365.

Nicol, "Prospective Overruling: A New Device for English Courts?" (1976), 39 Mod. L. Rev. 542.

Noland, "Stare Decisis and the Overruling of Constitutional Decisions in the Warren Years", [1969] Val. U.L. Rev. 401.

Oliphant, "A Return to Stare Decisis" (1928), 14 A.B.A.J. 71.

Orchard, "*Stare Decisis* in the Court of Appeal" (1980), N.Z.L.J. 380.

Prott, "Refusing to Follow Precedents: Rebellious Lower Courts and the Fading Comity Doctrine" (1977), 51 Aust. L.J. 288.

Prott, "When Will a Superior Court Overrule its own Decision?" (1978), 52 Aust. L.J. 304.

Raphael, "Stare Decisis in the Ontario Court of Appeal: *Delta Acceptance v. Redman*", 27 U. of T. Fac. L. Rev. 112.

Rickett, "Precedent in the Court of Appeal" (1980), 43 Mod. L. Rev. 136.

Rogers, "Perspectives or Prospective Overruling", 36 U.M.K.C. L. Rev. 39.

Rudden, "Courts and Codes in England, France and Soviet Russia", 48 Tul. L. Rev. 1010.

St. John, "Lords Break from Precedent: An Australian View", 16 Int. and Comp. L.Q. 808.

Schaeffer, "Control of 'Sunburst': Techniques of Prospective Overruling", 42 N.Y.U. L. Rev. 631.

Schaeffer, "New Ways of Precedent" (1967), 2 Man. L.J. 255.

Schaeffer, "Precedent and Policy" (1966), 34 U. Chic. L. Rev. 3.

Schmidhauser, "Stare Decisis, Dissent and the Background of the Justices of the Supreme Court of the United States" (1962), 14 U. of T.L. J. 194.

Schreiver, "Authority of International Judicial Practice in Domestic Courts", 23 Int. and Comp. L.Q. 681.

Seligson, "Use of Unreported Cases in California", 24 Hastings L.J. 37.

Shapiro, "Toward a Theory of Stare Decisis", [1972] 1 J. Legal Studies 125.

Silverman, "Panacea for a Judgment" (1971), 9 Alta. L. Rev. 397.

Sobeloff, "Tax Effect of State Court Decisions", 21 Tax Law 507.

Stone, "1966 and All That! Losing the Chains of Precedent", 69 Colum. L. Rev. 1162.

Stone, "The Lords at the Crossroads — When to 'Depart' and How!" (1972), 46 Aust. L.J. 483.

Stone, "On the Liberation of Appellate Judges: How Not To Do It!" (1972), 35 Mod. L. Rev. 449.

Stone, "The Ratio of the Ratio Decidendi" (1969), 22 Mod. L. Rev. 597.

Stone, "A Court of Appeal in Search of Itself: Thoughts on Judges' Liberation" (1971), 71 Colum. L. Rev. 1420.

Summers, "Two Types of Substantive Reasons: The Core of a Theory of Common Law Justification" (1978), 63 Cornell L. Rev. 707 at 730-35.

Tancelin, "Exemple d'application de regle du precedent et d'interpretation stricte du droit statutaire" (Mar.-Apr. 1980), 40 R. Barreau Que. 364.

Traynor, "Quo Vadis, Prospective Overruling: A Question of Judicial Responsibility" (1977), 28 Hastings L. J. 533.

Tur, "Varieties of overruling and judicial law-making: prospective overruling in a comparative perspective" (1978), 23 Juridicai Rev. 33.

Weiler, "Legal Values and Judicial Decision-Making" (1970), 48 Can. Bar Rev. 1.

Wesley-Smith, "*Per incuriam* doctrine" (1980), 15 J. Soc. Pub. T.L. 58.

Whitehead, "The Supreme Court of Canada and the Stare Decisis Doctrine" (1967), 15 Chitty's L.J. 146.

Williams and Myers, "Stare Decisis and the Pooling of Non-Executive Interests in Oil and Gas", 46 Mer. L. Rev. 1013.

Wright, "Precedent" (1942), 4 U. of T.L. J. 247.

Zellick, "Precedent in the Court of Appeal, Criminal Division", [1974] Crim. L.R. 222.

Practice Statement (Judicial Precedent), [1966] 1 W.L.R. 1234.

CASES

A.G.B.C., re; Re Diebolt, [1980] 3 W.W.R. 193, 4 M.V.R. 167 (B.C.S.C.).

A.G. Ont. v. Can. Temperance Fed., 1 C.R. 229, [1946] 2 W.W.R. 1, [1946] A.C. 193, 85 C.C.C. 225, [1946] 2 D.L.R. 1.

A.V.G. Mgmt. Science Ltd. v. Barwell Dev. Ltd., [1979] 2 S.C.R. 43, 92 D.L.R. (3d) 289, [1979] 1 W.W.R. 330, 8 R.P.R. 1, 24 N.R. 554.

Banque Can. Nat. v. Gingras, [1977] 2 S.C.R. 554, 1 B.L.R. 149, 15 N.R. 598, 76 D.L.R. (3d) 91.

Bell v. R., [1979] 2 S.C.R. 212, 9 M.P.L.R. 103.

Binus v. R., [1967] S.C.R. 594, [1968] 1 C.C.C. 227.

Brook v. Calgary, [1971] 5 W.W.R. 96 (S.C.C.).

Broome v. Cassell & Co. Ltd., [1971] 2 Q.B. 254, [1971] 2 All E.R. 187, affirmed [1972] A.C. 1027, [1972] 1 All E.R. 801 (H.L.).

Cameron v. C.P.R., [1918] 2 W.W.R. 1025, 11 Sask. L.R. 227, 42 D.L.R. 445 (C.A.).

C.P.R. v. Anderson, [1936] S.C.R. 200, 45 C.R.C. 1, [1936] 3 D.L.R. 145.

Chekaluck v. Sallenback, [1948] 1 W.W.R. 510, [1948] 2 D.L.R. 452 (Alta. C.A.).

Conder v. North Star Const. Co. (1979), 17 B.C.L.R. 186, 12 R.P.R. 313, 106 D.L.R. (3d) 673, (S.C.).

Daoust, Lalonde & Cie Ltée v. Ferland, [1932] S.C.R. 343, [1932] 2 D.L.R. 642.

Delta Acceptance Corp. v. Redman, [1966] 2 O.R. 37, 55 D.L.R. (2d) 481 (C.A.).

Domenco v. Domenco (1963), 44 W.W.R. 549, 41 D.L.R. (2d) 267 (Man.).

Dowsett v. Edmunds, [1926] 3 W.W.R. 447, 22 Alta. L.R. 292, 46 C.C.C. 330, [1926] 4 D.L.R. 796 (C.A.).

Doyle, Re (1974), 6 Nfld. & P.E.I.R. 479 (Nfld.).

Ellwood Robinson Ltd. and Ohio Dev. Co., Re (1975), 7 O.R. (2d) 556.

First Independent Bank v. Proby (1966), 57 W.W.R. 360 (B.C.).

Fraser v. R., [1963] S.C.R. 455, 40 D.L.R. 707.

General Brake & Clutch Services Ltd. v. W. A. Scott & Sons Ltd., [1975] W.W.D. 158, 59 D.L.R. (3d) 741 (Man. C.A.).

Guenette, Ex parte; Ex parte Wood (1975), 27 C.C.C. (2d) 279 (B.C.).

Harrison v. Carswell, [1975] 6 W.W.R. 673, 25 C.C.C. (2d) 186, 62 D.L.R. (3d) 68 (S.C.C.).

Jeremy v. Fontaine, [1931] 3 W.W.R. 203, [1931] 4 D.L.R. 556 (Alta.).

Lancashire v. Highley, [1917] A.C. 352.

London Tramways Co. v. London County Council, [1898] A.C. 375 (H.L.).

MacDonald v. Vapour Can. Ltd., [1977] 2 S.C.R. 134, 22 C.P.R. (2d) 1, 7 N.R. 477, 66 D.L.R. (3d) 1.

McKibbon and R., Re (1981), 34 O.R. (2d) 185, 61 C.C.C. (2d) 126, affirmed 35 O.R. (2d) 124, 64 C.C.C. (2d) 441, leave to appeal to S.C.C. granted 35 O.R. (2d) 124n, 64 C.C.C. (2d) 441n (S.C.C.).

Marvco Color Research Ltd. v. Harris (1980), 11 R.P.R. 112, 27 O.R. (2d) 686, 107 D.L.R. (3d) 632, 36 N.R. 90, affirmed 30 O.R. (2d) 162, 115 D.L.R. (3d) 512, which was reversed 26 R.P.R. 48, 141 D.L.R. (3d) 577, 45 N.R. 302 (S.C.C.).

Meurer v. McKenzie (1977), 2 C.P.C. 109, 73 D.L.R. (3d) 477, reversed on other grounds [1978] 1 W.W.R. 114, 4 B.C.L.R. 349, 81 D.L.R. (3d) 388 (C.A.).

Motherwell v. Motherwell, [1976] 6 W.W.R. 550 (Alta. C.A.).

Nedco Ltd. v. Clark, 41 D.L.R. (3d) 565, reversed [1973] 6 W.W.R. 425, 43 D.L.R. (3d) 714 (Sask. C.A.).

P. v. P. (1980), 25 A.R. 412 (Fam. Ct.).

Pac. Press Ltd. v. R., [1977] 5 W.W.R. 507, 38 C.R.N.S. 295, 37 C.C.C. (2d) 287 (B.C.S.C.).

Prudential Exchange Co. v. Edwards, [1939] S.C.R. 135, 71 C.C.C. 145, [1939] 1 D.L.R. 465.

Quinn v. Leathem, [1901] A.C. 495.

Regent Holdings Ltd. v. McKay (1972), 25 D.L.R. (3d) 615, affirmed on other grounds 35 D.L.R. (3d) 259 (B.C.C.A.).

R. v. Barrett, [1980] 4 W.W.R. 339, 15 C.R. (3d) 361, 54 C.C.C. (2d) 75, 31 A.R. 499 (C.A.).

R. v. Beaney, [1969] 2 O.R. 71, [1970] 1 C.C.C. 48, 4 D.L.R. (3d) 369.

R. v. Constable Transport Ltd., [1967] 1 O.R. 357, [1967] 2 C.C.C. 167, 60 D.L.R. (2d) 577.

R. v. Cotterhill (1977), 3 Alta. L.R. (2d) 37 (Dist. Ct.).

R. v. Davis (1974), 74 D.T.C. 6595, 21 C.C.C. (2d) 507 (B.C.).

R. v. Dawood, 31 C.R.N.S. 382, [1976] 1 W.W.R. 262, 27 C.C.C. (2d) 300 (Alta. C.A.).

R. v. Dennis, 28 C.R.N.S. 268, [1975] 2 W.W.R. 630, 22 C.C.C. (2d) 152, 56 D.L.R. (3d) 379 (B.C.).

R. v. Dickie; R. v. Pomerleau, 13 W.W.R. (N.S.) 545, 110 C.C.C. 168, [1955] 2 D.L.R. 757 (Alta.).

R. v. Govedarov (1974), 25 C.R.N.S. 1, 3 O.R. (2d) 23, 16 C.C.C. (2d) 238, affirmed (sub nom. *R. v. Popovic and Askov*) 32 C.R.N.S. 54, 25 C.C.C. (2d) 161, 62 D.L.R. (3d) 56 (S.C.C.).

R. v. Kartna (1979), 2 M.V.R. 259 (Ont. H.C.).

R. v. Kennedy, [1980] 4 W.W.R. 577, 6 M.V.R. 178 (Alta. Q.B.).

R. v. McInnis (1973), 23 C.R.N.S. 152, 1 O.R. (2d) 1, 13 C.C.C. (2d) 471 (C.A.).

R. v. Maika (1974), 27 C.R.N.S. 115, 17 C.C.C. (2d) 110 (Ont. C.A.).

R. v. Mankow (1959), 30 C.R. 403, 28 W.W.R. 433, 124 C.C.C. 337 (Alta. C.A.).

R. v. Mueller (1975), 32 C.R.N.S. 188, 29 C.C.C. (2d) 243 (Ont. C.A.).

R. v. Ostridge (1979), 22 Nfld. & P.E.I.R. 123, 58 A.P.R. 123, 2 M.V.R. 160 (P.E.I. S.C.).

R. v. Robertson (1975), 29 C.R.N.S. 141, 21 C.C.C. (2d) 385 (Ont. C.A.).

R. v. Santeramo (1976), 36 C.R.N.S. 1, 32 C.C.C. (2d) 35, leave to appeal to S.C.C. granted 32 C.C.C. (2d) 35n (S.C.C.).

R. v. Simpson (1968), 63 W.W.R. 606, 67 D.L.R. (2d) 585 (B.C.).

R. v. Tenta, 3 C.R.N.S. 263, 64 W.W.R. 7, [1968] 4 C.C.C. 237, 67 D.L.R. (2d) 536 (Alta. C.A.).

Reid v. Sigurdson (1979), 32 C.B.R. (N.S.) 170, 17 B.C.L.R. 117, reversed 37 C.B.R. (N.S.) 146, 26 B.C.L.R. 336, 118 D.L.R. (3d) 555 (C.A.).

Robins v. Nat. Trust Co. Ltd., [1927] 1 W.W.R. 692, [1927] A.C. 515, [1927] 2 D.L.R. 97.

S. v. S. (1973), 41 D.L.R. (3d) 621 (Man.).

Safeway Stores Ltd. v. Harris, 56 Man. R. 146, [1948] 1 W.W.R. 337 (sub nom. *Can. Safeway Ltd. v. Harris*), varied 56 Man. R. 167, [1948] 2 W.W.R. 211, [1948] 4 D.L.R. 187 (C.A.).

Searle v. Wallbank, [1947] A.C. 341.

Shaw v. City of Regina, [1944] 1 W.W.R. 433, [1944] 2 D.L.R. 223, affirmed [1945] S.C.R. 42, [1945] 1 D.L.R. 353.

Stuart v. Bank of Montreal, 41 S.C.R. 516, affirmed [1911] A.C. 120.

Trimble v. Hill (1879), 5 App. Cas. 342 (P.C.).

Wallace v. Wallace (1976), 28 R.F.L. 335, 70 D.L.R. (3d) 375 (Sask. Q.B.).

Ward, Re (1975), 20 R.F.L. 173, 9 O.R. (2d) 35, 59 D.L.R. (3d) 361.

Weiss v. R., [1980] 5 W.W.R. 93, 19 B.C.L.R. 207, 108 D.L.R. (3d) 253 (S.C.).

Western Can. Fire Ins. Co., Re; Cowper's Case (1915), 7 W.W.R. 1365, 8
　　Alta. L.R. 348, 30 W.L.R. 648, 22 D.L.R. 19 (C.A.).
Will v. Bank of Montreal, [1931] 2 W.W.R. 364, [1931] 3 D.L.R. 526
　　(Alta.).
Wolf v. R., 27 C.R.N.S. 150, [1974] 6 W.W.R. 368, [1975] 2 S.C.R. 107, 17
　　C.C.C. (2d) 425, 47 D.L.R. (3d) 741.
Woloszczuk v. Onyszczak (1976), 14 O.R. (2d) 732, 1 C.P.C. 129, 74 D.L.R.
　　(3d) 554.
Woods Manufacturing Co. Ltd. v. R., [1951] S.C.R. 504, 67 C.R.T.C. 87,
　　[1951] 2 D.L.R. 465.
Wray v. R., [1974] S.C.R. 565, 10 C.C.C. (2d) 215, 33 D.L.R. (3d) 750.
Yakymiw v. Yakymiw; Kerr v. Kerr, 5 W.W.R. (N.S.) 385, 60 Man. R. 118,
　　[1952] 4 D.L.R. 578 (C.A.).
Young v. Bristol Aeroplane Co., [1944] K.B. 718.

The above selection of cases includes a review of the Canadian
jurisprudence on this topic up to 1983. However, for a full review of all
the relevant cases up to 1967, readers should consult MacGuigan,
"Precedent and Policy in the Supreme Court" (1967), 45 Can. Bar Rev.
627; and for a further review of developments up to 1980, readers should
consult the two articles written by Professor Bale, cited earlier.

TREATISES

Cross, *Precedent in English Law*, 3rd ed. (1977).
Frank, *Courts on Trial* (1949).
Frank, *Law and the Modern Mind* (1970).
Friedmann, *Legal Theory*, 5th ed. (1967).
Goldberg, *Equal Justice* (1971).
Llewellyn, *The Common Law Tradition: Deciding Appeals* (1960).
Montrose, *Precedent in English Law and Other Essays* (1968).
Murphy & Reuter, *Stare Decisis in Commonwealth Appellate Courts* (1982).
Phillips, *A First Book of English Law*, 7th ed. (1977).
Pound, *Law Finding Through Experience and Reason* (1960).
Rudd, *The English Legal System* (1962).

11

THE RULES AND PRINCIPLES OF STATUTORY INTERPRETATION

In recent years, many old and settled principles at common law have been replaced or modified through legislative enactment at all levels of government. This phenomenon has been brought about both by principal legislation by Parliament and the various provincial legislatures and by regulations, ordinances, by-laws, statutory instruments and Orders in Council enacted by inferior legislative bodies. The result has been a proliferation of enactments dealing with all aspects of modern life, business, and relations between persons.

In addition, in the past quarter century the state of man's knowledge has rapidly increased. This has resulted in the development of complex modern technology in all fields in the natural and applied sciences. Similarly, in the social sciences, and particularly in the area of economics, man has devised new ways of looking at problems in society and new approaches in devising solutions to those problems. Society in the computer age is a matrix of complex institutions, riddled with complex problems. The law must reflect and respond to these complexities. The result is that much recent legislation has had to be expressed in complex language, and the first problem that the reader of the law faces is comprehending the language contained in many recent statutes.

THE PROBLEM OF COMPLEXITY

For example, the following provisions of the Income Tax Act, 1970-71-72 (Can.), c. 63, constitute only one part of one section of the Act. In reading the section, the reader might consider the simple question of what the section is saying:

66(1) A principal-business corporation may deduct, in computing its income for a taxation year, the lesser of

    (a)   the aggregate of such of its Canadian exploration and development expenses as were incurred by it before the end of the taxation year, to the extent that they were not deductible in computing income for a previous taxation year, and

    (b)   of that aggregate, an amount equal to its income for the taxation year if no deduction were allowed under this subsection, subsection 66.1(2) or section 65, minus the deductions allowed for the year by sections 112 and 113.

(2) A corporation (other than a principal-business corporation the principal business of which is described in subparagraph (15)(*h*)(i) or (ii)), whose principal business is production or marketing of sodium chloride or potash or whose business includes manufacturing products the manufacturing of which involves processing sodium chloride or potash, may deduct, in computing its income for a taxation year, the drilling and exploration expenses incurred by it in the year on or in respect of exploring or drilling for halite or sylvite.

(3) A taxpayer who is an individual or a corporation other than a principal-business corporation may deduct, in computing his income for a taxation year, the lesser of

    (*a*) the aggregate of such of his Canadian exploration and development expenses as were incurred by him before the end of the taxation year to the extent they were not deductible in computing his income for a previous taxation year, and

    (*b*) of that aggregate, the greater of

        (i) such amount as the taxpayer may claim, not exceeding 20% of the aggregate determined under paragraph (*a*), and

        (ii) the amount, if any, by which the aggregate of

            (A) such part of his income for the taxation year as may reasonably be regarded as attributable to the production of petroleum or natural gas from wells in Canada or to the production of minerals from mines in Canada,

            (B) his income for the taxation year from royalties in respect of an oil or gas well in Canada or a mine in Canada,

            (C) the amount, if any, included in computing his income for the year by virtue of paragraph 59(3.2)(*b*) or (*c*), and

            (D) the aggregate of amounts included in computing his income for the year by virtue of any of paragraphs 59(2)(*a*), (*c*) and (*d*) and subsection 59(2.1)

        exceeds

            (E) the aggregate of amounts deducted in computing his income for the year under subsection 64(1) in respect of property described in paragraph 59(1.2)(*b*), or under subsection 64(1.1) or (1.2), if no deductions were allowed under this subsection, subsection 66.1(3) or section 65.

        exceeds

        (iii) the amount of any deduction allowed by the *Income Tax Application Rules, 1971* in respect of this subparagraph in computing his income for the year.

(4) A taxpayer who is resident throughout a taxation year in Canada may deduct, in computing his income for that taxation year, the lesser of

    (*a*) the aggregate of such of his foreign exploration and development expenses as were incurred by him before the end of the taxation year to the extent they were not deductible in computing his income for a previous taxation year, and

    (*b*) of that aggregate, the greater of,

        (i) such amount as the taxpayer may claim not exceeding 10% of the aggregate determined under paragraph (*a*), and

(ii)   the aggregate of

(A)   such part of his income for the taxation year as may reasonably be regarded as attributable to the production of petroleum or natural gas from wells outside Canada or to the production of minerals from mines outside Canada,

(B)   his income for the taxation year from royalties in respect of an oil or gas well outside Canada or a mine outside Canada, and

(C)   the aggregate of amounts each of which is an amount, in respect of a foreign resource property or a property referred to in subsection 59(3) that has been disposed of by him, equal to the amount, if any, by which

(I)   the amount included in computing his income for the year by virtue of section 59 in respect of the disposition of the property,

exceeds

(II)   the amount deducted under section 64 in respect of the property in computing his income for the year,

if no deduction were allowed under this subsection, subsection 66(1) or (3), 66.1(2) or (3) or section 65.

If the reader has mastered an understanding of the above provisions, perhaps he might consult the regulations to the Anti-Inflation Act, 1974-75-76 (Can.), c. 75, which were at least equal in complexity to the above provisions.

Dr. Max Wyman, a former President of the University of Alberta, a former Chairman of the Alberta Human Rights Commission and a member of the Board of Review investigating Provincial Courts in the province of Alberta, recently made certain observations on the Canadian legal system. Since he is a lay person, his observations contain a certain objectivity which arises out of a first exposure to our legal system. In an addendum to the Board of Review's formal report in May of 1975 he made these remarks concerning "the language of the law:"

The law belongs to the people who have chosen to be governed by that law. It is not the private domain of the bar, the bench, and the police. For this reason, it seems to me to be axiomatic that the law should be written in the language of the people, not the archaic, stilted and sometimes meaningless language that is now being used. This does not mean that each person should be capable of being his or her own lawyer. Far from it. The complexity of our society will ensure that highly-trained legal personnel will have important roles to play in the years to come. Nevertheless, reasonably educated people should be able, if interested, to read and understand the laws they are expected to obey. Those who are in difficulty with the law should be able, with legal help, to understand the nature of their difficulties, the alternatives that are open to them, and to make a reasoned choice from among those alternatives.

At the present time, it is extremely doubtful that even highly educated people can understand the language in which the law is written. In some extreme cases, even members of the legal profession have difficulty in providing an unequivocal interpretation of some laws.

In Gulliver's Travels, Jonathan Swift made many a pungent and ironical comment about the laws and customs of eighteenth century England. Gulliver describes in some detail the laws of Brobdignag, one of which dealt with the language of the law:

No law of that country must exceed in words the number of letters in their alphabet, which consists only in two and twenty. But indeed few of them extend even to that length. They are expressed in the most plain and simple terms, wherein those people are not mercurial enough to discover above one interpretation. And to write a comment upon any law is a capital crime. As to the decision of civil causes, or proceedings against criminals, their precedents are so few, that they have little reason to boast of any extraordinary skill in either.

The laws of Canada might improve considerably if we were to follow the simplicity of the laws that were used to govern the land of the giants. Even then, over two hundred years ago, Swift was not enamoured with the reliance that English law placed on precedents.

These comments suggest that legislative draftsmen in Canada are not accomplished in performing their trade. On the contrary, however, legal drafting in Canada is an art which has been acknowledged and appreciated throughout the common law world. Canadian draftsmen are often sought by emerging nations in the Third World to draft their basic constitutions as well as the provisions of their regular statutes. Also, there is a substantial and important division of the Department of Justice of Canada in Ottawa concerned solely with the drafting of legislation. In addition, several law schools in Canada now provide courses in legal drafting; and recently there have been Canadian texts published dealing with the related concerns of legal writing and legal drafting. So the problem lies not in a lack of Canadian expertise in drafting, but rather in the fact that complex laws couched in complex statutory language must be used in order to resolve contemporary matters. In addition, historically, we in the common law world, are relatively inexperienced in drafting laws while the civil or Napoleonic codes of Europe date back to the early Roman codification for their origins. Nations employing a civil or Napoleonic code thus share a much vaster experience in reducing propositions to statutory language, an experience spanning several centuries.

THE PROBLEM OF AMBIGUITY: DETERMINING LEGISLATIVE INTENT

The major problem in dealing with statutes is the ambiguity often found in statutory language. Sometimes, of course, the ambiguity is intentional. More likely, however, it is totally unintentional. Often a statute must be applied in an area, or in connection with a fact situation, not within the contemplation of the drafter of the statute. In order to assist a judge in interpreting such provisions, various rules of statutory interpretation have been developed. In addition, courts have recognized and are receptive to the use of various aids in interpretation. Also, the entire interpretative process is conducted in the context of various presumptions recognized in law which serve as a guide to the judge in interpreting statutes.

The interpretation of ambiguous statutory provisions is a somewhat subjective process. A judge may select a particular rule of statutory interpretation or use a particular aid to interpretation and decide not to be receptive to an alternative rule or aid in interpretation. Nonetheless, that subjective exercise must be conducted in the context of an objective search for legislative intention. As one writer put it:

> In many modern cases, the principle that courts are bound to follow "legislative intention" has been taken to mean that in determining the effect of a statute in cases of interpretative doubt, the judge should decide in such a way as will advance the general objectives which, in his judgment, the legislators sought to attain by enactment of the legislation . . . Thus the principle that doubtful questions should be resolved in accordance with "legislative intention" requires, in this signification of "intention" that the judge interpret the statute not in the light of his own personal notions of justice and expediency, but in the light of the legislative conceptions of justice and expediency which underlie the policy of the enactment.[1]

It is important to realize that the process of interpreting ambiguous statutes represents a significant part of the judicial function, especially at the appellate levels; that is, judges spend a large part of their time in interpreting ambiguous statutes. That is why an understanding of the process by which they conduct this exercise is necessary.

1. RULES OF CONSTRUCTION

The fundamental rule in interpreting ambiguous statutes is that a judge must ascertain the intent of the legislature in enacting the statute. Legislative intent is one of the many fictions throughout the law that serves a useful purpose. Another example of a legal fiction arises in the law of negligence, where in order to determine whether a defendant has breached a standard of care, we resort to an objective test: whether the defendant has conducted himself in accordance with the standard expected of a "reasonable man." In reality, of course, there is no such person who is reasonable in all circumstances and in all situations. Likewise, in reality there is no such single or, for that matter, collective legislative intent in any legislative body. There are opposition parties who do not share the same political views as the government in respect of a given piece of legislation; there are backbenchers of the governing party who do not share the views of the government in respect of a particular piece of legislation but do not complain owing to the dictates of party discipline; there may even have been dissent within the cabinet in discussions preceding the introduction of a piece of legislation. However, notwithstanding its somewhat artificial nature, the notion of legislative intent must be regarded as another one of those legal fictions which serve a useful purpose.

In order to determine the intent of the legislature in enacting a given ambiguous statute, a judge may resort to one of the three major canons of construction. First, the "literal" or "plain meaning" rule requires

---

[1]Jones, "Statutory Doubts and Legislative Intention" (1940), 40 Colum. L. Rev. 157.

that if the precise words used are plain and unambiguous, the judge is bound to construe them in their ordinary sense, even though such a construction might lead to an absurdity or a manifest injustice. The corollary of the above is that any legislative omissions or errors are not to be inferred. Secondly, the "golden" rule requires that, in interpreting an ambiguous statute, the grammatical and ordinary sense of the words is to be adhered to, unless that would lead to some absurdity or some repugnance or inconsistency with the rest of the instrument, in which case the grammatical and ordinary sense of the words may be modified only so far as to avoid that absurdity and inconsistency.[2] Finally, the "mischief " rule requires that, in interpreting an ambiguous statute, the judge must consider four things: First, what was the common law before the making of the Act? Secondly, what was the mischief and defect for which the common law did not provide? Thirdly, what remedy did the legislature resolve upon to cure the mischief and defect? Finally, what was the true reason for the remedy? After entertaining those four questions, the judge must then construe the legislation so as to suppress the mischief and advance the remedy. The above definitions of the three canons of construction are taken from various early cases but they have been restated many times in various forms.

A statute may be enacted for one of two reasons: to codify the existing common law, or to remedy a defect present within the existing common law. Some statutes, called interpretation statutes, are enacted solely for the purpose of providing guidelines for interpreting other statutes enacted within the same jurisdiction. Many of these interpretation statutes contain provisions deeming these other statutes of the same jurisdiction to be remedial in nature. As a result, this seems to invite the application of the mischief rule in interpreting an ambiguous provision, although as indicated earlier judges may select the particular canon of construction that they prefer in the circumstances and interpret the ambiguous provisions in accordance with that canon of construction.

In addition to these three canons of construction, there are three more or less grammatical rules of construction. These rules, usually expressed in Latin, are as follows. First, the "noscitur a sociis" rule is that a general word, following a group of specific words, takes its meaning from those specific words. Similarly, if an ambiguous general word is followed by specific words, the ambiguous word takes its meaning from those words that follow it. For example, in one case it was held that the word "interest" in the phrase "interest, annuities, or other annual payments" means annual interest.

---

[2]See, e.g., *R. v. Wilson* (1978), 6 B.C.L.R. 231 (S.C.); and *R. v. Boylan* (1979), 8 C.R. (3d) 36 (Sask. C.A.).

The second grammatical rule of construction is the "ejusdem generis"[3] rule. It is very similar to the previous one and, in fact, some writers have suggested that they both are the same. This rule is that a general phrase (rather than a general word as in the previous rule) takes its meaning from the specific words that precede it. For example, if a statute contained a provision to the effect that "no dogs, cats or other animals may wander in public places without being controlled by means of a leash," under this rule the general phrase "or other animals" would take its meaning from the preceding specific words, with the result that it would probably be interpreted to mean a domesticated animal, rather than, for example, wild game.

The third grammatical rule of construction is the "expressio unius, exclusio alterius" rule. Under this rule, the express mention or inclusion of one word or phrase implies the exclusion of another word or phrase. A good example of this rule was set out by John Willis in an article entitled "Statute Interpretation in a Nutshell" (1938), 16 Can. Bar Rev. 1 at 8 is as follows:

> If I have living in my house my wife, my children, two old aunts and my mother, and a friend says "Bring the family to our picnic, Sunday", what does he mean by "family"? — my wife and children only, or my whole ménage? If he adds, "your mother comes under that heading, you know", by specially mentioning my mother he shews, it may be said, that he was using "family" in the narrow sense of "wife and children": result, the aunts are not invited — *expressio unius, exclusio alterius,* the express mention of one person or thing implies the exclusion of other persons or things of the same class not mentioned.

Willis then concludes, as many others have concluded that this rule of construction is unreliable and is very rarely applied by a court. However, see the recent case of *Crease v. Metro. Toronto Police Commrs. Bd.* (1976), 11 O.R. (2d) 459, 66 D.L.R. (3d) 403, in which the rule was applied. See also *R. v. Baig* (1979), 23 O.R. (2d) 730 (Dist. Ct.).

2. AIDS TO STATUTORY INTERPRETATION

In addition to all of the foregoing rules of construction, there are various aids available to assist a judge in determining the legislative intent behind the enactment of an ambiguous statutory provision. Again, there is an element of subjectivity in that a judge may choose to use one aid and ignore another. While some aids are clearly inadmissible in evidence others may be admitted depending upon the receptivity of the individual judge.

The following is a list of aids in interpreting ambiguous statutory provisions. Some of these aids are intrinsic to the statute containing the ambiguous provisions, while others are purely extrinsic in nature.

---

[3]Some recent examples of the application of this rule may be found in *Tiedmann v. Basiuk* (1977), 4 Alta. L.R. (2d) 127 C.P.C. 192, 5 A.R. 435 (T.D.); *Bell v. North Vancouver School Dist. 44* (1979), 16 B.C.L.R. 94 (S.C.); *Frehlick v. McLenehan*, [1980] I.L.R. 1-1270, 114 D.L.R. (3d) 310, 3 Sask. R. 340 (C.A.); and *R. v. Twoyoungmen* (1979), 16 A.R. 413 (C.A.).

(a) Interpretation Statutes

There are in Canada interpretation statutes at the federal level and in every province as well. The federal Interpretation Act applies to all federal statutes and the various provincial Interpretation Acts apply to all statutes within a given provincial jurisdiction. These statutes contain some general rules in interpreting statutes. Some of the typical rules are to the effect that a preamble to a statute shall be read as part of a statute, while any marginal notes explaining the purport of a given section are not to be read as part of the statute; that any words importing male persons in any statute include female persons; and that any words in the singular include the plural and any words in the plural include the singular.

In addition to these general rules, specific words are defined for purposes of all statutes within the given jurisdiction governed by the particular interpretation statute. For example, the federal Interpretation Act defines such words as "holiday", "radio-communication", and "standard time" for the purposes of all federal statutes.

(b) Definition Sections

Many statutes contain sections defining specific words used in the particular statute. Some statutes, like the Criminal Code of Canada, have a substantial definition section at the beginning of the Act. In addition, the Criminal Code is divided into various parts and there is a definition section at the beginning of each part. Moreover, on occasion, there are definition provisions at the beginning of some sections.

(c) Context

In determining legislative intent, a legitimate exercise is to examine the context in which an ambiguous provision is found, i.e., to examine other sections of the same statute.

(d) Other Statutes

A judge may resort to an examination of other statutes in order to determine the intent of the legislature in enacting an ambiguous provision in an instant statute.[4] However, in doing so he must remain within the bounds of two constraints. First, any other statute must have the same or similar subject matter to that contained in the instant statute. Secondly, the other statute must, presumably, have been enacted by the same legislative body as that which passed the instant statute. Unless they were both enacted by the same legislative body, it would be artificial to use the other statute in entertaining questions related to legislative intent. Although the notion of legislative intent is a legal fiction, the courts must treat that fiction with logical consistency.

---

[4]See *Goulbourn v. Ottawa-Carleton*, [1980] 1 S.C.R. 496, 100 M.B.R., 491, 12 O.M.B.R. 126 [sic] 101 D.L.R. (3d) 1 (S.C.C.); and *R. v. Croft* (1979), 35 N.S.R. (2d) 344, 62 A.P.R. 344 (C.A.).

(e) Legislative History

In Canada, a judge may make only limited use of the legislative history of a statute containing an ambiguous provision. Such use is confined to examining any amendments made to the statute, the prior existence of any predecessor statutes now repealed, and like matters. A judge may not examine any of the legislative debates contained in Hansard nor any speeches given by, for example, the minister responsible for the bill, nor any proceedings or reports of a parliamentary committee, nor any other extrinsic aid of that nature. Similarly, a judge may not consult the transcript of a royal commission of inquiry, even though that royal commission recommended the very enactment of the ambiguous statute. The foregoing are general rules arising out of judicial custom and convention, so it is not surprising to find the occasional exception to these rules: for example, in *Re Ombudsman Act* (1970), 72 W.W.R. 176, 10 D.L.R. (3d) 47 (Alta.), the report of the Clement Commission (investigating whether there existed a need for the establishment of an ombudsman in the province of Alberta) was admitted in a subsequent challenge to the jurisdiction of that office.[5]

The theory behind this rule is that a statute is an embodiment of all the components of its legislative history; the final enactment is deemed to include, through the plain meaning of its words, the sum total of all the debates, committee reports and other constituent elements of its legislative history. In contrast, in the United States, all elements of legislative history, including debates in Congress and other legislative bodies, reports of congressional committees, etc., are admitted in determining legislative intent.

There is a body of opinion that the American experience has gone too far. For example, in an article entitled "The Rule Against the Use of Legislative History: 'Canon of Construction or Counsel of Caution?' " (1952), 30 Can. Bar Rev. 769 at 788, the author D.G. Kilgour states:

> . . . If legislative history was freely admitted and indiscriminately used, there would be a tendency to give it an exaggerated place. In the United States its free admission has led to the quip that "only when legislative history is doubtful do you go to the statute".

Notwithstanding the danger posed by fully adopting the American position, there is some suggestion that Canada will, at the very least, shift direction towards the United States rule, at least in respect of constitutional cases. Professor Barry Strayer wrote in his 1968 treatise on *Judicial Review of Legislation in Canada* that in the course of constitutional adjudication it is necessary to adduce evidence in respect of both "legislative" facts and "adjudicative" facts. In respect of the former, he

---

[5]See also *N.B. Liquor Corp. v. C.U.P.E., Loc. 963* (1978), 21 N.B.R. (2d) 441, 37 A.P.R. 441, reversed [1979] 2 S.C.R. 227, 25 N.B.R. (2d) 237, 79 C.L.L.C. 14,209, 97 D.L.R. (3d) 417, 51 A.P.R. 237, 26 N.R. 341.

argues for the admissibility in court of such evidence as statements by members of legislative bodies, reports of royal commissions and parliamentary committees and like matters. In this desire to adopt, at least in part, the American position, Canada does not stand alone. For example, para. 54 of the Report of the Law Commission and the Scottish Law Commission on the Interpretation of Statutes states, in part:

> If the intention of Parliament is not to be treated as a mere figure of speech, it can hardly be denied in principle that proceedings in Parliament may be relevant to ascertain that intention.

(f) Treatises and Dictionaries

Some treatises have been written by learned authors on the process of statutory interpretation. Generally speaking, judges are receptive to an invocation to these treatises in order to verify a rule or principle of statutory interpretation. The two most influential of such treatises are *Craies on Statute Law*, 4th ed. (1971), and Maxwell, *The Interpretation of Statutes*, 12th ed. (1969).

In attempting to define particular words and phrases reference may be made to definitions from well respected general dictionaries. If, however, the word or phrase is legalistic in nature, judges will be receptive to definitions provided in law dictionaries.

(g) Text of the Statute in the Other Official Language

This aid in interpretation applies in Canada, to statutes which in their official text are published in both of our official languages, English and French. More particularly, it applies to Canadian, New Brunswick, and Manitoba statutes. As an aid in determining the legislative intent in enacting any of those statutes, it is perfectly legitimate to resort to an examination of the official text of the statute in both official languages (see the case of *Pfizer Co. v. Dep. M.N.R. for Customs and Excise* (1975), 6 N.R. 440, 24 C.P.R. (2d) 195, 68 D.L.R. (3d) 9 (S.C.C.)). Sometimes, a word or phrase might appear to be ambiguous, having regard only to the English text, but examination of that word or phrase in the French text might provide clarity as to the legislative intention and therefore avoid the ambiguity.[6]

(h) Miscellaneous Aids in Interpretation

The above list of aids in interpretation is not meant to be exhaustive. Indeed, from time to time, courts are receptive to aids not referred to

---

[6]For a view of a similar issue in the event that one text is clear and unambiguous, see *R. v. O'Donnell*, [1979] 1 W.W.R. 385, 46 C.C.C. (2d) 208 (B.C.C.A.). See also Beaupré, *Construing Bilingual Legislation in Canada* 1981, and *Cardinal v. R.*, [1980] 1 F.C. 149, 97 D.L.R. (2d) 402, affirmed (sub nom. *Cardinal v. Can.*), [1980] 2 F.C. 400, 109 D.L.R. (3d) 366, 32 N.R. 209 (C.A.).

above. For example, there is recent case authority to the effect that a court will examine international conventions and treaties in interpreting an ambiguous provision in a domestic statute.

Reference was made earlier to the admissibility of the preamble and the inadmissibility of marginal notes. There remain two similar matters to consider. First, the question arises as to the admissibility of various headings within a statute as aids in interpretation. Unless there is a statutory provision to the contrary (such as that which exists in the province of Ontario to the effect that such headings are not part of a statute), the common law position applies, which is that headings within a statute may be characterized as preambles and, as such, are admissible in determining legislative intent. A more difficult question relates to the title of a statute. Most statutes contain two titles, a long one and a short one. The law appears to be that both those titles form an integral part of the statute, but the long title is more reliable as an aid in interpretation.

3. PRESUMPTIONS IN STATUTORY INTERPRETATION

Following is a list of various presumptions regarding statutory interpretation which have arisen through pronouncements made in various cases and through the operation of custom and convention at common law. In examining these, the reader must bear in mind that some are archaic and therefore of little use to the modern judge.

(a) Presumption in Criminal or Penal Statutes

The presumption is that statutes of this nature are to be construed strictly and in favour of the accused.

(b) Presumption in Taxation Statutes

The presumption in respect of statutes of this nature is that they must be construed strictly, the charging sections in favour of the taxpayer and the exemption sections in favour of the government. In addition, there are many special rules of construction which apply uniquely to taxation statutes and which expand upon the above presumption.

(c) Presumption Against Alteration of the Law

This presumption, often expressed as a presumption against fundamental change, imports the notion that statutory enactments are presumed not to alter the common law. Such a notion is based upon the presumption that the legislative body knows the law; therefore, in the absence of an express provision in a given statute altering the existing common law, it is presumed that that statute is confirmatory of the common law.

However, this presumption is rebuttable by express language contained in the statute[7]. Moreover, this presumption is probably very unreliable in any case, in view of the provision contained, for example, in the federal Interpretation Act, to the effect that all statutes are deemed to be remedial in nature.

(d) Presumption Against Strict Criminal Liability

Unless a provision expressly creates a strict liability offence, it is presumed that every criminal offence contains a mens rea component (i.e., a mental or intentional component of some nature) which must be proved beyond a reasonable doubt.

(e) Presumption Against Retroactivity

One of the best statements of this presumption is set out in *Maxwell on Interpretation of Statues:*[8]

> . . . upon the presumption that the legislature does not intend what is unjust rests the leaning against giving certain statutes a retrospective operation. They are construed as operating only in cases or on facts which come into existence after the statutes were passed unless a retrospective effect is clearly intended. It is a fundamental rule of . . . law that no statute shall be construed to have a retrospective operation unless such a construction appears very clearly in the terms of the Act, or arises by necessary and distinct implication.

The author then cites R.S. Wright J. in the case of *Re Athlumney*, [1898] 2 Q.B. 547 at 551-52:

> Perhaps no rule of construction is more firmly established than this — that a retrospective operation is not to be given to a statute so as to impair an existing right or obligation, otherwise than as regards matter of procedure, unless that effect cannot be avoided without doing violence to.the language of the enactment. If the enactment is expressed in language which is fairly capable of either interpretation, it ought to be construed as prospective only.[9]

(f) Presumption Against Ousting the Jurisdiction of the Courts

This presumption is so firmly entrenched in the law that in the area of judicial review by courts of superior jurisdiction of administrative decisions, a statutory privative clause, with few exceptions, will not prevent a superior court from exercising this review jurisdiction. In other words, even if an enabling statute establishing an administrative tribunal con-

---

[7]See *Coles v. Roach* (1980), 25 Nfld. & P.E.I.R. 172, 112 D.L.R. (3d) 101, 68 A.P.R. 172 (P.E.I.S.C.); see also *Greater Niagara Transit Comm. v. Matson* (1977), 16 O.R. (2d) 351, 78 D.L.R. (3d) 265 (H.C.).

[8]Langan, *Maxwell on Interpretation of Statutes,* 12th ed. (London: Sweet & Maxwell, 1969), at p. 215.

[9]See also *Re Peel and Viking Houses* (1977), 16 O.R. (2d) 765, 36 C.C.C. (2d) 137, affirmed 16 O.R. (2d) 632, 36 C.C.C. (2d) 337 (C.A.).

tains a provision to the effect that any decision of that tribunal is not subject to judicial review by courts of superior jurisdiction, notwithstanding such a clause, courts of superior jurisdiction, with few exceptions, will be receptive to the process of judicial review. This will be discussed further in the next chapter, containing an introduction to administrative law.

(g) Presumption of Crown Immunity

This is a two-fold presumption. First, it is presumed that at common law, the Crown enjoys tortious immunity. This immunity arises out of the prerogative vested in the Crown. However, with the enactment of various Crown liability statutes in most jurisdictions, tortious immunity has now been lost. Secondly, this presumption also extends to statutory law, with the effect that no statute can bind the Crown in right of the Dominion or in right of a province unless that statute expressly states otherwise.

(h) Miscellaneous Presumptions

In addition to the foregoing, there are some miscellaneous presumptions which might serve as aids in construction. For example, there is a presumption against surplusage which requires a court to consider each word in a statute, on the theory that a legislative body enacted each word of the statute with a particular purpose in mind. Secondly, there is the presumption referred to in the Latin phrase generalia specialibus non derogant[10] to the effect that when two or more statutes of the same jurisdiction are applicable to a given factual situation, in the event of conflict between the various statutes, the more specific statute takes precedence over the general statute. In addition, there is the related presumption expressed in the Latin phrase leges posteriores priores contrarias abrogant to the effect that when two or more statutes of the same jurisdiction are applicable to a given factual situation and both statutes are of equal specificity, if they conflict with each other the more recent statute takes precedence over the older one. However, there is a presumption against the implied repeal of the older statute; a judge must make every effort to reconcile the two, if possible. Finally there is the important presumption contained in the Latin phrase de minimis non curat lex to the effect that the law does not concern itself with trifles, nor with trivial acts or omissions, nor with inconsequential breaches.

Some of the rules and principles of statutory interpretation find their source in judicial custom or convention. Some are statutory in nature,

---

[10]See, e.g., *Re Strachan and Melford* (1979), 102 D.L.R. (3d) 761 (Sask. Q.B.); see also *Re Wheeler*, [1979] 2 S.C.R. 650, 25 N.B.R. (2d) 209, 9 M.P.L.R. 161, 97 D.L.R. (3d) 605 (sub nom. *R. v. Wheeler*), 51 A.P.R. 209, 26 N.R. 323 (S.C.C.).

such as those arising out of provisions contained in the various interpretation statutes. Most, however, arise out of judicial pronouncements in early cases. There is no better example of this than the mischief rule, one of the three major canons of construction. That rule arose out of the decision in *Heydon's Case* (1584), 3 Co. Rep. 7a, 76 E.R. 637.

(i) Drafting Errors

On occasion, the courts have to deal with drafting errors on the part of our legislative bodies. Generally speaking, the role of the courts in these instances is to correct the drafting error in order to give effect to the intention of the legislating body. See *R. v. Flaman* (1978), 43 C.C.C. (2d) 241 (Sask. C.A.); *R. v. Findlay* (1977), 3 B.C.L.R. 321 (Prov. Ct.); and *R. v. Paul* (1978), 39 C.C.C. (2d) 129 (Ont. C.A.); see also *Re Ont. Ombudsman and Ont. Min. of Housing* (1979), 103 D.L.R. (3d) 117, affirmed (sub nom. *Re Ombudsman of Ont. and R.*), 30 O.R. (2d) 768 (C.A.), where it was held that a court may fill a gap in legislation so as to make it logically perfect and so as to give effect to the intent of the legislature.

Notwithstanding the somewhat dated sources of these various rules they are being presently applied by our courts. In this connection, the reader will find in the bibliography set out at the end of this chapter many very recent cases which apply these old rules to new fact situations.

The whole question of ambiguity is best summed up by reference to certain remarks made by Dr. Max Wyman in his addendum to the Report of the Alberta Board of Review. In that addendum, referred to earlier, Dr. Wyman makes these comments:

> Some of the words of a language must always remain undefined. This does not mean, however, that such words are devoid of meaning. It does imply that the meaning conjured up in the minds of people might be different for different people. Since those who legislate must use a language to communicate their thoughts to those who adjudicate, it is certain that in some instances the message that is sent will be different from the message that is received. This is a defect of all systems of law, and it cannot be avoided. It does not mean, however, that a society must condone vague and carelessly worded laws. Quite the opposite. Recognizing the existence of defects of this type, those who write the law must strive for clarity and precision, knowing full well that perfect clarity and absolute precision can never be obtained.

As an exercise in applying the various rules and principles of statutory interpretation, consider the five problems set out in the appendix to this chapter.

APPENDIX

PROBLEM ONE

ACME Foods Ltd., a company incorporated under the laws of the province of Manitoba, was engaged in the business of processing and packing instant coffee. In 1970, in the course of its business, the company decided to bolster sales by initiating a promotion in which the company placed on each jar of coffee a label containing the words "10 cents off regular price."

The finished product was then distributed through a local distributor to various retail outlets. In purchasing the coffee from the manufacturer, the distributor obtained a 10 cents reduction in the purchase price per jar and in turn passed on the reduction to the various retailers. The retailers then sold the coffee at a price of 10 cents less than the regular price which existed at the time that the promotion began.

The "cents off " promotion continued for some eighteen months, at which time many consumers complained that the reduced price had by that time become the regular price, and, as such, the price after eighteen months should be a further 10 cents off the now reduced regular price. As a result, various consumers complained to the Combines Investigation Branch of the Department of Consumer and Corporate Affairs. The Branch conducted an investigation, after which ACME Foods Ltd. was prosecuted for misleading advertising under the provisions of the Combines Investigation Act, R.S.C. 1970, c. C-23.

At that time, the relevant provisions of the said Act were as follows (the Combines Investigation Act has since been substantially amended, but these amendments should be ignored for the purpose of this problem):

37.(1) Every one who publishes or causes to be published an *advertisement* containing a statement that purports to be a statement of fact but that is untrue, deceptive or misleading or is intentionally so worded or arranged that it is deceptive or misleading, is guilty of an indictable offence and is liable to imprisonment for five years, if the advertisement is published

(a) to promote, directly or indirectly, the sale or disposal of property or any interest therein, or

(b) to promote a business or a commercial interest.

The various elements that must be established in order to support a conviction were as follows. First, the accused company must have caused to be published an advertisement. Secondly, the advertisement must have contained a statement which purported to be a statement of fact. Thirdly, the statement must have been untrue, deceptive or misleading. And fourthly, the advertisement must have been published to promote the sale of coffee. Assume that there was sufficient evidence to commit the accused company to trial providing the court could establish that a label on a coffee jar constitutes an "advertisement" under the provisions of the Act set out above.

Counsel for the accused argued that a label is merely a "representation" and not an "advertisement." In support of this argument, he cited the provisions of s. 36 of the same Act. Essentially, s. 36 prohibited a similar and related offence to that contained in s. 37. However, s. 36 referred specifically to the making of a *representation* to the public. The argument by counsel was simply that Parliament, in using the term "representation" in s. 36, had intended a wider scope than that encompassed in s. 37, which refers only to "advertising," that is, a distinction must be made between representations generally and advertising, and Parliament had made this very distinction in using different terminology in the two sections. Counsel then concluded that while a coffee jar label may constitute a representation, it does not constitute an advertisement as required under s. 37.

Counsel for the Crown, however, cited the definition of advertisement contained in the Food and Drugs Act, R.S.C. 1970, c. F-27, s. 2, which states that an advertisement "*includes any representation* by any means whatever for the purpose of promoting directly or indirectly the sale or disposal of any food, drug, cosmetic or device."

Counsel for the Crown then made reference to the Report of the Standing Committee of the House of Commons on Finance, Trade, and Economic Affairs, which report was released prior to the enactment of s. 37. That report stated in part as follows:

> The Committee feels that stronger measures are necessary in order to protect the consumer. As a result, all representations to the public, in whatever form, from manufacturers, distributors and retailers alike, should be fair and honest.

There appeared to be no decided cases which could be argued in order to support one side or the other as to whether a coffee jar label does in law constitute an advertisement. Accordingly, the judge must rely upon the above arguments of counsel as well as upon the generally accepted rules and principles of statutory interpretation. How would the judge likely rule on the narrow question as to whether a coffee jar label constitutes an advertisement?

PROBLEM TWO

In response to a City of Toronto by-law imposing certain restrictions on dog owners requiring control of dogs in public areas, the local Canine Association suggested that it was only fair that the same controls be imposed upon cat owners as well.

As a result, in response to a successful lobbying effort the Municipal Council of the City of Toronto enacted a cat by-law.

Essentially, that law placed the same restrictions on cats as those placed on dogs in the previous by-law and, in particular, required that cats must remain on leashes while in public places.

Shortly after the enactment of the by-law, the owner of a game farm situated around Toronto (the site of an African Big Game Safari) was seen walking along the Toronto lake front accompanied by his pet cheetah. The cheetah was not on a leash. An enthusiastic young police officer, in his first week on the job, upon seeing the game farm owner and his pet cheetah and assuming that a cheetah is, biologically, a member of the cat family, immediately summonsed the owner and charged him under the provision in the cat by-law prohibiting the walking of cats in public areas without a leash.

At the trial of this matter, a dispute in law arose as to what constitutes a "cat" for the purpose of the by-law. Counsel for the Crown pointed to the definition of "cat" in the introductory section of the by-law.

That definition stated as follows: "cat includes all species of animals possessing feline characteristics."

Reference was then made to the Webster's New International Dictionary in respect of three definitions:

1. "Cat" was defined as "a carnivorous mammal (felis catus) which has long been kept by man in a domestic state."

2. "Cheetah" was defined as "an animal of the cat family."

3. "Feline" was defined as "catlike, of or pertaining to the genus Felis or family Felidae."

In addition to the foregoing, reference was made to the debate in Municipal Council which preceded the enactment of the by-law. In particular, the speeches of several aldermen were cited, including the following remark:

I agree with the proponents of this by-law. It is about time that we took measures to ensure that these little pests are kept out of the garbage cans of Toronto.

Counsel for the accused emphasized that the wording "little pests" was suggestive that the intent of the by-law was directed at small, domestic cats and not at large game, such as a cheetah.

In addition, counsel for the accused also made reference to the provisions contained in the preamble of the cat by-law. In particular, he cited the following provisions in the preamble:

In recognition of the requirement of sanitation and the danger to health if standards are not maintained, and in recognition of the harmful effect of unsupervised domesticated cats upon sanitation standards, it is hereby enacted . . .

In addition, counsel for the accused cited the definition of "dog" in the dog by-law. In particular, "dog" was defined as follows:

"Dog" includes all species of animals possessing canine characteristics, but excludes animals possessing those characteristics which are not normally domesticated.

Counsel for the accused argued that the latter phraseology in the above definition should have been, but unfortunately was not, contained in the definition of "cat" in the cat by-law; however, counsel for the Crown suggested it was specifically left out in order that the cat by-law control not only domesticated animals but undomesticated animals as well, such as cheetahs.

Assume that the rules and principles of statutory interpretation apply, as they do in interpreting municipal by-laws, in the same way as in interpreting any other statutory enactment. In applying the three major canons of construction, how would the judge rule in this case? Also, would the judge be receptive to any or all of the above arguments of counsel?

PROBLEM THREE

Assume that the Benchers of the Law Society of Alberta were required to make a determination as to whether two lawyers were guilty of conduct unbecoming a barrister and solicitor.

The particular provision which defines "conduct unbecoming a barrister and solicitor" is set out in Pt. 3 of the Legal Profession Act, R.S.A. 1980, c. L-9, s. 47 [re-en. 1981, c. 53, s. 20]. More specifically, s. 47 of the said Act provides as follows:

47 (1) Except as otherwise provided in this Part, the question of whether the conduct of a member or student-at-law is conduct deserving of sanction shall be determined by the Benchers or, on appeal, by the Court of Appeal.

(2) Any act or conduct of a member or a student-at-law that

(a)   is incompatible with the best interests of the public or the members of the Society, or

(b)   tends to harm the standing of the legal profession generally,

is conduct deserving of sanction within the meaning of this Part, whether or not that act or conduct is disgraceful or dishonourable and whether or not that act or conduct relates to the practice of law.

(3)   Without restricting the generality of subsection (2), conduct deserving of sanction includes incompetently carrying on the practice of law and incompetently carrying out duties or obligations undertaken by a member or a student-at-law in his capacity as a member or student-at-law.

It was alleged that lawyer A was guilty under s. 47(2) of the Act set out above by virtue of a conviction under s. 320(1)(a) [am. 1972, c. 13, s. 29; 1974-75-76, c. 93, s. 31] of the Criminal Code, R.S.C. 1970, c. C-34. The relevant provisions of the Criminal Code are set out as follows:

319. (1) A false pretence is a representation of a matter of fact either present or past, made by words or otherwise, that is known by the person who makes it to be false and that is made with a fraudulent intent to induce the person to whom it is made to act upon it.

(2) Exaggerated commendation or depreciation of the quality of anything is not a false pretence unless it is carried to such an extent that it amounts to a fraudulent misrepresentation of fact.

(3) For the purposes of subsection (2) it is a question of fact whether commendation or depreciation amounts to a fraudulent misrepresentation of fact.

320. (1) Every one commits an offence who

(a) by a false pretence, whether directly or through the medium of a contract obtained by a false pretence, obtains anything in respect of which the offence of theft may be committed or causes it to be delivered to another person . . .

(2) Every one who commits an offence under paragraph (1)(a)

(a) is guilty of an indictable offence and is liable to imprisonment for ten years, where the property obtained is a testamentary instrument or where the value of what is obtained exceeds two hundred dollars; or

(b) is guilty

(i) of an indictable offence and is liable to imprisonment for two years, or

(ii) of an offence punishable on summary conviction,

where the value of what is obtained does not exceed two hundred dollars.

It was further alleged that lawyer B was also guilty under s. 47(2) of the Legal Profession Act by virtue of a conviction under s. 171(a)(i) of the Criminal Code. This conviction arose out of lawyer B's public display of excitement immediately after the Edmonton Eskimos won the Grey Cup. Section 171 [am. 1972, c. 13, s. 11; 1974-75-76, c. 93, s. 9] of the Criminal Code is set out as follows:

171. (1) Every one who

(a) not being in a dwelling-house causes a disturbance in or near a public place,

(i) by fighting, screaming, shouting, swearing, singing or using insulting or obscene language,

(ii) by being drunk, or

(iii) by impeding or molesting other persons,

(b) openly exposes or exhibits an indecent exhibition in a public place,

(c) loiters in a public place and in any way obstructs persons who are there, or

(d) disturbs the peace and quiet of the occupants of a dwelling-house by discharging firearms or by other disorderly conduct in a public place or who, not being an occupant of a dwelling-house comprised in a particular building or structure, disturbs the peace and quiet of the occupants of a dwelling-house comprised in the building or structure by discharging firearms or by other disorderly conduct in any part of a building or structure to which, at the time of such conduct, the occupants of two or more dwelling-houses comprised in the building or structure have access as of right or by invitation, express or implied,

is guilty of an offence punishable on summary conviction.

In applying each of the three major canons of construction and any other rules and principles of statutory interpretation that might be appropriate, what is likely to be the decision of the benchers on the narrow question as to whether the behaviour of each of the two lawyers amounts to "conduct unbecoming a barrister and solicitor" as defined in s. 47(2) of the Legal Profession Act?

PROBLEM FOUR

A person was charged that he fraudulently and without colour of right used a telecommunication facility contrary to s. 287(1)(*b*) [re-en. 1974-75-76, c. 93, s. 23] of the Criminal Code. The accused had obtained access to data contained in a university computer. He did this through the use of a remote terminal connected to the central computer by electric wires.

The wires and the electrical signals which flowed through them provided the means by which data was transmitted between the various terminals and the central unit. The accused's defence was that the above system does not constitute a telecommunication facility within the meaning of the Criminal Code.

The Criminal Code defines a telecommunication facility as follows:

> 287.(2) In this section and in section 287.1, "telecommunication" means any transmission, emission or reception of signs, signals, writing, images, sounds or intelligence of any nature by radio, visual, electronic or other electromagnetic system.

See *R. v. McLaughlin* (1979), 51 C.C.C. (2d) 243, affirmed [1980] 2 S.C.R. 331.

PROBLEM FIVE

The reader might also consider the intriguing question as to whether God is a person. See the facts and the decision on *R. v. Davie* (1980), 17 C.R. (3d) 72 (B.C.C.A.), presently under appeal to the Supreme Court of Canada, which concerned itself with this very issue. See also the case comment, Meehan's "Candid Confessions" (1981), 59 Can. Bar Rev. 817, which discussed the above decision.

SELECTED BIBLIOGRAPHY ON THE RULES AND PRINCIPLES OF STATUTORY INTERPRETATION

TREATISES

Allen, C. K., *Law in the Making*, 4th ed. Oxford: Clarendon Press, 1946.
Anson, W. R., *Law and Custom of the Constitution*, New York: Johnson Reprint Corp., 1970.
Beaupre, R. M. *Construing Bilingual Legislation in Canada*, Toronto: Butterworths, 1981.

Clifford, *History of Private Bill Legislation*, Butterworths, 1885.

Craies on Statute Law, 7th ed. Sweet & Maxwell, 1971.

Cross, R., *Statutory Interpretation*, Butterworths, 1976.

Driedger, E. A., *The Composition of Legislation, Legislative Forms and Precedents*, 2nd ed. Ottawa: Department of Justice, 1976.

Driedger, E. A., *The Construction of Statutes*, Butterworths, 1974.

Kiralfy, A. K. R., *The English Legal System*, 4th ed. Sweet & Maxwell, 1967.

Maxwell, P. B., *Interpretation of Statutes*, 12th ed. Sweet & Maxwell, 1969.

Odgers' Construction of Deeds and Statutes, 5th ed. Sweet & Maxwell, 1967.

Pearce, D. C., *Statutory Interpretation in Australia*, Melbourne: Butterworths, 1974.

Phillips, O. H., *A First Book of English Law*, 6th ed. Sweet & Maxwell, 1970.

Walker, R. J. and M. G. Walker, *The English Legal System*, 3rd ed. Butterworths, 1972.

Wilberforce, E., *On Statute Law*. Stevens, 1881.

Wilson, G., *Cases and Materials on the English Legal System*, 3rd ed. Sweet & Maxwell, 1973.

The Law Commission and the Scottish Law Commission, *The Interpretation of Statutes*. London: H.M.S.O., 1969.

ARTICLES

Canada

Bisson, Alain-François, "L'Interaction Des Techniques de Redaction et Des Techniques D'Interprétation Des Lois" (1980), 21 CD:D 511.

Boulois, J. "L'Interprétation du Droit Ecrit Par le Juge: Rapport de Synthèse" (1978), 13 Thémis 85.

Corry, "Administrative Law; Interpretation of Statutes" (1939), 1 U.T.L.J. 286.

Corry, "The Use of Legislative History in the Interpretation of Statutes" (1954), 32 Can. Bar Rev. 624.

Coté, Pierre André "Les Règles D'Interprétation Des Lois: Des Guides et Des Arguments" (1978), 13 R.J.T. 275.

Davis, "Legislative History and the Wheat Board Case" (1953), 31 Can. Bar Rev. 1. (See also, on this article, the letter from Milner (1953), 31 Can. Bar Rev. 228.)

Driedger, "A New Approach to Statutory Interpretation" (1951), 29 Can. Bar Rev. 838.

Driedger, E. A. "Statutes: The Mischievous Literal Golden Rule" (1981), 59 Can. Bar Rev. 780.

Driedger, "Statutory Drafting and Interpretation; Canadian Common Law" (1971), 9 Co. I. Dr. Comp. 71.

Friedmann, "Statute Law and Its Interpretation in the Modern State" (1948), 26 Can. Bar Rev. 1277.

Hopkins, "The Literal Canon and the Golden Rule" (1937), 15 Can. Bar Rev. 689.

Jodoin, A. "L'Interprétation Par Le Juge Des Lois Penales" (1978), 13 Thémis 49.

Kernochan, John M. "Statutory Interpretation: An Outline of Method" (1976), 3 Dalhousie L.J. 333.

Kilgour, "The Rule Against the Use of Legislative History: 'Canon of Construction or Counsel of Caution?' " (1952), 30 Can. Bar Rev. 769. (See also, on this article, the letters from MacQuarrie (1952), 30 Can. Bar Rev. 1087; Milner (1953), 31 Can. Bar Rev. 228.)

Krauss, Michael "L'Interprétation des Lois, Histoire Législative, 'La Queue qui Revue Le Chien' " (1980), 58 Can. Bar Rev. 756.

Laskin, "Interpretation of Statutes — Industrial Standards Act Ontario" (1937), 15 Can. Bar Rev. 660.

Lyman, "The Absurdity and Repugnancy of the Plain Meaning Rule of Interpretation" (1969), 3 Man. L.J. 253.

MacDonald, "Constitutional Interpretation and Extrinsic Evidence" (1939), 17 Can. Bar Rev. 77.

Mallory, "Parliamentary Scrutiny of Statutory Instruments in Canada: A Proposal" (1970), 4 Ottawa L.J. 296.

Master, "Difficulties of Judicial Interpretation of Legislative Draftsmanship" (1971), 2 Rep. Fam. L. 1.

McDonnell, T. E. "Statutory Interpretation 'Acceptable' Tax Planning, Courts Role in Filling in the Gaps in Tax Legislation" (1981), 29 Can. Tax. J. 188.

McGregor, "Literal or Liberal? Trends in the Interpretation of Income Tax Law" (1954), 32 Can. Bar Rev. 281.

McGregor, "Interpretation of Taxing Statutes, Whither Canada?" (1968), 16 Can. Tax J. 122.

Meiklem, "Legislative Expression and Transformational Generative Grammar" (1970), 5 U.B.C.L. Rev. 57.

Rémillard, G. "L'Interprétation Par Le Juge Des Règles Ecrites en Droit Constitutionnel au Canada" (1978), 13 Thémis 59.

Sanagan, "The Construction of Taxing Statutes" (1940), 18 Can. Bar Rev. 43.

Scott, "*M.F.F. Equities v. The Queen:* Statutory Interpretation" (1972), 18 McGill, L. J. 145.

Smith, "Statutory Drafting and Interpretation: Comparative Summing Up" (1971), 9 Col. I. Dr. Comp. 155.

Smith, "The Interpretation of Statutes" (1970), 4 Man. L.J. 212.

Todd, "Statutory Interpretation: Literal versus Context" (1956), 34 Can. Bar Rev. 458.

Willis, "Statute Interpretation in a Nutshell" (1938), 16 Can. Bar Rev. 1.

Wood, "Statutory Interpretation: Tupper and the Queen" (1968), 6 Osgoode Hall L.J. 92.

Zahn, J. B. "Language and the Law: Towards a Linguistic Understanding" (1977), 25 Chitty's L.J. 109.

The Report of the Manitoba Commissioners, Interpretation Act, [1966] Conf. of Commissioners on Uniformity of Legislation in Canada 66.

The Interpretation Act, [1967] Conf. of Commissioners on Uniformity of Legislation in Canada 123.

The Report of the Alberta Commissioners, the Interpretation Act and the Statutes Act, [1971] Conf. of Commissioners on Uniformity of Legislation in Canada 25.

United Kingdom, Australia and New Zealand

Barwick, "Divining the Legislative Intent" (1961), 35 A.L.J. 197.

Bennion, Francis "The Science of Interpretation" (1980), 130 New L.J. 493.

Bennion, "Statutory Drafting and Interpretation: England" (1971), 9 Co. I. Dr. Comp. 115.

Brazil, "Legislative History and the Sure and True Interpretation of Statutes in General and the Constitution in Particular" (1961), 4 U.Q.L.J. 1.

Brett, "The Theory of Interpreting Statutes" (1956), 2 U.Q.L.J. 99.

Burrows, J.F. "The Problem of Time in Statutory Interpretation" (1978), N.Z.L.J. 253.

Fiocc, J. G. "Current Approaches to Statutory Interpretation" (1980), N.Z.L.J. 53.

Harrison, "Methods of Statutory Interpretation in the House of Lords" (1955), 2 U.Q.L.J. 349.

Hartt, "An Attempt at the Meaning of Statutes" (1956), 2 U.Q.L.J. 264.

Mayor, "The Interpretation of Statutes" (1955), 29 A.L.J. 204 (followed by a discussion of the article on pp. 215-23).

Montrose, "Judicial Implementation of Legislative Policy" (1957), 3 U.Q.L.J. 139.

Snell, J. "Trouble in Oiled Waters: Statutory Interpretation" (1976), 39 Modern Law Rev. 402.

Statute Law Society, Report of the Committee appointed by the Society to Examine the Failing of the Present Statute Law System. Sweet & Maxwell, 1970.

Statute Law Society, Statute Law: The Key to Clarity: First Report of The Committee Appointed to Propose Solutions to the Deficiencies of the Statute Law System in the U.K. Sweet & Maxwell, 1972.

Todd, "Statutory Interpretation and the Influence of Standards" (1953), 2 Annual L. Rev. 526.

Turner, "An Approach to Statutory Interpretation" (1950), 4 Res Judiciate 237.

Ward, "A Criticism of the Interpretation of Statutes in the New Zealand Courts" (1963), N.Z.L.J. 293.

United States

Anon, "A Re-Evaluation of the use of Legislative History in the Federal Courts" (1952), 52 Col. L. Rev. 125.

Curtis, "A Better Theory of Legal Interpretation" (1949), 4 Record of The Association of the Bar of the City of New York 321.

Perman, Marc R. "Statutory Interpretation in California: Individual Testimony as an Extrinsic Aid" (1981), 15 U.S.F.L. Rev. 241.

Evans, Jeffrey, Merle "Void For Vagueness — Judicial Response to Allegedly Vague Statutes" (case note *State v. Zuanich* (1979), 593 Pzd. 1314 (Wash.)) (1980), 56 Washington L.R. 131.

Frankfurter, "Some Reflections on the Reading of Statutes" (1947), 2 Record of the Association of the Bar of the City of New York 213; (1947), 47 Col. L. Rev. 527.

Hart and Sacks, "The Legal Process: Basic Problem in the Making and Application of Law" (Cambridge, Mass., tentative ed., 1958) (Unpublished but available in certain libraries).

Jackson, "The Meaning of Statutes: What Congress Says or What the Court Says" (1948), 34 Amer. Bar Assn. J. 535.

Landis, "A Note on 'Statutory Interpretation' " (1930), 43 Harvard L. Rev. 886.

McCallum, "Legislative Intent" (1966), 75 Yale L.J. 754.

Radin, "Statutory Interpretation" (1930), 43 Harvard L. Rev. 863.

CASES

Acadian Pulp & Paper Ltd. v. Minister of Municipal Affairs (1973), 6 N.B.R. (2d) 755, 41 D.L.R. (3d) 589 (C.A.).

Administration de la Voie Maritime de Saint-Laurent v. Candiac Dev. Corp., [1978] C.A. 499.

Alta. Govt. Telephones v. Bauer, [1975] W.W.D. 30 (Alta.).

Re Atlantic Pet Food Supply Inc., 19 N.B.R. (2d) 602, 30 A.P.R. 602, reversed (sub nom. *Atlantic Petfood Supply Inc. v. Adrice P. Cormier Ltd.*), 22 N.B.R. (2d) 81, 39 A.P.R. 81 (C.A.).

Re A.G. Man. and National Energy Bd. (1974), 48 D.L.R. (3d) 73 (Fed. Ct.).

Aves v. Public Utilities Bd. of Commrs. (1973), 39 D.L.R. (3d) 266, 5 N.S.R. (2d) 370 (C.A.).

Re Bains and Superintendent of Ins. (1973), 38 D.L.R. (3d) 756 (B.C.C.A.).

Barrett v. Winnipeg (1891), 19 S.C.R. 374.

Bell v. Grand Trunk Ry. Co. of Can. (1913), 48 S.C.R. 561, 16 C.R.C. 324, 15 D.L.R. 874.

Bell v. North Vancouver School Dist. 44 Bd. of Trustees (1979), 16 B.C.L.R. 94 (S.C.).

Re Bolling and Pub. Service Staff Rel. Bd., [1978] 1 F.C. 85, 77 D.L.R. (3d) 318 (C.A.).

Re Black & Decker Mfg. Co. and R., [1973] 2 O.R. 460, 11 C.C.C. (2d) 470, 10 C.P.R. (2d) 154, 34 D.L.R. (3d) 308 (C.A.).

Brueckner v. Govt. of Man., [1973] 3 W.W.R. 214 (Man.).

C.E. & V. Holdings v. Assessment Appeal Bd., [1975] 4 W.W.R. 667 (B.C.).

Campbell Soup Co. v. Farm Products Marketing Bd. (1975), 10 O.R. (2d) 405, 36 D.L.R. (3d) 401, affirmed 16 O.R. (2d) 256, 77 D.L.R. (3d) 725 (C.A.).

Can. Financial Co. v. O'Neill (1977), 26 N.B.R. (2d) 221, 55 A.P.R. 221 (Co. Ct.).

Can. Indemnity Co. v. A.G.B.C., [1975] 3 W.W.R. 224 (B.C.).

Can. Life Assur. Co. v. Rieb, [1943] 1 W.W.R. 759 (Alta.).

Re C.P. Ltd. and Can. Tpt. Comm., [1979] 2 F.C. 808, 99 D.L.R. (3d) 52, affirmed [1980] 1 S.C.R. 319, 33 N.R. 157.

Canbra Foods Ltd. v. Overwater, [1978] 1 W.W.R. 231, 84 D.L.R. (3d) 350, 7 A.R. 506, affirming 71 D.L.R. (3d) 603 (Alta. C.A.).

Candlish v. Min. of Social Services, [1978] 3 W.W.R. 515, 5 R.F.L. (2d) 166, 85 D.L.R. (3d) 716 (Sask. Q.B.).

Cardinal v. R., [1980] 1 F.C. 149, 97 D.L.R. (3d) 402, affirmed (sub nom. *Cardinal v. Canada*) [1980] 2 F.C. 400, 109 D.L.R. (3d) 366, 32 N.R. 209 (C.A.).

Re Carfrae Estates Ltd. and Stavert (1976), 13 O.R. (2d) 537 (Div. Ct.).

Central Can. Potash Co. v. A.G. Sask., [1975] 5 W.W.R. 193, 57 D.L.R. (3d) 7 (Sask.).

Re Century Aviation Services Ltd. and Indust. Rel. Bd. (1976), 69 D.L.R. (3d) 176 (B.C.S.C.).

Coles v. Roach (1980), 25 Nfld. & P.E.I.R. 172, 112 D.L.R. (3d) 101, 68 A.P.R. 172 (P.E.I. S.C.).

Continental Finance Corp. v. Junico Ltd., [1978] 3 W.W.R. 759, 29 C.B.R. (N.S.) 65 (Man. Q.B.).

Cooligan v. Br. Amer. Bank Note Co. (1979), 1 C.H.R.R. D/52 (Human Rights Trib.).

Cowieson v. Atkinson (1974), 52 D.L.R. (3d) 401 (Man. C.A.).

Crease v. Toronto Bd. of Police Commrs. (1976), 11 O.R. (2d) 459, 66 D.L.R. (3d) 403.

Drewery v. Century City Developments Ltd. (No. 2) (1975), 6 O.R. (2d) 299, 52 D.L.R. (3d) 523 (C.At (1979), 35 N.S.R. (2d) 60, 106 D.L.R. (3d) 739, 62 A.P.R. 60 (C.A.).

Dymond v. Stirling (1977), 21 Nfld. & P.E.I.R. 297, 56 A.P.R. 297 (Nfld. Dist. Ct.).

Excelsior Lumber Co. v. Ross (1914), 6 W.W.R. 367, 19 B.C.R. 289, 16 D.L.R. 593 (C.A.).

Frehlick v. McLenehan, [1980] I.L.R. 1-1270, 114 D.L.R. (3d) 310, 3 Sask. R. 340 (C.A.).

Re Garet and Criminal Injuries Compensation Ordinance, [1975] 5 W.W.R. 36, 29 C.R.N.S. 391 (N.W.T.).

Good Electric Ltd. v. Thorne (1979), 24 Nfld. & P.E.I.R. 525, 107 D.L.R. (3d) 220, 65 A.P.R. 525 (P.E.I.S.C.).

Goulbourn v. Ottawa-Carleton, [1980] 1 S.C.R. 496, 10 O.M.B.R. 491, 12 O.M.B.R. 126, 101 D.L.R. (3d) 1, 29 N.R. 267.

Greater Niagara Transit Comm. v. Matson (1977), 16 O.R. (2d) 351, 78 D.L.R. (3d) 265 (H.C.).

Greenshields v. R., [1958] S.C.R. 216, [1959] C.T.C. 77, 17 D.L.R. (2d) 33.

Halifax Harbour Services Ltd. v. Maritime Telegraph & Telephone (1979), 38 N.S.R. (2d) 541, 69 A.P.R. 541, reversed 40 N.S.R. (2d) 448 (C.A.).

Re Harris and Min. of Community and Social Services (1975), 8 O.R. (2d) 721, 59 D.L.R. (3d) 169.

Harvard Realty Ltd. v. Dir. of Assessment (1979), 35 N.S.R. (2d) 60, 106 D.L.R. (3d) 739, 62 A.P.R. 60 (C.A.).

Re Hassard and Toronto (1908), 16 O.L.R. 500 (C.A.).

Re Hayes, [1931] 1 W.W.R. 301, 12 C.B.R. 225, 25 Sask. L.R. 257.

Heppner v. Min. of Environment (Alta.) (1977), 4 Alta. L.R. 139, 80 D.L.R. (3d) 112, 6 A.R. (sub nom. *Heppner v. Alta.*) (C.A.).

Hobby Ranches Ltd. v. R. (1978), 8 B.C.L.R. 247, 94 D.L.R. (3d) 529 (S.C.).

Hopper v. Mun. Dist. of Foothills No. 31, [1975] 2 W.W.R. 337, 7 L.C.R. 97 (Alta.).

Houde v. Que. Catholic School Comm., [1978] 1 S.C.R. 937, 80 D.L.R. (3d) 542, 17 N.R. 451.

Hourie v. Petti, [1975] 5 W.W.R. 254, 15 R.F.L. 210, 45 D.L.R. (3d) 306 (Man. C.A.).

I.A.F.F., Loc. 209 v. Edmonton (1979), 9 Alta. L.R. (2d) 119, 15 A.R. 594 (C.A.).

Re Jurisdiction of a Province to Legislate Respecting Abstention from Labour on Sunday (1905), 35 S.C.R. 581, 25 C.L.T. 77 (sub nom. *Re Sunday Laws*).

Juster v. R., [1974] 2 F.C. 398, [1974] C.T.C. 681, 28 D.T.C. 6540, 49 D.L.R. (3d) 256 (C.A.).

Ex parte Krachan (1975), 24 C.C.C. (2d) 114 (Ont.).

Kryworuchka v. Sask. Land Bank Commn., [1974] 5 W.W.R. 360 (Sask.).

Re Lamb (1979), 25 O.R. (2d) 23 (Co. Ct.).

Lawson v. Wellesley Hospital (1975), 9 O.R. (2d) 677, 61 D.L.R. (3d) 445 (C.A.).

Logan v. Bd. of School Trustees (1973), 6 N.B.R. (2d) 782 (C.A.).

M.G.E.A. and Man., Re, [1978] 1 S.C.R. 1123, [1977] 6 W.W.R. 247, 79 D.L.R. (3d) 1, 17 N.R. 506.

M. & M. Bulk Milk Service Ltd. v. Highway Tpt. Bd., [1979] 6 W.W.R 330, 102 D.L.R. (3d) 566 (Man. Q.B.).

M.R.T. Invts. Ltd. v. R., [1976] 1 F.C. 126, 29 D.T.C. 5224 (C.A.).

Re Mahon (1975), 8 O.R. (2d) 511, 21 R.F.L. 362 (Dist. Ct.).

Re McIntyre Porcupine Mines Ltd. and Morgan (1921), 49 O.L.R. 214, 62 D.L.R. 619 (C.A.).

McLaren v. McLaren (1979), 24 O.R. (2d) 481, 8 R.F.L. (2d) 301, 100 D.L.R. (3d) 163 (Ont. C.A.).

McLean v. Pilon (1978), 7 B.C.L.R. 99 (S.C.).

McNeil v. N.S. Bd. of Censors, [1978] 2 S.C.R. 662, 25 N.S.R. (2d) 128, 84 D.L.R. (3d) 1, 36 A.P.R. 128, 19 N.R. 570.

Malczewski v. Sansai Securities Ltd., [1975] W.W.D. 35 (B.C.).

Man. Fisheries Ltd. v. R., [1976] 1 F.C. 8, 58 D.L.R. (3d) 119.

Man. Fisheries Ltd. v. R., [1978] 1 S.C.R. 101, 88 A.L.R. (3d) 462.

Marcotte v. Deputy A.G. Can., [1976] 1 S.C.R. 108, 19 C.C.C. (2d) 257, 51 D.L.R. (3d) 259.

Martin v. Chapman, [1980] 1 F.C. 72, 14 R.F.L. (2d) 15, 107 D.L.R. (3d) 698.

Menzel v. R., [1978] C.T.C. 351, 78 D.T.C. 6237, 22 N.R. 61 (Fed. C.A.).

Re Metro. Toronto & Region Conservation Authority, [1973] 2 O.R. 531, 34 D.L.R. (3d) 483, reversed [1973] O.R. 1005, 39 D.L.R. (3d) 43.

Min. of Tpt. for Ont. v. Phoenix Assur. Co. (1975), 54 D.L.R. (3d) 768 (Can.).

Re Mobile Ad Ltd. and Scarborough (1974), 5 O.R. (2d) 203, 50 D.L.R. (3d) 191 (C.A.).

Morgentaler v. R., 30 C.R.N.S. 209, [1976] 1 S.C.R. 616, 20 C.C.C. (2d) 449, 53 D.L.R. (3d) 161.

Morrison v. M.N.R., [1928] Ex. C.R. 75, [1928] 2 D.L.R. 759.

N.B. Liquor Corp. v. C.U.P.E., Loc. 963 (1978), 21 N.B.R. (2d) 441, 37
   A.P.R. 441, reversed [1979] 2 S.C.R. 227, 97 D.L.R. (3d) 417, 25
   N.B.R. (2d) 237, 79 C.L.L.C. 14, 209, 51 A.P.R. 237, 26 N.R. 341.
Re Noah (1961), 36 W.W.R. 577, 32 D.L.R. (2d) 185 (N.W.T.).
Northwestern Utilities Ltd. v. Edmonton, [1979] 1 S.C.R. 684, 7 Alta. L.R.
   (2d) 370, 88 D.L.R. (3d) 161, 12 A.R. 449, 23 N.R. 565.
Re Ombudsman Act, [1974] 5 W.W.R. 176, 46 D.L.R. (3d) 452 (Sask.).
Re Ont. Ombudsman and Ont. Min. of Housing (1979), 26 O.R. (2d) 434, 103
   D.L.R. (3d) 117, affirmed (sub nom. *Re Ombudsman of Ont. and R.*)
   30 O.R. (2d) 768, 117 D.L.R. (3d) 613 (C.A.).
Ottawa v. Can. Atlantic Ry.; Ottawa v. Montreal & Ottawa Ry. (1903), 33
   S.C.R. 376.
Oznaga v. Société d' Exploitation des Lotteries et Courses du Québec, [1979]
   C.S. 186, reversed [1981] 2 S.C.R. 113, 40 N.R. 7.
Palomba v. R. (1975), 32 C.R.N.S. 31, 24 C.C.C. (2d) 19 (Que. C.A.).
Re Peel and Viking Houses (1977), 16 O.R. (2d) 765, 36 C.C.C. (2d) 137,
   affirmed 16 O.R. (2d) 632, 36 C.C.C. (2d) 337 (C.A.).
Re Peel Condominium Corp. No. 11 (1974), 4 O.R. (2d) 543, 48 D.L.R. (3d)
   503.
Pfizer Co. v. Dep. M.N.R., [1977] 1 S.C.R. 456, 24 C.P.R. (2d) 195, 68
   D.L.R. (3d) 9, 6 N.R. 440.
Re Pic-N-Save Ltd., [1973] 1 O.R. 809, 32 D.L.R. (3d) 431, affirmed on
   other grounds [1973] 3 O.R. 200, 19 C.B.R. (N.S.) 42, 36 D.L.R.
   (3d) 334 (C.A.).
Pimvicska v. Pimvicska, [1974] 6 W.W.R. 512, 50 D.L.R. (3d) 569 (Alta.).
Presbyterian Church Trustee Bd. v. R., [1979] 1 F.C. 632, 9 L.C.R. 301
   (C.A.).
Re Price (1973), 8 N.B.R. (2d) 620.
Re Proc and Min. of Community and Social Services (1974), 6 O.R. (2d) 624,
   19 R.F.L. 82, 53 D.L.R. (3d) 512.
Pub. Utilities Bd. of Commrs. v. N.S. Power Corp. (1976), 18 N.S.R. (2d)
   692, 75 D.L.R. (3d) 72 (C.A.).
R. v. Allen (Donald B.) Ltd. (1975), 11 O.R. (2d) 271, 65 D.L.R. (3d) 599
   (D.C.).
R. v. Baig (1979), 23 O.R. (2d) 730 (Dist. Ct.).
R. v. Basaraba, [1975] 3 W.W.R. 481 (Man.).
R. v. Bernier, [1978] C.S.P. 1095.
R. v. Boyce (1975), 28 C.R.N.S. 336, 7 O.R. (2d) 561, 23 C.C.C. (2d) 16
   (C.A.).
R. v. Boylan (1979), 8 C.R. (3d) 36, reversing 41 C.C.C. (2d) 497 (Sask.
   C.A.).
R. v. CAE Industries Ltd., [1977] 2 S.C.R. 566, 72 D.L.R. (3d) 159, 31
   C.P.R. (2d) 236, 13 N.R. 624 (sub nom. *CAE Indust. Ltd. v. Can.*).

R. v. Cadboro Bay Holdings Ltd., [1977] C.T.C. 186 (Fed. T.D.).

R. v. Church of Scientology of Toronto (1974), 4 O.R. (2d) 707, 18 C.C.C. (2d) 546.

R. v. Cook (1979), 25 N.B.R. (2d) 54, 51 A.P.R. 54 (C.A.).

R. v. Couche (1975), 31 C.R.N.S. 250 (Ont.).

R. v. Croft (1979), 35 N.S.R. (2d) 344, 62 A.P.R. 344 (C.A.).

R. v. Dagley (1979), 32 N.S.R. (2d) 421, 54 A.P.R. 421 (C.A.).

R. v. Demeter (1975), 6 O.R. (2d) 83, 19 C.C.C. (2d) 321, affirmed 10 O.R. (2d) 321, 25 C.C.C. (2d) 417 (C.A.).

R. v. Dubois, [1935] S.C.R. 378, [1935] 3 D.L.R. 209.

R. v. Dworkin Furs Ltd. (1976), 12 O.R. (2d) 460, 77 C.L.L.C. 14,071, 30 C.C.C. (2d) 452 (C.A.).

R. v. Dwyer, [1975] 4 W.W.R. 54, 23 C.C.C. (2d) 129 (B.C.).

R. v. Eaton, [1973] 4 W.W.R. 101, 11 C.C.C. (2d) 80 (B.C.).

R. v. Faulkner (1977), 39 C.R.N.S. 331, 37 C.C.C. (2d) 26 (N.S. Co. Ct.).

R. v. Findlay (1977), 3 B.C.L.R. 321 (Prov. Ct.).

R. v. Goodbaum (1977), 1 C.R. (3d) 152, 38 C.C.C. (2d) 473 (Ont. C.A.).

R. v. Govedarov (1975), 25 C.R.N.S. 1, 3 O.R. (2d) 23, 16 C.C.C. (2d) 238, affirmed on other grounds (sub nom. *R. v. Popovic and Askov*) 32 C.R.N.S. 54, 25 C.C.C. (2d) 161, 62 D.L.R. (3d) 56 (S.C.C.).

R. v. Johnston (1979), 20 A.R. 524, 52 C.C.C. (2d) 57 (Q.B.).

R. v. Kolot, [1973] 6 W.W.R. 527, 13 C.C.C. (2d) 417 (B.C.).

R. v. Krentz, [1976] 6 W.W.R. 527, 31 C.C.C. (2d) 450 (B.C.).

R. v. Laserich, [1977] 4 W.W.R. 703, 36 C.C.C. (2d) 285, 4 A.R. 148 (N.W.T. C.A.).

R. v. McLeod, 10 C.R. 318, [1950] 2 W.W.R. 456, 97 C.C.C. 366 (B.C. C.A.).

R. v. McLaughlin (1979), 12 C.R. (3d) 391, 19 A.R. 368, 51 C.C.C. (2d) 243, affirmed [1980] 2 S.C.R. 331, 18 C.R. (3d) 399, [1981] 1 W.W.R. 298, 113 D.L.R. (3d) 386, 53 C.C.C. (2d) 417, 32 N.R. 350, 23 A.R. 530.

R. v. Mallet (1975), 32 C.R.N.S. 73, 26 C.C.C. (2d) 457 (Que.).

R. v. Mansour (1977), 25 Chitty's L.J. 284, 36 C.C.C. (2d) 493, affirmed [1979] 2 S.C.R. 916, 2 M.V.R. 1, 101 D.L.R. (3d) 545, 47 C.C.C. (2d) 129, 27 N.R. 476.

R. v. Maroney (1974), 27 C.R.N.S. 185, 18 C.C.C. (2d) 257 (S.C.C.).

R. v. Miller and Cockriell, 33 C.R.N.S. 129, [1975] 6 W.W.R. 1, 24 C.C.C. (2d) 401, 63 D.L.R. (3d) 193, affirmed [1976] 5 W.W.R. 711 (S.C.C.).

R. v. Nabis, [1974] 6 W.W.R. 307, [1975] 2 S.C.R. 485, 18 C.C.C. (2d) 144, 48 D.L.R. (3d) 543.

R. v. Nielsen, [1974] 2 W.W.R. 379, 15 C.C.C. (2d) 224, 43 D.L.R. (3d) 634 (Y.T.).

R. v. O'Donnell, [1979] 1 W.W.R. 385, 46 C.C.C. (2d) 208 (B.C.C.A.).

R. v. Parkway Chrysler Plymouth Ltd. (1976), 32 C.C.C. (2d) 116, 28 C.P.R. (2d) 15 (Ont. C.A.).

R. v. Pasek, [1974] 3 W.W.R. 759 (Alta.).

R. v. Paul (1978), 39 C.C.C. (2d) 129, reversing 1 C.R. (3d) 173 (Ont. C.A.).

R. and Provincial Treasurer of Alta. v. Can. Northern Ry. and C.N.R., [1923] 3 W.W.R. 547, [1923] A.C. 714, [1923] 3 D.L.R. 719.

R. v. Raiche, [1975] W.W.D. 114, 24 C.C.C. (2d) 16 (Sask. Q.B.).

R. v. Rolland (1975), 31 C.R.N.S. 68, 27 C.C.C. (2d) 485 (Ont. C.A.).

R. v. Smith, [1980] 3 W.W.R. 591, 52 C.C.C. (2d) 290, 110 D.L.R. (3d) 636, 5 Man. R. (2d) 250 (Man. Co. Ct.).

R. v. Sommerville, [1973] 2 W.W.R. 65, [1974] S.C.R. 387, 9 C.C.C. (2d) 493, 32 D.L.R. (3d) 207.

R. v. Stefaniuk and Babiak, [1974] 4 W.W.R. 540 (Man.).

R. v. The Gulf Aladdin, [1977] 2 W.W.R. 677, 34 C.C.C. (2d) 460 (B.C.C.A.).

R. v. Tremblay, [1975] 3 W.W.R. 589, 23 C.C.C. (2d) 179, 58 D.L.R. (3d) 69 (Alta. C.A.).

R. v. Welsh (1977), 15 O.R. (2d) 1, 32 C.C.C. (2d) 363, 74 D.L.R. (3d) 748 (C.A.).

R. v. Wilson (1978), 6 B.C.L.R. 231 (S.C.).

R. v. Wildsmith (1974), 16 C.C.C. (2d) 479 (N.S.C.A.).

Re Regional Mun. of Ottawa-Carleton and Voyageur Colonial Ltd. (1975), 5 O.R. (2d) 601, 51 D.L.R. (3d) 161 (Dist. Ct.).

Rocca Group Ltd. v. Muise (1979), 22 Nfld. & P.E.I.R. 1, 102 D.L.R. (3d) 529, 58 A.P.R. 1 (S.C.C.).

Re Rockcliffe Park Realty Ltd. (1975), 10 O.R. (2d) 1, 62 D.L.R. (3d) 17 (C.A.).

Royal Bank v. Riehl, [1978] 6 W.W.R. 481, 28 C.B.R. (N.S.) 211 (Alta. Dist. Ct.).

Re St. Anne's Tower Corp. of Toronto (1973), 1 O.R. (2d) 717, 41 D.L.R. (3d) 481.

Sale v. Wills, [1972] 1 W.W.R. 138, [1972] I.L.R. 1-453, 22 D.L.R. (3d) 566 (Alta.).

Re Sam Richman Invt. (London) Ltd. (1974), 6 O.R. (2d) 335, 52 D.L.R. (3d) 655.

Sanderson v. Russell (1979), 9 R.F.L. (2d) 81 (Ont. C.A.).

Schofield v. Glenn, [1927] 2 W.W.R. 183, [1927] 3 D.L.R. 188, 21 Sask. L.R. 494, reversed on merits [1928] S.C.R. 208, [1928] 2 D.L.R. 319.

Re Shell Can. Ltd. and Dir. of Investigation and Research, 29 C.R.N.S. 361, [1975] F.C. 184 (sub nom. *Re Combines Investigation Act*), 22 C.C.C. (2d) 70, 55 D.L.R. (3d) 713 (C.A.).

Silliker v. Newcastle (1974), 10 N.B.R. (2d) 118.

Re Strachan and Melfort (1979), 102 D.L.R. (3d) 761 (Sask. Q.B.).

S.S. Marina Ltd. v. North Vancouver, [1976] 3 W.W.R. 284, 54 D.L.R. (3d) 13 (B.C.C.A.).

Re Telegram Publishing Co. and Zwelling (1973), 1 O.R. (2d) 592, 41 D.L.R. (3d) 176, 74 C.L.L.C. 14, 210 (Dist. Ct.).

Re Teperman & Sons (1974), 5 O.R. (2d) 507, 50 D.L.R. (3d) 675.

Tony Murray Assoc. Ltd. v. Morris (1980), 26 Nfld. & P.E.I.R. 31, 72 A.P.R. 31 (Nfld. T.D.).

Transco Mills Ltd. v. Louie, [1975] W.W.D. 141, 59 D.L.R. (3d) 665 (B.C.S.C.).

Union Gas Ltd. v. Dawn; Tecumseh Gas Storage Ltd. v. Dawn (1977), 15 O.R. (2d) 722, 2 M.P.L.R. 23, 76 D.L.R. (3d) 613 (Div. Ct.).

United Assn. of Journeymen and Apprentices of Plumbing and Pipe Fitting Industry v. Bd. of Industrial Relations, [1975] 2 W.W.R. 470, 49 D.L.R. (3d) 708 (Alta. C.A.).

Victoria School Trustees Bd. Dist. No. 61 v. C.U.P.E. (1976), 71 D.L.R. (3d) 139 (B.C.S.C.).

Victoria v. Bishop of Vancouver Island, [1921] 3 W.W.R. 214, [1921] 2 A.C. 384, 59 D.L.R. 399.

Western Mines Ltd. v Childs (1974), 51 D.L.R. (3d) 145 (B.C.).

Re Wheeler, [1979] 2 S.C.R. 650, 25 N.B.R. (2d) 209, 9 M.P.L.R. 161, 97 D.L.R. (3d) 605 (sub nom. *R. v. Wheeler*), 51 A.P.R. 209, 26 N.R. 323.

Worthington v. Robbins, 56 O.L.R. 285, [1925] 2 D.L.R. 80.

Zavitz v. Brock (1974), 3 O.R. (2d) 583, 46 D.L.R. (3d) 203 (C.A.).

Re Zong and Commr. of Penitentiaries, [1975] F.C. 430, 22 C.C.C. (2d) 553, affirmed 29 C.C.C. (2d) 114, 10 N.R. 1 (C.A.).

12

FAIRNESS AND NATURAL JUSTICE IN THE ADMINISTRATIVE PROCESS

INTRODUCTION

Administrative law is a division of what was earlier defined as "public law". An administrative body or tribunal conducts its affairs or renders its decisions in accordance with standards usually set out in the enabling statute which establishes the administrative body. Every administrative decision is presumably rendered, not in accordance with any benefit that might accrue to an interested party affected by the administrative decision, but rather in conformity to statutory or regulatory guidelines directed at serving the public interest. For example, assume an application is made by a private interest, such as a radio station, to the Canadian Radio-Television and Telecommunications Commission for a renewal of its licence to broadcast. Even though the renewal of the licence would primarily benefit a private business interest, the theory holds that the C.R.T.C. will render its decision on the basis of whether such a renewal is in accordance with public interest. In order to determine what constitutes public interest, the members of the commission must first look to any guidelines that might be suggested in the enabling statute, including, especially, those provisions establishing the commission and defining its jurisdiction. The administrative body may have to look at regulations passed pursuant to the enabling Act, for example by order in council, in order to determine those guidelines, or, in the absence of any written guidelines in the forms described above, the commission may itself have to be the judge as to what constitutes the public interest served by the regulatory jurisdiction of the particular administrative tribunal. In respect of broadcasting, for example, such guidelines might include the broadcasting of a minimum number of hours of Canadian content. For the private interest to have its licence renewed, it must ensure that it conducts its private business in accordance with those particular guidelines.

THE IMPORTANCE OF ADMINISTRATIVE LAW

Probably no area of law has grown so significantly in recent years as administrative law. Not too many years ago, administrative law was rarely taught in the law schools, nor was it considered an important branch of the law. However, since World War II and especially since the

1960's, there has been a proliferation of legislation at both the federal and provincial levels of government delegating authority to inferior tribunals composed of persons possessing expertise in particular areas to set policy and render decisions accordingly. In addition to reducing the workload of the primary legislative bodies this development has theoretically created expert bodies, better qualified to resolve the complex problems that arise in these particular areas. For example, the C.R.T.C. is better able and has more time than Parliament to deal with the technical questions which arise in respect of the various applications made before that body. Also, a commission is often invested with a budget sufficiently great to allow it to hire a permanent staff and, on occasion, to pay outside consultants, in order to assist the members of the commission in rendering appropriate decisions.

THE PROCESS OF DELEGATION

Legislative (or policy-making) authority can be delegated by a sovereign legislative body owing to the doctrine of parliamentary sovereignty.[1] The Parliament of Canada and all of the provincial legislatures in Canada are constitutionally able to conduct this delegation process, subject to the following constraints. First, the delegation must relate to a matter within the sovereign jurisdiction of the particular legislative body, as set out in the Constitution Act of 1867; that is, a superior legislative body cannot delegate to any inferior tribunal powers which it does not itself possess.

The second constraint relates to what is referred to as "interdelegation". The basic rule concerning interdelegation is that Parliament may not delegate any of its powers under the Constitution Act of 1867, to any or all of the provincial legislatures, nor may a provincial legislature delegate any of its powers to Parliament.[2] However, as a result of two later cases,[3] it is now constitutionally permissible for Parliament to delegate any powers it possesses to an inferior body created by a provincial enactment. In other words, Parliament may delegate a matter within its legislative jurisdiction to a subordinate tribunal created under a valid provincial law, but it may not delegate to the provincial legislature itself. The reverse is also true in respect of constitutionally permissible interdelegation between a provincial legislature and a subordinate agency created by federal statute.

---

[1]See *Hodge v. R.* (1883), 9 App. Cas. 117 (P.C.).

[2]This classic position was set out in *A.G.N.S. v. A.G. Can.*, [1951] S.C.R. 31, [1950] 4 D.L.R. 369 (*Nova Scotia Interdelegation Case*).

[3]*P.E.I. Potato Marketing Bd. v. H.B. Willis Inc. and A.G. Can.*, [1952] 2 S.C.R. 392, [1952] 4 D.L.R. 146, and *Coughlin v. Ont. Highway Tpt. Bd.*, [1968] S.C.R. 569, 68 D.L.R. (2d) 384.

This constitutionally permissible interdelegation, however, is itself subject to certain constraints.[4] Although Parliament, for example, may delegate any of its exclusive powers to a subordinate agency created by a provincial statute, it must limit the delegation in order to avoid an abdication of jurisdiction. That is to say, Parliament cannot delegate all of its authority under a given enumerated head of the Constitution Act of 1867. Thus, if Parliament wishes to delegate its constitutional authority to enact legislation in the area of interprovincial trade in a given commodity to an inferior tribunal created by a provincial statute, it may do so, providing it does not delegate all of its authority over interprovincial trade to that body.

A second constraint on delegation is the doctrine delegatus non potest delegare (a delegate may not re-delegate). This so-called "delegatus" rule is a general rule of administrative law that applies in respect to any delegation from a superior legislative body in a given jurisdiction of an inferior body within that same jurisdiction. Thus, if a provincial legislature delegates rule-making authority to an inferior body created by the legislature, that inferior body cannot re-delegate to a further inferior body unless: (1) the enabling statute expressly allows for a re-delegation; or (2) re-delegation is implied by the necessary intendment of the enabling statute. Thus, for example, when an enabling statute provides for a delegation of authority to a particular minister of the Crown to perform some act such as the issuing of licences, obviously, if the minister were to personally undertake that task, it alone would occupy his time day in and day out. Accordingly, it must be a necessary intendment of the enabling statute that the minister delegate that authority to appropriate persons, either on his staff or in the appropriate division of his department.

The inferior bodies to which authority is delegated are referred to as boards, commissions, tribunals, agencies, etc., and among the most common recipients of delegated authority are municipal councils. These bodies may already be in existence at the time the delegation is made or they may be newly created to receive such powers. The powers that they receive may include the power to formulate policy and to make rules or the power to make decisions or both. The delegated authority, if in the nature of rule-making, may generically be described as the power to make statutory instruments. These statutory instruments may take the form of by-laws, regulations, orders-in-council, ordinances, etc., the particular terminology depending upon the nature of the given delegate. For example, the provincial legislature commonly delegates authority to a municipality to make rules. In that context, the subordinate agency (i.e. the municipal council) is delegated authority to make rules (i.e. enact by-laws).

---

[4]There is a significant interrelationship between constitutional and administrative law. In the U.K., for example, constitutional law consists, in a large part, of what Canadians regard as administrative law. In Canada, the two areas are highly intertwined.

CLASSIFICATION OF ADMINISTRATIVE TRIBUNALS

Traditionally it is important to distinguish administrative tribunals in terms of their function because judicial review of administrative action and the application by our courts of the prerogative remedies for denial of a rule of natural justice have been limited to only one category of administrative tribunals: those which exercised a judicial or quasi-judicial function. With the development of the doctrine of fairness the need for classification has been somewhat reduced. Nevertheless a study of this area of the law still requires some understanding of the traditional classification.[5]

First, those administrative tribunals which are delegated a rule-making authority exercise a "legislative" function. Those kinds of tribunals set policy and generally have a wide discretion. Therefore the courts will intervene only where such a tribunal has exceeded its statutory jurisdiction or failed to perform its statutory duties or abused its powers.

Second, an administrative tribunal may exercise an "administrative" function. An administrative function is one in which the delegate renders decisions on the basis of the general policy set out in its enabling statute. In rendering such decisions, it has considerable discretion to set specific policy. An example of this kind of tribunal is the National Parole Board. A court may intervene in these proceedings for the same reasons that it may intervene in the case of legislative tribunals. However, it may also intervene where a decision has been made in breach of the doctrine of fairness.

The third kind of administrative tribunal exercises a ministerial or executive function which entails no exercise of discretion. For example, a body that issues automobile licences has no authority not to issue such a licence where an applicant pays the appropriate fee, signs the appropriate documents and in every way meets all the requirements. These tribunals set no policy whatsoever and their exercise of authority can be reviewed for the same reasons as that of a legislative tribunal.

The fourth type of administrative tribunal exercises a "judicial" or a "quasi-judicial" function. These tribunals also set no policy and therefore render decisions on the basis of a pre-set policy. An example of a judicial tribunal is a provincial court. A provincial court judge, on the basis of evidence adduced, finds an accused guilty or innocent of an

---

[5]The confusion of terminology in respect of the categorization of the various types of functions exercised by administrative tribunals is discussed in detail by the Honourable Mr. Justice J. C. McRuer in the now classic McRuer Report, arising out of the Royal Commission of Inquiry into Civil Rights in the Province of Ontario. See, in particular, Report 1, vol. 1, c. 1, in which Mr. Justice McRuer distinguishes among the various types of functions exercised by administrative tribunals and comments upon the confusing terminology in attempts at classification.

offence. The setting of policy as to what constitutes an offence is done by Parliament and is reflected in the provisions of the Criminal Code under which the provincial court judge operates. Theoretically, this kind of tribunal has very little discretion—if the evidence supports a conviction, there must be a conviction — although, in fact, there is considerable discretion in the sentencing process. However, even this exercise of discretion is done in accordance with pre-set policy as contained in the Criminal Code. The decisions of tribunals of this nature are the only ones that may be subjected to judicial review, strictly defined and quashed for non-compliance with the rules of natural justice.

In terms of their roles in setting policy and exercising discretion, the four kinds of administrative tribunals may be placed on a spectrum or a continuum. At one end, with a large policy-setting role and possessing a large amount of discretion, are the legislative tribunals. At the other end, with no policy-setting role and no discretion, are the ministerial or executive tribunals. The administrative and quasi-judicial tribunals fall in between.

It is important to realize that a given tribunal may exercise different kinds of functions at different times. For example, normally a municipal council exercises a legislative function, but on occasion an applicant may request a municipal council to render a decision which could substantially affect his rights. For this limited purpose, the municipal council will be exercising a quasi-judicial function.

A determination as to whether a given tribunal is judicial or quasi-judicial in nature often presents difficulties for a court. As a result, from time to time, the courts have enunciated various tests in order to distinguish a tribunal exercising this type of function from other tribunals. It is probably sufficient, although simplistic, to define a judicial or quasi-judicial tribunal as one which exercises a function by which the tribunal has "the power to adjudicate upon matters involving consequences to individuals".[6]

In the First McRuer Report, similar definitions are offered as to what constitutes a judicial or quasi-judicial administrative tribunal. It states that:

> [a] power is primarily "judicial" where the decision is to be arrived at in accordance with governing rules of law; in their application policy enters in only to the limited extent already discussed in connection with the exercise of judicial power. This type of decision will be referred to as a "judicial decision".[7]

---

[6]Gelinas, "Judicial Control of Administrative Action: Great Britain and Canada", [1963] Public Law 140 at 160.

[7]First Report, vol. 1, c. 1, p. 28.

In a brief comment Mr. Justice McRuer states that the obligation to act judicially constitutes a requirement "to follow . . . minimum standards of fair procedure".[8]

In addition, Professor H.W.R. Wade provides a definition of a "judicial" or "quasi-judicial" tribunal as follows:

> Is this administrative power one which deprives some individual of his rights or liberties, so that he must be given the elementary justice of a hearing before his rights are destroyed by administrative action?[9]

GROUNDS FOR JUDICIAL REVIEW OF ADMINISTRATIVE DECISION-MAKING[10]

When a sovereign legislative body, either Parliament or the legislature of a province, enacts a law granting a subordinate tribunal authority to make regulations or render decisions in respect of a particular matter, obviously the rights of individuals are affected by the decision of that tribunal. In order that such rights may be protected, a body of rules has developed at common law, breach of which will cause the decision of administrative tribunals to be quashed by the courts:

1. CONFORMITY TO ENABLING STATUTE

Just as a sovereign legislative body may only enact laws within its constitutional jurisdiction, so an administrative tribunal may only enact rules or make decisions within the parameters of the authority granted to

---

[8]*Ibid*, p. 29.

[9]"The Twilight of Natural Justice?" (1951), 67 L.Q.R. 103 at 108.

[10]In the following scheme, Mr. Justice McRuer sets out all the various grounds in defining the jurisdiction of the courts in quashing decisions of administrative tribunals. This list is set out in the First McRuer Report, vol. 1, p. 247. In respect of the fourth item contained in the following list, namely, the issue of bias, see the case of *Greenhut v. Scott*, [1975] 4 W.W.R. 645, 56 D.L.R. (3d) 634 (B.C.).

The following are grounds on which the courts have held decisions or actions by tribunals exercising judicial or administrative power to be invalid:

"(1) Unconstitutionality of the statute purporting to confer the power;
"(2) Invalidity of the appointments of the members of the tribunal;
"(3) Absence of preliminary matters of fact, law or mixed law and fact;
"(4) Bias or the absence of impartiality of members of the tribunal;
"(5) Failure to comply with the mandatory procedural requirements;
"(6) Exceeding scope or area of matters that may be decided: absence of collateral matters of fact, law or mixed law and fact;
"(7) Use of the power for an improper purpose, or the taking into account of extraneous or wrong considerations;
"(8) Failure to comply with the method required by the statute to make a decision;
"(9) Failure to comply with statutory requirements to render the decision legally effective;
"(10) Fraud of a party, misleading the tribunal; and
"(11) Any error of law on the face of the record of the proceedings before the tribunal, whether within its power or not, are an application in the nature of certiorari."

it by its governing statute. If a tribunal does exceed these parameters, an individual whose rights are adversely affected by these actions may ask that a court of law adjudge that the board is not acting competently in accordance with its enabling statute. To use an extreme example, a provincial agricultural marketing board cannot issue drivers' licences. Such an action will be declared ultra vires, that is, outside of the legal jurisdiction of the board, and thus be rendered null and void.

2. JURISDICTIONAL FACT DOCTRINE

The jurisdictional fact doctrine was described by Mr. Justice Roach in *Re Ont. Labour Relations Bd. and Bradley* as follows:

> When an inferior Court or tribunal or body, which has to exercise the power of deciding facts, is first established by Act of Parliament, the legislature has to consider what powers it will give that tribunal or body. It may in effect say that, if a certain state of facts exists and is shewn to such tribunal or body before it proceeds to do certain things, it shall have jurisdiction to do such things, but not otherwise. There it is not for them conclusively to decide whether that state of facts exists, and, if they exercise the jurisdiction without its existence, what they do may be questioned, and it will be held that they have acted without jurisdiction.[10.1]

An example of the application of this doctrine may be found in the case of *Bell v. Ont. Human Rights Comm.*[11] The anti-discrimination provisions contained in the Ontario Human Rights Code[12] specifically limit the scope of the Act to cover only those instances of racial discrimination which arise in respect of a denial of accommodation in self-contained dwellings. Upon an application for a writ of prohibition, a judge of the Trial Division of the Supreme Court of Ontario held that a board of inquiry had no jurisdiction to hear the matter unless and until the preliminary or jurisdictional fact, namely, that the facility was a self-contained dwelling, was present. Since, in this particular case, the facility was not a self-contained dwelling, the judge held that this ended the matter, and the board of inquiry had no jurisdiction to hear the matter further. Although this decision was overruled in the Appellate Division of the Supreme Court of Ontario, it was subsequently affirmed in the Supreme Court of Canada. This was, incidentally, the first and one of the few times the Supreme Court of Canada has heard a matter arising out of a provincial anti-discrimination statute.[13]

[10.1][1957] O.R. 316 at 326, 8 D.L.R. (2d) 65 (C.A.).

[11][1971] S.C.R. 756, 18 D.L.R. (3d) 1.

[12]1961-62 (Ont.), c. 93 [now R.S.O. 1980, c. 340].

[13]For a detailed discussion of the jurisdictional fact doctrine, particularly as it relates to the above case, see Hogg, "The Jurisdictional Fact Doctrine in the Supreme Court of Canada: *Bell v. Ontario Human Rights Commission*" (1971), 9 Osgoode Hall L. 203.

3. ABUSE OF POWER

If an administrative tribunal enacts subordinate legislation or conducts its affairs and renders its decisions in bad faith (in male fides or in the absence of bona fides), its decision and the subordinate legislation will be declared ultra vires the authority of the tribunal and, therefore, of no effect. This notion of bad faith encompasses the allied notions of dishonesty, fraud and malice.[14] In addition, the court will nullify a decision and subordinate legislation that have been made for "improper purposes", that is, improper having regard to the policy objectives establishing the tribunal.[15] In determining whether the tribunal has done something for an improper purpose, the court will entertain considerations relating to the intention of Parliament or a provincial legislature in enacting the particular legislation under which the tribunal was established. Finally, a court will attack the decision of an administrative tribunal, as constituting an abuse of power, if the decision is based upon irrelevant considerations. This, however, is of narrow and limited application.

4. RULES OF NATURAL JUSTICE

As indicated above, the requirement that an administrative tribunal adhere to the rules of natural justice is applicable only to those administrative tribunals which exercise a judicial or quasi-judicial function. If such a tribunal is not conducting its affairs in accordance with these rules, a court of superior jurisdiction of a province, in the case of a provincially constituted administrative tribunal, and the Federal Court, in the case of a federally constituted administrative tribunal, will entertain the process of judicial review and grant the appropriate prerogative writ in order to withdraw the jurisdiction of the tribunal to hear a particular matter, or, if the matter has already been determined, to quash the decision of that tribunal.

There are two fundamental rules of natural justice, under which are subsumed many sub-rules. The two basic rules, as expressed in Latin terminology, are the audi alteram partem and the nemo judex in sua causa rules.

The audi alteram partem rule dictates that both parties to a dispute must be heard. It requires that there must be a fair hearing,[16] that each

---

[14]See, *e.g.*, *Roncarelli v. Duplessis*, [1959] S.C.R. 122, 16 D.L.R. (2d) 689.

[15]See the case of *Madoc v. Quinlan*, [1971] 3 O.R. 540 at 541, 21 D.L.R. (3d) 136. In that case, a judge of the Trial Division of the Supreme Court of Ontario held that the township of Madoc, as a subordinate agency of the provincial government having authority to enact by-laws, could not prohibit a rock music festival on the defendant's farm, under the guise of exercising its regulatory and licensing authority, "even if the vast majority of the inhabitants of the municipality wish that the holding of such a festival be prohibited. It is trite law that a municipal council cannot prohibit under the guise of regulation."

[16]See *Blais v. Basford*, [1972] F.C. 151 (C.A.).

party must receive notice of the hearing, and that each party must be allowed to obtain legal representation. Moreover, during the course of the hearing each party must be allowed to rebut the evidence adduced, and to cross-examine witnesses.[17]

The *nemo judex in sua causa* rule requires the exclusion of all forms of bias from tribunal proceedings. If bias is proven the invocation of this rule of natural justice renders a tribunal's decision null and void.

Although the requirement that a given tribunal conduct its affairs in accordance with natural justice applies only to judicial or quasi-judicial tribunals, recent case law suggests that, with respect to bias, irrespective of the categorization of the function exercised by the tribunal, the courts will treat it as an abuse of power and nullify the decision.

5. DOCTRINE OF FAIRNESS

In the United Kingdom, during the 1960's, a major development in administrative law evolved with the judicial creation of the doctrine of fairness. A similar development occurred in Canadian law, but not until some time later. The breakthrough was the now landmark decision of the Supreme Court of Canada in the case of *Nicholson v. Haldimand-Norfolk Police Commrs. Bd.*[18] followed by the equally important decision of the Supreme Court of Canada in *Martineau v. Matsqui Institution Disciplinary Bd. No. 2*[19] As a result of these cases a court of superior jurisdiction may now review decisions of inferior tribunals on the ground that they were made in a manner that was procedurally unfair. In the same way that conformity with the full range of natural justice requirements varies according to the extent to which a tribunal is required to act judicially, so the requirements of procedural fairness vary from tribunal

---

[17] In the First McRuer Report, vol. 1, p. 137, the Honourable Mr. Justice McRuer defines the audi alteram partem rule in terms of the following constitutent elements:

1. Notice of the intention to make a decision should be given to the party whose rights may be affected.
2. The party whose rights may be affected should be sufficiently informed of the allegations against his interest to enable him to make an adequate reply.
3. A genuine hearing should be held at which the party affected is made aware of the allegations made against him and is permitted to answer.
4. The party affected should be allowed the right to cross-examine the party giving evidence against his interest.
5. A reasonable request for adjournment to permit the party affected to properly prepare and present his case should be granted.
6. The tribunal making the decision should be constituted as it was when the evidence and argument were heard.

[18] [1979] 1 S.C.R. 311, 78 C.L.L.C. 14,181, 88 D.L.R. (3d) 671, 23 N.R. 410.

[19] [1980] 1 S.C.R. 602, 13 C.R. (3d) 1, 15 C.R. (3d) 315, 50 C.C.C. (2d) 353, 106 D.L.R. (3d) 385, 30 N.R. 119.

to tribunal. The doctrine of fairness is part of the rules of natural justice, indeed it might be regarded as the core or central requirement of natural justice. As Mr. Justice Dickson said in *Martineau, supra*:

> It is wrong, in my view, to regard natural justice and fairness as distinct and separate standards and to seek to define the procedural content of each. In *Nicholson, supra*, the Chief Justice spoke of a "notion of fairness involving something less than the procedural protection of the traditional natural justice". Fairness involved compliance with only some of the principles of natural justice. Professor de Smith, *Judicial Review of Administrative Action* (1973), 3rd ed., p. 208, expressed lucidly the concept of a duty to act fairly:
>
>> In general it means a duty to observe the rudiments of natural justice for a limited purpose in the exercise of functions that are not analytically judicial but administrative.
>
> The content of the principles of natural justice and fairness in application to the individual cases will vary according to the circumstances of each case, as recognized by Tucker, L.J., in *Russell v. Duke of Norfolk et al.*, [1949] 1 All E.R. 109 at p. 118.[20]

The importance of the doctrine of fairness is underscored by the declaration of the Supreme Court of Canada that it applies not only to judicial or quasi-judicial tribunals, but also to tribunals exercising an administrative function. To give meaningful effect to this declaration, the Supreme Court of Canada also held (in *Martineau*) that a writ of certiorari will lie to quash a decision of a tribunal, exercising a judicial or quasi-judicial function or exercising a purely administrative function, for reason that the decision was made in a procedurally unfair manner. This development represents the first time that an order in the nature of certiorari has issued in respect of a tribunal that was neither judicial nor quasi-judicial. However, it is nonetheless restricted in the following way: a writ of certiorari will only lie, with respect to tribunals exercising an administrative function, for a breach of the doctrine of fairness.

Certiorari is still unavailable to quash decision of tribunals exercising ministerial or legislative functions. This, coupled with the fact that the rules of natural justice (as they are traditionally known) still apply only to judicial or quasi-judicial tribunals, leaves the question of categorization or classification of function as an important issue.

Mr. Justice Dickson, in the *Martineau* case, summarizes this major development in the law as follows:

> The authorities, in my view, support the following conclusions:
> 1. *Certiorari* is available as a general remedy for supervision of the machinery of Government decision-making. The order may go to any public body with power to decide any matter affecting the rights, interests, property, privileges, or liberty of any person. The basis for the broad reach of this remedy is the general duty of fairness resting on all public decision-makers.
> 2. A purely ministerial decision, on broad grounds of public policy, will typically afford the individual no procedural protection, and any attack upon such a

---

[20]106 D.L.R. (3d) 385 at 411-12.

decision will have to be founded upon abuse of discretion. Similarly, public bodies exercising legislative functions may not be amenable to judicial supervision. On the other hand, a function that approaches the judicial end of the spectrum will entail substantial procedural safeguards. Between the judicial decision and those which are discretionary and policy-oriented will be found myriad decision-making processes with a flexible gradation of procedural fairness through the administrative spectrum. That is what emerges from the decisions of this Court in *Nicholson*, supra. In these cases an applicant may obtain *certiorari* to enforce a breach of the duty of procedural fairness.

3.   . . . The fact that a decision-maker does not have a duty to act judicially, with observance of formal procedure which that characterization entails, does not mean that there may not be a duty to act fairly which involves importing something less than the full panoply of conventional natural justice rules. In general, courts ought not to seek to distinguish between the two concepts, for the drawing of a distinction between a duty to act fairly, and a duty to act in accordance with the rules of natural justice, yields an unwieldly conceptual framework. The *Federal Court Act*, however, compels classification for review of federal decision-makers. . . .

8.   In the final analysis, the simple question to be answered is this: Did the tribunal on the facts of the particular case act fairly toward the person claiming to be aggrieved? It seems to me that this is the underlying question which the Courts have sought to answer in all the cases dealing with natural justice and with fairness.[21]

For a good discussion of some of the earlier cases involving the application of the doctrine of fairness see D.P. Jones, "Administrative fairness in Alberta" (1980), 18 Alta. L.R. 351. This article is expanded upon in a major paper delivered by the same author which appears in C.I.A.J., Judicial Review of Administrative Rulings (Montreal: La Revue du Barreau du Quebec, 1983).

The reader should also bear in mind the important remarks of Mr. Justice Dickson quoted earlier concerning the relationship between the concepts of fairness and natural justice.

The doctrine of fairness, or indeed the doctrine of fairness and the rules of natural justice, cannot be considered in isolation from the constitutional requirements of s. 7 (and other sections) of the Canadian Charter of Rights and Freedoms. Section 7 guarantees that "everyone has the right to life, liberty and security of the person and the right not to be deprived thereof except in accordance with principles of fundamental justice". It is reasonable to predict that the courts, in interpreting the phrase "principles of fundamental justice", will look to previous court decisions which have given meaning to the concepts of "fairness" and "natural justice" in administrative law. Likewise, in further defining these latter concepts, the courts will be likely to look at decisions interpreting "fundamental justice" in s. 7 of the Charter.

---

[21]106 D.L.R. (3d) 385 at 412.

ERROR OF LAW ON THE FACE OF THE RECORD

Often an enabling statute requires a tribunal to keep a record of its proceedings and it is not uncommon for this to be done voluntarily even in the absence of such a statutory requirement. The major part of a record is the tribunal's reasons for its decisions. If there is an error of law on the face of this record, a court of superior jurisdiction has the inherent authority to grant the remedy of certiorari to quash the decision of a tribunal. Where tribunals do not maintain a record, there can, of course, be no error of law on the face of the record, with the result that a court will not grant a writ of certiorari.

PROCEDURE FOR CHALLENGING DECISION OF ADMINISTRATIVE TRIBUNALS.

1. WHEN THEY ARE ULTRA VIRES ENABLING LEGISLATION

The usual way in which a matter of this nature is litigated is by way of an action for declaration. The procedure will differ, of course, from province to province, depending upon the various rules of practice or rules of court of the individual provinces. However, generally speaking, an action for declaration is commenced either by way of a statement of claim or by way of a notice of motion. A challenge of this nature is available to quash the decisions of all administrative tribunals, irrespective of the categorization of the particular function exercised by a given tribunal.

2. WHEN THEY CONSTITUTE AN ABUSE OF POWER

Matters of this nature are brought before the courts in a variety of proceedings, depending upon the circumstances. An action for a declaration is available. Also an application for an injunction (again depending upon the particular rules of court of particular provinces) may be brought either by way of statement of claim or notice of motion, although before a court will entertain such an application the applicant must have the requisite locus standi. Because of this, in some circumstances, the appropriate action is a relator action brought by the Attorney General of the province at the instance of another person.

In addition, an action for damages, including both general and punitive damages, appears to be available where a tribunal exercises a public duty in bad faith, acting maliciously, and for an improper purpose. From a recent decision of the Manitoba Court of Appeal,[22] it does not appear to be absolutely imperative that the action be made on the basis of a recognizable and actionable tort at common law.

---

[22]*Gershman v. Man. Vegetable Producers' Marketing Bd.*, [1976] 4 W.W.R. 406, 69 D.L.R. (3d) 114.

Challenges on the basis of an abuse of power are available to quash the decision of all administrative tribunals, irrespective of the categorization of their particular functions.

3. WHEN A JUDICIAL OR QUASI-JUDICIAL TRIBUNAL HAS BREACHED A RULE OF NATURAL JUSTICE

The process of judicial review, strictly defined, is available only with regard to those tribunals exercising a judicial or quasi-judicial function. In respect of federally constituted tribunals, an application for judicial review is made to the Federal Court.[23] In respect of provincially constituted tribunals, an application for judicial review is made to the courts of superior jurisdiction in the province. In particular, these applications are made to the trial division of the supreme court of a province or, in those provinces where the court possessing trial jurisdiction is constituted as a separte court, to that separate court.

In making such an application, the applicant is asking the court to exercise its inherent jurisdiction to grant a prerogative remedy. There are various types of prerogative remedies, and the applicant will request the one which is appropriate to his particular circumstances.

The prerogative (or extraordinary) remedies are in the form of writs, known as prerogative writs, each having its own unique effect. For example, the granting of a writ of certiorari or, in some provinces, an order in the nature of certiorari quashes the decision of an administrative tribunal, while the granting of a writ of prohibition prohibits an administrative tribunal from hearing the particular matter which is the subject of the application for judicial review.

A writ of mandamus compels a public official to perform an act which he has a statutory duty to perform, and it is not limited to persons or tribunals exercising a judicial or quasi-judicial function. A writ of quo warranto prevents the continued exercise of unlawful authority or power on the part of a public official, although this remedy is, in fact, of rare and limited application. Finally, there is the prerogative remedy of habeas corpus. If an application for a writ of habeas corpus is granted, it invalidates the unlawful incarceration of the subject. This, of course, is primarily applicable in the area of criminal law.

Generally speaking, and again this may vary from province to province, an application for a prerogative writ is commenced by way of notice of motion and, in some instances, by way of statement of claim.

Decisions of tribunals exercising a judicial or quasi-judicial function may also be challenged by way of an application for an injunction or by way of an action for declaration.

---

[23]In this connection, reference may be made to the particular provisions of the Federal Court Act, set out later in this chapter.

4. When a Judicial or Quasi-Judicial Tribunal or an Administrative Tribunal has Breached the Doctrine of Fairness

As indicated above, certiorari is now available to quash decisions of judicial or quasi-judicial tribunals and of purely administrative tribunals for reason that these tribunals, in making their decisions, did so in breach of the requirements of procedural fairness.

PRIVATIVE CLAUSES

One of the reasons underlying the increase in the number of administrative tribunals in recent years is the desirability of placing the authority to render decisions and to make subordinate legislation in the hands of those persons possessing a degree of expertise in the particular matter being regulated. In addition, neither Parliament nor a provincial legislature has the time to deal with all of the various regulatory and/or decision-making matters which presently fall into the hands of administrative tribunals.

In order to permit these tribunals to conduct their affairs in an expeditious and efficient manner, the conventional wisdom is that their decisions ought to be final and binding and not subject to interference by the courts. To promote this end, two legislative developments have occurred. First, there is a noticeable lack of appeal provisions from the decisions rendered by administrative tribunals in many of the enabling statutes. Secondly, the enabling statutes often contain what are referred to as "privative clauses" which have the effect, at least in theory, of excluding from the jurisdiction of our courts the judicial review of decisions rendered by administrative tribunals. There are, however, various formulae of privative clauses, with each type of clause differing in the extent to which it excludes the jurisdiction of the court. Some only exclude the jurisdiction of the court in respect of judicial review, strictly defined, and are therefore directed at preventing courts from granting certain prerogative remedies. Others are wider and attempt to exclude the jurisdiction of the courts in reviewing the decisions of administrative tribunals, in any respect and for any reason. Set out below is s. 108 of the Labour Relations Act, R.S.O. 1980, c. 228, which is a typical privative clause:

108 No decision, order, direction, declaration or ruling of the Board shall be questioned or reviewed in any court, and no order shall be made or process entered, or proceedings taken in any court, whether by way of injunction, declaratory judgment, certiorari, mandamus, prohibition, quo warranto, or otherwise, to question, review, prohibit or restrain the Board or any of its proceedings.

Generally speaking, the courts have resented these attempts by Parliament and the provincial legislatures to exclude judicial review from their jurisdiction. Thus, through a process of statutory interpretation, the courts have largely ignored the privative clauses or have given little effect to them. In response, Parliament and the provincial legislatures have attempted to strengthen the effect of privative clauses by the use of wording which is directed at achieving an iron-clad exclusion of the court's jurisdiction in these matters. One example of a privative clause which has been successful in this regard is s. 5 of An Act to Amend the Succession Duty Act, 1970 (B.C.), c. 45, considered in *Executors of Woodward Estate v. Minister of Finance*:

> . . . and the determination of the Minister is final, conclusive, and binding on all persons and, notwithstanding section 43 or 44 or any other provision of this Act to the contrary, is not open to appeal, question, or review in any Court, and any determination of the Minister made under this subsection is hereby ratified and confirmed and is binding on all persons.[24]

It remains to be seen how the courts will interpret the above and other variants of privative clauses in the future. The desire on the part of Parliament and the provincial legislatures to exclude the jurisdiction of the courts continues to exist and, at the very least, it is predictable that the courts will do their best to avoid the application of this exclusion, wherever possible.

It is important to distinguish the process of appeal from the process of judicial review. The common law rule is that a right of appeal is statutory in nature; no right of appeal exists unless it is specifically provided for in a particular statute. In contrast (with the exception of some recent provincial enactments, especially those in the province of Ontario, as well as provisions contained in the Federal Court Act), the process of judicial review is conducted in accordance with an inherent jurisdiction vested in courts of superior jurisdiction to grant prerogative remedies.

STATUTORY ENACTMENTS IN ADMINISTRATIVE LAW

Recently, statutes have been enacted to codify the process of judicial review. In respect of federally constituted administrative tribunals, the enactment of the Federal Court Act represents a major and significant development in the law. In respect of provincially constituted administrative tribunals, the enactment of a scheme of three Ontario statutes represents an important model of legislative reform in the area of administrative law. Following is a brief review of the above enactments.

1. FEDERAL COURT ACT

Under the Federal Court Act,[25] enacted pursuant to Parliament's legislative authority under s. 101 of the Constitution Act of 1867, Parlia-

---

[24][1973] S.C.R. 120, [1972] 5 W.W.R. 581, 27 D.L.R. (3d) 608 at 612, [1972] C.T.C. 385.
[25]R.S.C. 1970, c. 10 (2nd Supp.).

ment established a new court, called the Federal Court of Canada, replacing the former Exchequer Court of Canada. It was constituted in two divisions, a Trial Division and an Appeal Division (the latter may also be referred to as the Court of Appeal or the Federal Court of Appeal). The Federal Court was granted exclusive original jurisdiction over certain matters and concurrent jurisdiction in respect of other matters. One of its most important functions is a general supervisory role over the affairs of federal administrative tribunals.[26] In particular, under the provisions contained in s. 18 of the Act, the Trial Division has exclusive, original jurisdiction, with respect to those tribunals falling within the scope of s. 2, to issue:

(a) an injunction,
(b) a writ of *certiorari*,
(c) a writ of prohibition,
(d) a writ of *mandamus*,
(e) a writ of *quo warranto*

or to grant declaratory relief . . . This jurisdiction extends, in addition, to other proceedings designed to obtain equivalent relief such as actions against the Attorney General for a declaration.[27]

Notwithstanding these provisions, much of the jurisdiction assigned to the Trial Division is taken away and given to the Appeal Division by virtue of the provisions contained in s. 28 of the Act:

28.(1) Notwithstanding section 18 or the provisions of any other Act, the Court of Appeal has jurisdiction to hear and determine an application to review and set aside a decision or order, other than a decision or order of an administrative nature not required by law to be made on a judicial or quasi-judicial basis, made by or in the course of proceedings before a federal board, commission or other tribunal, upon the ground that the board, commission or tribunal

(a) failed to observe a principle of natural justice or otherwise acted beyond or refused to exercise its jurisdiction;

(b) erred in law in making its decision or order, whether or not the error appears on the face of the records; or

(c) based its decision or order on an erroneous finding of fact that it made in a perverse or capricious manner or without regard for the material before it.

Section 28(3) makes it clear that in the event that a given matter falls within s. 28, the Trial Division is deprived of jurisdiction in respect of that matter.

---

[26]In s. 2 of the Act, "federal board, commission or other tribunal" means "any body or person having, exercising or purporting to exercise jurisdiction or powers under an Act of the Parliament of Canada other than a superior, district or county court of a province or other body set up by provincial legislation": see Jackett, *The Federal Court of Canada: A Manual of Practice*, (1971), p. 18.

[27]*Ibid*.

In this connection, one commentator made these observations:

By virtue of section 28 of the Act, the Court of Appeal has exclusive original jurisdiction in respect of all decisions of a "judicial or quasi-judicial" nature. What was previously a factor in certiorari, prohibition, and natural justice cases only, now becomes crucial in virtually every application for review, for on the issue of whether a function is of a judicial or administrative nature depends the questions of whether the matter is within the jurisdiction of the Court of Appeal or the Trial Division. Finally, the jurisdiction concept retains a place in the law, for, in section 28(1) (a), the Act allows review where an administrative authority has "acted beyond or refused to exercise its jurisdiction".[28]

In addition, consider the provisions contained in s. 29 of the Act:

29.(1) Notwithstanding sections 18 and 28, where provision is expressly made by an Act of Parliament of Canada for an appeal as such to the Court, to the Supreme Court, to the Governor in Council or to the Treasury Board from a decision or order of a federal board, commission or other tribunal made by or in the course of proceedings before that board, commission or tribunal, that decision or order is not, to the extent that it may be so appealed, subject to review or to be restrained, prohibited, removed or otherwise dealt with, except to the extent and in the manner provided for in that Act.

Many commentators have described the effect of the above provisions as being confusing and unnecessarily complex.

Section 31 of the Act permits an appeal to the Supreme Court of Canada from the decisions of the Federal Court; however, leave to appeal must first be obtained from either the Federal Court of Appeal or from the Supreme Court of Canada itself.

2. PROVINCIAL ENACTMENTS

Administrative law reform at the provincial level has not occurred in a substantial way across Canada. One exception is the striking model of reform in the province of Ontario, following a somewhat interesting legislative history. In 1964, the Ontario government introduced legislation which granted wide-ranging investigatory powers to the then recently established Ontario Police Commission. That bill, referred to as the "Police Bill" or "Bill 99", caused a storm of publicity in the legislature, in the press, and in the public at large. As a result of that controversy, the legislation was dropped, the minister responsible for the legislation resigned, and the government appointed the former Chief Justice of the Trial Division of the Supreme Court of Ontario, the Honourable J.C. McRuer, to conduct a Royal Commission of Inquiry into Civil Rights in the Province of Ontario. As a result of this royal commission, the now classic McRuer Report was published, in which certain recommendations were made in connection with the reform of administrative law.

---

[28]Mullan, "The Federal Court Act: The Misguided Attempt at Administrative Law Reform" (1973), 23 U. of T. L.J. 14. See also other articles contained in the selected bibliography appearing at the end of this chapter.

Subsequently, these recommendations were adopted in the form of new Ontario legislation in the early 1970's. In particular, the Ontario legislature enacted the Statutory Powers Procedure Act, 1971 (Ont.), c. 47, the Judicial Review Procedure Act, 1971 (Ont.), c. 48, the Judicature Amendment Act, 1970 (No. 4) (Ont.), c. 97, and the Judicature Amendment Act, 1971 (Ont.), c. 57.[29]

The Statutory Powers Procedure Act sets out various procedures to which administrative tribunals must adhere in the course of conducting their affairs. Essentially, the Act is a codification of the rules of natural justice and dictates that administrative tribunals must conform to these requirements. It also requires that an administrative tribunal maintain a record of its proceedings. This remedies the defect at common law where an application for certiorari on the basis of an error of law on the face of the record must necessarily fail in the absence of a record.

Under the provisions of the Judicial Review Procedure Act, "judicial review through the prerogative remedies of prohibition, certiorari, mandamus, and the equitable remedies of a declaratory judgment and an injunction, are all replaced by one 'Application for Judicial Review'."[30]

And finally, under the two Judicature Amendment Acts referred to above, a new division was created in the Supreme Court of Ontario, namely, the Divisional Court, in order to specifically deal with the judicial review of administrative action. The judges of the Divisional Court are those appointed to the Trial Division of the Supreme Court and they share responsibilities in both of these divisions.

GROWTH OF GOVERNMENT BUREAUCRACY

The increase in the number of administrative tribunals has been matched by the growth in government bureaucracy. The public service, at all levels of government, has expanded to a considerable degree in the past few years. Many people feel that the bureaucracy has lost touch with the average citizen. Indeed, we have all experienced frustration in attempting to resolve a particular matter with a department of government assuming we have overcome the initial problem in attempting to locate the appropriate party with whom to deal. In order to mitigate these and other concerns, many provinces have enacted ombudsman legislation.

---

[29]For a comprehensive review of the above legislative history, see Tarnopolsky, *The Canadian Bill of Rights* (McClelland and Stewart, 1975). Although the reform of administrative law has been conducted in a substantial way only in the province of Ontario, other provinces have enacted some statutory provisions in connection with administrative law. See, for example, the Alberta Administrative Procedures Act, R.S.A. 1980, c. A-2.

[30]Tarnopolsky, *op. cit.*, p. 63.

The institution of the ombudsman arose in Sweden and, in the modern era, developed significantly in New Zealand. Since that time, the institution has come to North America and, in 1967, following the recommendation of the Clement Commission, Alberta became the first province in Canada to have a legislative ombudsman. In recent years, virtually all provinces in Canada have enacted similar ombudsman legislation. In addition, in 1976, the International Ombudsman Institute was established in Alberta as a resource centre and clearing house in respect of materials of interest to ombudsmen around the world. The first international meeting of ombudsmen was held in Edmonton in 1976, and the second in Jerusalem in 1980, and the third is to be held in Stockholm in 1984.

Another aspect of concern in connection with government bureaucracy relates to the storage and usage of personal information contained in government data banks. Reference should be made to the privacy provisions contained in the Privacy Act,[31] which address the issue of the individual's access to information concerning himself stored in government data banks. Reference might also be made to the protection of privacy provisions in the Criminal Code. It is interesting to note that the institution of the ombudsman has, thus far, developed only at the provincial level, whereas the protection of privacy, with some exceptions (for example, the Privacy Act, R.S.B.C. 1979, c. 336), has developed primarily at the federal level.

Akin to the foregoing developments is the enactment, at both the federal and provincial levels, but primarily at the federal level, of freedom of information statutes. Freedom of information legislation, generally speaking, is designed to give a citizen access to government information. It differs from federal privacy legislation in that the privacy provisions relate to an individual's access to and use of personal information in government data banks concerning himself, whereas freedom of information legislation relates not to personal information but to government information in the nature of "public business".[32] Both the so-called "privacy" provisions and the so-called "freedom of information" provisions were recently enacted by Parliament as part of a single access to government information package in 1982 and proclaimed into force in 1983. As indicated above, the privacy provisions are a strengthened version of an earlier enactment contained in the Canadian Human Rights Act. However, the freedom of information provisions are contained in a new law, which followed a somewhat checkered legislative history — among other things, private members' bills, a government "Green Paper", a bill introduced by the Conservative government, and the eventual

---

[31] 1980-81-82-83 (Can.), c. 111 (Sched. II). The Act was originally enacted [1976-77, c. 33] as Part IV of the Canadian Human Rights Act.

[32] See the Access to Information Act, 1980-81-82-83 (Can.), c. 111 (Sched. I).

enactment of the new package in 1982 by the Liberal government. Freedom of information is an area of law which has developed significantly in the United States, and, no doubt, will be of significant import, in future years, in Canada.

CONCLUSION

The development of administrative law in recent years represents an important component of Canadian legal history. We have seen how the law has responded to the consequences of regulatory control over virtually all aspects of human affairs[33] and how the law strives, sometimes imperfectly, to ensure that under a regime of regulatory control there is, at the very least, a minimum standard of fairness and justice in the administrative process.

Administrative law is more than a single, substantive area of the law. It transcends all of the major divisions of the law. The direction that it takes in ensuring the achievement of justice and fairness in the administrative process, may assist in providing an answer to the perplexing question as to adaptability of the law to changing social conditions.

SELECTED BIBLIOGRAPHY OF TREATISES, ARTICLES AND OTHER MATERIALS ON ADMINISTRATIVE LAW

TREATISES

Canada

Angus, Wm. H., *Cases and Materials on Administrative Law*, Toronto: York University, 1977.

Canadian Institute for the Administration of Justice, *Judicial Review of Administrative Rulings*. La Revue du Barreau de Quebec: Montreal, 1983.

Garant, P., *Droit Administratif*. Les Editions Yvon Blais Inc.: Montreal, 1981.

Laux, F., *The Administrative Process: Cases, Notes and Other Materials*, 5th ed. University of Alberta: Edmonton, 1981.

Law Society of Upper Canada, *Practice and Procedure before Administrative Tribunals*. De Boo: Toronto, 1953.

Reid, *Administrative Law and Practice*, 2nd ed. Butterworths: Toronto, 1978.

---

[33]For some excellent summaries as to the extent of regulatory control over modern life, and, in particular the growing use of the order-in-council (including its effect on civil liberties), see the Financial Post, 23rd December 1978 and the editorial of 3rd November 1979; the Toronto Star, 7th January 1979 and the Globe and Mail, 3rd October 1981.

Great Britain

Allen, *Law and Orders,* 3rd ed., Nature and Scope of Delegated Legislation and Executive Power. Stevens: London, 1965.

Benjafield, *Principles of Australian Administrative Law,* 4th ed. Law Book Co.: Sydney, 1971.

Borrie, *Elements of Public Law* 2nd ed. Sweet & Maxwell: London, 1970.

Clarke, *Constitutional and Administrative Law.* Sweet & Maxwell: London, 1971.

de Smith, *Constitutional and Administrative Law,* 2nd ed. Penguin Education: Harmondsworth, 1973.

de Smith, *Judicial Review of Administrative Action,* 3rd ed. Stevens: London, 1973.

Foulkes, *Introduction to Administrative Law,* 3rd ed. Butterworths: London, 1972.

Ganz, *Administrative Procedures.* Sweet & Maxwell: London, 1974.

Garner, *Administrative Law,* 4th ed. Butterworths: London, 1974.

Garrett, *Administrative Reform the Next Step.* Fabian Society: London, 1973.

Griffith and Street, *Principles of Administrative Law,* 4th ed. Pitman: London, 1967.

Jackson, *Natural Justice.* Sweet & Maxwell: London, 1973.

Jennings, *The Law and the Constitution,* 5th ed. University of London Press: London, 1959.

Phillips, *Constitutional and Administrative Law,* 5th ed. Sweet & Maxwell: London, 1973.

Reid, *The Administrative Process.* Butterworths: London, 1971.

Schwartz and Wade, *Legal Control of Government.* Clarendon Press: Oxford, 1972.

Wade, *Administrative Law,* 3rd ed. Clarendon Press: Oxford, 1971.

Wade and Bradley, *Constitutional Law,* 8th ed. Longman: London, 1970.

Wheare, *Maladministration and its Remedies.* Stevens: London, 1973.

Yardley, *Source of English Administrative Law,* 2nd ed. Butterworths: London, 1970.

ARTICLES

Angus, "The Individual and the Bureaucracy: Judicial Review — Do We Need It?" (1974), 20 McGill L.J. 178.

Alarie, J. et G. Boisvert, "Les criteres de repartition des normes entre la loi et le reglement" (1980), 21 cahiers 567.

Arthurs, H.W., "Rethinking administrative law: a slightly dicey business" (1979), 17 Osgoode Hall, L.J.1.

Arthurs, H.W., "Recognizing administrative law" (1981), Admin. Law Conf. 2.

Atkey, "The Statutory Powers Procedure Act, 1971" (1972), 10 Osgoode Hall L.J. 155.

Atkey, R.G., "Freedom of Information: The problem of confidentiality in the administrative process" (1980), 18 U.W.O.L. Rev. 153.

Atkinson, W.J., "La discretion administrative et la mise en ouevre d'un politique" (1978), 19 cahiers 187.

Atkinson, W.J. et M.C. Levesque, "Delegation de pouvoirs et delegation de signature: l'exercise par des Fonctionnoures des pouvoirs confies a leau ministre" (1982), 42 R. du B. 327.

Barbe, R.P., "De certains aspects de la jurisdiction de la regie des services publics en matiere de troit municipal" (1978), 19 cahiers 447.

Belley, J.G., "La notion de protection du public dans la reforme du troit professional quebecois: une analyse socio-politique" (1980), 21 cahiers 673.

Blache, P., "Les aspects proceduraux de la lutte administrative contre la discrimination, et la charte des droits et libertes de la personne" (1976), 17 cahiers 875.

Branson, C.O.D. and H.R. Wade, "The British Columbia Judicial Review Procedure Act: procedural means for obtaining judicial review; comments" (1981), Admin. Law Conf. 156.

Brown, L.N., "The Council on Tribunals; a re-assessment in its 20th year" (1979), Aspects 1-25.

Brown, L.N., "La nouvelle justice naturelle: l'administrateur equitable et raisonnable" (1980), 21 cahiers 67.

Bruni, M.J. and K.F. Miller, "Practice and procedure before the energy resources conservation board" (1982), 20 Alta. L. Rev. 79.

Castrilli et al., "An environmental impact assessment statute for Ontario with commentary" (1975), Environmental Management 319.

Corry, "The Prospects for the Rule of Law" (1955), 21 Can. J. of Econ. and Pol. Sci. 405.

Cote, "Droit civil et droit administratif au Quebec" (1976), 17 cahiers 825.

Couture, "Introduction to Canadian Federal Administrative Law" (1972), 22 U. of T.L.J. 47.

Dessault, "Relationship between the Nature of the Acts of the Administration and Judicial Review: Quebec and Canada" (1967), 10 Can. Public Administration 298 at 317.

Doern, "Regulatory Process, performance and reform; concluding observations" (1978), Regulatory Process 1.

Doern, "The Regulatory process in Canada" (1978), Regulatory Process 1.

Driedger, "Subordinate Legislation" (1969), 47 Can. Bar Rev. 1.

Dussault et Pelletier, "Le professionel fonctionnaire face aux mecanismes d'inspection profesionnelle et de discipline institues par le code des professions" (1977), 37 R. du B 2.

Dussault, "L'equilibre entre les pouvoirs judiciaire, legislatif et executif: rupture ou evolution?" (1979), 22 Can. Pub. Admin. 196.

Dussault, "Le role du juriste fonctionnaire dans l'amenagement des relations entre l'administration et les citoyens" (1981), 24 Can. Pub. Admin. 8.

Edmond, "A critical evaluation of the evironmental protection laws in the Maritime Provinces (and more particularly the Nova Scotia Environmental Protection Act)" (1975), Environmental Management 258.

Estey, "Usefulness of the Administrative Process" (1971), Lectures of Law Society of Upper Can. 307.

Estey, "The right to know the case against you in administrative law" (1981), Cambridge Lecture 228.

Estrin, "The legal and administrative management of Ontario's air resources 1967-74" (1975), Environmental Management 182.

Evans, "Judicial review in Ontario; recent developments in the remedies" (1977), 55 Can. Bar Rev. 148.

Evans, "Remedies in administrative law" (1981), Lectures L.S.U.C. 429.

Fera, "Review of Administrative Decisions Under the Federal Court Act" (1971), 14 Can. Public Administration 580.

Filion, "Le pouvoir discretionnaire de l'administration exerce sous forme de normes administratives: les directives" (1970), 20 cahiers 855.

Flick, "L'abus de pouvoirs en droit administratif Canadien et quebecois" (1978), 19 cahiers 135.

Gagnon, "The case of the elusive regulations" (1977), 1 Legal Med. 247.

Garant, "Le Protecteur de citoyen et le droit administratif" (1979), Aspects 26.

Gauthier, "Le processus dicisionnel de liberation conditionelle" (1981), 14 Criminologue 2:16.

Gelinas, "Judicial Control of Administrative Action: Great Britain and Canada", [1963] Public Law 140.

Glenn, "L'amenagement du territoire en droit public quebecois" (1977), 23 McGill L.J. 242.

Glenier, "Controle administratif du pouvoir contractuel de l'administration municipale" (1982), 84 R. du N. 247.

Grey, "Discretion in administrative law" (1979), 17 Osgoode Hall L.J. 107.

Grey, "Can fairness be effective?" (1982), 27 McGill L.J. 360.

Hendry, "Some Problems in Canadian Administrative Law" (1967), 2 Ottawa L. Rev. 71.

Hogg, "Is Judicial Review of Administrative Action Guaranteed by the British North American Act?" (1976), 54 Can. Bar Rev. 716.

Hogg, "The Supreme Court of Canada and Administrative Law: 1949-1971" (1973), 11 Osgoode Hall L.J. 187.

Houle-Rousseau, "La notion d'enrichissement sans cause en droit administratif quebecois" (1980), 19 cahiers 1039.

Issalys, "The professions tribunal and the control of ethical conducts among professionals" (1978), 24 McGill L.J. 588; (1979), Aspects 222.

Janisch, "Policy making in regulation: towards a new definition of the status of independent regulatory agencies in Canada" (1979), 17 Osgoode Hall L.J. 46.

Janisch, "Administrative tribunals in the 80's rights of access by groups and individuals" (1981), 1 Windsor Yearbook Access Justice 303.

Janisch, "The role of the independant regulatory agencies in Canada" (1978), 27 U.N.B. L. Rev. 83.

Jones, "Administrative Progress in Alberta" (1980), 18 Alta. L. Rev. 357.

Kenniff, "Les Recentes reformes legislatives en droit Municipal Quebecois: Bilan et Perspective d'avenir" (1981), 12 R.D.U.S. 3.

Kernaghan, "Political control of administrative action: Accountability or Window Dressing?" (1976), 17 Cahiers 927.

Kerr, "Telephone rate Regulation in New Brunswick and rate regulation process" (1977), 26 U.N.B.L.J. 69.

Kenniff and Giroux, "The law relating to the protection and Quality of the Environment in Quebec" (1975), Environmental Management 213.

Lafond, "La loi sur l'amenagement et l'urbanisme" (1981), 12 R.B.U.S. 43.

Lalonde, "Les regres vs. le citoyen; raport d'atelier" (1978), 38 R. du B. 496.

Lambert, "Administrative Law; Reform of the Public Law Remedies in England" (1978), 56 Can. Bar Rev. 668.

Lawford, "Appeals Against Administrative Decisions: The Function of Judicial Review" (1962), 5 Can. Public Administration 50.

Lemieux, "Supervisory judicial control of federal and provincial public authorities in Quebec (1979), 17 Osgoode Hall L.J. 133; (1979), Aspects 147.

Lemieux, "Les reactions de la doctrine a la creation du droit pour les juges en droit administratif" (1980), 21 cahiers 277.

Levesque-Crevier, "La motivation en droit administratif" (1980), 40 R. du B. 535.

Longtin et Bouchard, "Vers une revision du processus et du codre d'elaboration de la decision administrative au Quebec" (1981), 22 cahiers 159.

Loughlin, "Procedural Fairness: A study of the crisis in administrative law" (1978), 28 U. of T.L.J. 215.

Lowery and Smith, "Judicial Review of and Appeals from Conservation Board Orders" (1969), 7 Alta. L. Rev. 443.

Lucas and McCallum, "Looking at environmental Impact assessment" (1975), Environmental Management 306.

McAllister, "Administrative Law" (1963), 6 Can. Bar J. 439.

MacCrimmon, "The British Columbia Judicial Review Procedure Act: Procedural Means for Obtaining Judicial Review" (1981), Admin. Law Conf. 98.

Macdonald, "A bibliography of legislation relating to administrative law in Canadian jurisdictions" (1979), 27 Chitty's L.J. 83.

Macdonald, "Judicial review and procedural fairness in administrative law" (1980), 25 McGill L.J. 560; (1980), 26 McGill L.J. 1.

Macdonald, "The commissions of inquiry in the perspective of administrative law" (1980), 18 Alta. L. Rev. 366.

Macdonald and Paskell-Meade, "Administrative Law: Annual Survey of Canadian Law" (1981), 13 Ottawa L. Rev. 671.

MacDowell, "Law and Practice before the Ontario Labour Relations Board" (1978), 1 Advocates Q. 198.

Mackay, "Human rights in Canadian Society: Merchanisms for Raising the Issues and Providing Redress" (1981), 4 Dalhousie L.J. 739.

McDonald, "Contradictory Government Action: Estopped of Statutory Authorities" (1979), 17 Osgoode Hall L.J. 160.

McRuer, "Control of Power" (1979).

Millward, "Judicial Review of Administrative Authorities in Canada" (1961), 39 Can. Bar Rev. 351.

Mitchell, "The Relationship Between Government and Administration Tribunals" (1973), 39 Man. Bar News 52.

Molot, "Administrative Law": Annual Survey of Canadian Law, Part 2 (1969), 3 Ottawa L. Rev. 465.

Molot, "Administrative Discretion and Current Judicial Activism" (1979), 11 Ottawa L. Rev. 336.

Morden, "Recent Developments in Administrative Law" (1967), Lectures of Law Society of Upper Can. 275.

Mullan, "Judicial Restraints on Administrative Action: Effective or Illusory?" (1976), 17 cahiers 913.

Mullan, "Recent developments in Nova Scotian Administrative Law" (1978), 4 Dalhousie L.J. 467.

Mullan, "Developments in Administrative Law: the 1978-79 term" (1980), Supreme Court L.R. 1.

Mullan, "Developments in Administrative Law: the 1979-80 term" (1981), Supreme Court L.R.1.

Mullan, "Procedural fairness: Nicholson and the tasks ahead" (1981), Admin. Law Conf. 219.

Mullan, "Natural justice and fairness, substantive as well as procedural standards for the review of administrative decision making?" (1982), 27 McGill L.J. 250.

Mullen, "The Federal Court Act: A Misguided Attempt at Administrative Law Reform" (1973), 23 U. of T.L.J. 14.

Mullen, "Reform of Judicial Review of Administrative Action: The Ontario Way" (1974), 12 Osgoode Hall L.J. 125.

Neilson, "Administrative Remedies: the Canadian Experience with Assurances of Voluntary Compliance in Provincial Trade Practices legislation" (1981), 19 Osgoode Hall L.J. 153.

Pacquet, "The regulatory process and economic performance" (1978), Regulatory Proc. 34.

Paskell-Meade, and Macdonald R.A. "Administrative law" (1981), 13 Ottawa L. Rev. 671.

Patterson, "Practice and Procedure Before the Ontario Environmental Appeal Board" (1982), 3 Advocates Q. 181.

Pepin, "Les regies vs. Le Citoyen; explication du theme" (1978), 38 R. du B.

Pepin, "Le pouvoir reglementaire et la Charte de la langue Francaise" (1978), B Themis 107.

Pepin, "Droit administratif; chroniques regulieres" (1979), 39 R. du B. 121.

Pepin, "Droit administratif; chroniques regulieres" (1981), 41 R. du B. 161.

Pepin, "Droit administratif; chroniques regulieres" (1982), 42 R. du B. 269.

Plunkett and Lightbody, "Tribunals, Politics and Public Interest: The Edmonton Annexation Case" (1982), 8 Can. Pub. Policy.

Quinn and Trebilcock, "Compensation, transition Costs and Regulatory change" (1982), 32 U. of T. L.J. 117.

Rankin et al., "Procedural fairness: Nicholson and the tasks ahead; comments" (1981), Admin. Law Conf. 237.

Reid, "Administrative Law; Rights and Remedies", [1953] Law Society of Upper Can. Spec. Lect. 1.

Riddell, "Procedures before the Ontario workmens compensation Board" (1977), 1 Advocates' Q.46.

Rivest, "Les politiques du regulation et la modelle d'edelman: une analyse en fonction de la Sante dans l'industrie de l'amiante" (1979), 22 Can. Pub. Admin. 290.

Rivest, "Les Politiques de Regulation et le Modele d'edelman: Une Analyse en Fonction de la Sante dans l'industrie de l'amiante" (1979), 22 Can. Pub. Admin. 290.

Robertson, "The use of official notice by administrative tribunals" (1980), 6 Queen's L.J. 3.

Rousseau, "Le recours en cassation dans le Contentieux Municipal" (1980), 21 cahiers 715.

Roman, "Regulatory Law and Procedure" (1978), Regulatory Proc. 68.

Rutherford, "Legislative Review of Delegated Legislation" (1969), 47 Can. Bar Rev. 352.

Schachter, "Controlling the Ministers" (1978), 16 Alta. L. Rev. 388.

Scott, "Administrative Law 1923-1943" (1948), 26 Can. Bar Rev. 268.

Slayton, "Competitive applications before the Canadian Radio-Television and Telecommunications Commission" (1981), 59 Can. Bar Rev. 571.

Smillie, "Jurisdictional Review of Abuse of Discretionary Power" (1969), 47 Can. Bar Rev. 623.

Smith, "Practice and procedures before the environmental assessment board" (1982), 3 Advocates' Q. 195.

Sproule, "The uranium mining industry in Saskatchewan: control regulation and related constitutional issues" (1979), 43 Sask. L. Rev. 65.

Taylor, "The new despotism — fifty years later" (1979), 37 Advocate 417.

Taylor, "The appearance or justice: a sober second look at statutory tribunals, despotism and the rule in R. v. Sussex" (1981), Admin. Law Conf. 211.

Trebilcock, "The consumer interest and regulatory reform" (1978), Regulatory Proc. 94.

Trudel et Plotte, "La reglementation des infrastructures de telecommunications au Quebec" (1978), 13 Themis 139.

Wade, "Anglo-American Administrative Law; Some Reflections" (1965), 81 L.Q. Rev. 357.

Wade, "Some Anglo-Canadian comparisons and contrasts" (1981), Admin. Law Conf. 197.

Wexler, "The forms of action and administrative law" (1981), Admin. Law Conf. 292.

Willis, "Administrative Law in Canada" (1939), 53 Harvard L. Rev. 251.

Willis, "Administrative Law in Canada" (1961), 39 Can. Bar Rev. 251.
Willis "Canadian Administrative Law in Retrospect" (1974), 24 U. of
    T.L.J. 225.
Willis, "Civil Rights — A Fresh Viewpoint" (1965), 13 Chitty's L.J. 224.
Willis, "Three Approaches to Administrative Law" (1935), 1 U. of T.
    L.J. 53.
Yates, "The lawyer in the regulatory process" (1980), Alta. L. Rev. 70.
Zimmerman, "Synergy and the Science court: Scientific Method and
    the Adversarial System in Technology Assessment" (1980), 38 U.
    of T. Fac. L. Rev. 170.

OTHER MATERIALS

Alberta, Legislative Assembly Special Committee on Boards and Trib-
    unals, Report, 1965.
Administrative Law Conference, Proceedings, 1979. University of British
    Columbia: Vancouver, 1981.
Administrative Law Remedies, H.N. Janisch (ed.), 1973.
Individual End of Bureaucracy, Baum (ed.), 1974.
Current Issues in Adminstrative Law, H.N. Janisch (ed.), 1974.
Law Society of Upper Canada, *New Directions in Administrative Law*
    (Phonotape).
Ontario, Royal Commission of Inquiry Into Civil Rights, Report, 1968.
Canada, Royal Commission on Government Organization, Report, 1962-63.
Ontario, Committee on the Organization of the Government in Ontario,
    Report, 1959.
Great Britain, Committee on Administrative Tribunals and Enquiries,
    Report, 1957.
Great Britain, Committee on Minister's Powers, Report, 1932.
Canada, Special Committee on Statutory Instruments, Report, 1969.
Scotland, Scottish Law Commission, Memorandum No. 14, Remedies
    in Administrative Law, 1970.
Great Britain, Law Commission, Working Paper No. 40, Remedies in
    Administrative Law, 1971.
Canadian Law Reform Commission, *Independent Administrative Agencies.*
    Canada Law Reform Commission: Ottawa, 1980.
Ontario Economic Council, *Government Regulation.* Ontario Economic
    Council: Toronto, 1978.
Mildon, *Administrative Law.* Communities and the Legal Resource Cen-
    tre: Edmonton, 1977.
Ontario Regulatory Reform Program, *Achievements in Regulatory Reform
    in Ontario. Toronto, 1982.*

SOME RECENT CASES

Bowen v. Edmonton, [1977] 6 W.W.R. 344, 3 M.P.L.R. 129, 4 C.C.L.T. 105, 80 D.L.R. (3d) 501, 8 A.R. 336 (T.D.).

Campeau Corp. v. Calgary, 7 Alta. L.R. (2d) 294, 12 A.R. 31 (C.A.).

C.U.P.E., Loc. 963 v. N.B. Liquor Corp., 97 D.L.R. (3d) 17, 25 N.B.R. (2d) 237, [1979] 2 S.C.R. 227, 79 C.L.L.C. 14, 209, 51 A.P.R. 237.

Delanoy v. Pub. Service Comm. Appeal Bd., [1977] 1 F.C. 562 (C.A.).

Heppner v. Min. of Environment (Alta.) (1977), 4 Alta. L.R. (2d) 139, 80 D.L.R. (3d) 112, 6 A.R. 154 (sub nom. *Heppner v. Alta.*).

Kane v. Univ. of B.C. Bd. of Gov., [1980] 3 W.W.R. 125, [1980] S.C.R. 1105, 18 B.C.L.R. 124, 110 D.L.R. (3d) 311, 31 N.R. 214.

Klymchuk v. Cowan (1964), 47 W.W.R. 467, 45 D.L.R. (2d) 587 (Man.).

Martineau v. Matsqui Institution Inmate Disciplinary Bd. No. 2, [1978] 1 S.C.R. 118, 33 C.C.C. (2d) 366, 74 D.L.R. (3d) 1, 14 N.R. 285.

Matsqui Institution Inmate Disciplinary Bd. v. Martineau, [1978] 2 F.C. 637, 40 C.C.C. (2d) 325, 22 N.R. 251, reversing [1978] 1 F.C. 312, 37 C.C.C. (2d) 58 (C.A.).

Nat. Cablevision Ltd. v. La regie des services publics, [1975] C.A. 335 (Que.).

Nicholson v. Haldimand-Norfolk Police Commrs. Bd., [1979] 1 S.C.R. 311, 78 C.L.L.C. 14, 181, 88 D.L.R. (3d) 23 N.R. 410.

Tegon Dev. Ltd. v. Edmonton City Council (1977), 5 Alta. L.R. (2d) 63, 81 D.L.R. (3d) 543, 8 A.R. 384, affirmed 121 D.L.R. (3d) 760, 24 N.R. 269 (S.C.C.).

Re Vardy (1976), 8 N.R. 91, 9 Nfld. & P.E.I.R. 245, 34 C.R.N.S. 349, 28 C.C.C. (2d) 164 (sub nom. *Vardy v. Scott*), 66 D.L.R. (3d) 431 (S.C.C.).

13

NEW DIRECTIONS

INTRODUCTION

Generally speaking, the substantive law in each of the various divisions of law is always undergoing change. This change is effected either by way of the evolutionary process by which the common law develops through judicial pronouncements in recently decided cases, or by way of new statutory and/or regulatory enactments. Many new statutes are legislating in areas of human concern not previously covered by formal enactment. This is not to say that all of the substantive areas of the law are undergoing major revision. However, at the very least, one could readily argue that change is endemic to our legal system, if not a fundamental and central characteristic of that system.[1]

Aside from the substantive and procedural changes in the various divisions of the law, there have been some fundamental changes in the Canadian legal system as a whole. These developments have occurred to some extent because many persons are questioning the basic presumptions underlying our legal system. Modern thinkers are attempting to re-evaluate the role of law in contemporary society and to seek devices permitting the law to adapt to changing social conditions. In addition, there are related questions being asked in connection with the reform of antiquated laws. The updating of these laws can take the form of simple reform on an ad hoc basis, or alternatively, it might take the form of a major revamping of a particular area of the law.

The law must respond to new problems. However, the manner in which the law responds to these problems often gives rise to considerable controversy. For example, one recent issue relates to the need and advisability of selective, mandatory wage and price controls in Canada.

---

[1]The most dramatic example of this was the "patriation", in 1982, of our so-called "new constitution". What is particularly significant about that event is the incorporation in the new constitution of a domestic amending formula (actually, there is more than one formula, the use of a particular one depending upon the nature of the proposed amendment). Therefore, in future, further constitutional changes will likely occur, as it is now easier to effect constitutional change without having the necessity to resort to a request to the U.K. Parliament to bring about the change. Also, there is no longer any ambiguity as to precisely how to effect a constitutional change. In the past, there was considerable uncertainty as to what the conventional requirements were to amend the old B.N.A. Act and, indeed, as to the status of convention itself in our legal system.

In this example, the question, first, is whether a legislative response is the appropriate one in attempting to resolve complex economic issues. Given that there is a consensus that a legislative response is appropriate, then a second question relates to the form and substance of that response.

The process of law reform in Canada is perhaps made more difficult than in other sovereign nations owing to certain constitutional restraints. For example, there have been many recent developments in relation to the creation of a unified family court in Canada. Neither the federal government nor any province could entertain such a notion without regard to the serious constitutional constraints in conducting such a reform. Similarly, there are currently some proposals in connection with the creation of a single court of trial jurisdiction in criminal matters. Again, this can never happen unless there is federal/provincial co-operation. Moreover, in June of 1983, the Supreme Court of Canada held that it was unconstitutional to do so given the constraints flowing from s. 96 of the Constitution Act of 1867. Also, there are constitutional constraints on a province in enacting consumer protection legislation, owing to the prohibitions presently contained in the federal Combines Investigation Act, R.S.C. 1970, c. C-23. In the event that there is an operational incompatibility between the provisions contained in the provincial consumer protection legislation and the Combines Investigation Act, the doctrine of federal paramountcy would apply. Constitutional constraints notwithstanding, the process of law reform in Canada has now become a well-developed and institutionalized component of the Canadian legal system.

In addition, there are other broad changes which will, in the long run, affect the form and structure of the existing legal system and the processes by which that system operates. These developments will, no doubt, play a major role in the evolution of our system and in its capability of adapting, not only to changing social conditions at present, but also to future realities.

TECHNOLOGY AND THE LAW

Generally speaking, the law and modern technology have each grown to a level of substantial sophistication but their paths have never crossed. Consider, for example, the following editorial comment:

> In many ways our courts still function as if electricity had never been discovered. When a trial is in progress, for example, a court reporter laboriously writes down the proceedings in shorthand, and then transcribes them at night. The result is delay and expense in preparing the transcripts which are necessary for an appeal; and indeed the record of the witness' testimony may not be available if anyone wants to refer to it later at the same trial. Chief Justice Estey points out that a great deal of time and trouble could be saved by transcribing the testimony electronically.
>
> Another use of electronics he suggested would be to take the testimony of witnesses living in distant places. Flying such a witness to Ontario and providing him with meals and lodging during the trial can be a heavy expense to the party who needs his evidence.

Why not have his evidence taken in his own home town before a TV camera, and show the video tape at the trial? The judge and jury could not only hear what the witness had to say, but listen to the tone of his voice and observe his behaviour under questioning just as if he were in court — and probably at a fraction of the cost of securing his physical presence.[2]

One area of some development, however, is the application of computer technology to legal research. The entire question of electronic legal retrieval systems falls under the general heading of "jurimetrics". In Canada, there have already been some significant developments in the area of jurimetrics. For example, there exists a Jurimetrics Committee of the Canadian Bar Association. The objectives of that committee are set out as follows:[3]

1. to provide information and advice to the Canadian Bar Executive on questions arising from the Jurimetrics area;

2. to provide exposure for the members of the Association to developments in the Jurimetrics area through presentations at such occasions as the annual meeting;

3. to encourage activities for projects in the Jurimetrics area where deemed appropriate;

4. to maintain close contact with similar organizations in other Bar Associations and with other appropriate groups such as the Computer Law Committee of the Canadian Law Information Council.[4]

Indeed, one of the recent projects of that committee was the preparation of a commentary on a report on electronic legal retrieval systems prepared by Professor Philip Slayton for the federal Department of Communications. In that report, Professor Slayton reached the following conclusions:

1. Retrieval systems have been developed with little regard for how lawyers actually think, and to the extent they reflect those processes, they may do so accidentally.

2. Retrieval systems may impose certain alien logical structures on the verbal symbols of law, and thereby affect legal thought and ultimately substantive law.

3. Retrieval systems cannot operate by way of analogy, a key feature of legal thought.

4. Retrieval systems cannot be used satisfactorily to retrieve legal concepts.

5. Retrieval systems (unlike an ordinary library situation) do not allow for random conceptual searching, a creative process meeting a crucial need of both the practising lawyer and the judge.

6. Retrieval systems may accentuate existing social inequalities by providing superior legal information for large law firms and government agencies, at the expense of small firms and solo practitioners who normally represent weak clients.

7. Retrieval systems may seriously affect the stability of the doctrine of legal precedent by keeping the information out of the system and by encouraging through information overload rejection of information as the basis for legal thought.

---

[2]The Toronto Star, 5th June 1975.

[3]The Law Society of Upper Canada established a computer-assisted legal research service in March of 1983, utilizing the "Quic/Law" computer for Canadian cases and statutes and the "Westlaw" system for U.S. materials.

[4]Special Committee on Jurimetrics, Canadian Bar Association, Report to 1974 Mid-winter Meeting, p. 1.

8. Retrieval systems may destroy the ability of judges to make law by imposing a myriad of specific rules and by filling legal *lacunae*.[5]

The application of computer technology to legal research was originally embarked upon in 1968 by the Faculty of Law and the Computing Centre of the University of Montreal in a project known as DATUM. Similarly, in 1969, a joint project was undertaken by Queen's University and the federal Department of Justice known as Quic/Law. Through these pioneering efforts, the notion of computerized legal retrieval systems has advanced from mere concept to a substantial and operational reality. Moreoever, since that time, other ambitious and sophisticated projects have followed. Some law schools contain courses in their curricula relating to computers and the law and, no doubt, it can be predicted that most law libraries will shortly contain terminals as part of a nationwide computerized system.

However, it has been suggested by Professor Slayton and others that this will have the effect of favouring clients of large and established law firms, in that only those law firms will be able to afford the installation of a terminal in their offices.

In the United States there are, at present, two computer systems to assist lawyers in the conduct of legal research. These are the Lexis System of Mead Data Central and the Westlaw System of West Publishing Company.[6]

The underlying object, of course, in developing computerized legal retrieval systems, relates to the recent proliferation of statutory and regulatory enactments at all levels of government, as well as the massive number of cases decided and recorded in the case reports.[7] The obstacles,

---

[5]*Ibid.*, Appendix 1. See also Appendix 2 for a selected bibliography on "Computer and the Law".

[6]For further information see (1976), 62 Amer. Bar Assn. J. 320, including a bibliography of additional materials on this topic.

[7]An alternative device directed at assisting lawyers in conducting legal research (and particularly directed at lawyers practising alone or in small groups) is the concept of a research service. Services of this nature began recently in the United States, and have not, as yet, to a major extent, reached Canada.

A description of this service is set out as follows in Time Magazine, 16th September 1974:

"One way for the small firm to have a fighting chance, at reasonable rates, is to turn to a research company manned by lawyers. There is now a handful of these in the U.S. doing legal spade work. The largest and most aggressive is The Research Group Inc., with offices in Cambridge, Mass., Ann Arbor, Mich., and Charlottesville, Ve. — all cities with major university law libraries. The Group gears its services to smaller firms, which constitute an important market; about three-quarters of the private attorneys in the U.S. work in offices that have three lawyers or fewer.

"The company will prepare basic analyses of statutes and precedents in question, draw up briefs, develop strategy or seek grounds for appeal. It claims to be competent in most legal specialties, from admiralty law to zoning. Relying solely on old-fashioned search and analysis, not computers, The Group, charges its customers $17.50 an hour

of course, relate to the high cost, as well as the restricted availability, at present, of such systems; however, it is also predictable that, as these systems become widespread, the cost will fall.

In addition, it is likely that, for purposes of transcribing proceedings of courts and administrative tribunals, electronic technology and modern science have much to contribute to the efficient operation of the Canadian legal system.[8] One recent example of this contribution may be found in the province of Ontario, where the registration of personal property security is conducted on a province-wide computerized basis: see the Personal Property Security Act, R.S.O. 1980, c. 375 [am. 1981, c. 2 and c. 58].

THE LEGAL PROFESSION:
PUBLIC IMAGE AND PUBLIC ACCOUNTABILITY

It is axiomatic and often said that the law belongs to all members of society, not only to lawyers and judges.[9] However, this notion has attracted little more than lip service until recently. Both the legal profession and members of the public at large have come to accept that we all share a proprietary interest in the law and in the legal process. As a result, courses in law for laypersons are now being taught in many institutions, and books and pamphlets designed for laypersons on particular areas of the law are being widely disseminated in order to educate members of the general public in respect of their rights and duties under the law. In fact, the teaching of law has now extended into the high schools.[10] In addition, through university departments of extension or continuing education, courses in specialized areas of the law are being offered for members of the business community.

— a bargain compared with the average $40.00 that individual lawyers routinely charge for their own time. The difference can mean substantial savings for the client.

"The staff that churns out this cut-rate research consists of 50 lawyers, most of them under 30, and some 150 third-year law students who work part-time."

[8]Indeed, U.S. Supreme Court justices now have and use computer keyboards in their respective offices to assist in the preparation of their opinions. See U.S. News & World Report, 30th October 1978. In the U.S., the American Bar Association Consortium for Professional Education and the A.B.A. Section of Science and Technology have recently produced a videotape on "Computer-Assisted Legal Research". For a further discussion of new technology and the canadian legal system, see the Financial Post, 26th September 1979 and 1st August 1981.

[9]For a greater public awareness, the Canadian Bar Association now annually conducts "Law Day", during which, in each province, the C.B.A. sets up panels and other information - disseminating formats for the general public. This includes, for example, open house at the court house in some provinces.

[10]In the United States, there is a move to ensure that high school courses on law are offered throughout the nation: The New York Times, 13th October 1974.

Some other instances of educational programs designed for the general public are as follows. First, an organization known as the "Toronto Community Law School" (and there are other similar organizations in major cities throughout Canada), has recently offered courses in the law of real estate transactions, income tax law, mental health law, small claims court procedure, consumer protection law, marriage and divorce law, criminal law, municipal law, and wills.

Similarly, law students at the University of Toronto established a few years ago what is referred to as "Lawline". Essentially, this service provides free legal advice in the areas of consumer law and landlord and tenant law, and it offers assistance to those persons engaged in disputes with government agencies. This project is especially directed at those Toronto residents who cannot speak the English language. Along similar lines, in 1978, Calgary Legal Guidance and the Public Relations Section of the Alberta Branch of the Canadian Bar Association established a bi-weekly half-hour phone-in television program called "Law Line". And similarly, the Law Society of Upper Canada, together with the Ontario Branch of the Canadian Bar Association, recently established a similar service called "Dial-a-Law": see Communique, 25th February 1983.

These educational and assistance programs are to a large extent designed to assist those persons who cannot afford to retain the services of lawyers and who are not eligible to receive legal aid. In addition, many persons are simply eager to learn about various areas of the law. One can easily find in many bookstores "do-it-yourself" or "self-help" books on various areas of the law. There are, of course, some obvious dangers in assuming that one is able to attack a legal problem without the professional advice of a trained lawyer.[11] However, the popularity of these volumes is well established and suggests, at the very least, that there is a need for a wider dissemination of legal advice among the general public.

In summary, members of the public have demanded a greater understanding of the law.[12] People have come to realize that a knowledge of the law is consistent with responsible citizenship, and that an awareness of the law is vital in confronting the complex issues arising daily in business and in personal life.

---

[11]See an interesting article entitled "When to Take the Law into Your Own Hands", Money Magazine, March 1975, p. 59.

[12]For a complete review of this subject see Friedland, Access to the Law (Toronto: Carswell/Methuen, 1975). One recent phenomenon relates to the establishment of interprovincial branch law offices. This, of course, is not a significant concern to the general public — it is a phenomenon having to do with the major, corporate-oriented law firms. In fact, it led to one of the first cases litigated under the mobility rights section of the new Charter of Rights. For further information concerning the concept of interprovincial law firms, see Clarry, "Inter-Provincial Law Firms" (1982), 16 L.S.U.C. Gazette 266.

It is likely that historians will look at the mid-1960's as marking the onset of what might be described as the "consumer era". One can, for example, point to Ralph Nader's work in the United States, the development of consumer protection associations throughout the North American continent and the enactment of consumer protection legislation at all levels of government. Consumerism has, in addition, spread to the professions. As a result, members of society regard themselves as consumers of professional services and in turn, the professions must now, of necessity, regard themselves as accountable to the consumers that they serve. Even though the profession of law is a self-governing profession, it is necessary that an element of accountability be included within the boundaries of self-government. This has led to lay representation on the governing bodies of some provincial law societies. For example, in Ontario there is provision for the appointment of four lay members to the governing body or "benchers" of the Law Society of Upper Canada. These four benchers serve, not only on the governing body of that law society, but also on many of the committees of the benchers. Some provincial law societies do not have lay benchers, but it is predictable that as consumerism develops further, the notion of lay representation in the decision-making process of provincial law societies will become widespread across Canada.

The public image of the legal profession is, unfortunately, not always a positive one. There are many possible reasons for this; however, one can point to the feeling shared by at least some consumers of legal services that lawyers are excessively compensated for the work that they do. It flows from this that many persons are not able to afford the services of lawyers. One development, however, which is directed at alleviating this concern is the growth of legal aid.

Legal aid is operated under differing authorities, varying from province to province. In some provinces, legal aid is run by the provincial government while in others it is run either by the provincial law society or by the provincial law society in association with the provincial government. In yet other provinces, it is operated by special provincial societies mandated by statute for that purpose.

The funding of legal aid also varies from province to province; it is funded in some provinces by direct government grants for that purpose and, in others, by provincial law foundations. Provincial law foundations receive their moneys from the interest earned on lawyers' trust accounts.

In general, legal aid is available only to those persons who are unable to afford to retain their own lawyers. The recipients of legal aid must first establish, to the satisfaction of the appropriate officials, that they are in need of financial assistance. Secondly, the particular matter for which they are seeking legal advice and assistance must be a matter covered by the particular legal aid plan. If these two preconditions are satisfied, the recipient will be granted a legal aid certificate and will then be able to pick the lawyer of his choice for the required advice. In some cases, legal aid may offer only partial assistance, depending upon the financial ability of the recipient to bear at least part of the costs of legal services rendered.

As stated above, only certain items are covered by a given legal aid plan. As a result, there are those who cannot afford a lawyer, yet cannot obtain legal aid for reason that the matter for which they are seeking assistance is not covered by the particular legal aid plan. A recent development directed at remedying this situation is the creation, at various law schools across Canada, of legal aid societies. These organizations provide student legal services. In some law schools, student legal services are integrated into the curriculum as part of a clinical program. The first, and the largest of such organizations, is the Parkdale Community Legal Services, operated under the auspices of Osgoode Hall Law School of York University in Toronto. Consider the following remarks made by the director of Parkdale Community Legal Services:

> On March 14, 1975, the report of the Government-appointed Task Force on Legal Aid (the Osler Report) was published. It unanimously recommended a substantial expansion in the scope of legal aid and the adoption of new techniques of delivering legal aid services aimed at making these services truly accessible to all, including immigrants.

> The report points out that the total annual expenditure on legal aid by the province amounts to about half of the annual operating budget of one of the large community colleges — an expenditure, the report suggests, that is no longer an adequate reflection of the priority which the province ought to give to ensuring access of less fortunate members of our society to courts and tribunals . . .

> And the limitations in the success of the Ontario Legal Aid Plan in meeting the needs of the community for financially assisted legal services is not the fault of the Legal Aid Plan administrators or the Law Society, as public criticism tends to suggest.

> The administrators of the Ontario Legal Aid Plan have been remarkably successful in making free or financially assisted legal services available, having regard to limitations imposed by the legislation by which they are controlled. That legislation was modern when it was first proposed by the Law Society in 1965-66 but its inadequacies in the light of the growth in the need for assisted legal assistance since that time were apparent several years ago.

> This reluctance to pay the price for the handmaidens and machinery of law enforcement is particularly difficult to understand when one considers the extent to which this society has embraced law itself as the ultimate magic.

> We live in a society which is inundated with legislation-created law. To an extent never before envisaged in a democratic society, there is no social or economic activity, or indeed any aspect of our life, that is not shaped and colored and in the end defined by legislation.

> There is, apparently, no social problem that cannot be solved by some carefully drafted legislation.

> The man who cannot afford legal assistance, whose legal rights in years gone by might fairly be said to have consisted mainly of defences — against the police, Crown, landlord — is now the beneficiary of innumerable legislated benefits and rights.

He has pension benefits, medical benefits, hospital benefits, welfare benefits, workmen's compensation benefits, employment benefits and unemployment benefits. He has rights against his landlord and his used-car dealer. He has the right not to be discriminated against (the Human Rights Code, Employment Standards Act, Labor Relations Act, etc.), nor to be taken advantage of (credit and consumer protection legislation) and he has the right to insist that all of the tribunals and agencies administering those new benefits treat him fairly and with justice . . .

And yet it is self-evident that rights and benefits that cannot be enforced are worse than useless. Robert F. Kennedy, speaking at the University of Chicago Law School in 1964 on the subject of poverty law, made the point that "unasserted, unknown, unavailable rights are no rights at all."

It is apparent that known but unenforceable rights are worse than no rights at all. They are a trap and a delusion and a source of socially destructive bitterness and frustration.[13]

One outgrowth arising from the development of legal aid is the concept of duty counsel. Duty counsel, essentially, is a lawyer retained by legal aid for the purpose of representing persons appearing in court who are not otherwise represented by a lawyer. In the province of Ontario, duty counsel now provides representation in respect of involuntary admissions to mental facilities. Moreover, a former director of Ontario's legal aid plan has been appointed to head an experimental team of full-time duty counsel to serve in the provincial courts at City Hall in Toronto. This appointment arises out of the deliberations of a committee of the Law Society of Upper Canada, which noted that the present system of duty counsel involved a lack of continuity and supervision among the lawyers acting as duty counsel, and suggested that many lawyers acting as duty counsel were inexperienced and rather uninterested in the area of criminal law. As a result, the concept of a permanent staff acting as duty counsel was initiated, on an experimental basis, on 1st April 1977.[14] The result of this experiment, hopefully, will be that the services of duty counsel will eventually be administered by lawyers who, after a time, will become professionally experienced in this area. Accordingly, those persons not represented by their own lawyers will ultimately receive better service.[15]

An issue somewhat related to legal aid is that of prepaid legal insurance. This has not been promoted in Canada to any considerable extent; however, there is a movement in that direction. For example, the Quebec Branch of the Canadian Bar Association proposed, a few years ago, a prepaid legal insurance scheme for middle income earners; it was suggested at that time that an annual premium in the vicinity of $100 to

---

[13]These remarks were made by Professor S. R. Ellis, in an article contained in the Toronto Globe and Mail, 28th June 1975.

[14]See the Toronto Globe and Mail, 19th January 1977.

[15]A related phenomenon, in the United States, is the establishment of the so-called "public-interest" law firms. These firms are primarily concerned with public issues. For example, in New York, there is a women's rights law clinic. For further details on the development of those public-interest law firms, see the New York Times, 27th April 1980.

$150 would be appropriate. The proponents of the proposed plan pointed to similar programs now in operation in some of the American states.[16]

At the centre of issues such as legal aid and prepaid insurance is the fact that lawyers generally command a high fee for their services. This is not to say, of course, that the fee, in most circumstances, is unjustified. In fact, a lawyer usually performs a sophisticated service, having the ability to do so only after years of rigorous training and experience. Nonetheless, the high price of lawyering and the need for legal aid and prepaid insurance plans all suggest that there is a problem relating to the unavailability of legal services for many persons in society.[17] Even middle income earners are not hesitating to challenge the high price of legal services. For example, many clients are exercising their rights to tax their lawyers' bills before a taxing master or other appropriate official.[18]

There can be no doubt that the public perception of the legal profession includes the notion that lawyers are expensive. In a study conducted by the Contemporary Research Centre of Toronto, prepared for the Ontario Task Force on Legal Aid, it was discovered that three-quarters of the persons living in Ontario, over the age of sixteen, think that lawyers are too expensive.[19] Accordingly, if lawyers are to remedy this somewhat negative aspect of their professional image, an expansion of legal aid, the development of prepaid legal insurance schemes, and other measures will be necessary.

One other measure, often suggested, is the notion that fees would be lowered if lawyers were allowed to advertise their services. There exists

---

[16]As a result of a recent congressional amendment to the Taft-Hartley Act, both labour and management can now contribute to legal insurance funds. The result is, according to a former chief counsel of the House Special Subcommittee on Labor, "prepaid legal services will now be in the mainstream of collective bargaining", so that, according to legal experts, in the next few years 70 per cent of all Americans and 50 per cent of all lawyers will be involved in group insurance plans: see Time Magazine, 23rd September 1974. Again, for a further discussion of this issue, see Chapter 9, *supra*.

[17]One way of addressing the problem of availability appears to lie, in part, in placing law offices in commonly travelled public places. For example, in British Columbia, several operations, each designated as "The Law Office" are located at various Sears stores. Similarly, in Edmonton, there is a law office located at the Hudson's Bay store.

[18]In addition, as a result of the enactment of comprehensive amendments to the Combines Investigation Act in 1975, there is now new regulation of fee setting practices by local bar associations. Similarly, in the United States, in a recent decision of the Supreme Court of the United States, it was held that bar associations which set mandatory billing fees are subject to the provisions of the Sherman Anti-trust Act. For a description of the background of that decision, see Newsweek Magazine, 30th June 1975.

[19]Recently, the issue arose in several provinces as to whether law firms should be permitted to accept credit cards in payment of their professional fees. The question, essentially, relates to whether such a practice would be in the nature of unprofessional conduct. In this connection, there was no uniformity of opinion among the various provincial law societies.

presently, across Canada, some ethical prohibitions against advertising by lawyers. The suggestion is, quite simply, that if lawyers were allowed to advertise freely, this would have the effect of lowering their fees through greater competition at the market place. Consider, for example, the following comments made by New York Times columnist William Safire:

> The services for which doctors and lawyers charge fees is a "market"; when medical or bar associations deny other qualified practitioners of the services entry to that market by means of advertising, that is a monopoly practice.
>
> Because the barriers set up by professional associations against advertising so obviously restrain trade, Joseph Sims, of the anti-trust division of the U.S. department of justice, recently suggested to the New York State Bar Association, that it consider modifying its canon of ethics: "Perhaps the rule should be worded so as to prohibit only that type of solicitation which is false, misleading, undignified or champertous."
> . . .The professions will one day be considering the how, and not the if, of advertising. Never, say never; such a flat statement is out of place in the field of anti-trust.[20]

Very recently, Michigan became the first state in the United States to permit lawyers to advertise their fees and other information concerning themselves. As a result of changes to Michigan's Code of Professional Responsibility, approved by the Michigan Supreme Court, lawyers will be permitted to list fees and other information in the yellow pages of the local telephone directory. Also, as a result of a recent suit launched by the United States Justice Department against the American Bar Association, alleging that the American Bar Association's ban on advertising constituted a restraint of competition, many states are considering the alteration of existing rules banning advertising by lawyers. As a result of the above suit, the American Bar Association amended its Code of Ethics in order to allow for fee advertising in the yellow pages.[21] If one examines a typical wide-circulation U.S. newspaper, one sees in it many advertisements for lawyers. As a result of the *Jabour* case, one is starting to see the same phenomenon in Canada, although Canadian ads are still less flamboyant than those in U.S. newspapers. The *Jabour* case and advertising by lawyers generally is discussed in Chapter 9.

A LIFETIME OF EDUCATION

The process of legal education is discussed at some length in Chapter 9 but for our present purposes a brief review of some current developments is appropriate. One recent change in respect of the training of lawyers is that native and mature persons, owing to affirmative action

---

[20]Edmonton Journal, 9th September 1974.

[21]See the Toronto Globe and Mail, 18th January 1977. See also V. Alboini, "A Lawyer's Limited Practice in Ontario — The Time for more Appropriate Recognition" (1976), 10 Law Society Gazette 154, and the reports appearing in the January and February 1977 editions of the National, published by the Canadian Bar Association. In addition see "Let Lawyers Advertise?", U.S. News & World Report, 28th February 1977.

programs in some law schools, now have a greater opportunity than ever before to enter the legal profession, and presumably with respect to native persons, to serve their own, previously unserviced, communities. Also, it is encouraging to note the substantially greater number of women now entering the legal profession, and it is predictable that this trend will increase in the years to come.

Another current phenomenon in legal education is the competitive number of persons desiring to enter the legal profession. This is reflected not only in the number of applications to all of the law schools across Canada, but also in the job market, both in obtaining articles of clerkship following graduation from the law schools and in obtaining employment after being called to the bar. One result of the growing number of new lawyers is the number of law school graduates now engaging in various different capacities of legal work and indeed entering into other fields. A lawyer can act as an advisor to the government, conduct legal research on behalf of the government, act as counsel to the government in litigation, or assist in the drafting of legislation. He may act as counsel for the corporation or work in a corporation's legal department or use his law degree as an adjunct to his business activities for a company. He may decide to enter the teaching profession; or he may combine a law career with another profession. For example, there are many persons in Canada who hold both law and medical degrees, and these persons often act as coroners or engage in advisory work for the government or for private industry in connection with medico-legal matters.

Also as a result of the increasing number of persons entering the legal profession, many new lawyers are moving to smaller urban as well as rural communities to service previously underserviced areas. Some new lawyers are devoting a substantial portion of their practice to work under the various provincial legal aid plans. Others are entering into alternative modes of practice, such as "storefront" operations, and there is, for example, an organization known as the Law Union, which consists of several lawyers possessing a common ideology. Those lawyers are particularly interested in certain areas of the law, such as landlord and tenant and immigration law.

The training of lawyers itself is presently the subject of much change. Under existing curricula, many law schools offer such educational opportunities as clinical legal services, a wide range of optional courses, and opportunities for specialization in given areas of the law. In addition, there have been other proposals for reform. For example, in Ontario, as a result of the report of the MacKinnon Committee,[22] there was consider-

---

[22]The Special Committee on Legal Education of the Law Society of Upper Canada. See also the Report of the Special Committee on Legal Education conducted by the Honourable Mr. Justice Roy J. Matas at the request of the Law Society of Manitoba and the Faculty of Law, University of Manitoba, 1979.

able debate as to whether the requirement that law school graduates serve one year under articles of clerkship should be removed. However, the Committee's recommendation to dispense with the articling requirement was dropped. In addition, also in Ontario, a review is being conducted by the Law Society of Upper Canada in connection with a substantial restructuring of the present bar admission course in that province. Other provinces are conducting similar reviews.

In addition, two provincial law societies, in Ontario and Alberta, have issued reports recommending the adoption of the notion of accredited specialization in certain areas of the law. Moreover in Ontario

> a plan allowing lawyers to advertise their competence in a specific field of law has been endorsed by the governing body of the Law Society of Upper Canada.
>
> It would be the first time such advertising has been allowed in Canada. To qualify, lawyers would be required to show that they have practised in a particular field of law for a set period of time — perhaps three to five years.
>
> To maintain their accreditation, lawyers would be required to take a refresher course sponsored by the law society once every two years following accreditation.[23]

Finally, irrespective of the mode of practice or the nature of work in which a lawyer is engaged, all lawyers must undertake continuing legal education throughout their professional lives. This is facilitated by attendance at seminars and conferences, the regular utilization of up-to-date publications, audio-visual aids, etc. Although continuing legal education is voluntary at present, it is predictable that it will, in future, become a mandatory requirement for continuing certification.

LAW REFORM

One of the most provocative and perplexing questions relates to the adaptability of the law in response to changing social conditions.[24] One of the ways that the law has responded to changing social conditions is the development of the concept of permanent law reform commissions at all levels of government. Virtually every province in Canada has a law reform commission, although not all provinces call them by that name. In addition, the Law Reform Commission of Canada conducts work in respect of those matters which are, constitutionally, within federal jurisdiction. These law reform bodies, in the usual case, are mandated by statute[25] to conduct research, with a view to subsequent reform of the law, in those areas falling within their respective constitutional jurisdictions. After proposals for legislative reform are formulated, they are forwarded, in the first instance, to the Attorney General of the province or, in the case of the Law Reform Commission of Canada, to the Minister of

---

[23]The Toronto Globe and Mail, 22nd February 1977.

[24]See Freidmann, *Law in a Changing Society*, 1964.

[25]In the case of the province of Alberta, however, the Institute of Law Research and Reform was established under an agreement between the University of Alberta, the Department of the Attorney General and the Law Society of Alberta.

Justice. Often, the proposals for reform are then referred to the whole of the cabinet for consideration, and ultimately, if approved, to the legislative body for enactment.

The usual manner in which a law reform commission operates is as follows. This description is, of course, an oversimplification of the process of law reform, and it obviously differs significantly from province to province. Upon the request of government (or, in respect of some law reform commissions, upon the request of members of the legal profession, members of the legislature, other interested parties or at their own instance), research is conducted in a particular area of the law. A project is usually led by a full-time member of the law reform body, although outside consultants and advisors are significantly utilized. The initial research usually gives rise to a research paper which is then refined and altered in form. This produces a working paper or a memorandum for discussion which essentially, is in the nature of a white paper for consideration and review by members of the public and the legal profession. A final report is then prepared, reflecting the various submissions received in response to the working paper or memorandum for discussion.

When a given matter is finally referred to the cabinet, it is sometimes accompanied by draft legislation. The cabinet can act upon it, modify it or reject it.[26]

Generally speaking, at the provincial level, the reports of the various law reform commissions have led to considerable legislation. Unfortunately, however, at the federal level, there has been, to date, little legislative action taken in respect of the various recommendations made by the

---

[26]The Director of the Alberta Institute of Law Research and Reform describes the process of law reform in Alberta in this way:

> The process starts with research by the Institute staff or by consultants. It involves consultation with lawyers and other professionals, experts in various disciplines, and groups affected by a particular law.

> The Institute then considers the issues involved and issues a report, usually with draft legislation attached.

> It sends its reports to the Attorney General and to any other minister concerned with the subject matter. It also makes its reports public and sends them to those who express interest in them.

> It is, of course, for the government and the Legislature to decide whether or not to act upon the Institute's recommendations, but they have so far been receptive to them.

> The Institute chooses its own reform projects, though with due regard to the suggestions of the government and the Legislature. Its choices are governed by its capabilities, by the apparent need for reform, and by the desirability of maintaining a balance between reforms which primarily involve technical law and reforms which more clearly involve social policy.

See W. H. Hurlburt, "Institute of Law Research and Reform — A Report", [1978] Without Prejudice 10.

Law Reform Commission of Canada. The reason for this, probably, is that the federal proposals for reform are of a more controversial nature, whereas provincial proposals are usually of little controversy because they are in the nature of a modification of what might be referred to as "lawyer's law", i.e., those issues of law which are highly technical in nature.

There are various ancillary benefits arising out of the work conducted by law reform commissions, aside from their primary achievements in conducting a reform of the law. For example, the reports of the various law reform commissions represent an important contribution to the literature in the areas being researched. Often, these reports contain a comprehensive, well-researched and well-prepared review of the law in a particular area. This review is often of invaluable assistance to both teachers and students of the law, as well as to practising members of the legal profession.[27] Secondly, various projects and experiments are conducted which, in themselves, are valuable. For example, in connection with a criminal law project conducted for the Law Reform Commission of Canada, the Borough of East York in the Municipality of Metropolitan Toronto altered the usual procedures followed in the course of criminal justice investigation. The normal policing practices were pre-empted in order to permit the employment of an alternative way of enforcement and remediation. These experimental projects conducted by law reform commissions often lead to the formulation of new concepts. For example, the concept of "diversion", in the area of criminal law, arose in part out of the above research and experimental work conducted by the Law Reform Commission of Canada. Accordingly, aside from the primary function of the reform of the law, there are many additional benefits that arise out of the process of law reform.[28]

The concept of a law reform commission is not unique to Canada. In fact, it is fairly widespread now throughout the whole of the common law world.

---

[27]Two examples of this are as follows. First, a national publication of the Canadian Bar Association often contains excerpts from reports of the Law Reform Commission of Canada. It is hoped that this will arouse interest among the members of the profession and that, consequentially, there will be greater reaction, in the form of submissions, in response to the particular report set out. However, as an ancillary benefit, no doubt many lawyers use these excerpts for purposes of an up-to-date review of law in a particular area. Secondly, Dean Martin Freidland of the University of Toronto recently conducted research for the Law Reform Commission of Canada, the result of which was later published in the form of a treatise entitled Access to the Law. That treatise represents a major contribution to the literature for it contains the results of his research, underscores the importance of providing access to the law for members of the public at large, and contains recommendations which, if adopted, might ultimately serve that end.

[28]For a more detailed review of the process of law reform see Bowker, "Organized Law Reform in Alberta" (1969), 19 U. of T.L.J. 376; Thomas, "The Manitoba Law Reform Commission: A Critical Evaluation", [1975] 2 Dalhousie L.J. 417; and Lyon, "Law Reform Needs Reform" (1974), 12 Osgoode Hall L.J. 21. See also "Barristers and Solicitors: Prospects for the Lawyer as a Reformer" (1976), 15 U.W.O.L. Rev. 59.

Consider the following remarks delivered by Mr. Justice Patrick Hartt, a former chairman of the Law Reform Commission of Canada, to the Convocation of the Law Society of Upper Canada, held on 20th March 1975:

We decided to seek reform of the law through public persuasion rather than resort immediately to Parliamentary amendment. This decision was made with the confidence that the concept of law could be redefined in a non-positive, value-laden way, and the citizens of Canada could be persuaded to actually participate in its reformulation.

This decision of the Commission has been criticized as being idealistic and unrealistic. It might well be expecting a lot, but in a pluralistic, truly democratic society, nothing less will suffice. In these turbulent times, the rule of law may be a very fragile thing, but we must never let ourselves forget that the alternatives to it are a series of profoundly unpleasant options. And if increased public involvement is the only way that a rule of law can be maintained, and in my opinion it is, then surely we would be very foolish indeed not to try. Otherwise, we shall have no choice but to live, or possibly die, with the consequences. What we are really talking about is a society in which the citizens are not simply joined collectively together by the threat of coercive state, but rather one in which they are united from within themselves, by agreement on core values and a shared desire to secure their common goals. This should be carried out within a supportive community that would develop an environment, leaving everyone as free as possible to reach their maximum potential as human and spiritual beings, free for each to find his own centre.

As temporary members of a non-elected commission, it is certainly not our task to impose our views and values on the public. In the first instance, it is our responsibility to provide accurate, understandable and clearly articulate realistic alternatives. By so doing, the public is reminded and made aware of the values which they actually hold, or "ought to hold" if they are to be consistent to a particular view of society. In addition, the implications of the holding of certain values become apparent.

But, in my personal opinion, the Commission ought to go further and actually assert what, in their opinion, are the values which should constitute the law's substance. Being only an advisory body, their views can, of course, be accepted or rejected. It then remains for the law to be brought into better alignment with the accepted values. In short, there is a role to be played in assisting the public to put morality back firmly into the centre of the law . . .

We must discover and develop new unifying principles capable of giving a general orientation to a fragmented society, and the law and its processes must be directed primarily to compatible goals of synthesis and reconciliation. No society or community can exist unless a significant number of people can agree upon, or at least tacitly accept, a basic value structure.

Above all, we cannot look to legislative enactment alone to save us. Only laws rooted in popular sentiment can be enforced. Laws violating this sentiment merely arouse resentment. If our sentiments are superior, we will have superior laws. In the end, good men and women will support only those undertakings which they feel instinctively to be just. If our instincts are civilized, we will have civilized laws. Law reform cannot be better or worse than the society which generates it. In the end, I am satisfied we get what we really deserve.[28a]

In addition, consider the following remarks on law reform, in general:

Reforming laws means more than changing them; it means improving them. The two don't always go together. Cromwell's Parliament once passed an act outlawing Christmas — a change admittedly, but was it an improvement. Was the new law a true reflection of the social need?

[28a] "Law Reform Through Consciousness-Raising" (1975), 9 Law Soc. Gazette 132.

. . . Alteration of law for alteration's sake was not enough: new laws must truly reflect society's needs and constitute some genuine progress. But how can we be sure of making real progress . . .

Before knowing where to go we must be quite clear where we stand; before knowing what alterations to make to our law, we need to understand all aspects of the legal situation — not only what the law prescribes but also what its purpose is, how it operates, which is the best way of altering it, and, last but not least, how far alteration will make any difference. This raises questions about the very nature of law reform itself, on which we have begun a fundamental jurisprudential investigation.

The usual coming of departure for law reformers has been the letter of the law. Sometime, indeed the actual working of the law can be the major problem. Laws suffering from what Bentham termed "overbulkiness", from ambiguity or from sheer obscurity impose too great a strain on courts and lawyers, but worse still, fail to provide satisfactory rules and guidelines for society.

Often, however, the letter of the law isn't the main problem. The rules, themselves, not just their wording, may need change. Official practice — the operation of the rules — may need to alter. The values which those rules enshrine may be untenable or no longer be the values of the society those rules serve. Or again, the rules themselves may be misunderstood.[29]

There are those, however, who are critical of the various reports issued by the Law Reform Commission of Canada, and indeed one critic, a former president of the Canadian Association of Police Chiefs, made these remarks:

[The Law Reform Commission of Canada has outlived its usefulness and should be dissolved immediately . . . the Commission's latest recommendation to abolish sentences of life imprisonment for those convicted of rape or manslaughter is intolerable.] The working paper reflects the thinking of an academic, social reformist without any real appreciation of the impact of such implementation . . . The law reform commission might do well to consider that there are also recidivists, too much crime and too many victims.[30]

Just as our courts and legislatures are institutions within the Canadian legal system, permanent law reform commissions have also become institutions within that system. The process of institutionalized law reform represents a vital opportunity for the law to be adaptable to changing social conditions:

Law reform is like a never-ending relay race. As soon as one objectionable law is dealt with another takes its place. Just as the price of freedom is eternal vigilance, so the price of justice is eternal effort. The law reformer's race is never over. One lap complete, the next begins.[31]

One dramatic change in our law, in recent years, might be described as a move towards a liberalization in the law. Perhaps "liberalization" is the improper term; this development might be considered rather as a

---

[29]Law Reform Commission of Canada, Third Annual Report, 1974.
[30]The Globe and Mail, 25th June 1975.
[31]Law Reform Commission of Canada, Fifth Annual Report, 1976.

fundamental change in the relationship between the individual and the law.

On one hand, it can be argued that virtually every area of human affairs and human concern is controlled and regulated by law. On the other hand, there is current evidence to suggest that the law is abandoning certain areas in which it previously exercised control. For example, it is no longer an offence in Canada to attempt to commit suicide. As well, there are other, recent amendments to the Criminal Code which implement the government's view as of 1968 "that the government has no place in the bedrooms of the nation".

The counter argument to this suggestion of "liberalization" is in the area of economic regulation, where it appears that the law has entered some fields which were previously unoccupied. One can easily point to several examples, such as the program of selective mandatory wage and price controls in the mid-1970's, the enactment of foreign investment review legislation, the recent and prospective comprehensive amendments to our anti-combines legislation, major revisions in our income tax law, and many others. In other words, one could argue that in the matter of economic regulation, the law has developed in such a way as to exercise an unprecedented domain over individual and corporate affairs, while in the area of personal morality, such as the matters raised above, as well as in connection with changes proposed by some in the areas of obscenity, abortion, possession and trafficking of "soft" drugs, etc., the law has abandoned this field to the dictates of individual morality.

The law, generally speaking, has drifted toward liberalization in a second sense. There are legislative developments which suggest that the law has become, essentially, more humanitarian. For example, virtually every province has anti-discrimination legislation and, since 1977, there has been federal legislation in the same field.[32] In addition, the Canadian Bill of Rights was enacted in 1960. The impact of the Canadian Bill of Rights has not proven to be particularly significant. However, what remains to be seen is the effect of the new Canadian Charter of Rights and Freedoms. If any instrument suggests a drift toward "liberalization" in the "humanitarian" sense, it would have to be the new Charter. Only future historians and lawyers will be able to judge, ultimately, what effect our entrenched constitutional Charter will have. In addition, as indicated in the preceding chapter, there is now federal (and some provincial) legislation providing for freedom of information and for privacy.[33] Virtually every province has a legislative ombudsman and

---

[32]See the Canadian Human Rights Act, 1976-77 (Can.), c. 33.

[33]See Access to Information and Privacy Act, 1980-81-82-83 (Can.), c. 111. On the other hand, anti-discrimination legislation might be regarded as constituting the opposite of a liberalizing effect. In this sense, anti-discrimination laws restrict the individual's freedom of choice (i.e., his freedom to discriminate), the exercise of which was previously permissible under the law.

there are proposals for a federal ombudsman. One might also conclude that the abolition of capital punishment was consistent with this trend.

CONCLUSION

Broadly defined, the role of law is to ensure that the affairs of all persons in society are conducted in an orderly manner and in accordance with particular social objectives.[34] The role of lawyers, again broadly defined, is to ensure the effective, orderly regulation of the affairs of all persons in society and, at the same time, to ensure that such regulation is conducted in a manner consistent with the preservation of individual rights. It is always a balancing question, that is, one must always balance the protection of individual liberties against the preservation of the integrity of society as a whole, an integrity that flows from orderly regulation.

One interesting approach, in answer to the question as to the effectiveness of the law in achieving its social objectives, is contained in a recent treatise by Richard A. Posner, entitled *Economic Analysis of Law*,[35] in which the author conducts an analysis of the role of law in terms of economic principles, seeking to answer the fundamental question whether the law leads to economically correct solutions. He concludes, for example, in respect of the law of contracts, that the basic function of the law of contracts is to minimize breakdowns in the process of exchange. In addition, he observes that the economic function promoted in connection with negligence liability is not compensation for the victim, but rather deterrence of non-cost-justified accidents. Finally, in respect of the relationship between poverty and the criminal law, he states:

> Poverty imposes costs on the nonpoor that warrant, on strictly economic grounds and without regard to ethical or political considerations, incurring some costs to reduce it. For example, poverty in the midst of a generally wealthy society is likely to increase the incidence of crime. One important cost of a criminal career, the forgone income of a legitimate alternative occupation, will be low for someone who has little earning capacity in legitimate occupations, while the proximity of wealth increases the expected return from crime, or stated another way, the cost of honesty.[36]

Another view advanced, on occasion, is that the lawyer has a role which might be described as that of a "social engineer". To some extent, the concept of social engineering is implicit in the lawyer's participation in the process of law reform, as well as the large participa-

---

[34]An example of the articulation of a particular social objective may be found in the area of anti-competition law. Specifically, the 1969 Interim Report of the Economic Council of Canada promoted the specific social objective of achieving, by way of legislative reform, economic efficiency through the instrumentality of greater competition at the market place.

[35]2nd ed. (Boston: Little Brown & Co., 1977).

[36]*Ibid.*, p. 350.

tion of lawyers, generally, in the legislative process. Certainly, it is not illegitimate for a lawyer to regard himself as a social engineer; however that legitimacy is lost, no doubt, when a lawyer, in advancing a particular cause, conducts himself in a manner constituting unprofessional conduct.

Mark Green, a Washington lawyer and author of a treatise entitled *The Other Government: The Unseen Power of Washington Lawyers*, recently made these remarks:

> It is an article of faith among lawyers, especially business lawyers, that they should zealously advocate their clients' cause without worrying about its moral unpopularity or social impact. "Any lawyer who surrenders this independence or shades this duty by trimming his professional course to fit the gusts of popular opinion in my judgment not only dishonors himself but disparages and degrades a great profession," wrote the venerable Wall Street attorney John W. Davis in 1924. "What is life worth, after all, if one has no philosophy of [one's] own to live by."
>
> Admirers consider this soaring response the classic explanation of the lawyer's proper role. But others wonder exactly what philosophy it was that required Davis to devote his professional life to the House of Morgan.
>
> A half century later, the law-for-hire ethic is still controversial. When, if ever, should a lawyer tell a client that a proposed argument or policy is unjust? Lawyers who answer that anything goes in legal combat overlook the fact that law is very much a *public* profession. Because lawyers are "officers of the court" licensed by the state and granted a monopoly of access to the judicial process. Louis Brandeis came to regard them as a kind of public utility, trustees of justice for us all. As he enjoyed saying, a lawyer should represent not merely his client, but the situation.[37]

Consider, in addition, the following remarks made by Dr. Max Wyman, in connection with the Canadian legal system:

> Having said this, I am impelled to voice the deep concern I have about the vast ignorance that exists about the law and the legal process, an ignorance that exists both within and without the legal profession. It is almost unbelievable that the law and the legal process in Canada have no philosophical base, a base that should give purpose and scope to that law and to that legal process. It is inexcusable that there does not exist a definitive empirical base by means of which society can measure the effects that those laws have on the lives of people.
>
> Our laws have grown like Topsy, without purpose, without scope, and without knowledge of their effect. With three-quarters of the twentieth century now passed into history, it is inexcusable that a twentieth century system of laws and a twentieth century system of legal procedures still remains to be written.
>
> My concern is heightened because of the high respect I have for the law and the legal process. That law and that legal process should be the mirror of civilization as it is now, or might be in the future, not of a civilization that existed hundreds of years ago. In Canada, that mirror has become distorted and opaque, and now reflects a grotesque image of civilization as it now has become.[38]

---

[37]Newsweek Magazine, 16th June 1975.

[38]Comments on the Criminal Law and the Legal Process, Alberta Board of Review, Provincial Courts (1975), p. 1. See also the following recent articles: Totenberg, "Behind the Marble, Beneath the Robes", New York Times Magazine, 16th March 1975; "America's Lawyers: 'A Sick Profession' " and "Why Courts are in Trouble", U.S. News & World

The role of law and lawyers in modern society is not the subject of universal agreement; rather it is the subject of considerable controversy. The law cannot, realistically, be regarded as the panacea of all the problems faced by contemporary society. However, it represents probably the best opportunity for members of society to collectively achieve desired social objectives. In turn, the legal system must be regarded as the structural framework in which the realization of this opportunity is brought about. It is the task of judges and lawyers to ensure that, within the framework, the law becomes an operational reality available to all persons that it governs, administered with its desired social objectives in mind.

It is not enough that modern legal thinkers simply devise new directions in our law. Any changes in our law and in our legal system must ultimately be designed to improve the quality of Canadian democracy. The test that must be applied in measuring the desirability of any new directions relates to the effects of those directions on the quality of democratic life and the preservation of individual freedom in a liberal, democratic society.

As indicated earlier, the law may be viewed as an opportunity to achieve international peace and progress, domestic tranquility and major advancements in the quality of life. Moreover, the dictates of justice, fairness and equity demand that the Canadian legal system, in performing its functions, fulfil a promise. A judgment as to the success of Canadian law and the Canadian legal system, in fulfilling its promise and opportunity, is ultimately in the hands of future historians. It is incumbent upon lawyers, judges and members of society at large to ensure that our legal system does, indeed, fulfil its promise. In other words, as members of the legal profession in Canada or as members of the public at large, we jointly have the challenge, if not the shared responsibility, to mould the judgment of history. In short, to borrow the words of s. 1 of our new Charter of Rights and Freedoms, we must preserve and protect the "free and democratic society" that Canadians cherish. By the pursuit of innovative new directions, we can ensure that the Canadian legal system will continue to endure as a cornerstone of liberty and democracy in Canada.

Report, 25th March 1974 and 31st March 1975 respectively; and "Too Much Law", Newsweek Magazine, 10th January 1977. See also the following treatise: Auerbach, *Unequal Justice: Lawyers and Social Change in Modern America* (New York: Oxford University Press, 1975), and a review thereof in the New York Times Book Review, 25th January 1976.

INDEX

ABORIGINAL RIGHTS
  See CANADIAN CHARTER OF RIGHTS AND
    FREEDOMS; CIVIL LIBERTIES; CON-
    STITUTION ACT, 1982.

ABORTION, 86, 326

ACADIA, 133

ACCESS TO INFORMATION ACT, 91,
  298

ACT OF SETTLEMENT, 185, 192

ACT OF UNION, 136

ADJUDICATION, 109-111

ADJUDICATIVE FACTS, 257

ADMINISTRATIVE DECISION-MAK-
  ING
  See also ADMINISTRATIVE LAW; ADMIN-
    ISTRATIVE TRIBUNAL; DELEGATION;
    REMEDIES, prerogative.
  abuse of power, 283, 287, 288
    bad faith, 287, 291
      dishonesty, 287
      fraud, 287
      malice, 287, 291
      improper purpose, 287
      irrelevant considerations, 287
  conformity to enabling statutes, 285-286
  delegatus non potest delegare, 38, 282
  error of law on the face of the record,
    285, 291, 295
  fairness, 1, 219, 234, 283, 288-290
  judicial review of, 283, 284, 287, 293,
    294
  jurisdictional fact doctrine, 286
  privitive clauses, 293-294
  rules of natural justice, 1, 287-290, 295,
    296, 297
    audi alteram partem, 287
    nemo judex in sua causa, 287

ADMINISTRATIVE LAW, 20, 22, 280-
  308
  See also ADMINISTRATIVE DECISION-
    MAKING; DELEGATION; INTERDELE-
    GATION; LAW, public; REMEDIES
  constitutional law, and, 282
  delegation, See DELEGATION
  Federal Court Act, 84, 117, 185, 290,
    294-296
  growth of government bureaucracy,
    297-299
  importance of, 280-281
  the individual and bureaucracy, the, 297
    See also OMBUDSMAN
  Police Bill, 296
  powers of, 282

process of delegation, 281-282
provincial enactments, 296-297
statutory enactments, 294-297
subordinate legislation
  See LEGISLATION, subordinate

ADMINISTRATIVE TRIBUNAL, 20, 38,
  83, 84, 109, 116, 117, 260, 280
  administrative function of, 283, 284, 289
  agencies, 282
  boards, 282
  classification of, 283-285, 289
  commission, 282
  executive function of, 283, 284
  federal, 84, 180, 295
  inferior legislative body, 281
  judicial function of, 283, 285, 287, 289,
    292, 295
  legislative function of, 283, 284, 289
  ministerial function of, 283, 284, 289
  municipal councils, 282, 284
  procedure for challenging decisions of
    abuse of power, 291-292
    breach of doctrine of fairness, 293
    breach of rule of natural justice, 292
    ultra vires enabling legislation, 291
  provincial, 84, 116, 180
  quasi-judicial, 283, 284, 285, 287, 289,
    292, 295
  royal commission of inquiry, 87, 174,
    204
  tribunals, 174, 282, 288

ADMIRALTY, 121

ADVOCATE
  See LAWYERS

AFFIRMATIVE ACTION, 319-320

ALBERTA, 44, 52, 62, 116, 118, 119, 123,
  125, 156, 257, 321
  Administrative Procedures Act, 297
  Bill of Rights, 62
  Council on Aging, 106
  Human Rights Commission, 152, 251
  Individual's Rights Protection Act, 62
  Institute of Law Research and Reform,
    321, 322
  Provincial Court Act, 118

ALBERTA ACT, 44

AMENDMENT
  See CONSTITUTION, Canadian, amend-
    ment of; CONSTITUTION, Canadian,
    amending formula

AMERICAN BAR ASSOCIATION, 183,
  319
  Committee on the Federal Judiciary,
    183